Contents

Introduction

Great natural beauty and world-famous cultural sites (whether a throbbing metropolis or the heart of a medieval town), magnificent churches and monasteries, mighty castles and fortresses – with a rich cultural legacy and some of the most beautiful scenery on earth, Europe has a wealth of fascinating places to visit. Travel within Europe is also easier than ever, now that passport formalities have been all but abolished and the euro has been adopted in twelve European Union countries.

Twenty-six painstakingly researched routes will take you through the scenic and cultural highlights of Europe: on the trail of the Hanseatic League in the Baltic; following the Nordkapp route in Norway or the Via Appia in Italy; or perhaps a tour across Portugal, through the Alpine passes, or around the cities of the Golden Ring in Russia.

The Route descriptions

An introductory section in each chapter summarizes the route and presents the scenic and cultural highlights of each country and region. There then follows a description of the important towns and sights along the route, with road information and directions, all illustrated with lavish color photography. The towns and sights are consecutively numbered and cross-referenced with the maps at the end of each chapter.

Each route is provided with an information panel containing important travel tips regarding the length of each journey, how much time to allow, local traffic laws, weather, the best time to travel, and useful links and addresses. Interesting aspects of local culture and scenery are featured in sidebars. Additional highlighted sections in the sidebars contain information about worthwhile detours.

City maps

Extra pages featuring detailed maps and comprehensive tourist information are provided for the cities through which the routes pass.

Touring maps

Special touring maps at the end of each chapter chart the course of each route and the most important cities and sights. The main route is clearly identified and complemented with additional suggestions for interesting detours. A set of pictograms (see list opposite) identify the location and nature of the most important sights along the route and exceptionally interesting destinations are featured in photographs with short captions at the edges of the maps.

Images:
Pages 2–3: The Old Town of Berne in the twilight (above); the Houses of Parliament and Big Ben in London (below). Pages 4–5: St Ursanne on the River Doubs in the Swiss Canton of Jura. Pages 6–7: The suspension bridge across the Danube in Budapest.

**Natural features
and landscapes**

- mountainous area
- active volcano
- rocky scenery
- canyon
- cave
- glacier
- river course
- waterfall/rapids
- lakes
- geyser
- national park (wildlife)
- national park (vegetation)
- national park (cultural feature)
- national park (scenic)
- nature reserve
- coastal area
- beach
- zoo
- fossil finds
- wildlife reserve
- whale watching

**Cultural features
and events**

- prehistoric and early period
- Greek antiquity
- Roman antiquity
- Etruscan
- Judaica
- church/monastery

- Phoenician culture
- prehistoric rock painting
- Viking culture
- cultural landscape
- castle/fortress
- palace
- historic industrial building
- memorial
- observatory
- historic cityscape
- skyline
- feasts and festivals
- museum
- theater
- expo
- Olympic town
- monument/memorial
- markets
- military feature/battlefield
- lighthouse
- notable bridge

**Sporting and
leisure activities**

- racetrack
- mineral baths/spa
- bathing resort
- leisure park
- casino
- racecourse
- port
- sea route

The Dream Routes

Iceland ponies in the marshes near Reykholt in the south-west of the island.

Iceland

Fire and ice: archaic landscapes on the world's largest volcanic island

This legendary island in the North Atlantic delivers spectacular natural encounters with primordial force: formidable basalt mountains, vast lava fields, mighty glaciers, meandering glacial streams, thundering waterfalls, and much more. All the more comforting, then, when you encounter villages with a centuries-old cultural tradition on the periphery of seemingly infinite, untouched expanses.

Iceland, the largest volcanic island on earth, is just 300 km (186 mi) from Greenland, but nearly 1,000 km (621 mi) from western Scandinavia. The "wayward end of the world" is what the Vikings called these inhospitable shores close to the Arctic Circle when they settled here in the 9th century and set up one of their first free states.

Today, this 103,000-sq-km (3,976-sq-mi) island has 270,000 inhabitants who live primarily off fishing, sheep farming, cat-

Fishing boats in the port at Ólafsvik.

tle and horse breeding, aluminum production, and vegetable farming in greenhouses heated by geothermal energy. Iceland offers visitors unique encounters with nature in its original state, where elemental forces still reign free.

The capital of Iceland, Reykjavík, is full of charm and does boast a number of interesting things to see, but the real destinations on the "Island of Fire and Ice" are outside of the city. The other small towns, such as Akureyri and Húsavík in the north or Egilsstadir on the east of the island, are set in very picturesque locations but their buildings are mostly recent or even totally new. Masonry, concrete and corrugated iron have long since replaced the old peat bricks and traditional thatched roofs of the scattered individual homesteads. Significant cultural monuments are not to be found

anywhere on the island. Iceland's most outstanding attraction is its magnificent landscape. Admittedly, it is no image of pastoral tranquility, but rather one of dramatic activity, extreme wilderness and tremendous diversity.

The four essential elements dominate the island with breathtaking intensity. The air is so fresh and clear that when the weather is good – which is fortunately much more often the case than one would expect here – you can see for over 100 km (62 mi).

Water is available in excess and seems to be absolutely everywhere you look, from meandering rivers, powerful waterfalls, cold and warm lakes located atop hot and cold springs, and of course the famous geysers. More than ten percent of the island is covered in glaciers, with one quarter of the ice surface alone

Massive gurgling mud baths such as this one in Namarskard on Lake Mývatn are typical of Iceland.

On the south coast a 25-m-wide (82-ft) glacial river from the Myrdalsjökull in Skógafoss plunges 62 m (203 ft).

belonging to Europe's largest glacier, Vatnajökull. Indeed, the island owes its name to its numerous glaciers.

Given all of that, however, the earth element is still the most spectacular. Vast areas of land are covered with recently cooled lava, transforming Iceland into an open-air geology museum that reveals how our planet looked during the different phases of its early development.

As a result, however, the inhabitable areas are limited to a few coastal regions. The rest of the island is shaped by steep cliffs and fjords that extend into the interior, which in turn features expansive plateaus, lava fields, deserts of stone, sand and ash, table mountains, glaciers, and active and extinct volcanoes. Today, Surtur, the mythical leader of the fire giants, still leaves fascinating traces of his work all around the island. By

stoking the fires deep within the earth, he makes the glowing, viscous magma rise from the depths, melt the earth's crust and erupt in furious explosions. The island itself is actually the tip of a submerged mountain that forms part of the Mid-Atlantic Ridge, where the American and Eurasian tectonic plates drift apart. For visitors, it is a sort of sample gallery of geological shapes, from volcanic craters and cinder fields to tuff cones and countless other whimsical lava formations. Geysers discharge their fountains of scalding water at regular intervals while mud baths bubble away and fumaroles and solfataras smolder. The plentiful thermal springs provide relaxation for Icelanders and their guests all year round and many houses have a bathing pool with volcanically heated water right outside the door.

Steam rises from the boiling hot fumaroles at Haverarond in Lake M'yvatn.

Leif Eriksson

Leif Eriksson, legendary Viking sea-farer and predecessor of Christopher Columbus, looks out over the rooftops of Reykjavík towards the ocean from his pedestal in front of Hallgríms church. Eric the Red, his father, may not have a statue but he was no less famous. After being banished from Norway, he discovered Greenland from his base in Iceland in 982 and founded its first European settlement. It was from this new colony that the then 30-year-old Leif put to sea in around 1000, with thirty-five men, to begin his famous voyage of discovery. The "Greenland Saga" reports that he landed in North America at around the same latitude as Baffin Island,

Statue of Leif Eriksson in Reykjavík.

which he called Helluland ("flat stone land"). From there he is said to have sailed as far as New England, following the Labrador Current southwards. This he christened "Vinland" because he found vines growing there.

Another contemporary source, how-ever, claims that Leif, "the Happy One", as he was known in his day, had heard from a fellow countryman named Bjarni Herjólfsson about the existence of a foreign land to the west before undertaking his legendary voyage. It was a land that the latter is said to have seen some fourteen years previously after losing his way during a storm.

Ultimately, Leif went down in history as the first European to have set foot on American soil and, in 1930, was posthumously granted this imposing monument in Reykjavík by the U.S. Congress to mark the occasion of the 1,000th anniversary of the first meet-ing of the Althing.

Iceland's ring road: Anyone circling the island of fire and ice on the roughly 1,500-km-long (932-mi), almost completely paved, coastal road (Route 1) will become acquainted with most of the facets of this unique natural paradise, but a number of detours from the ring road into the interior are certainly worthwhile.

① **Reykjavík** Iceland's capital, which is also the country's cultur-al, transport, and economic cen-ter, is on the northern edge of a peninsula on the south-west coast. Its climate benefits from the mild currents of the Gulf Stream. When it was granted its charter at the end of the 18th century, there were just 200 peo-ple settled in the "smoky bay" ("Reykjavík" in Icelandic). Now, including suburbs and outlying towns, the population has grown to around 160,000 – roughly sixty percent of the country's inhabitants.

The city tour begins at the main square, Austurvöllur, which is home to the oldest parliament in the world, a cathedral, and the time-honored Hotel Borg. The city's most prominent fea-ture is the Tjörnin, a small lake in the city center. The new city hall, the National Gallery and some upscale residential villas line its shores. To the south are the National Museum and the Árni Magnússon Institute, home to the medieval saga manu-scripts. The council buildings, originally designed as a prison, and the bronze statue of Ingólfur Arnarson, one of Rey-kjavík's first settlers, are located closer to the port.

On a hill to the south-east of town, Hallgríms church watches over the city with the Leif Eríksson monument standing tall before it. Right next door is the Ásgrímur Jónsson Collection,

donated to the state by the Icelandic landscape artist who died in 1958. The Natural History Museum, Einar Jónsson's collec-tion of sculptures, as well as the Árbaer Open Air Museum and the Laugardalslaug swimming pool are also worth a visit.

② **Hraunfossar** Roughly 25 km (15 mi) north of the town of Borganes it is worth taking a detour along the Hálsasvei-tarvegur (Route 518) to an im-pressive natural spectacle not far from the Húsafell country estate: the Hraunfossar "lava waterfalls", a multitude of small springs that cascade over a basalt lip into the Hvítá glacial river. Nearby, there is a similar natural attraction called the Barnafoss Waterfall.

③ **Akureyri** With 15,000 in-habitants, this "pearl of the north" is located at the end of the Eyjafjördur and is the coun-try's third largest town. It is also the transport center for the north coast thanks to its ship-yard, airport and port.

The well-organized local history museum and botanical gardens provide an introduction to the history, flora and fauna of the surrounding region. The Nonná-hús, a monument to local chil-dren's book author Jón Sveins-son, alias Nonni, may be interesting for literature fans. The city also serves as a starting point for hiking trips into the

Travel information

Route profile
Length: 1,400 km (870 mi), without detours
Time required: min. 8–10 days
Start and end: Reykjavík
Route: Reykjavík, Akureyri, Mývatnsee, Egilsstadir, Stafafell, NP Skaftafell, Vík, Skogar, Thingvellir

Traffic information:
Many gravel roads. Be careful of varying depths when cross-ing rivers. The following laws are very strictly enforced for drivers: 0.0 mg alcohol limit for drivers; maximum speed limit in towns 50 km/h (30 mph), on gravel roads 80 km/h (50 mph), on tarred roads 90 km/h (60 mph). The majority of the roads in the interior are first opened in July.

For more information on road conditions call:
0354/17 77 (8am–4pm)
or go to:
www.vegag.is
If you are driving a diesel vehicle you will be required to pay a weight tax on arrival.
www.icetourist.de

When to go:
Summer is the best time, but don't expect very high temper-atures.
Weather in English:
Tel: 0902 / 06 00
www.vedur.is

Other information:
Here are a few sites to help you prepare for your trip:
www.icelandtouristboard.com
www.iceland.org

fascinating interior, for example to the region around the Hlidarfjall at an elevation of up to 1,200 m (3,937 ft).

4 **Goðafoss** Some 40 km (25 mi) east of Akureyri, the roaring Skjálfandaðfljót River makes its way from the stony expanse of the Sprengisandur plain down toward the ocean over a 10-m (33-ft) escarpment. Despite the relatively short drop, the width and quantity of water make Goðafoss one of the most impressive and deservedly famous falls in Iceland.

Its name, "Waterfall of the Gods", comes from Thorgeir, the speaker of the Althing. He is said to have thrown the statues of his former house gods into the river here in the year 1000 because the Icelandic parliament decided that Icelanders should convert to Christianity. Norwegian King Olaf had threatened a timber embargo, which would have crippled shipbuilding, an essential industry for the island.

5 **Mývatn** Located about 30 km (19 mi) east of Goðafoss, Lake Mývatn was formed only about 3,500 to 2,000 years ago by lava discharged during two volcanic eruptions. It is 37 sq km (14 sq mi) in size but only 4–5 m (13–16 ft) deep and fed by hot springs.

The diversity of plant life here is nearly singular on the planet for such northern latitudes. Mosses, grasses, ferns, herbs and birch trees grow along the shore and on the numerous islands. During the summer months, massive swarms of midge flies form over the warm water. Together with the insect larvae, they provide food for the wealth of fish and waterfowl here, thousands of which nest in the many bays, making the region a paradise for birdwatchers.

The Lake Mývatn area is considered one of Iceland's most spectacular landscapes. It is also located in one of the island's most active volcanic zones. Beautiful lava formations are scattered all along the very well-signposted hiking trails. The Dimmuborgir, or "Dark Fortresses", consist of bizarrely shaped formations with small caves and arches. The best view over the pseudo-crater in and around Lake Mývatn can be enjoyed from the rim of the Hverfjall crater, a 170-m-high (558-ft) cinder cone.

6 **Krafla** The area surrounding the 818-m (2,683-ft) volcano just a few miles north-east of Lake

Mývatn is one of Iceland's most tectonically unstable zones. Considered extinct at the beginning of the 18th century, the 2,000-year-old Krafla suddenly buried the entire region under a thick layer of lava and ash following a violent eruption. The ultimate result was a dazzling, emerald green tuff cone with a crater lake some 320 m (1,050 ft) in diameter.

In 1975, the volcano came to life again for nearly a decade. Its bubbling, steaming sulfur springs have since remained a very popular attraction and are the most visible indication of ongoing volcanic activity.

7 **Húsavík/Tjörnes** Instead of following the shortest route along the ring road east of Lake Mývatn, it is definitely worth taking a detour around the Tjörnes Peninsula, which is especially fascinating from a geological point of view. A good 30 km (19 mi) after the turnoff near Reykjahlið you will pass Grenjadarstadur, a peat homestead built in around 1870. It was abandoned in 1949 before being turned into a folk museum. The little town of Húsavík, which mainly survives off fishing and fish-processing, has managed to make a name for itself as a tourist destination with a particular focus on whale watching. With commercial whaling

now a thing of the past in Iceland, local fishermen now take seaworthy holidaymakers out on their cutters for a day's worth of whale watching in the summertime.

8 **Jökulsárgljúfur and Dettifoss** Compared to the rest of Iceland, the climate around Ásbyrgi, the "Fortress of the Gods", is mild and the contours of the landscape quite gentle. A birch forest covers the valley where, legend has it, Odin's six-legged horse shaped a mighty, semi-circular cliff with its hoof. There are the two roads from here that follow the canyon upstream along the edge of the escarpment toward Dettifoss. The eastern of the two is in better condition, while the western one is bumpier and thus

less crowded. Jökulsárgljúfur National Park, founded in 1973, encompasses the canyon-like Jökulsá á Fjöllum valley section between Ásbyrgi and the Dettifoss Waterfall. With a length of

1 The river feeding the Goðafoss begins far to the south.

2 The waterfalls at Hraunfossar, near Húsafell, cascade down from a lava field.

3 The bizarre Dimmuborgir cliff landscape at Lake Mývatn.

4 Volcanic landscape at Reykjahlið, north-east of Lake Mývatn.

5 The Breiðamerkurjökull flows into the Jökulsárlón glacial lagoon on the south side of the Vatnajökull.

Detour

Herðubreið and Askja

Anyone turning off shortly before Grimsstadir, west of the Jökulsá á Fjöllum River, and heading south on the F88 – navigable only with four-wheel drive vehicles – will get a good look at Iceland's interior. The route takes you from the Hrossaborg crater to the southern ring road, the Mývatnsöraefi (or midge lake desert) and the Ódádahraun

Top: Herðubreið volcano.
Bottom: A view inside the Askja crater.

desert. The area is lined with vast lava fields, bleak stony expanses, and the occasional shield volcano. You will only seldom come across patches of green vegetation, which grow where water is able to seep through the volcanic soil to the surface. Herðubreið (about 50 km/31 mi) south of Hrossaborg) is one such oasis. A cabin provides somewhat spartan accommodation at the foot of the Herðubreið, imposing, 1,682-m-high (5,519-ft) table volcano.

If the weather is good, you should take a drive to the Dyngjufjöll volcano massif. Just the 40 km (25 mi) jaunt past the magnificent Jökulsa Canyon, the Dragon Gorge (Drekagil), and the Vikrahraun lava flow is worth the extra time.

After roughly a 30-minute walk you get a spectacular the view of the Askja, a 45-sq-km (17-sq-mi) crater with Iceland's deepest lake.

Gullfoss, the "Golden Waterfall", is one of the country's loveliest and most impressive waterfalls in the south-west of the island and is close to a famous geyser. For the last 10,000 years, the waters of the Hvíta River, which begins underneath the Langjökull Glacier, have plunged over two 32-m-high (105 ft) precipices to

form an impressive gorge about 35 m (115 ft) deep and 2.5 km (1.6 mi) long. The river's average flow is 109 cu m/sec (3,849 cu ft/sec), but during the spring snowmelt it can increase to 2,000 cu m/sec (70,629 cu ft/sec).

Detour

Hekla and Landmannalaugar

Route 26 takes you past Iceland's most famous volcano, the snow-capped Hekla (1,491 m/4,891 ft), on

Top: Hekla Volcano.
Bottom: Landmannalaugar.

the way to Landmannalaugar. The ryolith rock mountains glisten with a range of hues and there are paths leading to a number of spectacular sulfur springs.

Geysir/Gullfoss

You can reach the Geysir thermal area via Flúðir, 15 km (9 mi) before the Selfoss turnoff on Route 30. The geyser, which can blast water up to 60-m (199-ft) into the air, only

A look at Strokkur Geyser.

came back to life in 2000. The Strokkur Geyser is even more active and shoots its boiling stream about 25 m (82 ft) into the sky every five to ten minutes. Just 10 km (6 mi) to the north-east is the Gullfoss, Iceland's most famous waterfall.

206 km (128 mi), the "glacier river from the mountains", as its name translates, is Iceland's second-longest. It is fed from the northern edge of the Vatna-jökull Glacier and intersects the ring road at Grímsstadir. About 20 km (12 mi) upstream is where it plunges into the Dettifoss Waterfall over five formidable rock faces into a deep gorge. Iceland has a number of magnificent waterfalls, but few will make the same impression as Dettifoss. With a span of about 100 m (328 ft), the gray-brown floodwaters of the Jökulsá á Fjöllum drop 44 m (144 ft) into a canyon between vertical basalt walls. In the summer the flow rate reaches up to 1,500 cu m/sec (52,972 cu ft/sec). This makes the Dettifoss Waterfall the mightiest in Europe by a long shot.

A drive from here to the Herðu-breið volcano and the Askja caldera makes for a very worthwhile detour. You'll come to the turnoff about 36 km (22 mi) after Reykjahlið.

⑨ Egilstaðir/Fjorde Eastern Iceland's administrative and commercial center is on the ring road in a mostly agricultural area of the country. It is also a heavily wooded area. A worthwhile destination in these parts is the more than 100-m-high (328-ft) Hengifoss Waterfall on the northern shore of the long and narrow Lake Lögurinn. The ring road follows the coast once you pass Reydarfjördur and affords spectacular views of the wild ocean.

⑩ Stafafell A historical homestead stands on the edge of the Jökulsá á Lóni Delta about 30 km (19 mi) before Höfn, the only port on the entire south coast. Once a vicarage, it now serves as a youth hostel from which you can set off on hikes into the varied landscapes of the Lonsoraefi wilderness region.

⑪ Jökulsárlón About 70 km (43 mi) beyond Höfn, where the impressive ice tongue of the Breidarmerkurjökull Glacier extends to within a few hundred yards of the sea, the ring road takes you right past the island's glacial lake. Glistening a blue-white hue in the lagoon, giant icebergs from the edge of the glacier evoke an atmosphere akin to Greenland.

⑫ Skaftafell National Park Skaftafell National Park, established in 1967, extends from the area around Vatnajökull, Ice-

land's largest glacier, to the south as far as the ring road and provides a multitude of scenic attractions. Within the national park, signposted hiking trails take you into dense forests such as the one in Núpstadaskogar, along extensive wetlands and marshes to dilapidated but intact homesteads, and to the Svarti-foss Waterfall surrounded by basalt pillars.

Between Fagurhólsmri and Kirk-jubaejarklaustur the ring road now traverses the black sand and scree expanse of the Skeiðar-ársandur. A glacier run here was caused by an eruption of the Lóki volcano below the Vatnajökull Glacier. The melted glacial ice under the Vatnajökull ice cap then surged into the sand in a giant flood wave.

⑬ Vík The big attraction at Iceland's "southern cape" are the bird cliffs at Dyrhólaey, around 20 km (12 mi) away. A number of common North Atlantic seabird species live here at varying levels of the cape. Right at the top are the Atlantic puffins, which hide their tunnels in the grass tufts. On the cliffs beneath them are the kittiwakes and fulmars. You

can take a boat tour from the black sand beach. A lighthouse 100 m (328 ft) up on the cliffs is a popular viewing point.

⑭ Skógafoss The catchment area of the Skógar river, which crosses the road south-east of the mighty Mýrdalsjökull is a good stopover for two reasons. The first is the Skógafoss, a waterfall that is 62 m (203 ft) high surrounded by meadows. You can see the falls from above and below, which is what makes it a special place. Secondly, the meticulously detailed folk museum in Skógar deserves a visit. About 7 km (4 mi) beyond Hella it is worth taking a detour to the Hekla volcano and through the Landmannalaugar thermal region. Back on the ring road, instead of taking the direct return route to Reykjavík, take a detour via Route 30, which passes by the Gullfoss Waterfall and the Strokkur Geyser. Route 35 will then take you directly back to the ring road. Before that, however, you should to take a look at the church in Skálholt, which was a Viking center in the Middle Ages and boasts lovely glass windows. The main road takes you past Lake

þingvallavat towards þingvellir, the last stop.

⑮ þingvellir The renowned Thingfeld lies on the northern shore of Lake þingvallavatn. The lava plateau bordering the All Men's Gorge to the west is a very interesting geological area and the historical heart of the country.

It was this "Holy Free State" that became the former Icelandic Free State in the year 930 and it was here that the legendary Althing, the oldest democratic parliament in the world, met annually all the way up until 1798. It was also here that the Icelanders declared themselves a republic on June 17, 1944.

1 Glaciers reflected on a lake in the Skaftafell National Park.

2 The water from Svartifoss, "The Black Waterfall", plunges over an impressive basalt cliff into a basin shaped like an amphitheater.

3 Rock needles in front of the coastal cliffs at Vík, Iceland's southern-most point.

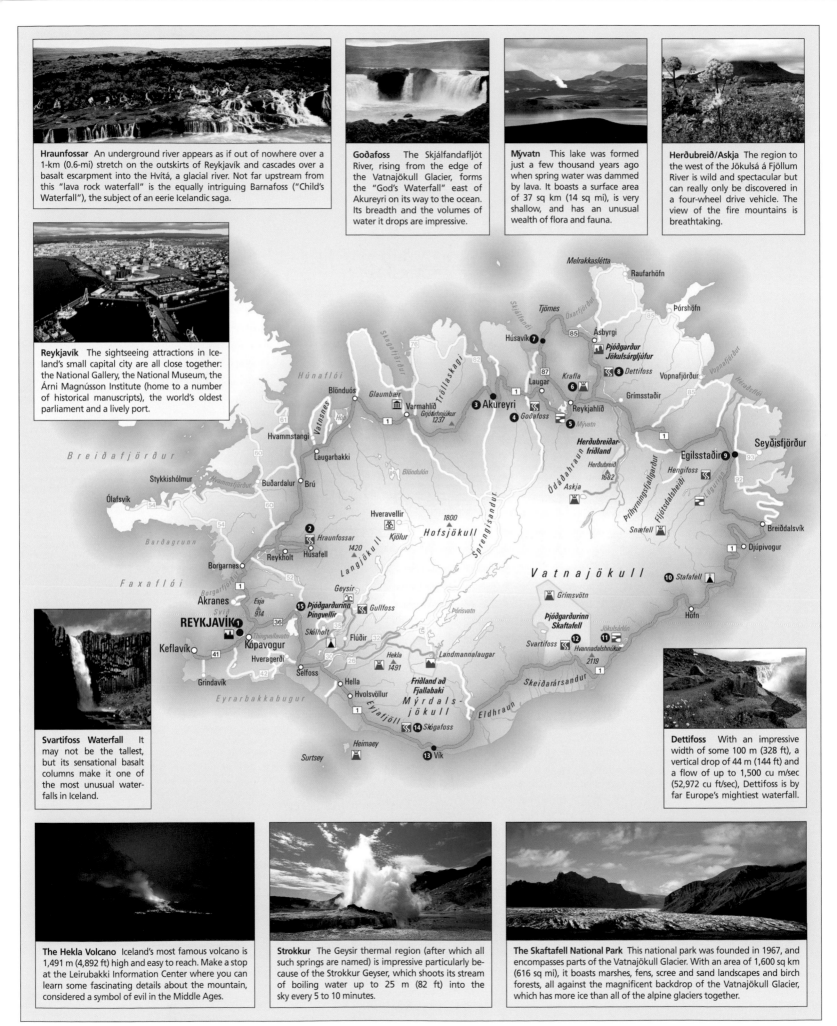

Hraunfossar An underground river appears as if out of nowhere over a 1-km (0.6-mi) stretch on the outskirts of Reykjavík and cascades over a basalt escarpment into the Hvítá, a glacial river. Not far upstream from this "lava rock waterfall" is the equally intriguing Barnafoss ("Child's Waterfall"), the subject of an eerie Icelandic saga.

Goðafoss The Skjálfandafljót River, rising from the edge of the Vatnajökull Glacier, forms the "God's Waterfall" east of Akureyri on its way to the ocean. Its breadth and the volumes of water it drops are impressive.

Mývatn This lake was formed just a few thousand years ago when spring water was dammed by lava. It boasts a surface area of 37 sq km (14 sq mi), is very shallow, and has an unusual wealth of flora and fauna.

Herðubreið/Askja The region to the west of the Jökulsá á Fjöllum River is wild and spectacular but can really only be discovered in a four-wheel drive vehicle. The view of the fire mountains is breathtaking.

Reykjavík The sightseeing attractions in Iceland's small capital city are all close together: the National Gallery, the National Museum, the Árni Magnússon Institute (home to a number of historical manuscripts), the world's oldest parliament and a lively port.

Svartifoss Waterfall It may not be the tallest, but its sensational basalt columns make it one of the most unusual waterfalls in Iceland.

Dettifoss With an impressive width of some 100 m (328 ft), a vertical drop of 44 m (144 ft) and a flow of up to 1,500 cu m/sec (52,972 cu ft/sec), Dettifoss is by far Europe's mightiest waterfall.

The Hekla Volcano Iceland's most famous volcano is 1,491 m (4,892 ft) high and easy to reach. Make a stop at the Leirubakki Information Center where you can learn some fascinating details about the mountain, considered a symbol of evil in the Middle Ages.

Strokkur The Geysir thermal region (after which all such springs are named) is impressive particularly because of the Strokkur Geyser, which shoots its stream of boiling water up to 25 m (82 ft) into the sky every 5 to 10 minutes.

The Skaftafell National Park This national park was founded in 1967, and encompasses parts of the Vatnajökull Glacier. With an area of 1,600 sq km (616 sq mi), it boasts marshes, fens, scree and sand landscapes and birch forests, all against the magnificent backdrop of the Vatnajökull Glacier, which has more ice than all of the alpine glaciers together.

The round Doonagore watchtower on the coast of County Clare.

Ireland

Out and about in the land of the Celts

Ireland is a natural phenomenon in itself. The sandy beaches, striking cliffs, moor landscapes, glistening lakes and green hills are the core of its attractions. But Ireland is more than a natural history museum. It possesses a rich folk tradition that is testimony to the island's vibrant spirit.

Ireland is both an island and a divided nation. The Republic of Ireland (Éire) makes up about four-fifths of the island, while the smaller Northern Ireland is still part of the United Kingdom. As different as they might be, both parts of the island have their very own appeal. The spectrum of landscapes is broad and the natural environment is largely pristine. The central lowlands are surrounded by modest mountain ranges that rise to peaks of more than 1,000 m (3,281 ft) only in the south-west. Despite their relatively small size, however, many of these mountains rise quite strikingly out of the ocean.

The Carrauntoohil (1,038 m/3,406 ft), for example, offers magnificent views of fjord-like bays on the west coast that even appear to change shape in the rapidly shifting light. Lighthouses there defy the relentless pounding of waves on desolate craggy peninsulas. On the flatter coastal sections the sandy beaches provide a contrast to the steep cliffs that surround them. Moorland and countless lakes disappear behind the buttes and green hills of the interior. Indeed, Ireland shows its calmer side on the east coast where the shore is less fragmented, the ocean more tranquil and the surf more placid.

In general, it is not without reason that Ireland has earned epithets like such as "The Green Island" or the more ostentatious "Emerald Isle". Of course, the island does not possess any precious stone mines, but after one of the frequent rain showers, the green appears to take on a special luminosity in the sunlight.

The moors in the interior of the island are scattered with individual fields and meadows. According to a Gaelic saying, the grass in the Irish meadows grows so quickly that if you leave a stick lying in the grass you won't be able to find it again the next day. These fertile areas have been targeted by invaders and op-

One of the many pubs in the little villages on the Dingle Peninsula.

A sensational view of the Cliffs of Moher, one of Ireland's most impressive scenic attractions.

Cutters waiting to put to sea in the port of Dingle on the peninsula of the same name.

portunists since the island's discovery. Word quickly reached mainland Europe of the cows in Ireland having enough food in their pastures the whole year round, making winter storage of fodder unnecessary. To be certain, agriculture remains the backbone of the Irish economy today, with statistics attributing one sheep to each of the roughly 5.1 million inhabitants.

Irish lore and music provide a window into the soul of the Irish people. The Irish harp, for example, is the national instrument, hence its appearance on all Irish Euro coins. It is also a very well-read society, in keeping with a long literary tradition. There are libraries and bookshops on almost every street corner. The famous Trinity College Library in Dublin comprises some 2.8 million volumes and one of its greatest treasures is the 9th-century Book of Kells, one of the loveliest medieval Irish manuscripts. Ireland's cultural tradition is also characterized by a wealth of myths and sagas in which fairies and hobgoblins often play starring roles. Even today, the Giant's Causeway, a craggy portion of Ireland's north coast, is shrouded in legend. You can hear all about it over a Guinness or a glass of Irish whiskey in one of the cozy pubs.

Part of Ireland's special attraction also lies in its contrasts. While time appears to stand still in the more remote coastal regions, and the howling wind makes you wonder how those rustic, thatched-roof cottages can withstand the harsh elements, things in Dublin and Belfast are entirely different. There, visitors who are interested in getting a taste of the country's urban culture are certainly in for a treat as well.

In the south and west of Ireland, the coast is rugged and features many secluded bays.

The Irish Pub

After fighting through the crowd to the bar, the guest calls out, "a pint of ..." to the man behind the counter. In return he receives the appropriate quantity of his selected "poison", either a Guinness, Harp, Kilkenny or any number of other elixirs. Naturally, a "half pint" also exists,

The Stag's Head, one of Dublin's oldest pubs, is a popular meeting place.

but it is not considered worthy of an Irishman. Some of the more traditional Irish pubs generally tend to be more male dominated affairs that can quite often get loud and raucous. Indeed, it is here in the pubs that the Irish are at their most Irish.

There are a number of basic rules that visitors should attempt to keep in mind when visiting the pub: pay for your beer (or whiskey) as soon as it is placed on the bar for you. Tipping is not expected but it is appreciated. Closing time is closing time, especially if the police station is nearby.

Once around the island: The circular route takes you along wide roads following the coast, from Dublin clockwise around the whole of Ireland, including the counties of Northern Ireland. Fascinating landscapes, lively towns and historical buildings invite visitors to linger a while.

1 Dublin (see page 21)

2 Powerscourt Estate Gardens An impressive park with lovely Italian and Japanese gardens, areas of untouched nature and man-made lakes directly on the southern outskirts of Dublin. The ambiance here is further augmented by a castle-like country home, which was fully restored following a fire in 1974.

From here, a side trip to the Powerscourt Waterfall is well worth it. The clearly posted signs lead you to Ireland's highest falls, where the Dargle River plunges 130 m (427 ft) over a granite cliff.

3 Glendalough About 30 km (19 mi) south of the waterfall, one of Ireland's most wonderfully situated monasteries has stood the test of time amidst the scenic surroundings of the "Valley of the Two Lakes". Known for his reclusive ways, St Kevin founded this isolated monastery in the 6th century. Despite his efforts, other pilgrims followed soon after and the complex grew. The focal point of the former settlement is now the 33-m-high (108-ft) round tower, which is visible from a distance and was both a lookout post and a place of refuge. Most visitors limit their visit to the ruins on the lower

lake, but those on the upper lake are no less interesting and in fact more peaceful to explore. From Glendalough there is a road leading west toward the heart of the Wicklow Mountains, which peak at 924 m (3,032 ft). There are scenic hiking trails leading to the mountain lakes of Lough Dan and Lough Bray. From the mountains you return to the coastal road, then continue southward to Enniscorthy, 50 km (31 mi) away.

4 Jerpoint Abbey At Enniscorthy, which features a towering fortress close to the island's southern tip, it is worth leaving the coastal road to take a side road westward into the interior. The Cistercian Jerpoint Abbey (12th century) on the shores of Little Arrigle is one of Ireland's best-preserved monastery ruins. The route then continues to the north-west to what is the interior's loveliest town, Kilkenny.

5 Kilkenny The 17,000 residents of Kilkenny enjoy life in a medieval jewel of a town featuring narrow alleyways, half-timbered stone houses and myriad historical buildings. The town's landmark is the tower of St Mary's Cathedral (19th century), which stands 65 m (213 ft) tall. Kilkenny Castle, a fortress built by the Normans, towers high

above the River Nore and is one of the most famous in Ireland. The ostentatious Long Gallery has antique furniture and portraits of former lords of the manor. Even the buildings lining Kilkenny's main streets are not short on grandeur, and some of the pubs with their stained-glass windows seem to be in competition with the churches for attention. From Kilkenny the route continues westward to Cashel.

6 Cashel The Irish are well aware of the cultural importance of this town of just 2,500 residents. The music and theater events at the Brú Ború Heritage Center are renowned throughout the country.

Most visitors to Ireland, however, are drawn to the Rock of Cashel, an imposing limestone cliff with the ruins of a fortress towering over the broad Tipperary plains. Starting in the 5th century, the fortress was the seat of the kings of Munster whose dominions extended for centuries over large areas of southern Ireland. At the end of the 11th century, the complex passed into the hands of the Catholic Church. It was later plundered by English troops under Oliver Cromwell in 1647 before being

1 The gentle, rolling landscape reflected in the port at Ballycrovane in County Cork.

Travel information

Route profile
Length: approx. 1,200 km (746 mi)
Time required: 2–3 weeks
Route (main locations): Dublin, Kilkenny, Cashel, Cork, Killarney, Ring of Kerry, Limerick, Cliffs of Moher, Galway, Clifden, Westport, Ballina, Sligo, Donegal, Londonderry, Giant's Causeway, Belfast, Dublin

Traffic information:
The Irish drive on the left. Four-wheel-drive vehicles are required only in very remote areas.

Weather:
In keeping with the motto "The only guarantee with Irish weather is that it's constantly changing", you are

advised to take both warm and rain-proof clothing. The mild-Atlantic climate keeps winter temperatures from sinking below 5°C (40°F), while July and August have an average temperature of 16°C (60°F).

Accommodation:
There are myriad options for bed and breakfast establishments in Ireland. They are a popular form of accommodation and are just about everywhere, even in the most remote corners.

Information
Here are a few sites to help you prepare for your trip:
www.discoverireland.com
www.travelireland.org
www.travelinireland.com

Dublin

The capital of the Republic of Ireland is over 1,000 years old and has always been worth a visit, albeit more for its celebratory flair than for its artistic treasures.

The Vikings, who were the first to settle in what is now Dublin, called their settlement Dyfflin, which basically meant "black puddle". Sound like a bad omen? Well, it must be said that Dublin's long history has indeed been largely determined by outside influences, particularly those of the neighboring English, whose first "colony" was, you guessed it, Ireland. Dublin was selected as the representative center of the Anglo-Irish administration, and yet, despite hundreds of years of rule, the city never fully gave in to British hegemony. Gaelic traditions of music, poetry, storytelling and debate have been ardently upheld in Ireland. It is no surprise, then, that the battle for Irish independence began in Dublin in 1916 with the Easter Uprising. And although today's vibrant, trendy Dublin is no longer Irish enough for some, it is still a very interesting city. The center of the metropolis on the Liffey is characterized by wide shop-

Top: The O'Connell Bridge over the River Liffey in Dublin.
Below: The library at Trinity College, Ireland's oldest university founded in 1592.

ping streets. A ride on a double-decker bus is a good laugh – preferably outside of the rush hour. Among the other must-see attractions are: the Gothic Christ Church Cathedral; the Gothic St Patrick's Cathedral; the historical Temple Bar nightlife area; Trinity College and lively university district; the National Gallery with a collection of Irish paintings; the National Museum of Irish cultural history; the National Botanic Gardens with 19th-century greenhouses.

Skellig Michael Monastery

The cells of the Skellig Michael Monastery are a well-preserved example of early Irish architecture. The stone-walled terraces support several stone huts whose domes rise up from square floor plans like beehives. Although the monastery complex was built without the use of mortar, it has withstood the merciless elements of the west coast since the 7th century.

From the mainland it is impossible to see this hidden treasure – a UNESCO World Heritage Site since 1996 – and the island's jagged, 217-m-high (712-ft) cliffs tend to ward off visitors. The 6th-century monks here were searching for a remote location for their sanctuary and their choice fell on Great Skellig, the largest of the Skellig Islands. The conditions on Great Skellig of course demanded a very spartan lifestyle. The monks clambered down from the monastery to the sea every day to catch their daily ration of fish, bartering part of their catch with passing sailors in exchange for corn and tools.

The 670 steps cut into the cliff still allow today's visitors to attempt the exhausting climb up to the

Skellig Michael is a desolate, 17-ha (42-acre) rock island.

complex, which was actually inhabited until the 12th century. The few stone crosses in the small cemetery commemorate the early residents of the monastery, where important manuscripts were produced.

Boats sail to the island between April and September only, and even in those months only when the sea is calm. The roughly 90-min crossing from Portmagee circles Little Skellig island, while the Skellig Experience exhibition on Valentia Island serves as an introduction and preparation for the spectacular Skellig Michael.

abandoned some 100 years later. In addition to the cathedral, its mighty walls also house Cormac's Chapel, a masterpiece of romanesque architecture, and the 28-m (92-ft) round tower. Another of Cashel's attractions is the Folk Village, an open-air museum that documents the region's history.

From Cashel the route continues south-west towards Cork, about 60 km (37 mi) away.

⑦ Cork The Republic's second-largest city after Dublin has about 125,000 people and is noticeably more "continental" than the capital. It also boasts a range of architectural treasures dating from the 18th and 19th centuries. The old town is situated on an island between two channels of the River Lee. The narrow alleyways, quaint canals and bridges lined with townhouses are reminiscent of Dutch towns.

Cork's landmark is St Ann's Shandon, a church built in 1722. The weather vane in the shape of a salmon on the top of the tower is visible from afar and is a good orientation point. A climb up the tower is rewarded with a panoramic view.

From Cork it is worth taking a detour to the town of Midleton, just 20 km (12 mi) to the east, or to Ballycrovane in the direction of Killarney.

⑧ Jameson Heritage Center Midleton is known primarily as the site of the island's largest whiskey distillery. A number of famous brands including Jameson, Tullamore Dew and Hewitts are distilled here. On the guided tour you'll learn a bit about the history and techniques of whiskey production.

⑨ Blarney Castle A second detour takes you along the by-pass road north of Cork to Blarney Castle (15th century). Visitors from all over the world flock to the ruins of this castle

10 km (6 mi) north-west of Cork to not just see the legendary Blarney stone but also give it a kiss. According to the legend, anyone kissing the stone will be endowed with eloquence and the power of persuasion, the word "blarney" being a synonym for flattery.

With its many handicraft and souvenir shops, the village of Blarney is quite tourist-oriented. The route back to the main road heading west, the N 22, follows portions of the Lee River.

⑩ Killarney This town is a popular starting point for exploring south-west Ireland. You won't be able to overlook the many horse-drawn coaches plying the roads inviting visitors to take a tour of the town. Killarney's sightseeing attractions include the National Museum of Irish Transport, with a collection of vintage cars, as well as a life-like model railway.

Most guests don't linger long in the town, though, for nearby awaits the spectacular landscape of Killarney National Park, which covers an area of approximately 100 sq km (39 sq mi) and features three scenic lakes: Upper Lake, Muckross Lake and Lough Leane, the largest of the three. The many small islands appear like dabs of green paint in the blue water, while the densely wooded hills rise gently from the shores. At a few locations, however, the mountains rise abruptly enough from the lake's edge to create sizable falls. One of these is the Torc Waterfall, which drops 18 m (59 ft) into Muckross Lake, marking the end of the Owengarriff River. Several monasteries and fortress ruins dot the surrounding lake landscape as well, including Muckross Abbey (ca. 1448) and Ross Castle (ca. 1420).

Up until the mid-17th century, some of these buildings formed the last of the Irish bastions in their fight against the English under Oliver Cromwell.

From the lake district, a number of roads lead to the Macgillcuddy's Reeks, a mountain chain that includes the Carrauntoohil, a 1,041-m (3,416-ft) peak.

⑪ Ring of Kerry In addition to the scenery of the Iveragh Peninsula, there are a number of picturesque locations in County Kerry that are worth a stopover. In Sneem, near the south coast, for example, the colorful houses of this picturesque town make a charming impression.

Only a few miles farther to the west is a 3-km-long (2-mi) road leading from the main road up to Staigue Stone Fort, a Celtic fortification dating from the 3rd/4th centuries.

The 3-km-long (2-mi) Caherdaniel beach has a Mediterranean atmosphere, with scenic sand dunes and boats for hire. The Derrynane House, a feudal country home in the Derrynane National Historic Park, commemorates Daniel O'Connell, an Irish national hero for his efforts in liberating Catholics from oppressive British laws. After the road

takes a turn to the north, a famous postcard scene awaits you behind the Coomakista Pass: a lonely row of houses on a cliff in Waterville that defies the strong winds blowing up from the ocean. From the main road, head westward to the fishing village of Portmagee where boats take you to the monastery island of Skellig Michael. The village is linked by a bridge to Valentia Island off the coast to the north. Accordion music emanating from the pubs is typical of the island's main town, Knight's Town.

Back on Iveragh you soon come to the main town on the peninsula, Cahersiveen, which has retained much of its charm despite the heavy tourism in the area. The village of Glenbeigh boasts the 5-km-long (3-mi) Rossbehy Beach, which seems to never end and proudly flies the sea-blue environmental flag indicating especially clean water. The Kerry Bog Museum nearby has an exhibition on the history of the now defunct peat cultivation trade.

Clonmacnoise Monastery

This monastery on the River Shannon is a must for anyone passing through the Irish Midlands. It is especially appealing for the contrast between its ruins and their surroundings. Founded in the 6th century by St Ciaran, the monastery's location was convenient even in the Middle Ages, but at that time the only safe way to reach the site was through the infamous Blackwater Moor.
Between the 7th and the 12th centuries, Clonmacnoise was an important center for scholars and artisans. Numerous valuable manu-

The town of Killorglin to the north-east nicely rounds off your visit to the Ring of Kerry with a choice of more than twenty pubs.

12 Dingle Peninsula A drive around the 48-km-long (30-mi) Dingle Peninsula is equally stunning as the Ring of Kerry, and you'll need to plan at least half a day for it. The alternating craggy cliffs and sandy bays are what

and monasteries. The tiny Gallarus Oratory stone church, with a shape reminiscent of a capsized boat, is one of the best-preserved early churches in Ireland. The Blasket Islands are just off the coast.

13 Tralee The main attractions in Tralee are the Kerry County Museum and the Blennerville Windmill, situated just outside of town and the largest still

14 Limerick The mighty Shannon River is spanned by several bridges at Limerick. Although the town does not appear particularly inviting at first glance, it does have a number of sights worth seeing. The oldest building in Limerick, which was founded by the Vikings in the 9th century, is St Mary's Cathedral, built on a hill in 1172.
No less imposing is King John's Castle, from 1200, has five round towers and impressive ramparts. The Hunt Museum has antique relics from all over Ireland.

15 Bunratty Castle und Folk Park North-west of Limerick, Bunratty Castle is yet another must for any itinerary. The most famous lords of this manor, from the 15th century, were the O'Briens. The rooms are magnificently furnished with antique furniture and tapestries, creating a unique atmosphere. Medieval-style banquets still take place here in the evenings. From the stout battlements to the dark dungeons, the complex provides a graphic portrayal of aristocratic life in Ireland. An entirely reconstructed medieval Irish farming village has also been erected in front of the castle in the Folk Park.
Continuing north for a mile or so you will come to the 12th-century Augustine Clare Abbey shortly before the town of Ennis. Ennis Abbey (13th/14th centuries) was once one of Ireland's largest and contains some high-quality medieval styling.
The small town is characterized by winding alleys and a lively music scene. Indeed, folk music seems to be everywhere here. From Ennis, the road continues

south-west through the interior before reaching Kilrush, one of Ireland's largest yachting ports, just before the Shannon widens and flows into the ocean. From here you continue along the west coast to one of the region's main attractions.

16 Cliffs of Moher The Cliffs of Moher are an absolutely breathtaking feat of nature. These vertical cliffs can be more than 200 m (656 ft) high and stretch over a length of 8 km (5 mi). The spectacular backdrop is accompanied by the cackle of countless sea birds. Visitors can venture up to the edge of the cliffs along the paths but the lack of protective barriers does mean that caution needs to be exercised.

1 County Kerry in the south-west of Ireland is a paradise for botanists and ornithologists.

2 The Macgillcuddy's Reeks mountain range in Kerry is located on the north-east of the Iveragh Peninsula.

3 Fingers of land reach out into the ocean on the Dingle Peninsula.

4 The Blasket Islands are Europe's westernmost point.

5 The Cliffs of Moher are among the many popular attractions in the west of Ireland. They extend over 8 km (5 mi) between Hags Head in the south and Aillensharragh in the north.

6 The town of Limerick is divided into three parts by the Shannon and Abbey Rivers.

**Top: The impressive Clonmacnoise ruins.
Below: Irish crosses in the Clonmacnoise cemetery.**

scripts as well as traditional Celtic gold and silver works were written and created here.
Although the monks were long able to withstand attacks from the Vikings and the Normans, in addition to a number of fires, their resistance against English soldiers in 1552 proved futile. The latter ultimately rendered the complex uninhabitable forever.
The site, measuring roughly one hectare (2.5 acres), encompasses the ruins of a cathedral and eight churches as well as copies of a number of high crosses and tombstones. The originals are displayed in the Visitor Center.
An audiovisual presentation provides interesting details on the lifestyle of the monks and on the significance of the individual buildings on the site.

Ring of Kerry

A highlight of any trip to Ireland is the roughly 200-km-long (124-mi) tour around the Iveragh Peninsula, which magnificently displays many of Ireland's most appealing features within a compact area The south coast is more rugged and fragmented into bays than the north coast. The road is good and parking is available at the various points of interest.

make this coastal landscape particularly appealing.
Coming from the south, you leave the main road at Castlemaine heading west. The sandy Inch Spit is a perfect beach for a swim. The main road then continues past several old fortresses

functioning windmill in Ireland. From Tralee the route heads north to Tarbet, where the road then follows the course of the Shannon River. On the way to Limerick it is worth making a stop in Glin and the Georgian Glin Castle, built in 1780.

Top: The coastal landscape at Connemara. Part of the peninsula is a national park containing moorlands, swamps, the mountain scenery of Twelve Ben and Glanmore Valley, and the area along the Polladirk River.

Bottom: The scenery at Doo Lough in County Mayo in the north-west of Ireland is breathtaking. The extensive Doo Lough is wedged between the Mweelrea and the Sheffry Mountains and is surrounded by dense forests.

Belfast

The Northern Irish capital has been the subject of largely negative head-lines in recent decades but they are quickly forgotten when you arrive in Belfast. The city is situated at the mouth of the Lagan River in a bay known as Belfast Lough.

Belfast is the political, economic and cultural center of Northern Ireland. The lively seaport, with a population of 300,000, has everything that makes a vibrant town into a city – a wealth of shopping opportunities, myriad restaurants, theaters and cinemas, and some architectural highlights.

Belfast was officially founded in the year 1177 with the construction of the Norman fortress, but even after it was captured by England there was no significant development of the settlement. By the mid-17th century, the town comprised no more than 150 houses. Just a few decades later, however, the Huguenots, driven out of France for religious reasons, built up a prosperous linen industry, with tobacco processing and ship-

Belfast's illuminated skyline along Belfast Lough.

building also providing further em-ployment opportunities and economic stimulus. The result was a dramatic rise in the number of immigrants from neighboring England and Scotland. Belfast became the capital of Northern Ireland in 1920.

The most important location in the city center is Donegall Square. It is home to some imposing Victorian buildings as well as the city's most prominent landmark: the grandiose city hall from 1906 with its striking copper dome. The Grand Opera House, which opened in 1894, is one of the most important concert halls in Great Britain. Just a stone's throw away is the famous Crown Liquor Saloon, a Victorian-style pub that is worth a visit just for its stylish stained-glass windows, marble décor and gas lamps.

17 The Burren In the town of Lisdoonvarna the R 476 heads south-east toward Leamaneagh Castle (17th century).

You will pass through a unique landscape on the way north known as the Burren, whose name is derived from the Irish word for "great rock" (boire-ann). In the 17th century, this limestone plateau, with numer-ous rifts and cleavages, was somewhat grimly described by one English military commander as follows: "No water for drown-ing, no trees for hanging, no soil for burying". Stone circles and other traces of settlement in this desolate region remain an enigma today.

The excavation of human bones here, however, has proven that the Poulnabrone dolmen, a col-lection of monoliths, served as a burial ground between 2500 and 2000 BC. The Burren is also known for its caves. One of them, the Aillwee Cave, can be visited and is set back somewhat from the road. Bring a jacket as the temperature in the caves is only 10 °C (50 °F) all year round.

18 Galway With a population of about 66,000, Galway is the largest town in western Ireland. It is also a university town and is characterized not only by its cozy alleyways and stone build-ings with wooden facades, but also for its pub and music scene. For car drivers the center of the town at Corrib is a nightmare, but it is a paradise for pedestri-ans and strollers. When the weather is good, street cafés get busy while musicians and artists display their prowess.

The renovated suburbs along the river are testimony to a high standard of living, a result of the high-tech boom of recent years. The town's best-known build-ings include the St Nicholas Church, built by the Normans in 1320, and the St Nicholas Cathe-dral from 1965, on the northern bank of the river.

From Galway, a good road heads east to Clonmacnoise Monastery about 65 km (40 mi) away.

19 Aran Islands The ferries to the craggy Aran Islands depart from Galway. The archipelago's main island, Inishmore, is a mountain bikers' paradise, but tours of the island are also offered via minibus or horse-drawn carriage. Recommended stops are the steep cliffs as well as the monastery and fortress ruins like Dun Aengus. The *Men of Aran*, a silent film from the 1930s, portrays the fishermen

doing what would appear even then to have been a tedious job.

20 Kylemore Abbey The land-scape west of Galway is defined by coastline, mountains and stark moorlands, all protected in part by the Connemara National Park. The route from Galway to-wards the west and north-west closely follows the coast and fea-tures many bays as well as Clifden Castle.

Kylemore Abbey, an enchanting 19th-century Benedictine abbey, is idyllically situated on Kylemore Lough. Part of the present-day national park land actually used to belong to the abbey. En route to the north it is worth taking a detour at Bangor to Blacksod Point.

21 Donegal Castle A mighty 15th-century fortress dominates the small town of Donegal. After several renovations, it now looks more like a castle, and the ban-queting hall alone is worth the entrance fee. Preserved in the style of the Jacobean era, it boasts a fireplace dating from this time. You leave the coast road at Donegal and head across the northern tip of Ireland toward Londonderry.

22 Londonderry You reach the walled town of Londonderry shortly after crossing the border into Northern Ireland. The city is known as Londonderry to Protestants here, while Catholics and residents of the Republic re-fer to it as Derry, a name derived from the Irish "Daire", meaning "oak grove". Houses in pastel hues characterize the cityscape. The walls of Derry, up to 9 m (30 ft) wide in places, are some of the most intact town forti-fications in all of Europe. The Tower Museum details the town's history and the Bloody Sunday Center tells of the Northern Ireland conflict.

23 Giant's Causeway The in-numerable basalt stones of the Giant's Causeway are the undis-puted highlight of the very scenic Antrim north coast. They are also shrouded in legend. One story tells of a giant who built a causeway so that his mistress, who lived on the Scottish island of Staffa, would be able to reach Ireland without getting her feet wet. No one knows the exact number of the mostly hexagonal basalt columns, but some of them measure up to 25 m (82 ft) in height.

The route then continues along the north-east coast of the North Channel, past Dunluce Castle, heading to Belfast and then leaving Northern Ireland again south of Newry.

24 Belfast (see sidebar left)

25 Bend of the Boyne Before reaching Dublin, it is worth stopping in the Boyne Valley near Slane. The valley features neothlithic passage graves. The grave built near Newgrange in 3200 BC remained untouched until 1960. It has a 19-m-long (62-ft) passage leading to the 6-m-high (20-ft) burial chamber with three side chambers.

1 Giant's Causeway: An estimated 35,000 hexagonal basalt columns rise out of this coastal formation to heights of up to 25 m (82 ft).

2 A prehistoric stone circle at Blacksod Point on the southern tip of the Mullet Peninsula.

3 On a cliff on the north coast of Antrim, Dunluce Castle (13th cen-tury) stands exposed to the whims of the rugged coast.

Blacksod Point The Mullet Peninsula is connected to the north-west Irish mainland by a narrow, sparsely inhabited spit of land. On the west, it is a wide rocky plateau with pebble beaches that are constantly pounded by the sea. A granite lighthouse stands at the southernmost tip of the island, at Blacksod Point. Tthe island cemetery here at the "End of the World" is also worth a visit.

Giant's Causeway The roughly 35,000 step-like basalt columns, most of which have a hexagonal shape and rise to heights of up to 25 m (82 ft), are the natural scenic highlight of Northern Ireland. Their origins are shrouded in legend but they are in fact a completely natural form of cooled, slow-flowing lava.

Dunluce Castle The well-preserved 13th-century castle ruins are located on a high cliff on the north coast of Antrim, only about 10 km (6 mi) west of the Giant's Causeway. As defiant as the former headquarters of the lofty MacDonnels and Lords of Antrim may appear today, the castle was in fact powerless in the face of the harsh coastal winds.

Connemara The area in the north-west of County Galway is a barren landscape of stone walls and moors where traditional rural culture has been well preserved. Its white beaches provide a stark contrast, and the Victorian resort town of Clifden is an ideal base from which to explore the area.

Bend of the Boyne Due to its ring-like fortifications, passage graves and cairns, this river valley in the Midlands near Dublin is considered to be the cradle of Irish civilization. The Newgrange passage grave from 3200 BC is particularly striking.

Clonmacnoise This especially attractive monastery on the Shannon was founded in the mid-6th century. It has been in ruins since its destruction by English soldiers in 1552.

Belfast The numerous Victorian buildings here make the Northern Irish capital and the port at the mouth of the Lagan River well worth a visit. The Grand Opera House and the domed city hall are two main attractions.

Cliffs of Moher The sandstone and shale cliffs, some of which are up to 200 m (656 ft) high, extend over 8 km (5 mi) from Hags Head to Aillenshragh.

Dublin Christ Church and St Patrick's cathedrals, as well as Dublin Castle, Trinity College, the National Gallery and the National Museum are all worth a visit in the Irish capital.

Skellig Michael The monastery shelters on the island of Great Skellig are examples of Irish architecture. The 700 steps give an indication of how tough monastic life must have been.

Rock of Cashel, County Tipperary On the lower reaches of the Shannon, this county is rich in farmland. St Patrick is alleged to have picked three-leaf clover on the Rock of Cashel in 450.

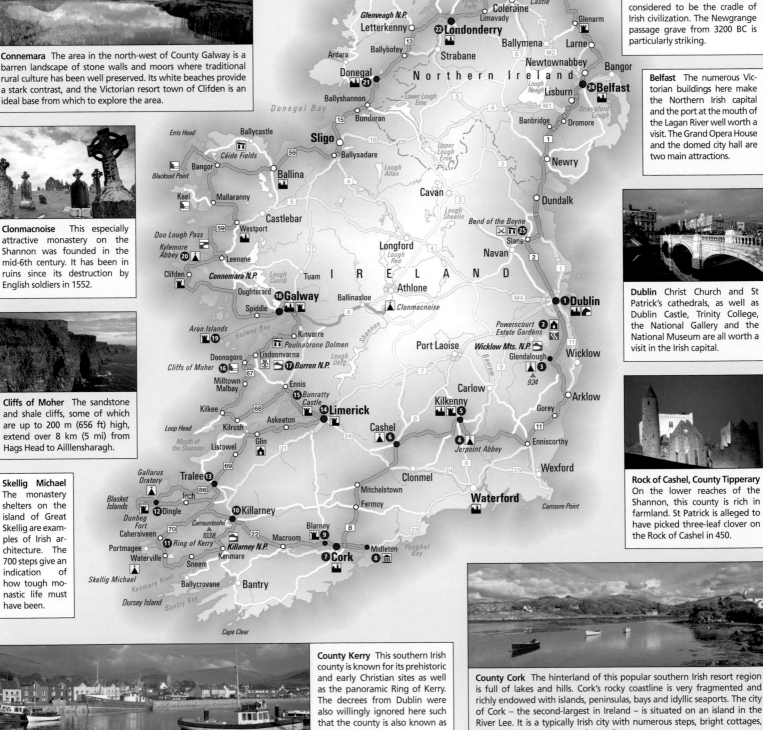

County Kerry This southern Irish county is known for its prehistoric and early Christian sites as well as the panoramic Ring of Kerry. The decrees from Dublin were also willingly ignored here such that the county is also known as "The Kingdom".

County Cork The hinterland of this popular southern Irish resort region is full of lakes and hills. Cork's rocky coastline is very fragmented and richly endowed with islands, peninsulas, bays and idyllic seaports. The city of Cork – the second-largest in Ireland – is situated on an island in the River Lee. It is a typically Irish city with numerous steps, bright cottages, attractive pubs and even a vineyard!

The summit of Buchaille Etive Mor is a challenge for mountain climbers.

Scotland

Clansmen, whisky and the solitude of the Highlands

Whether you're a romantic, a lover of the outdoors or a culture connoisseur, Scotland's raw beauty rarely fails to move the souls of people who make the journey there. Those who choose to experience the rugged, often solitary landscape of the Highlands and the rich history and tradition of this country will be rewarded with unforgettable memories.

Jagged escarpments covered in a lush carpet of green grass, deep lakes in misty moorlands, and torrential rivers tumbling down craggy valleys often typify our image of the Highlands and Scotland in general. But there is more to Scotland than the Highlands in the north, notably the interesting groups of islands to the west and a couple of lovely cities.
Glasgow and the capital, Edinburgh, offer modern city living, with cultural events, attractive shopping possibilities and renowned festivals, while idyllic sandy

'Clansmen' in Scottish national costume.

beaches await discovery, for example on the Western Isles. On the mainland, Scotland's first national parks were recently opened around the Cairngorm Mountains and Loch Lomond.
Poets such as Sir Walter Scott and the 'national poet of Scotland', Robert Burns, have written of this country's unique beauty. The modern revival of Gaelic music and language has long since spread beyond Scotland's borders, and Scottish customs like caber tossing and wearing kilts may seem peculiar to outsiders, but to the Scots they are part of their identity.
If you take one insider tip, make it this one: Scottish cooking. Once you have tried Angus steak, grouse or Highland lamb, you will no longer limit your praise of the country to single malt whisky. Having said that, there are about 110 whisky distilleries in Scotland, mainly

spread around the Highlands and on the Western Isles. These world-famous single malt elixirs age for up to thirty years in old whisky and sherry barrels.
Scotland's territory covers a total of 78,000 sq km (30,014 sq mi), roughly the top third of the island of Great Britain. Most of its many islands are part of either the Hebrides (Inner and Outer), the Orkneys or the Shetlands. During the last ice age, glaciers formed deep valleys throughout the region. When they melted, they left behind lochs (lakes) and firths (fjords) along the country's 3,700 km (2,300 miles) of coastline.
Among the characteristics of the Highlands, the most sparsely populated area of Scotland, are steep rock faces, heath-covered moors, deep lochs and rushing mountain streams. The Great Glen valley divides the Highlands into two

Eilean Donan Castle lies on Loch Duich in Glen Shiel and is linked to the mainland by a small dam and a bridge. The castle was rebuilt last century from its former ruins.

Kilchurn Castle on the northern edge of Loch Awe dates from the 15th century.

parts. South of the Highlands are the Lowlands, a fertile and densely populated area containing both Glasgow and Edinburgh. The Southern Uplands make up the border with England.

Despite what one might think, Scotland's oceanic climate rarely produces extreme weather conditions – but the weather really can change from sun to rain in a hurry. Wide areas of Scotland are renowned for their characteristic flora (heather, pine trees, ferns) and a wide variety of wildlife.

The Scots are the descendants of a mix of different peoples including the Picts, the Scots, who gave their name to the country, as well as the Scandinavians and the Anglo-Saxons. It was in the 9th century, under Kenneth MacAlpine, that Alba was founded, the first Celtic Scottish kingdom. From then on Scotland's history was plagued with struggles for independence and resistance against the ever-mightier forces of England. In 1707, the 'Acts of Union' created the Kingdom of Great Britain and with that came the end of Scotland's independence.

Things unfortunately went from bad to worse after that. The characteristic solitude of the Scottish landscape was a direct result of the Highland Clearances, a move by their own clan chiefs and aristocratic land owners in the 18th century to run small Highland and island farmers off their plots to make room for more lucrative sheep breeding.

After 300 years, Scotland now has its own parliament again, in Edinburgh, and about 5.1 million people. Although the official language is English, many Scots in the Highlands and on the Hebrides speak Scottish Gaelic, a Celtic language.

Tobemory with its colourful houses lies on the northern end of the Isle of Mull.

Detour

Blair Castle

At Arbroath the A933 makes its way west before you get to For-far, where the pink-grey walls of Glamis Castle appear through the trees. It is a place steeped in history, from the murder of Duncan by Macbeth to numerous ghost apparitions and the childhood tales of the late Queen Mother, who grew up here.

The trip then continues north-west to Blair Atholl via the Killiecrankie Pass, scene in 1689 of a bloody battle between the English and the Scots.

The origins of Blair Castle date back to the 13th century.

From there an alley lined with lime trees leads to Blair Castle, the residence of the Duke of Atholl. This fabulously equipped, brilliant white castle is among the most beautiful buildings in Scotland.

The Atholl Highlanders, as the Duke of Atholl's private army is called, are a curious band. Every year at the beginning of June an impressive parade is staged in front of the castle with a backing of bagpipe music.

A journey through Scotland: venerable buildings, mysterious stone circles and the occasional whisky distillery line your route, which begins in Edinburgh, takes you through the Highlands and ends in Glasgow. Detours to the Orkneys and Hebrides are highly recommended and can be easily organized from the various port towns.

① **Edinburgh** (see page 31). Your route begins in the cultural metropolis of Edinburgh, travelling initially north-westward towards Stirling.

② **Stirling** The charming city of Stirling, roughly 58 km (36 miles) west of Edinburgh, is built on the banks of the Forth at the point where it first becomes part of the tidal firth (fjord). It is often called the 'Gateway to the Highlands' and is dominated by a large castle. The oldest part of Stirling Castle dates back to the 14th century. The Church of the Holy Rood (cross), which was built in the 13th century, is historically significant in that it is one of the very few churches from the Middle Ages to have survived the Reformation in Scotland.

③ **Fife Peninsula** The Fife Peninsula juts out between the Firth of Forth and the Firth of Tay. In the 4th century the region here made up one of the seven Scottish kingdoms.

The northern coast of the Firth of Forth leads initially to Culross, a small town that blossomed as a trading center in the 16th cen-

tury. Wealthy trade houses have remained intact and make for an enchanting atmosphere here.

About 11 km (7 miles) to the east of Culross you'll come to Dunfermline, once a long-standing residence or 'burgh' of the Scottish kings. The ruins of the old castle, abbey and monastery can still be seen atop a hill to the south-west of the town.

A little further east, behind the Chapel Ness headland and between the coastal towns of Elie

1 View from the Nelson Monument of the Old Town and castle in Edinburgh.

2 The Scottish national sport of golf was already being played in the 15th century on the sandy beaches of St Andrews.

3 Glamis Castle was the childhood home of the late Queen Mother.

Travel information

Route profile
Length: approx. 1,200 km (745 miles), excluding detours
Time required: 2–3 weeks
Start: Edinburgh
End: Glasgow
Route (main locations): Edinburgh, Stirling, Dundee, Dunottar Castle, Ballater, Inverness, John o'Groats, Durness, Fort William, Inveraray, Glasgow

Traffic information:
Drive on the left in Scotland. Ferries connect the mainland with the various islands:
www.northlink-ferries.co.uk
www.scottish-islands.com

Weather:
The weather in Scotland is generally 'unsettled':

summers are relatively cool, winters on the coast are mild, but in the Highlands bitterly cold, and it can rain at any given moment.

When to go:
Between April and October is the best time. You can check weather forecasts at:
www.onlineweather.com

Accommodation:
An interesting option is a private bed & breakfast:
www.bedandbreakfast scotland.co.uk
www.aboutscotland.com

Information:
wikitravel.org/en/ Scotland
www.visitscotland.com
www.scotland.org.uk

Edinburgh

Both the Old Town and New Town of Scotland's capital have been listed as UNESCO World Heritage Sites, and both are a fascinating display of architectural unity and its exceptional cultural activity. Summer is especially lively during the renowned Edinburgh Festival weeks. The city has been the cultural center of the north since the 18th and 19th centuries, with famous authors such as Robert Burns and Sir Walter Scott making it their home.

The oldest core of the city, inhabited since the Bronze Age, is Castle Rock, a volcanic outcrop upon which King Edwin built the first castle in the 7th century – hence the name Edinburgh. The castle is still the city's eye-catcher but other higher buildings from the 17th century rise up around it like battlements.

The attractions most worthy of a visit in the Old Town include Edinburgh Castle, a large edifice with buildings from numerous eras, of which St Margaret's Chapel (11th century) is the oldest; the Scottish royal insignia in the castle's Crown Room; the Palace

Edinburgh Castle has served as a fort, a royal residence and a prison.

of Holyroodhouse, the Queen's official residence in Scotland; and the Royal Mile between her residence and the castle with its many side streets.

The New Town, built at the end of the 18th century, is home to the National Gallery of Scotland with one of Europe's most important collections of paintings, the Museum of Antiques for early and art history, and the Scottish National Gallery of Modern Art (20th-century art), all of which are worth a visit.

Detour

Balmoral Castle

This royal castle on the River Dee is in the Grampian Mountains, and thus within the limits of the Cairngorms National Park in Aberdeenshire. Prince Albert, Queen Victoria's consort, bought Balmoral Castle in 1846 and later had it replaced with a magnificent granite building in grand Scottish style.

He personally oversaw the interior decoration, which was inspired by Scottish hunting lodges, with large check patterns and floral designs on upholstery that bear witness to the country style. The royal family came here to get away from court ceremonies in London.

Cairngorms National Park, established in 2003, is Great Britain's largest national park and stretches from Grantown on the Spey to Angus Glens near Glamis. Twenty five per cent of Great Britain's endangered species live in the reserve and numerous rare plants

Top: Iconic Highland cattle graze in front of Balmoral Castle.
Bottom: A royal garden party.

grow only at the foot of the central Cairngorms range (Scottish Gaelic for "Blue Mountain"). The various moorlands, heath and forests are typical of the area. Fields and pasture typify the lovely Spey and Dee valleys.

Stone-Age monuments, medieval castles and towns steeped in tradition are testimony to the historical importance of the region.

and Crail, is a series of picturesque fishing villages, castle ruins and old churches.

④ St Andrews Continuing on around the north-east side of the peninsula you will come to the proverbial golfing mecca of the world, St Andrews, about 10 km (6 miles) north of Crail. This, the first ever golf club, was founded here in 1754, and it is still possible to play on the famous Old Course.

The 16th-century ruins of Blackfriars Chapel, at one time Scotland's largest church, are also worth a visit if golf isn't your cup of tea. There is a fabulous view of the grounds from the top of St Rule's Tower.

The route then follows the coast through Dundee to Montrose, about 12 km (8 miles) north of Arbroath. A worthy detour here takes you to Blair Castle, roughly 65 km (40 miles) inland from Arbroath.

⑤ Montrose This port town and 'burgh' is built like a defensive wall on the peninsula of a natural bay. The House of Dun Mansion, built in 1730, stands on the bank of the Montrose Basin. The coastline north and south of Montrose impresses with long sandy beaches and steep cliffs.

⑥ Dunnottar Castle Following the A92 to the north you'll reach one of Scotland's most

fascinating ruins just a few kilometers before Stonehaven – Dunnottar Castle. Built on a rock more than 50 m (60 yds) out to sea, the fortress is connected to the mainland only by a narrow spit of land.

In the 17th century, the Scottish imperial insignia were stored here. Nowadays, only the ruins of the turret, a barrack and the chapel remain of the once formidable construction.

⑦ Aberdeen This town is the capital of Europe's oil industry and one of the largest European ports. Despite its industrial leanings, however, there are a number of historic highlights to visit, including Kings College, St Andrew's Cathedral, St Machar's Cathedral and the Maritime Museum.

From Aberdeen the route leads inland to Ballater. (Here we recommend taking a detour to

Balmoral Castle about 50 km (31 miles) away. The mountain road (A939) then goes from Ballater through Colnabaichin to Tomintoul, the starting point of the whisky trail, before heading to Dufftown and Keith.

You then go west through the Spey Valley to Aviemore where the A9 takes you to Inverness.

⑧ Inverness This modern-day industrial center at the northern

The Orkney Islands

The Orkney Islands, of which only eighteen are inhabited, are around 30 km (19 miles) off the north-eastern coast of Scotland. They are best reached from the ferry ports of John o'Groats and Thurso.

Mainland, Hoy and South Ronaldsay are the larger of the islands in the archipelago, with rolling hills formed by glaciers from the last ice age. Despite their northerly location, the islands benefit from a comparatively mild climate caused by the warm Gulf Stream.

along the north coast towards Bettyhill past deserted beaches that are often only accessible by short footpaths. Dunnet Head is the most northern point of the Scottish mainland. The popular holiday destination of Thurso, which is also the ferry port for travel to the Orkney Islands, was the scene of a memorable battle between the Scots and the Vikings in 1040.

To the west of the village of Bettyhill, in the county of Sutherland, the A836 leads over the impressive Kyle of Tongue Fjord and on to Durness. Shortly before Durness is the Cave of Smoo, which was used as shelter by the Picts, then the Vikings, and later still by Scottish smugglers. Organized trips to Cape Wrath, the rocky outcrop on the north-westernmost point of Scotland, are offered from Durness.

1 The once strategic position of Dunnottar Castle is unmistakable: built on a solid rock promontory, a deep ravine separates the castle from the mainland.

2 Inverness is the 'capital' of the Highlands, and its business and administrative center.

3 View from the port over Aberdeen.

4 Mighty waves from the Atlantic crash against the cliffs of Cape Wrath on the north coast of Scotland. The lighthouse was built in 1828.

Top: An historic lighthouse.
Middle: The 'Standing Stones of Stennes', a prehistoric stone circle.
Bottom: Impressive rocky coast.

The inhabitants of the Orkneys, descendants of Scots and Scandinavians, live mostly from farming, fishing and tourism these days. Rock climbers and ornithologists are also fascinated by Britain's highest coastal cliffs (347 m/1,138 ft) on the island of Hoy, while the spectacular landscape and monuments, like the Stone-Age village of Skara Brae or the stone circle of Brodgar on Mainland, are popular with everyone who visits.

The Whisky Trail

The famous 110-km-long (68-mile) Speyside Malt Whisky Trail, which sets off from Tomintoul, is a well-signposted route leading past seven whisky distilleries. Among them are some well-known names such as Glenlivet, Glenfiddich and Glenfarclas.

tip of Loch Ness is the ideal starting point for trips to the home of 'Nessie', Urquhart Castle and into the wild and romantic Highland landscape.

Due to its exposed location, Inverness was regularly involved in military disputes, to the extent that few of its old buildings remain. Most of today's structures were erected in the 19th century.

9 East Coast of the North-west Highlands From Inverness the A9 (and the A99) snake northwards along the striking east coast. Various sites like Dunrobin Castle, Helmsdale Castle or the mysterious Bronze-Age rock lines near Greg Cairns are worth short visits on your way. One option is to take a long walk from the former fishing village of Wick out to the picturesque cliffs of Noss Head. Nearby are the ruins of Sinclair and Girnigoe Castles.

10 John o'Groats The village of John o'Groats is about 17 km (11 miles) north of Wick on the north-eastern tip of Caithness. Just before you get there, Warth Hill will offer an exceptional view of the area.

Ferries travel between John o'Groats, the Orkneys and the coastal seal colonies.

11 North Coast The A836 then takes you from John o'Groats

Detour

The Outer Hebrides

The Atlantic islands to the west of Scotland are made up of the southern Inner Hebrides, near the Scottish mainland, and the Outer Hebrides (Western Isles) farther out towards the northwest. The main islands of the Outer Hebrides are, from north to south, the double islands of Lewis and Harris, North Uist and South Uist, joined by a dam, and Barra. You can reach the Western Isles by ferry from Ullapool or from Skye, the largest of the Inner Hebrides islands, which include Rum, Coll, Tiree, Mull, Jura and Islay.

The Hebrides have a long and varied past. In 563 the Irish minister Columban the Elder (who later became St Columba) established a Celtic monastery on the small island of Iona and began the process of Christianizing Scotland. In the 8th century the islands were invaded by the Norwegian Vikings, who kept their rule over much of the region for many hundreds of years. It was only in 1266, after the signing of the Treaty of Perth, that the Scots regained the upper hand and the islands were henceforth run by the clans MacDougall and MacDonald. Their rulers were thereafter called 'Lord of the Isles'.

Today's visitors are met by a world in which life is still greatly influenced by natural forces and the isolation of the Atlantic. History and time have left some clear traces in the partly undulating moor and heath landscape. In geological terms the islands consist of the oldest rocks in the entire British Isles. Stone-Age graves, Celtic Christian ruins, Viking settlements and Scottish forts can all be found around the various Hebrides islands.

In addition to the historical attractions, the magnificent natural environment includes lakes and valleys, pristine white sand beaches, and rich animal and plant life that all help to attract a good number of adventurous tourists each year.

The Isle of Lewis and Harris

The two halves of the island of Lewis and Harris are connected by an isthmus and are not just the largest of the Western Isles, but the largest island around Great Britain after Ireland. Lewis and Harris have very differing landscapes: Lewis is littered with rocky hill ranges, fjords and bays, while Harris is covered with moors and heath. The A859 leads from the main town of Stornoway to south Harris, which is noteworthy for its fabulous sandy beaches. Don't miss the mysterious stone circles of Callanish on Lewis, which, like Stonehenge, were built thousands of years ago, presumably for cult rituals.

North Uist und South Uist

North and South Uist, and the island of Benbecula between them, are covered with countless lakes. Deep ocean bays line the east coast to such an extent that it resembles a series of islands that have grown together.

The Stone-Age burial chambers on North Uist and the low, reed-covered crofter houses, some of which have survived hundreds of years of wind and weather, are worth visiting.

The A865 leads all the way around North Uist and down to the southern tip of South Uist, passing the prettiest areas of the island on the way. The east coast of South Uist has two 600-m (2,000-ft) peaks – Beinn Mhór and Hecla.

Barra

Ferries from Ludag on South Uist to the small island of Barra, the southernmost island of the Outer Hebrides, only take about 40 minutes. Barra's small neighbouring islands include Berneray with it tall lighthouse.

The island, named after St Finbarr, is regarded as one of the prettiest islands of the Outer Hebrides due to the thousands of colourful flowers that grow

there. Kisimuil Castle, the old residence of the MacNeils, dominates the port of the main town, Castlebay.

The ring road, the A888, goes as far as Cille Barra in the north, with its ruins of a monastery built in the 12th century. A 12th-century chapel has been restored and houses some sacred objects. A cemetery lies on the hill.

1 Isle of Lewis: the monumental 'Standing Stones of Callanish' form a 13 m by 11 m (40 ft by 35 ft) circle and were erected around 1800 BC.

2 The Taransay Sound separates the island of Taransay from the south-west coast of Harris. This island of beautiful beaches is uninhabited.

3 Lovers of treeless, wild landscapes will be contented on the Isle of Lewis in the north of the Outer Hebrides.

4 This is the inlet of Loch Sealg on the east coast of Lewis at dusk. The natural life of this stretch of land has inspired many an artist.

1

2

3

Isle of Skye

Skye, the largest island of the Inner Hebrides, is known for being one of the wildest, roughest and yet most beautiful islands in Scotland. Mountains like the 1,009-m-high (3,310-ft) Cuillin Hills, or the Quiraing Hills and bizarre geological formations like the Old Man of Storr give the island its unique character.

Fog, brief showers and plentiful rainbows make a trip around this island an unforgettable adventure. Dunvegan Castle, lounging seal herds, the Talisker whisky distillery, otter colonies and other fun sights invite the traveller to make pleasant stops along the way.

Next to an open fire in a little restaurant offering local specialities like venison and raspberry dessert, you can imagine what may have come to pass on these remote islands while enjoying a glass of whisky and a Gaelic tune.

⑭ Eilean Donan Castle A bit further along the A87 is Eilean Donan Castle, a picturesque natural stone castle rising up from St Donan Island in Loch Duich. This edifice, which was badly damaged by the Jacobite Wars, was only rebuilt at the start of the 19th century.

Around 5 km (3 miles) from the castle, the A890 feeds into the A87, which leads to Kyle of Lochalsh. A toll bridge from there takes you over to the Isle of Skye. From Ardvasar in the south-west of Skye there is a ferry back to Mallaig on the mainland. Take the 'Road to the Isles' (A830) 40 km (25 miles) to the east to reach Fort William.

If you are short on time, travel directly from Eilean Donan Castle eastwards on the A87 and then turn south onto the A82 at Invergarry to reach Fort William.

⑮ Ben Nevis The highest mountain on the British Isles, at 1,344 m (4,409 ft), rises magnificently from the Grampian Mountains above Fort William. While the north-western face of the mountain is relatively easy to hike, the 460-m (1,509-ft) north-eastern rock face is reserved for experienced climbers.

Before travelling on to Glencoe, take the A828 15 km (9 miles) to Castle Stalker near Portnacroish.

⑯ Loch Rannoch Fort William is the starting point for a small detour by train into the other-

⑫ North-west Coast up to Ullapool The wild north-west portion of Sutherland is not your typical holiday destination. Its steep mountains and fjords, deep blue lakes and glistening waterfalls are too secluded for the average traveller. The impassable valleys and deserted coastlines have thus become a paradise for hikers, hunters and fishermen. Naturalists can observe seabirds, seals and dolphins and sometimes even whales from these remote environs. Innumerable small alcoves are perfect for a relaxing break.

A narrow road, the A838, then leads from Durness towards the south-west. Just before Scourie you can take the A894, which branches off towards Handa

Island, a seabird sanctuary with imposing cliffs where puffins and guillemots nest.

From Kylesku, which is further south, you can take boat trips to seal colonies and to Great Britain's highest waterfall along Loch Glencoul (200 m/656 ft).

If you want to follow the tiny roads along the coast, turn off after Kylesku on to the B869. Otherwise follow the wider roads, A837 and A835, south to Ullapool. This beautiful stretch passes Loch Assynt and the ruins of Ardvreck Castle.

If you are interested, you can take the ferries that travel from Ullapool on Loch Broom to Lewis in the Outer Hebrides, and the steamers that travel to the nearby Summer Isles.

After Ullapool, stay on the A835 until shortly after Corrieshalloch Gorge (61 m/200 ft), a ravine with waterfall, where you will turn onto the A832.

⑬ Inverewe Gardens After Little Loch Broom and Gruinard Bay you come to Loch Ewe and the Inverewe Gardens. These gardens were planted in 1862 and exhibit a wonderful collection of rhododendron and hibiscus bushes. Next you will come to Kinlochewe, in the Torridon Mountains, where the road to Shieldaig on the coast follows the Liathach Ridge out to a seabird sanctuary. Thrill seekers can then follow the tiny coastal road south from Shieldaig.

1 Eilean Donan Castle was destroyed in 1719 by the English because it was a Jacobite stronghold.

2 View from Loch Eil to the east with Ben Nevis.

3 Mountain stream in the snow-covered Highlands near Glencoe.

Top: Beinn Edra (611 m/2,005 ft) on the Trotternish Peninsula.
Middle: Dunvegan Castle in the north-west of Skye has been the official residence of the MacLeod Clan since the 11th century.
Bottom: The green cattle and sheep pastures are mainly down in the southern part of the Isle of Skye.

Top: Lismore is an island 14 km long (8.8 mi) and only 2.5 km wide (1.6 mi) on Loch Linnhe, north-west of Oban. The Gaelic name lios-mór ("Big Garden") refers to the fertile land on which three hundred types of wildflowers grow. The lighthouse stands at the south end of the isle on the Sound of Mull.

Bottom: The four-storey Castle Stalker in Argyllshire dates from the 15th century and stands proud on a small island in Loch Laich off the coast of Oban in southwest Scotland. Its strategic location made it almost impossible to attack.

Isle of Mull

Mull, one of the islands of the Inner Hebrides at the entrance to Loch Linnhe, has an unusual effect on visitors with its craggy, hilly landscape and castles. It is also one of the easier islands to reach by taking the quick ferry from Oban.

The west coast of Mull is particularly pretty. This is where you'll find The Burg nature reserve, among other things, and picturesque bays lining the northern side of the Ross of Mull Peninsula.

Just off the peninsula is the legendary Isle of Iona, the cradle of Christianity in Scotland, where the Celtic monk Columban the Elder

Abandoned boats on the coast of the Isle of Mull.

founded the first monastery here in 563. For a long time Iona was even the final resting place of Scottish, Norwegian and Irish kings. The island has been inhabited since the Stone Age, as archaeological digs have proven.

Also off the west coast of Mull is the Isle of Ulva, which was inhabited until the Highland Clearances in the middle of the 19th century before farmers were driven from their land in order to make way for more lucrative sheep farming.

wise intractable Rannoch Moor. Rannoch Station, a tiny house in the wide landscape of the moor, is one of the most isolated stations in Great Britain. Small ponds and trout-rich streams cross the boulder-scattered moor and marshland. To the east of the moor lies the impressively calm Loch Rannoch.

17 Glencoe The Glencoe Valley begins roughly 16 km (10 miles) to the south of Fort William and is one of Scotland's must-see destinations. After the Jacobite Risings of the 17th century, the English attempted to take control over Scotland by exploiting clan rivalries and disputes. So it was that in 1692, soldiers led by the Clan Campbell of Glencoe and loyal to the new king, William of Orange, massacred the opposing Clan MacDonald almost in its entirety. Women and children were apparently left to perish in the elements. An impressive monument marks this gruesome event.

Following the A82 you will soon cross the A85 at Tyndrum. If you are planning a trip to the Isle of Mull, follow the A85 west to Oban, a port on the Firth of Lorne. Ferries sail from here to Mull and the other islands of the Inner Hebrides.

18 Kilchurn Castle If you turn east from the A82 onto the A85, you will reach the northern tip of Loch Awe where you will find the ruins of the 15th-century Kilchurn Castle. The ruins were hit by lightning in the 18th century and completely abandoned. One of the turrets still lies upside down in the courtyard. Restored steamboats navigate Loch Awe, the longest freshwater loch in Scotland.

19 Inveraray The town of Inveraray, 15 km (9 miles) south of Loch Awe, was constructed alongside Loch Fyne according to plans drawn up in the 18th century by the Duke of Argyll. He had his castle built in artistically arranged gardens. A prison museum in the old Inveraray Jail is also worth a visit. You can appear in court there, and even be locked up.

20 Loch Lomond The A83 leads further east to the holiday destination of Loch Lomond, Scotland's largest loch in surface area. The area is loved by hikers, water-sports enthusiasts and families looking to take a steamboat trip to the islands.
In 2002, Loch Lomond and the Trossachs National Park was opened to the east of the lake.

21 Glasgow For culture fans this city is one of Europe's hot destinations. Renowned museums and galleries as well as countless cultural programs vie for your attention. The million-strong city on the Clyde River is also an important industrial center. To get an overview of Glasgow's various highlights and attractions, take a double-decker bus tour.
Only a few of the buildings in Scotland's largest city date back to before the 18th century. Among them are the Gothic St Mungo's Cathedral and the classical Pollok House. The Hunterian Museum (with works by Charles Rennie Mackintosh, for example), the Burrell Collection (art and craftwork) and the Gallery of Modern Art are worth a visit.

A little way out of town is the New Lanark textile mill from the 18th century, which was recently listed as a UNESCO World Heritage Site – one of four in Scotland. This interesting museum town provides insight into factory life at the start of the 19th century.

1 Kilchurn Castle in the shadow of the 1,125-m-high (3,691-ft) Ben Cruachan.

2 The inaccessible Rannoch Moor is Britain's largest uninterrupted moor. The landscape is made up of wild streams, crippled trees and thousands of boulders carried here by a glacier.

3 View over the industrial city and port of Glasgow.

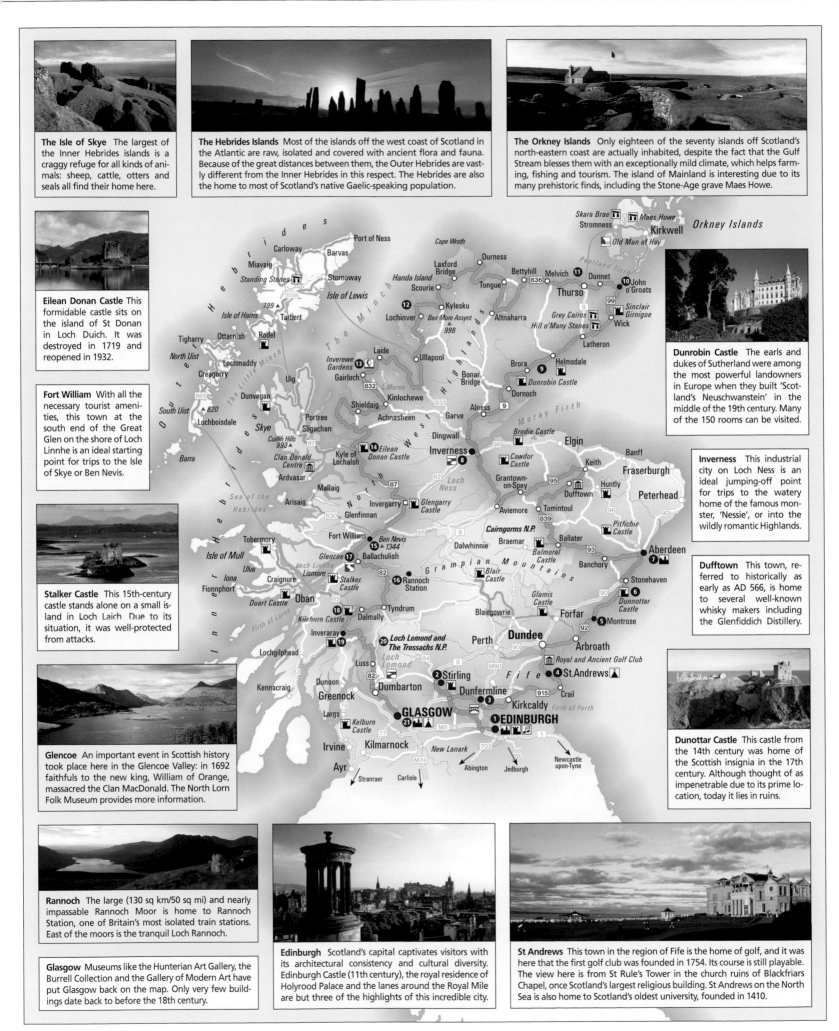

The Isle of Skye The largest of the Inner Hebrides islands is a craggy refuge for all kinds of animals: sheep, cattle, otters and seals all find their home here.

The Hebrides Islands Most of the islands off the west coast of Scotland in the Atlantic are raw, isolated and covered with ancient flora and fauna. Because of the great distances between them, the Outer Hebrides are vastly different from the Inner Hebrides in this respect. The Hebrides are also the home to most of Scotland's native Gaelic-speaking population.

The Orkney Islands Only eighteen of the seventy islands off Scotland's north-eastern coast are actually inhabited, despite the fact that the Gulf Stream blesses them with an exceptionally mild climate, which helps farming, fishing and tourism. The island of Mainland is interesting due to its many prehistoric finds, including the Stone-Age grave Maes Howe.

Eilean Donan Castle This formidable castle sits on the island of St Donan in Loch Duich. It was destroyed in 1719 and reopened in 1932.

Fort William With all the necessary tourist amenities, this town at the south end of the Great Glen on the shore of Loch Linnhe is an ideal starting point for trips to the Isle of Skye or Ben Nevis.

Stalker Castle This 15th-century castle stands alone on a small island in Loch Laich. Due to its situation, it was well-protected from attacks.

Dunrobin Castle The earls and dukes of Sutherland were among the most powerful landowners in Europe when they built 'Scotland's Neuschwanstein' in the middle of the 19th century. Many of the 150 rooms can be visited.

Inverness This industrial city on Loch Ness is an ideal jumping-off point for trips to the watery home of the famous monster, 'Nessie', or into the wildly romantic Highlands.

Dufftown This town, referred to historically as early as AD 566, is home to several well-known whisky makers including the Glenfiddich Distillery.

Dunottar Castle This castle from the 14th century was home of the Scottish insignia in the 17th century. Although thought of as impenetrable due to its prime location, today it lies in ruins.

Glencoe An important event in Scottish history took place here in the Glencoe Valley: in 1692 faithfuls to the new king, William of Orange, massacred the Clan MacDonald. The North Lorn Folk Museum provides more information.

Rannoch The large (130 sq km/50 sq mi) and nearly impassable Rannoch Moor is home to Rannoch Station, one of Britain's most isolated train stations. East of the moors is the tranquil Loch Rannoch.

Glasgow Museums like the Hunterian Art Gallery, the Burrell Collection and the Gallery of Modern Art have put Glasgow back on the map. Only very few buildings date back to before the 18th century.

Edinburgh Scotland's capital captivates visitors with its architectural consistency and cultural diversity. Edinburgh Castle (11th century), the royal residence of Holyrood Palace and the lanes around the Royal Mile are but three of the highlights of this incredible city.

St Andrews This town in the region of Fife is the home of golf, and it was here that the first golf club was founded in 1754. Its course is still playable. The view here is from St Rule's Tower in the church ruins of Blackfriars Chapel, once Scotland's largest religious building. St Andrews on the North Sea is also home to Scotland's oldest university, founded in 1410.

The most famous prehistoric construction in Europe – Stonehenge, erected around 3000 BC.

England

Magical locations in southern Britain

Ancient trading routes crisscross the south of England, and monumental stone circles bear witness to prehistoric settlements in the region. The Celts, the Romans, the Anglo-Saxons and the Normans came after the original inhabitants of the island and eventually transformed the magnificent natural environment here into a diverse cultural macrocosm with monuments, cathedrals, quaint fishing villages, parks and country houses.

Generally, the 'South of England' refers to the region along the south coast, extending northwards to Bristol in the west and London in the east. For some, however, the south only includes the coastal counties south of London like East and West Sussex, Hampshire and Dorset. Others think of just the south-east including London, while others of the south-west with Cornwall and Devon. In some references, the south even reaches up to the middle of England. Some areas, like Greater London (with around

Bodiam Castle near Hastings.

eight million inhabitants) are densely populated, whereas others like Dartmoor in Devon appear at first glance to be deserted. In the end, the South of England is unspecific, but Britons look at it as an area 'steeped in history' and known for its contrasts: picturesque cliffs and small sailing villages, busy seaside resorts and modern port towns, green pastures and barren moorland.

Indeed, the bustling metropolis of London dominates the south-east, while the more relaxed south-west has a real holiday feel to it. The area has always attracted writers and artists: Shakespeare, Jane Austen, Turner and Constable all lived here, or at least gave the south a recognizable face in their various works. Numerous nature reserves and magical, manicured gardens invite you to take peaceful walks.

Geologically speaking, the British Isles 'separated' from the continent roughly 700,000 years ago. At the time, there had been a land bridge connecting what is now England to the mainland, with a river running through (now the English Channel). The water trapped in the ice at the end of the ice age about 10,000 years ago was then released, causing sea levels to rise and gradually wash away the land bridge. The characteristic white limestone cliffs that we now see in places along the south coast like Dover and Eastbourne are the result of this 'river' flooding through the weakest point between the now divided land masses. The West Country consists mostly of granite, whereas the limestone is typical of the south-east. At the narrowest point in the channel, the Dover Strait, the distance between the United Kingdom and

The natural arch of Durdle Door on the Jurassic Coast of Dorset is the result of erosion by the pounding sea.

The western facade of Wells Cathedral is decorated with countless sculptures from the medieval period.

the European continent is only around 32 km (20 miles).

Demographically, countless generations have created a rich landscape in Britain. Due to the geographical proximity to the continent, the south was always the arrival point for immigrants, invaders and traders. In about 3500 BC, farmers and livestock breeders migrated to the island. The fortuitously warm Gulf Stream provided them and their modern-day ancestors with a relatively mild climate and even some subtropical vegetation. Natural resources like tin and copper also attracted invaders over the centuries.

England has not been successfully subdued by an enemy power since 1066, when the Normans under William the Conqueror emerged victorious at the legendary Battle of Hastings. The vulnerability of the south coast is revealed by countless castles and fortresses, and also by installations from World War II.

The varied history of settlements also features in the endless stories and myths that originate here. King Arthur and his Knights of the Round Table are among the prominent characters in these tales. Castles, cathedrals and grand old universities testify to the historical importance of the south while small fishing villages on the coast have developed into significant port towns that enabled the British Empire's rise to naval dominance. In return came exotic goods and peoples, changing yet again the cultural fabric of the traditional island inhabitants.

'High society' discovered the coast in the 19th century, and from then on vacationed in resort towns like Brighton and Eastbourne. Today the coastal economy relies primarily on services and tourism.

Tower Bridge is a masterpiece of Victorian engineering completed in 1894.

This dream route through the South of England begins in London and heads down to the coast, which it then follows west until bending northwards at Land's End back towards Oxford and eventually back to the capital, London. Along the way you will experience everything from fashionable seaside resorts and Roman ruins to awe-inspiring cathedrals, desolate moors and craggy cliffs.

Brighton

The well-known seaside resort of Brighton, which once attracted London's high society and even became a royal city of sorts, is still a wildly popular getaway for city dwellers and

Top: The Mughal-style Royal Pavilion is one of Brighton's main attractions. Bottom: Chandeliers in the banquet room of the Royal Pavilion.

beach lovers. One of the attractions is the Royal Pavilion from the 19th century, a palace built in Indian Mughal style with minarets, columns and an ostentatious interior. It is still used for exhibitions and concerts. Before the advent of cheap package holidays, Brighton was famous for its West Pier, which was unfortunately destroyed by fire and storms in 2003.

1 London (see pp. 44–47 for a detailed description of the sights and sounds that await you in England's capital).

2 Hastings Around 40 km (25 miles) south of London (A21) is possibly one of the most important battlefields in the long and distinguished history of the British Isles: Hastings, scene of the legendary battle in 1066 between Duke William of Normandy and the Saxon army under King Harold of England. The outcome of the Battle of Hastings was the coronation of the Duke of Normandy as the third king of England in Westminster following his victory. The first building he commissioned was the Battle Abbey on the site of the struggle.

Nearby Bodiam Castle is also worthy of a visit. Purportedly intended as a fortress to protect against French attacks during the Hundred Years War, it has come to light that it was actually more for show, a purpose it fits well: the castle is guarded by eight mighty towers and is artistically placed in the middle of a spring-fed moat.

3 Eastbourne and the Seven Sisters The traditional sea re-sort of Eastbourne, about 17 km (11 miles) west of Has-tings, is noteworthy for its wonderful sandy beaches and noble Victorian architecture. Just be-yond Eastbourne is the fascinating Seven Sisters Country Park, named after seven bright limestone cliffs on the coast. A short walk leads to the South Downs Way, which meanders along the shore and over the remarkable limestone landscape.

From Beachy Head, the highest limestone cliff in Britain at 163 m (535 ft), you get a breathtaking view over the English Channel and the 100-year-old lighthouse out in the sea. The postcard panorama of the Seven Sisters, however, is only visible from the next cliff, South Hill.

4 Portsmouth and the Isle of Wight The narrow coastal road now travels past the elegant seaside resort of Brighton towards Portsmouth, an old port and trading port that is home to the Royal Navy. Some of the attractions here include Lord Nelson's flagship from the Battle of Trafalgar (the most significant naval victory of the Napoleonic Wars), the Sea Life Center and the house where Charles Dickens was born.

Travel information

Route profile
Length: approx. 1,200 km (746 miles), excluding detours
Time required: 2–3 weeks
Start and end: London
Route (main locations): London, Hastings, Brighton, Portsmouth, Salisbury, Weymouth, Exeter, Torquay, St Austell, Land's End, Barnstaple, Bridgwater, Bath, Stratford-upon-Avon, Oxford, Windsor, London

Traffic information:
Drive on the left in Great Britain. The green insurance card is necessary.
Info: *www.theaa.com*

When to go:
Thanks to the Gulf Stream, the weather in southern

Britain is better than reputed with warm summers and mild winters. Recommended travel season: April to October. Further information available at:
www.onlineweather.com

Accommodation:
As well as hotels and guesthouses, bed-and-breakfast accommodation (B&B) is in private houses recommended. Useful information:
www.bedandbreakfast nationwide.com
www.accommodation britain.co.uk

Information:
British Tourist Office
www.visitbritain.com
London sights and travel
www. visitlondon.com

The cathedrals of Salisbury, Exeter and Winchester

Salisbury Cathedral was built between 1220 and 1258 in what is known as 'Early English' style to the Britons, an English Gothic form that identifies with the early-Gothic architectural style. The cathedral has the tallest spine in England.

The silhouette of the diocesan city of Exeter is dominated by the Cathedral Church of St Peter, built between the 11th and 14th centuries in 'Decorated' style. England's largest surviving collection of 14th-century sculptures cover

Ferries sail from Portsmouth to the Isle of Wight, the smallest county in England at 381 sq km (146 sq mi), once inhabited by the Romans. The island benefits from a varied landscape thanks to the warm Gulf Stream, which gives it a mild climate and allows colourful subtropical plants to blossom here between palm trees.

Off the west coast are three limestone formations – The Needles. At the base of the last rock outcrop, a lighthouse defies the constant pounding of the waves. Back on the mainland, we continue inland to Winchester, which was the capital of England until 1066, and then on to Salisbury. About 16 km (10 miles) to the north of the town lies Stonehenge.

5 **Stonehenge** It should come as no surprise that the most famous prehistoric site on the British Isles has been listed as a UNESCO World Heritage Site. Stonehenge is believed to have been erected in four stages between 3100 BC and 1500 BC by successors of the Bell-Beaker culture. The unbelievable 'engineering' and building capacity of these Stone-Age peoples inspires awe to this day: they transported eighty-two gigantic building blocks from the Welsh mountains, nearly 160 km (100 miles) away, presumably using rivers and rollers of some sort all the way to Stonehenge. Later, at the start of the Bronze Age, these blue stones were replaced by even larger sandstone blocks measuring 7-m (23-ft) high.

Indeed, the site was modified a number of times. Today two concentric stone circles make up the middle section. The outer circle, with a diameter of 30 m (98 ft), is made up of seventeen trilithons and two vertical monoliths with a horizontal stone. The inner circle is made up exclusively of monoliths. It is a source of discussion as to whether the site was used as a place of worship, an observatory or for monitoring the sun's behaviour. On the day of the summer solstice, the sun rises exactly over the Heel Stone, following the axis of the entrance, and throws its light through a stone window. Stonehenge has been a magical place for thousands of years. Celtic druids also used the site for their rites.

6 **Shaftesbury** About 20 km (12.5 miles) to the west of Salisbury, one of Britain's rare medieval hill towns continues to enchant visitors. Time seems to have stood still in Shaftesbury: ancient town walls and Gold Hill are reminiscent of a long forgotten time. The steep, cobbled lanes are lined with small, sometimes thatched houses and were at one time part of the pilgrimage route to the grave of Edward the Martyr, whose bones are now kept in Westminster Abbey. In the Middle Ages there was a prosperous Benedictine monastary here, but it was disbanded in 1539 and for the most part demolished.

The oft-photographed Gold Hill is classified today as Britain's prettiest street. From the top of

it you get a view over green, hilly pastureland that is interrupted only by lush, dark-green hedges.

The A350 then leads south, back to the coast, past Blandford and on to the coastal town of Swanage on the lovely Purbeck Peninsula.

7 **Corfe Castle and Swanage** On your way to Swanage it is worth stopping at Corfe Castle, a wild and romantic set of ruins out on a high promontory. In 1646 the fort fell through a betrayal on the part of Oliver Cromwell's soldiers and was almost totally destroyed.

Swanage is a charming seaside town at the end of the narrow Purbeck Peninsula. The Old Harry Rocks are just a walk away from here. Like the Needles on the Isle of Wight, the limestone rocks in this formation were formed by the emergence of the Alps over thirty million years ago.

8 **The Jurassic Coast** The coast between Swanage and Weymouth is not called the Jurassic Coast for nothing. The cliff formations here date from the period and because of their location are only partially accessible by car. In 2001 this stretch of coastline was classified a Natural World Heritage Site by UNESCO – the first site to be listed as such in the UK – because it documents nearly 185 million years of the earth's history.

The beaches and the cliffs here bear witness to periods within the Mesozoic Era, effectively the geological 'Middle Ages'. Ever

since the spectacular find of an Ichthyosaurus, an enormous fish dinosaur, in the 19th century, this area has also become world-famous among hobby fossil hunters.

Yet the region is also perfect for walks with breathtaking views. Shortly before Weymouth is the enchanting Lulworth Cove, a natural port with steep cliffs and golden sands. A footpath then leads you along the cliff edge to the impressive Durdle Door, a natural bridge that extends out into the ocean. St Oswalds Bay, with its fine sand beach, can also be reached from here by a steep path.

Between Weymouth and Exeter there are many small coastal villages that invite you for a break. In the dreamy village of Abbotsbury, the Swannery swan colony is home to about 1,000 swans, a sight to behold.

Chesil Bank is a gravel bank that is over 80,000 years old and stretches more than 29 km (18 miles). It resembles a pebble dune. Beyond the dune is a bird sanctuary in the brackish water of the lagoon.

9 **Torquay** Torquay is around 40 km (25 miles) south of Exeter on what is commonly known as the English Riviera. This 30-km-long (19-mile) stretch of coast

1 The white lighthouse of Godrevy, which sits atop an isolated rock, is not far from Gwithian in Cornwall. The lighthouse inspired Virginia Woolf's famous novel *To the Lighthouse*.

2 One of England's most recognizable medieval streets: Gold Hill in Shaftesbury.

3 The limestone cliffs of the Seven Sisters between Seaford and Eastbourne are visible from far away.

4 The Needles and lighthouse west of the Isle of Wight.

5 The yacht port of Torquay on the 'English Riviera' in Devon.

Top: Exeter Cathedral in Devon.
Bottom: The impressive quire of Salisbury Cathedral.

the western facade and include angels, kings and apostles. The lusciously decorated interior contains an impressive carved arch.

The city of Winchester was England's capital until 1066, a pivotal year in the island's history when the Normans invaded and conquered it. The transepts and tower survive from the Norman cathedral (1079) while the Perpendicular nave and choir loft (with vertical framework on the windows) are from the 14th century. At 170 m (560 ft), the cathedral is Europe's tallest medieval church.

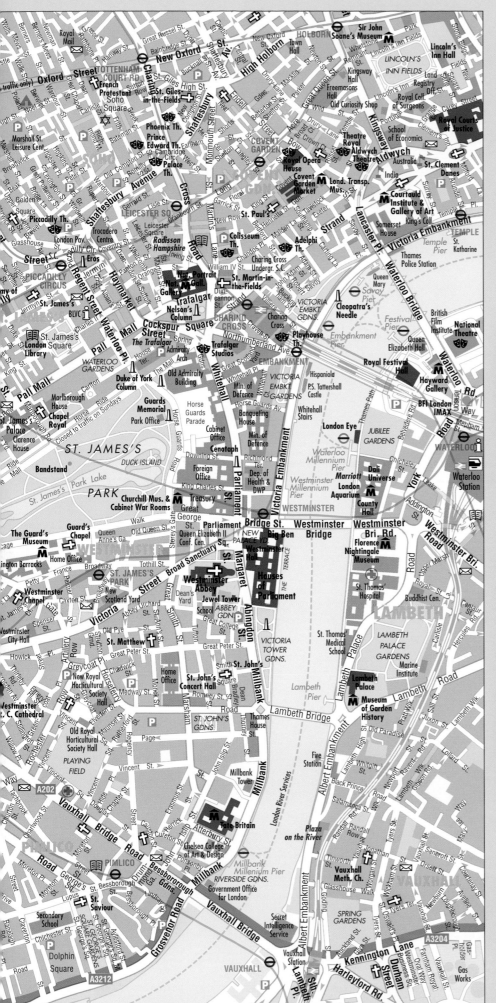

London

England's capital, London, is the seat of British government and an international financial center of massive proportions, but above all it is a cosmopolitan city in the truest sense of the word. For a few centuries, London was the heart of the British Empire, and this is still very much perceptible in its dynamic atmosphere. Due to numerous restrictions for cars in the city center, use of the excellent public transport network or a tour on a red sightseeing double-decker bus is highly recommended.

The western part of central London is typified by diversity – the administrative center of Whitehall in the historic district of Westminster; posh residential and business districts like Knightsbridge and Belgravia; busy squares like Piccadilly Circus and Trafalgar Square; and the fabulous parks like St James's and the Kensington Gardens. Starting with the district of Westminster, here is a handful of things to see, the first two being UNESCO World Heritage Sites: Westminster Abbey, the mighty Gothic church where English kings are crowned and buried (not to be confused with nearby Westminster Cathedral, a Catholic church from the 19th century), and the neo-Gothic Houses of Parliament on the Thames. Then we have the only remaining part of the original medieval building, Westminster Hall, and next to that the clock tower housing Big Ben (1858). Westminster Bridge crosses the Thames. After that we have Buckingham Palace (early 18th centu-

ry), the city residence of the Queen, Green Park and St James's Park, and the Tate Gallery with a first-class selection of English art.

In Whitehall you'll find 10 Downing Street, residence of the Prime Minister; the Palladian-style Banqueting House, opposite Horse Guards Parade for the Changing of the Guard; Trafalgar Square with Nelson's Column; the National Gallery with works from the

Top: Buckingham Palace – London residence of the Queen.
Middle: Bustling Trafalgar Square with Nelson's Column.
Bottom: Houses of Parliament with Big Ben.

16th to 20th centuries, the National Portrait Gallery; Hyde Park, a public park from the 17th century with the famous Speaker's Corner; Madame Tussaud's Wax Museum.

In Knightsbridge are the Victoria and Albert Museum, the largest arts and crafts museum in the world; the Natural History Museum, with a famous dinosaur section; the Science and Technology Museum; the legendary Harrods department store with something for everyone; and the younger and less conventional Harvey Nichols department store.

London

In 1851, when Great Britain was at the height of its imperial power and had just celebrated itself in a World Fair, London had around one million inhabitants. Today there are over twelve million people in Greater London and around eight within city limits – the latter makes it the largest city in Europe.

It began modestly almost 2,000 years ago, when the Romans conquered the island that is now England and founded Londinium on the Thames. Many peoples have come to the British Isles, but since William the Conqueror made London his capital in 1066, the city has remained the administrative center of Britain, not least due to its strategic position – near the continent, yet protected in an estuary. The first block of the Tower of London, the city's most venerated building, was in fact laid by William the Conqueror in 1078.

A large fortress and medieval royal residence, the Tower of London complex is centerd around the White Tower (11th century) and it is here that the Crown Jewels are on display. Another one of the most recognizable icons of London's cityscape is the Tower Bridge

center – and the famous London Stock Exchange from 1773.

In the West End you'll find countless theaters, cinemas, pubs and restaurants around Piccadilly Circus, London's most colourful square. Covent Garden, once a market, is now a pedestrian zone in the West End. The Royal Opera House and the British Museum, with a number of world-famous collections, are also here.

Interesting places in the Southwark area include the cathedral of the same name, which is the oldest Gothic church in London. It has a memorial for Shakespeare, whose Globe Theater was rebuilt nearby almost in its original form. The Tate Modern is a striking art museum in a disused power station across the Thames on the Millennium Footbridge. The Docklands and Canary Wharf both

Top: St Paul's Cathedral stands in the center of London.
Bottom: Walls from the 13th century protect the Tower of London.

(1894) with its double towers and distinctive bascule bridge.

In the City district of London you should take time to go to St Paul's Cathedral (1674–1710), a Renaissance masterpiece with a walkway that goes all the way around its dome. North of St Paul's Cathedral are the futuristic Barbican towers – a culture and arts

feature modern architecture – Canada Tower and Canary Wharf Tower, respectively. The latter is the tallest building in the UK at 244 m (800 ft). In Greenwich is the Royal Maritime Museum with sailing history, the historic Cutty Sark clipper ship, and the observatory, which crosses the prime meridian.

Through Dartmoor National Park

From Torquay, a route leads through Dartmoor National Park, a largely untouched area of moorland and forest on the south-west coast of England that covers approximately 945 sq km (363 sq mi) at an elevation of roughly 500 m (1,640 ft) above sea level. It is one of Europe's largest nature reserves.

Dartmoor is not a primeval landscape, but rather an area that has been cultivated for thousands of years. Numerous archaeological sites – remains of Stone Age villages, stone paths and circles, monuments such as burial sites, and more – testify to the extensive human presence here.

Heather-covered moor landscape in Dartmoor National Park.

An 800-km-long (500-mile) network of footpaths crisscrosses the countryside, and in some places the granite rises out of the earth in formations called tors, or craggy hills. Reddish-brown ferns, heather, windswept trees and shaggy Dartmoor ponies are among the park's simple selection of things to see, especially in the sparse western reaches. Tidy lanes and little villages are common on the more inhabited east side.

From Ashburton, a pretty town near idyllic Widecombe-in-the-Moor, your drive goes through the hilly landscape to Two Bridges, past Princetown with the infamous Dartmoor Prison. Tavistock, an earlier center for tin and copper mining, was famous for hundreds of years because of its rich Benedictine monastery.

has been given this name because of its numerous idyllic bays, palm-littered beaches, mild climate and its urbane atmosphere. Three towns – Torquay, Paignton and Brixham – have become known as Torbay, though they have kept their own individual styles. Elegant hotels, Victorian villas and countless bars and restaurants around the little port give the area a holiday feel.

After the impressive mountain road through Dartmoor National Park (with grades of up to twenty-five per cent), the A390 leads from Liskeard back down towards the coast and St Austell.

⑩ St Austell and the Eden Project Since the discovery of kaolin in the 18th century, the economic welfare of the town has been closely linked to the mining of this important base product used in the manufacture of porcelain. The story of china clay or 'white gold' is retold in St Austell's museum. The Eden Project was constructed over 14 ha (35 acres) on a disused kaolin quarry near Bodelva. In two gigantic greenhouses, gardeners have reproduced two climatic zones – tropical rainforest and Mediterranean. The greenhouses are densely populated with plants from these respective regions in order to allow a natural ecosystem to develop. In another area, a cool zone was set up, in which indigenous plants from Britain and exotic plants from temperate Cornwall flourish. The larger of the greenhouses, the Humid Tropics Biome, is the largest greenhouse in the world covering an area of 1,559 ha (4 acres) at a height of 55 m (180 ft).

⑪ Mevagissey The Lost Gardens of Heligan north of Mevagissy are every bit as fascinating as the Eden Project – strange, prehistoric fallen tree trunks lie amid a subtropical landscape with giant bamboo, ancient tree ferns and mysterious ponds. The gardens were initially planted in the 18th and 19th centuries, but then fell into a long dormant phase.

In 1990, the developer Tim Smit cut through the 5-m-thick (16-ft) thorn bushes and discovered a site that had been forgotten for nearly a hundred years. After a painstaking reconstruction of the original gardens, the microenvironment was saved. The 32-ha (80-acre) site includes a ravine, an enchanting Italian garden, a grotto and ancient

rhododendron bushes. Lost Valley, a jungle environment with a view over Mevagissey, is another highlight of the gardens.

⑫ Penzance The largest town in Cornwall lies 50 km (31 miles) to the west of here. A drive over the Penwith Peninsula to Land's End is definitely recommended. Due to its temperate climate, this striking region is also called the 'Cornish Riviera'.

Penzance was an important tin trading point for the Roman Empire and medieval Europe. The center of town, between Chapel Street and Market Jew Street, is the oldest part of

Penzance, where the long since vanished times of the seafarers can still be felt. The Barbican, which is an old storage house, and the Egyptian House (1830) are both worth visiting.

Opposite the town stands the old castle of St Michael's Mount on top of a granite island in the bay of the same name. This former Benedictine monastery came into the Crown's possession in 1535 and was then converted into a fortress. Historians date the founding of the monastery back to the 8th century. At that time Celtic monks had built a monastery on Mont St-Michel in Normandy, which is remarkably,

but not coincidentally, similar to its Cornish counterpart.

At low tide you can cross the bay on foot. At high tide there is a boat service. If you climb to the top of the 70-m-high (230-ft) outcrop, you'll get a fabulous view over Penwith Peninsula.

From Penzance, there is a 35-km (22-mile) road that leads round the peninsula to Land's End and on to St Ives.

⑬ Land's End The westernmost point of England is covered with an open moor and heath, and is absolutely riddled with archaeological treasures. Headstones from the ice age and

Bronze Age, Celtic crosses and entire villages that date back to times before the birth of Christ all bear witness to thousands of years of settlement in the area. The continual breaking of the waves from the Atlantic over the mighty rocks led the Romans to christen the place Belerion – Home of the Storms.

14 Scilly Isles About 40 km (25 miles) off the coast to the south-west lie the 140 Scilly Isles, which are reachable by ferry from Penzance. The 2,000 inhabitants, who live mostly from tourism and flower exports, are spread over only seven inhabited islands. With their rough granite rocks, white sandy beaches and turquoise bays, the Scilly Isles are best discovered on foot or by bicycle. A collection of the exotic palms and plants that traditionally flourish in this mild climate can be seen in the Abbey Garden at Tresco.

Back on the mainland, the often steep coastal road then follows the Atlantic coast around to St Ives. Ornithologists come here to find rare visitors like thrushes, New World warblers and vireos that have come over from America accidental on the omnipresent Westerlies. Some of the best observation points are the lighthouses.

15 St Ives Grey granite houses populate this former fishing village, which also happens to have one of Cornwall's most beautiful beaches. Numerous artists and sculptors have been coming here since the last century, fascinated by the light and landscape. The Tate Gallery has even opened

a 'branch' high above Porthmoor Beach where works by artists from St Ives are on display including paintings by Patrick Heron and Ben Nicholson, who lived here with his artist wife Barbara Hepworth. The village of Gwithian just up the road is also worth a stop.

The tiny fishing village of Port Isaac is near by, just off the A30. It has been spared a lot of the mass tourism that has become rampant in these parts, which makes it a refreshing alternative. The extremely steep streets probably put off a lot of visitors, so the best bet is to park the car above the village, and walk to Kellan Head on the coast.

16 Tintagel The legendary ruins on Tintagel Head are said to be the birthplace of King Arthur. Beyond the village of Tintagel a path leads over the cliffs to a green outcrop on the Atlantic that is crowned with crumbling ruin walls and can be reached via the steep staircase. As digs have proven, a Celtic monastery from the 5th century once stood here with a library, chapel, guest house, refectory and even a bath house.

The castle, however, whose ruins are also still visible, only dates back to the 13th century, a fact that would cast a doubt over the speculation of it being the birthplace of the legendary king of England.

And yet he who stands in the fog on the cliffs looking down at waves crashing by the dark entrance to Merlin's Cave can easily feel himself transported back to the times of King Arthur. The Norman church graveyard has a

number of half-buried tombstones telling tales of dead seamen and grieving widows.

The A39 leads further north from Tintagel along the coast, passing between Blackmoor Gate and Dunster across Exmoor National Park. In order to fully appreciate the coast and the moorland here, you should walk a section of the Somerset and Devon Coastal Path, from Bossington for example.

17 Glastonbury and Wells At Bridgwater, the coastal road A39 finally turns inland and leads to Glastonbury, a mythical place that attracts countless esoteric types. There are many reasons for the concentration of mystical and supernatural activity here: the remains of King Arthur are thought to be buried under the ruins of Glastonbury Abbey, and Glastonbury is often thought to be the legendary Avalon – a paradise to which Arthur was carried after his death.

Historical facts date the foundation of the first monastery back to the 7th century while the construction of England's largest abbey came around the year 1000 and the dissolution of the monastery in 1539.

The small city of Wells, on the other hand, is known for its glorious cathedral, the first Gothic building in all of England. The main section was completed in 1240, but the western tower and chapel came much later. The western facade was at one time covered with 400 figures, testimony to the skill of the medieval masons here – one picture book carved into the stone relates biblical and world history. Adjacent

to the cathedral is the Bishop's Palace, which is still used by the Bishop of Bath and Wells.

Bath, your next stop, is the cultural center of the county of Somerset and is around 30 km (19 miles) north of Wells on the A367.

18 Bath The Romans knew this hot-springs town as Aquae Sulis. They built magnificent swimming pools, Turkish baths and saunas, and turned the town into a meeting place for the Roman elite. Oddly, the unique baths were only discovered in the 18th century.

Bath's rebirth as a health resort began in earnest in the 19th century when the city's grandiose Georgian architecture, concerts and balls enticed London's upper class to enjoy the recuperative benefits of its historic facilities. Visitors could also admire the dignified limestone buildings such as Queen Square, Royal Crescent and Pulteney Bridge.

1 Kellan Head on the striking north-west coast of Cornwall.

2 Street in the picturesque town of St Ives.

3 The West of England begins in the Wiltshire countryside.

4 A great boulder near Lower Slaughter in the Cotswolds.

5 The cove of Port Issac on the west coast of Cornwall.

6 Land's End – in Cornish, Penn an Wlas – the steep, Atlantic-battered cliffs on the westernmost point of Great Britain.

The Romans in England

It's true, the Romans even ruled England, as Britannia, from around 55 BC to AD 410. After Julius Caesar's failed attempt, Emperor Claudius was the first to conquer the island all the way up to what is now Scotland, then called Caledonia, or 'Wooded Land'. Emperor Hadrian had built a wall there in around 122 BC to keep the fearsome Picts (Scottish predecessors) out of the Roman territories in

Bath: View of the Roman baths and the abbey.

England. The Romans remained on the island for a good 400 years.

The Romans selected Londinium as their capital and founded numerous other cities, with common suffixes like 'caster' or 'chester' being a throwback to the Roman word for fort. Some of their roads are still in use as well, for example the Fosse Way through the Cotswolds. When the Pict resistance grew too strong, the Romans retreated. Their ruins are now monuments.

Today, you can taste the healing waters and take in the atmosphere in the Pump Room.

A short detour of about 12 km (7.5 miles) via Chippenham leads you to the archaeological site at Avebury in Wiltshire. Avebury is home to the remains of England's largest and most impressive stone circle, made up of over 100 stones erected around 3,500 years ago. Nearby, the 40-m-high (130-ft) Silbury Hill looks like a pyramid, but it was not used as a burial site.

19 The Cotswolds The A429 takes you through the deep, wooded valleys and gentle hills of the Cotswolds, an area that has been populated since prehistoric times. After the Romans, the Cotswolds bloomed through the Middle Ages thanks to wool production. The region then sank into a long period of dormancy before being reawakened by tourism.

The typical Cotswolds architectural style and fairy-tale charm can be best seen in places such as Bouton-on-the-Water where golden stone buildings stand side-by-side with little bridges crossing streams in quaint and vivid meadows.

The town of Stow-on-the-Wold with its stone market hall sits atop a hill and was once a thriving sheep market. On the other side of the hill are the tiny villages of Upper Slaughter and Lower Slaughter, whose miniature appearance have made them into much-loved postcard images.

20 Stratford-upon-Avon The birthplace of William Shake-speare (1564) is the northernmost point of your route. In 1594, the famous playwright left for London, where he was able to establish his legendary reputation as actor and writer in one of the leading theater companies of the time. In 1610 he returned to his home town of Stratford, where he died in 1616. Despite thousands of tourists walking in the footsteps of the poet every year, Stratford has been able to retain some of its Shakespearian atmosphere.

Visitors can tour the house where the playwright was born, learn about his life and work in the Shakespeare Center, or watch one of his plays performed by the Royal Shakespeare Company in the Swan Theater. A boat trip on the Avon rounds off the visit.

The A44 towards Oxford passes the impressive Blenheim Palace at Moreton-in-Marsh.

21 Blenheim Palace This impressive palace near Oxford was finished in 1722 and is Britain's largest private home. It was originally a gift from Queen Anne to

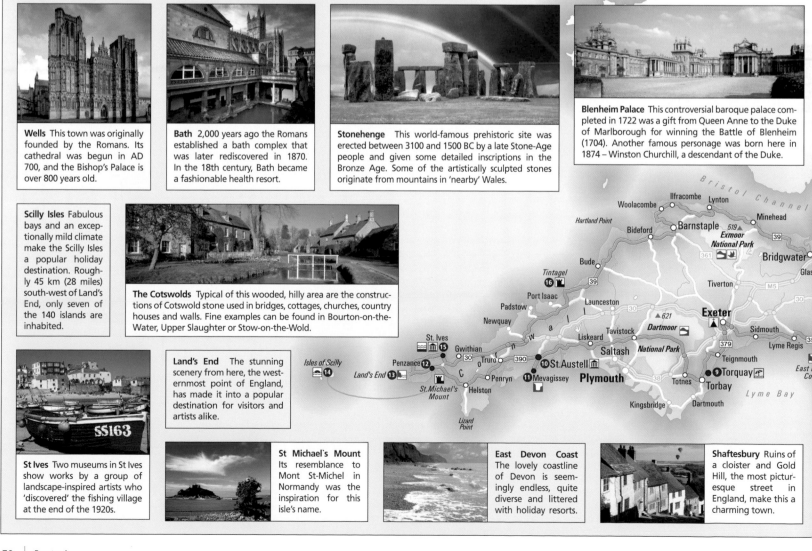

Wells This town was originally founded by the Romans. Its cathedral was begun in AD 700, and the Bishop's Palace is over 800 years old.

Bath 2,000 years ago the Romans established a bath complex that was later rediscovered in 1870. In the 18th century, Bath became a fashionable health resort.

Stonehenge This world-famous prehistoric site was erected between 3100 and 1500 BC by a late Stone-Age people and given some detailed inscriptions in the Bronze Age. Some of the artistically sculpted stones originate from mountains in 'nearby' Wales.

Blenheim Palace This controversial baroque palace completed in 1722 was a gift from Queen Anne to the Duke of Marlborough for winning the Battle of Blenheim (1704). Another famous personage was born here in 1874 – Winston Churchill, a descendant of the Duke.

Scilly Isles Fabulous bays and an exceptionally mild climate make the Scilly Isles a popular holiday destination. Roughly 45 km (28 miles) south-west of Land's End, only seven of the 140 islands are inhabited.

The Cotswolds Typical of this wooded, hilly area are the constructions of Cotswold stone used in bridges, cottages, churches, country houses and walls. Fine examples can be found in Bourton-on-the-Water, Upper Slaughter or Stow-on-the-Wold.

Land's End The stunning scenery from here, the westernmost point of England, has made it into a popular destination for visitors and artists alike.

St Ives Two museums in St Ives show works by a group of landscape-inspired artists who 'discovered' the fishing village at the end of the 1920s.

St Michael's Mount Its resemblance to Mont St-Michel in Normandy was the inspiration for this isle's name.

East Devon Coast The lovely coastline of Devon is seemingly endless, quite diverse and littered with holiday resorts.

Shaftesbury Ruins of a cloister and Gold Hill, the most picturesque street in England, make this a charming town.

John Churchill, the 1st Duke of Marlborough, after his defeat of Ludwig XIV in Blenheim, Bavaria (actually Blindheim near Höchstädt on the Danube). Blenheim Palace is recommended for a relaxing afternoon walk followed by tea. Many garden-lovers come here to visit the palace park, created by landscape gardener Capability Brown in typical English style.

㉒ Oxford The many spires of Oxford, especially Tom Tower of Christ Church and Magdalen Tower, are visible from the approach road. Oxford is known throughout the world as England's most prestigious university town. Its cathedral and the Picture Gallery, containing masterpieces from the Renaissance and baroque era, are worth a visit. Don't miss the Radcliffe Camera, Sheldonian Theater and the Bodleian Library with its five million books. A coffee break with a book can be taken in the Blackwell Bookshop with a view over Radcliffe Camera.
The college tour is a classic, and leads around the buildings of Merton College, Corpus Christi and New College, among others. Take a relaxing walk through the botanical gardens and its old greenhouses as well.

㉓ Windsor and Ascot Windsor Castle is in the Thames Valley west of London, and has been the primary residence of the English royal family since the Middle Ages. The fort, built in the 12th and 13th centuries, has been frequently remodelled over the years.
Many sections of Windsor Castle, one of the largest inhabited castles in the world, are open to the public. A trip to St George's Chapel and the Albert Memorial Chapel to view the burial sites of the monarchs is recommended. The Round Tower offers a wonderful view of the castle and the Great Park.
Opposite Windsor Castle is Eton College, founded in 1440–41. This exclusive private school favours a traditional English education with emphasis on the Classics and sport.
Windsor and Ascot, the famous racetrack, are separated only by a few kilometers. The Hippodrome, built in 1711 by Queen Anne, is among the most famous tracks in the world. From 1825 until 1945, the four-day Royal Meeting race was the only event staged there. Today twenty-five races take place each year.
The last stop now is London, with its historical monuments, impressive museums and world-famous churches.

1 Stratford-upon-Avon: the tower of the legendary Holy Trinity Church, site of William Shakespeare's grave.

2 Winston Churchill was born in 1874 in Blenheim Palace (UNESCO World Heritage Site), a baroque masterpiece.

3 The countless spires and towers of colleges and churches give the skyline of Oxford a dignified and unmistakable appearance.

3

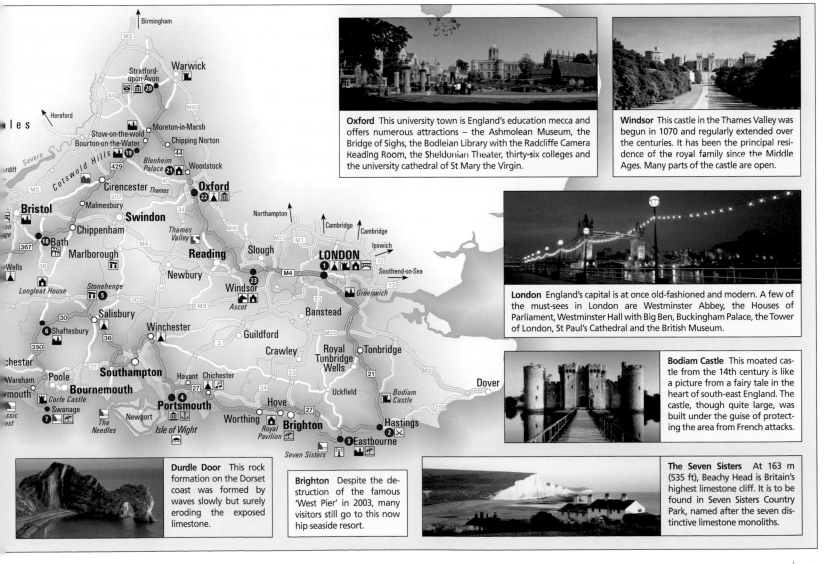

Oxford This university town is England's education mecca and offers numerous attractions – the Ashmolean Museum, the Bridge of Sighs, the Bodleian Library with the Radcliffe Camera Reading Room, the Sheldonian Theater, thirty-six colleges and the university cathedral of St Mary the Virgin.

Windsor This castle in the Thames Valley was begun in 1070 and regularly extended over the centuries. It has been the principal residence of the royal family since the Middle Ages. Many parts of the castle are open.

London England's capital is at once old-fashioned and modern. A few of the must-sees in London are Westminster Abbey, the Houses of Parliament, Westminster Hall with Big Ben, Buckingham Palace, the Tower of London, St Paul's Cathedral and the British Museum.

Bodiam Castle This moated castle from the 14th century is like a picture from a fairy tale in the heart of south-east England. The castle, though quite large, was built under the guise of protecting the area from French attacks.

Durdle Door This rock formation on the Dorset coast was formed by waves slowly but surely eroding the exposed limestone.

Brighton Despite the destruction of the famous 'West Pier' in 2003, many visitors still go to this now hip seaside resort.

The Seven Sisters At 163 m (535 ft), Beachy Head is Britain's highest limestone cliff. It is to be found in Seven Sisters Country Park, named after the seven distinctive limestone monoliths.

Autumn tundra in the Finnmark Province of Norway's far northern expanse.

Norway

Across fjord and fell: the spectacular natural world of northern Europe

Norway shares its borders with Russia, Finland and Sweden and is enveloped by the Norwegian Sea, the North Sea and the Skagerrak. It is a natural realm of truly unmatched beauty – alternately wild and delicate. One tip – make sure you allow plenty of time for the enormous distances.

As you might expect from industrious Scandinavians, the Norwegian mainland has an astonishingly well-maintained road infrastructure. In places where the rugged terrain would have you think the onward journey has come to an end, there appears a ferry, a tunnel or a bridge. Even the smallest hamlets and remote coastal villages are generally easy to reach. And yet progress in this expansive land inevitably takes longer than you've planned, mainly due to the unusual physical geography and strict speed limits. But you won't have to worry much about traffic jams and red lights.

The *Hurtigruten* is Norway's legendary passenger ship, which has been plying the 2,500 nautical miles between Bergen in the south and Kirkenes on the Russian border in the very north for well over a hundred years. It was originally used to transport post and supplies. Nowadays the permanent route, known as 'Imperial Road 1', has become famous as one of 'the world's most beautiful sea voyages'. From a geographical point of view, Norway is unlike any other European country. No other country in Europe is longer (1,752 km/1,089 miles), almost none is as narrow, and despite its odd shape it is

Mountain landscape in Kjerringøy in the north.

(without its polar provinces) three times the size of England.

Almost half of Norway is over 500 m (1,640 ft) above sea level. Its mountains are not particularly high – the highest does not even measure 2,500 m (8,200 ft) – yet nearly a quarter of the country is covered by alpine or high-alpine landscape, glaciers or wide, treeless plateaus at over 1,000 m (3,280 ft) altitude. The generally barren, high plateaus – known as fjells, or fells – are covered in snow for a large part of the year and consist mainly of moors, lakes and rivers.

Above the Arctic Circle and in the highland areas of the interior there is often no sign of human life at all. With the exception of Oslo, Bergen, Trondheim and Stavanger there is no town with more than 100,000 inhabitants in this relatively large country. Four out of five people live on

Historic warehouses in Bergen, member of the Hanseatic League from the 14th to 16th century.

View from the mountain of Aksala over Ålesund past the town center to the port.

the coast or the banks of a fjord. Norway's very craggy coastline, including the fjords and bays, is over 28,000 km (17,398 miles) long – more than half the circumference of the earth.

The country is very sparsely populated and, thanks to the Gulf Stream, free of ice all year. Were it not for these warm ocean currents, the Norwegian mainland would be covered with a crust of ice, as is the case in large areas of the Norwegian polar provinces. On the other hand, the Gulf Stream is also to blame for the high level of summer rainfall, which is common.

Norway's fjords – the most famous of which are Geirangerfjord, Hardangerfjord and Sognefjord – are the number one tourist attraction here. These former valleys and canyons of various sizes and shapes were carved out by massive gla-ciers and ultimately flooded by rising sea levels following the last ice age.

The short summer months in Norway are quite mild. North of the Arctic Circle – in the 'Land of the Midnight Sun' – summer days actually don't end and the special atmosphere during this time of year often inspires wild parties. The opposite is the case during the cold period, which is snowy and dark in the very north – no sun for two months straight.

Norway is not in the EU and still uses the Norwegian Krone as its currency. After hundreds of years of occupation and invasion by the Danes, the Swedes and the Germans, they feel they have earned this 'exclusivity'. But things are going swimmingly here – fishing and tourism, as well as plentiful oil and natural gas reserves in the North Sea, have made the beautiful 'Land of Utgard' quite prosperous.

Fishing boats in the port of Hamnøy on the Lofoten island of Moskenesøya.

Oslo

At the end of the fjord of the same name, stretching nearly 100 km (60 miles) inland and surrounded by wooded hills, is Norway's capital Oslo, a city dating back to the 11th century. Oslo was called Kristiania until 1925 and had varying political and industrial significance. Although the city is home to a mere half-million inhabitants, it is one of Europe's largest cities in surface area. It is the largest port in Norway and the country's trading and industrial center.

Worth seeing in the center of town: the new town hall (1931-1950), the city's trademark with a sumptuous interior and Europe's highest clock tower; Akershus Fort (from 1300), one of the country's most important medieval

Top: Oslo town hall.
Bottom: Akershus Castle.

buildings; Nasjonalgalleriet, the largest collection of paintings and sculptures in Norway; the royal castle (changing of the guard at 1:30 pm). Highlights outside the city center include Holmenkollen, a winter-sport resort with skiing museum; Munch-Museet; Vigelandpark (Frognerpark) with 200 monumental works in bronze and stone by Gustav Vigeland; Bygdöy peninsular museum with the Vikingskipshuset (three ships from the 9th century); Kon-Tiki Museet with the Thor Heyerdahls Raft (Kon-Tiki, RA I, RA II); Fram-Museet.

North Cape Route: On the 4,000-km (2,484-mile) trip to the North Cape you get to experience just about everything Norway's fascinating natural landscape has to offer: glaciers, waterfalls, mountains, high plateaus, rugged coastline and endless fjords. The cultural highlights include old port and mining towns, interesting stone carvings and charming old churches.

❶ Oslo (see sidebar left). From Oslo follow the coast to Kongsberg.

❷ Kongsberg The Mining Museum here casts you back to the times of silver mining, which ceased in 1957 after more than 330 years. In the Saggrenda pit you can see what is probably the world's first ever elevator – it consists of ladders that go up and down.

❸ Heddal and Eidsborg Norway's first stave church (1147) is in Telemark and has an outer gallery that was used to protect people from the weather and to store weapons.
Road 45 (direction Dalen) splits off towards the Eidsborg stave church at Ofte. The walls of the

church are covered with shingles, which is unusual. About 4 km (2.4 miles) beyond Rødal, Road 13 turns off towards Stavanger.
The E134 also passes through Hardangervidda further on.

❹ Hardangervidda Europe's largest plateau is a fascinating area for hiking and is home to rare wildlife. From Skarsmo our route leads north on Road 13. Alongside the road are the wild frothing waters of the Låtefossen. It is definitely worth a short detour (50 km/31 miles) from Kinsarvik, along the Eidfjord to Fossli, to the edge of the Vidda where the Vøringfossen Falls drop 170 m (557 ft) into the depths of Måbø Canyon.
From Kinsarvik, ferries cross the Utne to Kvanndal on the Hardangerfjord. The 'King of the Fjords' reaches far inland at a length of 179 km (111 miles) and a depth of 830 m (2,723 ft). The

Travel information

Route profile
Length: approx. 4,000 km (2,484 miles), excluding detours
Time required: at least 4 weeks, ideally 6–8 weeks.
Start: Oslo
End: The North Cape
Route (main locations): Oslo, Kongsberg, Bergen, Jotunheimen, Trondheim, Fauske, Narvik, Tromsø, Alta, North Cape

Traffic information:
This route requires some driving skill and good planning as the ferries are often fully booked. Drive on the right in Norway. Customs laws are strictly enforced. Headlights are obligatory even during the day. Bridges, tunnels and mountain pass roads mostly charge

tolls. Mountain roads are often only opened in June/July.

When to go:
The best time to go is from June to August. Even in these months, snowfall is common in the north and on the plateaus.

Accommodation:
Mountain inns, known as fjellstue or fjellstove, and chalets are attractive.

General information:
www.visitnorway.com
www.norway.org
www.norway.com
Customs:
www.toll.no

Stavanger and Lysefjord

Instead of the E134 south, you can take a spectacular mountain road (13) from Røldal to Stavanger. You will have to cross a good many fjords on this route.

Stavanger, founded in 1125, was still the center of the herring and fish-canning industry in Norway until just three decades ago. In 1970, plentiful oil reserves were discovered in the Ekofisk Field, instantly making Norway's third-largest town the oil capital of the country.

Top: A colourful port town.
Bottom: Stavanger Oil Museum.

As a result, some flamboyant buildings were erected, but much of the architecture still recalls the more tranquil times prior to the oil bonanza – the Canning History Museum, for example.

The old town is called Gamle Stavanger and has 173 listed wooden houses in cobblestone lanes. The Gothic cathedral (1125–1300) is noteworthy for being the purest example of medieval church building in Norway. The Kongsgaard, where the Danish kings stayed on their travels between the 14th and 19th centuries, appears spartan in contrast. The Valbergturm, an old fire watchtower and local icon, offers a good view of the town.

The long, narrow Lysefjord is among the prettiest in the country, plunging to a depth of 400 m (1,311 ft) and stretching 40 km (25 miles). Its stone walls rise as high as 1,000 m (3,300 ft).

An impressive suspension bridge spans the fjord at its western end. A boat trip to Lysefjord and the Prekestolen promontory – the Preacher's Pulpit – is a must.

house in Norway – 'Finneloftet' from the 13th century. Further along the route you should take a detour to Viksøyri (with a charming stave church) where you can see the Sognefjord about 40 km (25 miles) away. It is Norway's greatest fjord – 180 km (112 miles) long, in some places only 5 km (3 miles) wide, and up to 1,200 m (3,937 ft) deep.

⑦ Stalheimskleiva and Nærøyfjord About 13 km (8 miles) past Oppheim, a road leads to the Hotel Stalheim, which has wonderful views. Norway's steepest road leads round thirteen hairpin bends down to the Nærøyfjord. It is the narrowest one in the country with walls up to 1,200 m (3,937 ft) high.

Two impressive waterfalls are also on the route – the Stahl-heim-foss (126 m/413 ft) and the Sivlefoss (240 m/787 ft). The main road goes from Gud-vangen to Kaupanger and on to Songdal. The fjord route leads past Nærøyfjord, Aurlandsfjord and Sognefjord, among the most beautiful in Norway.

1 UNESCO World Heritage Site: the picturesque wooden houses of Bryggen in Bergen, once a member of the Hanseatic League.

2 An isolated farmstead in the bare fell landscape – Telemark in southern Norway.

3 The Vøringfossen falls cascade from the Hardanger Plateau into the deep and narrow Måbø Canyon.

4 The 800-year-old stave church of Borgund near Borlaug, deep in the Lærdal Valley.

route then leads over the plateau of Kvamskogen on to Bergen.

⑤ Bergen The most famous street in this old Hanseatic League town is Bryggen, a UNESCO World Heritage Site with picturesque warehouses right on the waterfront. The fishing port, the cathedral, the 12th-century church and the Gamle Bergen open-air museum are also worth visiting.

⑥ Viksøyri The E16 passes many lakes on the way to Voss, home of the oldest wooden

Lysefjord and the majestic rock promontory known as the Prekestolen ("Preacher's Pulpit") is one of south-west Norway's most popular nature attractions. Surrounded by cliff walls up to 1,000 m (3,300 ft) high, the narrow fjord is 40 km long (25 mi) and stretches east from Stavanger. You can reach Prekestolen

on foot or by car; the large viewing platform has no safety railings, so you look 600 m (1,900 ft) straight down into the abyss. Be careful – the height can be dizzying. The hiking trail to the promontory takes you through a pristine boulder landscape and is one of the most beautiful of its kind in Scandinavia.

Detour

Ålesund and the bird island of Runde

This little detour first takes you about 120 km (75 miles) out to Ålesund, an island town with stone buildings (unusual for Norway) that were built by art nouveau architects from all over Europe after a fire destroyed the place in 1904. It is this uniform view of the port town that makes a visit so worthwhile.

The main attractions of the town include a visit to the 189-m-high (621-ft) Aksla Mountain – from its terrace you can enjoy a great panoramic view over the town, the skerry (rock) belt and the Sunnmøre Mountains in the west. From the town park it's about 400 m (1,312 ft) to the viewpoint.

Top: Sheep on the cliffs. Bottom: A farmstead on the Kløfjellet.

The Atlanterhavsparken Aquarium displays marine flora and fauna local to this Norwegian coastal area. To the east of town is the Sunnmøren open-air museum with more than forty old houses and farms.

The island of Runde, which is only 6.4 sq km (2.5 sq mi), is a must for anyone who loves nature. Although only 150 people live there, up to 700,000 sea birds also call it home. You can get the best view of 'Bird Island', which hosts puffins, uria, razorbills and several varieties of gulls, by booking a boat trip around the island.

Even divers value the area as much as ornithologists – in 1725 a Dutch ship carrying nineteen cases of gold and silver coins sank off the island, as did a Spanish treasure ship in 1588!

Trollstigen

Surrounded by waterfalls, deep valleys and mountains as high as 1,760 m (6,316 ft), Norway's most photographed mountain pass, the Trollstigen, snakes its way from Langdal to Åndalsnes at elevations of up to 850 m (2,789 ft). Eleven hairpin bends with a gradient of ten per cent take some skill to master. The road was built in 1936 and winds along almost vertical rock faces. As a result, it is unfortunately closed to camper vans.

⑧ Borgund The best-preserved stave church in the country can be viewed by taking a short diversion inland after driving through the new 20-km (13-mile) Lærdals Tunnel on the E16.

The church was erected around 1150 and is known for its ornate carvings. The pagoda-shaped bell tower is next to the church.

⑨ Jotunheimen and Sognefjell road Norway's highest and most spectacular mountain pass runs from Sogndal to Lom. It climbs a steep, winding trail into the Jotunheimen Mountains where over two hundred peaks of at least 2,000 m (6,561 ft) form a bizarre ring. The two highest among them are Galdahøppigen at 2,469 m (8,100 ft) and Glittertind at 2,452 m (8,045 ft).

The Sognefjell is a plateau littered with lakes of all sizes. To the west of the road is Europe's largest mainland glacier, the Jostedalsbree, which is about 100 km (62 miles) long.

⑩ Urnes A small single-lane road now leads from Skjolden on the east bank of the Lustrafjord to the town of Urnes and an 11th-century stave church, the oldest of twenty-nine listed Norwegian stave churches and a UNESCO World Heritage Site. The robust design of the exterior is fascinating and the carvings of fable characters in the interior are lovely.

⑪ Geirangerfjord The route continues through some pretty landscape on its way to the Geirangerfjord, a 15-km (9-mile) arm of the Sunnylvsfjord. Its walls are up to 800 m (2,625 ft) high and many waterfalls feed into the fjord. The panorama from the viewpoint at Dalsnibba before Geiranger is fabulous.

The winding road 'Ornevein' (Eagle Route) leads up into the mountains offering frequent views over the fjord. After crossing the Nordalsfjord you get your first chance to turn off to Ålesund Island (80 km/50 miles). The main route then continues through the Gudbrands Gorge to the Trollstigen mountain road and on to Åndalsnes. Here you have a second possibility to head towards Ålesund about 120 km (74 miles) down the E136.

The E136 continues east in Romsdalen to Dombås, and from here

through the hilly mountainous countryside to the Dovrefjell.

⑫ **Dovrefjell** Norway's tallest mountain, Snøhetta, at 2,286 m (7,500 ft) dominates the plateau and you can get a great view from the road's highest point (1,026 m/3,366 ft). The national park is classified as the only remaining intact high-altitude ecosystem in Europe.
The road passes through Drivdalen to Oppdal with its modest open-air museum. On the way to Trondheim (E06) you will be presented with a diversion to the old mining town of Røros (120 km/74.5 miles), with a massive stone cathedral and some charming historic buildings.

⑬ **Trondheim** Trondheim was Norway's capital for quite some time. To this day, royal coronations still take place in the mighty Nidaros Cathedral, built in 1070 over the grave of Olav the Holy. The western facade has some particularly interesting sculptures. The Tyholt Television Tower, Fort Kristiansen and the cathedral tower all offer wonderful views over the rooftops of Trondheim.
The scenic E16 leads from Trondheim to Grong, following the banks of numerous fjords along the way. In Grong, Road 760 links up with the R17, the Kystriksveien. The E06 goes north towards Fauske, rolling through the charming Namdalen.

⑭ **Kystriksveien** The 560-km (348-mile) Kystriksveien is in effect the mainland counterpart to the legendary Hurtigruten coastal journey – one of Europe's dream routes. Many ferries ply the fjords and lakes in this region and the landscape is varied. But the coastal road requires a lot of time and money, and waiting times are to be expected for the various ferries. The crossing fees can indeed add up to a considerable sum.
A few kilometers beyond Sonja there is a small road to Mo I Rana where you can get back on the E06 to the Saltfjellet-Svartisen National Park.
The section of the coastal road north of the turnoff to Mo I

1 The Jostedalsbreen National Park, the 'Land of the Giants', in southern Norway protects the largest land glacier in Europe, which has four glacial tongues.

2 Picturesque fishing boats reflected in the Lusterfjord, a northern arm of the Sognefjord.

3 South of Oppdal lies the Dovrefjell National Park with Snøhetta (snow cap) in the background (2,286 m/7,500 ft), Norway's highest mountain just outside Jotunheimen.

4 Typical mountainous and fjord landscape in Nordland, the Norwegian province that straddles the Arctic Circle.

Detour

Røros

A number of buildings, hangars, pits and slag heaps recall an era when Røros was a great mining center. The oldest copper mine in

The church of Bergstaden Zir, built between 1780–1884.

town is a UNESCO World Heritage Site dating back to 1644.
The stone baroque church of Bergstaden Zir (1784) in the town center is surrounded by wooden buildings and is worth visiting. With a capacity of 2,000, it is the third-largest church in the country. It was reserved for miners who lived alongside the slag heaps or in the side streets in shacks. Rich citizens, civil servants and mine managers lived in the avenues and pleasant areas of town, as usual.

1

Detour

Lofoten and Vesterålen Islands

Lofoten and Vesterålen, its northern extension, have been popular holiday destinations for Norwegians since the 19th century. The grandiose scenery of mountains and sea, the colourful villages and the surprisingly mild climate make them exceptional even amid the already spectacular Norwegian landscape. Infrastructure here is excellent, with all the main islands connected to one another as well to the mainland by tunnels or bridges. Ferries take you to the smaller islands.

Both groups of islands reach 250 km (155 miles) out into the Norwegian Sea like a wildly shattered wall of stone, with snow-capped mountains and deep, verdant valleys. Because of the steep cliffs, often only the narrow coastlines are inhabited.

Colourful wooden houses – called Rorbuer – are built on stilts over the water. At places like Austvågøys, wonderful white sandy beaches are hidden

in the fjords and bays – not what one would expect this far north. The bird life on the islands is also impressive. In addition to the typical sea and migratory birds, majestic sea eagles are also at home here. The plant life on these once wooded islands is stunted but varied. Mountain, beach and meadow plants grow side by side.

Despite the fact that the Lofoten and Vesterålen are between 150 and 300 km (93–86 miles) inside the Arctic Circle, the air temperature, even in winter, rarely drops below freezing thanks to the warming effects of the Gulf Stream. Due to the constantly warm currents, the Vestfjord has become a preferred spawning-ground for herring and cod, which in turn benefits salmon and trout breeding in the fjords and bays.

Dried and cured cod are considered delicacies. From March to June they are to be found in their masses

2

drying on wooden racks. Dried fish chips, which like the vitamin C-rich cloudberries are easy to store for long periods, are beloved souvenirs for the 200,000 tourists who visit Lofoten every year.

The detour to Lofoten is a long 587-km (365-mile) drive, but the effort is definitely worth it. The best time of year to visit this stunning archipelago is from the end of May to the middle of July,

when the interplay of midnight sun and mountains will dazzle the uninitiated. Remember to bring your eye masks if you are sensitive to light when you sleep!

Another one of Lofoten's attractions that is worth visiting is Hinnøya, the northernmost medieval church in the world located in Harstad on Norway's largest island. Orcas and porpoises are a very common sight in the

Vestfjord, but a whale safari is still an unforgettable experience. They are offered from Andenes on the northern point of the northernmost Vesterålen island, Andøya, from June to September and you are likely to see sperm whales in the waters off the shore of the whaling station.

The museum in Stokmarknes on the Vesterålen island of Hadseløya tells of the legendary Hurtigruten liner, which

1 A scene typical for the archipelago – small fishing villages in front of impressive cliffs on the rare flat areas along the coast.

2 Hamnøy, sheltered at the entrance to the Reinefjord, is one of the oldest fishing villages on the Lofoten island of Moskenesøya.

3 Midsummer's night: from 2 May to 17 July the sun never sets on the north and west side of the Lofoten Archipelago.

4 The fishing village of Reine is surrounded by steep mountain scenery and considered to be one of the prettiest Lofoten villages. The red-painted Rorbuer houses that line the banks have been used by fishermen since the 12th century.

5 The *hjeller,* wooden racks used to dry fish (especially cod), are common sights on the Lofoten Islands.

was 'founded' here in 1881. Hadseløya has no fjords or bays, but is remarkable from a sporting point of view – its circumference is 42.195 km (26 miles 385 yards), precisely the length of a traditional marathon. Naturally, every year in August there is a race around the island.

Svolvær, the capital of the Lofoten on Austvågøya, is overshadowed by a craggy rock that is shaped like a goat, the Svolværgeita. Don't pass up trips to: the highest peak of the Lofoten islands, the Higravstindan at 1,146 m (3,758 ft); to Raftsund with the second-longest cantilever bridge in the world; and the boat trip to Raftsund in the Trollfjord, which has walls as high as 1,146 m (3,759 ft) in some places and narrow passages that are definitely among the best that the Norwegian landscape has to offer.

From February to April Kabelvåg is northern Norway's cod fishing center. During this time, thousands of fishing boats cast their nets into the waters of the Vestfjord. Around AD 600 there were Vikings living on Vestvågøya. Make sure to pay a visit to the 86-m-long (270-ft) Norman meeting hall in the reconstructed settlement at the Lofotr Museum in the town of Borg.

The 19th-century church in nearby Flakstad on the island of Flakstadøya is considered the prettiest church in the Lofoten Archipelago. Hamnøy, on the beautiful adjacent island of Moskenesøya, is a particularly rustic fishing village.

From Moskenes there is a regular ferry crossing to Bodø on the mainland, and from there you get back on the E06 to Fauske.

The classic Norwegian triple: In the unspoilt, uninhabited landscape of the Vesterålen off the north-western coast you will be surrounded by sky, mountains and fjords. The Steinlandsfjord is on the west side of the island of Langøya, which faces the open Atlantic. It is the second-largest island in Norway. The fjord is in

the middle of a vast, treeless mountainous region of breathtaking beauty and is basically the continuation of the Prestfjord, which goes deep into the island's interior. Langøya is one of the most mountainous parts of the Vesterålen region with peaks of up to 1,000 m (3,300 ft). It is also a great whale watching location.

Flora and fauna in the Finnmark

Long, cold winters with astounding temperatures of -40°C (-40°F) and short but pleasant summers are characteristic of the tundra of northern

Top: Musk oxen.
Bottom: Reindeer run wild here.

Norway. During the few snow-free weeks the small flora in this area seem to explode into berries and blossom, offering direct or indirect nourishment to animals like reindeer, Arctic hares, Arctic foxes, lemmings, snow owls, wolves, bears and lynxes.

In addition, a variety of whale species live in the coastal waters. But the most common encounters are with reindeer and mosquitoes!

Rana is called Helgeland-Salten, the 'Green Road'. A natural tidal spectacle is visible near Løding – every six hours the water trapped behind the 'Eye of the Needle' forces its way through the strait.

From Løding it is a 43-km (27-mile) drive back to the E06 at Fauske. An interesting alternative is the road through the Saltfjellet-Svaryisen National Park. Norway's second largest glacier is high in the Arctic Circle here. The tremendous glacier is hard to reach, however – gravel track turns off at Skonseng towards Svartisdalhytta. Inside the Arctic Circle and above the tree line, only moss and shrubs grow here. The road to Rognan on Saltdalsfjord leads through the high valley of Saltfjells, and then follows the eastern bank to Fauske. The E06 then goes north to Ulsvåg,

where you can turn off to Skutvik, the most important Lofoten port.

⑮ Narvik Swedish iron ore from Kiruna is shipped around the world from the permanently ice-free port of Ofotenfjord here. The warehouses and transport systems are best viewed from the panorama point up on Fagernessfjell (656 m/2,151 ft). Ferries also travel to Lofoten from Narvik. The E08 turns to Tromsø at Nordkjosbotn.

⑯ Tromsø Northern Norway's largest town ironically benefits from a mild climate. The Polarmuseet has interesting exhibits covering various international polar expeditions. The Tromsøbrua connects the island town to the mainland. Next to it is the town's icon – the pointed Arctic Cathedral (1965). Back on the

E06 you drive through some spectacular fjords.

⑰ Alta This town on the fjord of the same name is a center of Sami culture. The stone carvings of Hjemmeluft, which date back between 2,000 and 6,000 years, are definitely worth a visit. They depict animals, hunting and everyday scenes and are listed as a World Heritage Site. The Alta Canyon is also a must-see, with impressive depths of 500 m (1,634 ft) and a length of 15 km (9 miles).

The route then crosses the tundra landscape of Finnmarksvidda to the port town of Hammerfest. After that, the E06 crosses a plateau before the E69 turns off at Olderford towards the North Cape.

⑱ North Cape The road then heads past Porsangerfjord to the

ferry port of Kåfjord, where ferries travel to Honningsvag on the North Cape island of Magerøya. There is now a tunnel to the island. Across the harsh landscape we reach the North Cape, the end of our trip.

1 The Lyngenfjord is over 10 km (6 miles) wide and one of the prettiest in northern Norway.

2 The Finnmark is characterized by wild, harsh landscape, deep fjords, craggy coastal cliffs and expansive plateaus.

3 The midnight sun shines on the North Cape from May 14 to July 30, yet the Cape is often immersed in thick fog, rain or snow. A globe marks Europe's northernmost point.

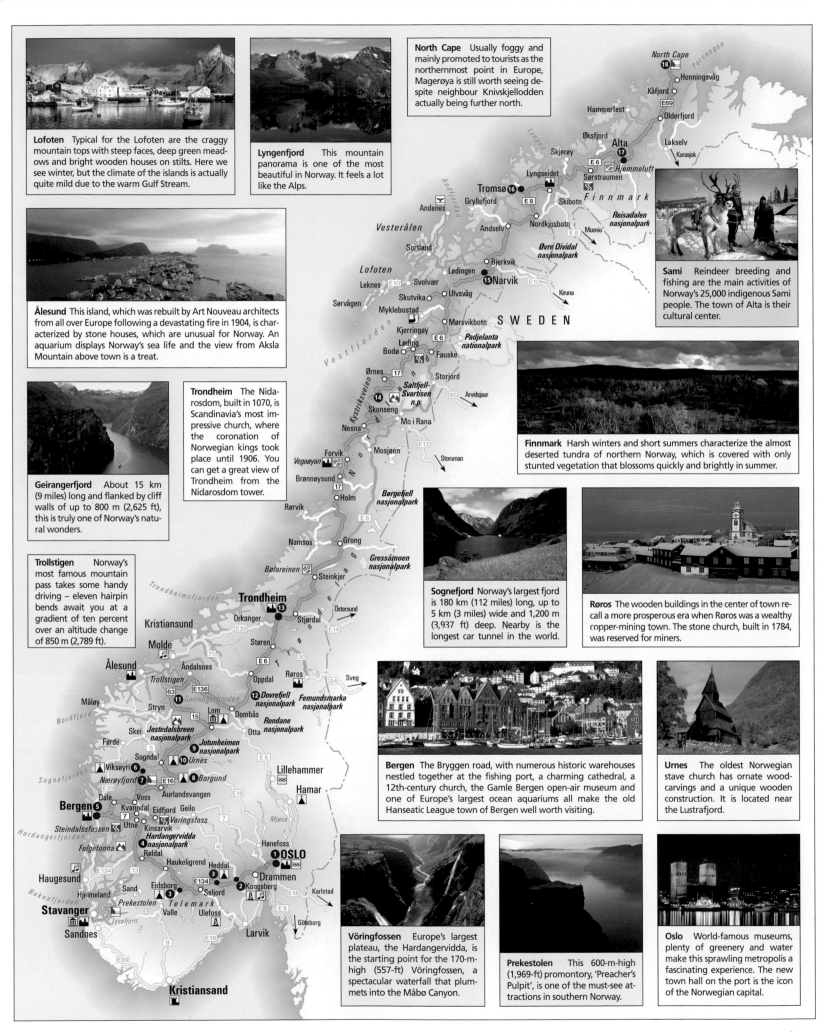

Lofoten Typical for the Lofoten are the craggy mountain tops with steep faces, deep green meadows and bright wooden houses on stilts. Here we see winter, but the climate of the islands is actually quite mild due to the warm Gulf Stream.

Lyngenfjord This mountain panorama is one of the most beautiful in Norway. It feels a lot like the Alps.

North Cape Usually foggy and mainly promoted to tourists as the northernmost point in Europe, Magerøya is still worth seeing despite neighbour Knivskjellodden actually being further north.

Ålesund This island, which was rebuilt by Art Nouveau architects from all over Europe following a devastating fire in 1904, is characterized by stone houses, which are unusual for Norway. An aquarium displays Norway's sea life and the view from Aksla Mountain above town is a treat.

Sami Reindeer breeding and fishing are the main activities of Norway's 25,000 indigenous Sami people. The town of Alta is their cultural center.

Trondheim The Nidarosdom, built in 1070, is Scandinavia's most impressive church, where the coronation of Norwegian kings took place until 1906. You can get a great view of Trondheim from the Nidarosdom tower.

Geirangerfjord About 15 km (9 miles) long and flanked by cliff walls of up to 800 m (2,625 ft), this is truly one of Norway's natural wonders.

Finnmark Harsh winters and short summers characterize the almost deserted tundra of northern Norway, which is covered with only stunted vegetation that blossoms quickly and brightly in summer.

Trollstigen Norway's most famous mountain pass takes some handy driving – eleven hairpin bends await you at a gradient of ten percent over an altitude change of 850 m (2,789 ft).

Sognefjord Norway's largest fjord is 180 km (112 miles) long, up to 5 km (3 miles) wide and 1,200 m (3,937 ft) deep. Nearby is the longest car tunnel in the world.

Røros The wooden buildings in the center of town recall a more prosperous era when Røros was a wealthy copper-mining town. The stone church, built in 1784, was reserved for miners.

Bergen The Bryggen road, with numerous historic warehouses nestled together at the fishing port, a charming cathedral, a 12th-century church, the Gamle Bergen open-air museum and one of Europe's largest ocean aquariums all make the old Hanseatic League town of Bergen well worth visiting.

Urnes The oldest Norwegian stave church has ornate woodcarvings and a unique wooden construction. It is located near the Lustrafjord.

Vøringfossen Europe's largest plateau, the Hardangervidda, is the starting point for the 170-m-high (557-ft) Vøringfossen, a spectacular waterfall that plummets into the Måbø Canyon.

Prekestolen This 600-m-high (1,969-ft) promontory, 'Preacher's Pulpit', is one of the must-see attractions in southern Norway.

Oslo World-famous museums, plenty of greenery and water make this sprawling metropolis a fascinating experience. The new town hall on the port is the icon of the Norwegian capital.

Many Swedes have holiday homes on the skerry coast, as here at Lake

Denmark and Sweden

Where the North Sea meets the Baltic: a journey around the Kattegat

Ever since the bold Öresund Bridge connected Denmark with Sweden, it has been much easier to explore the two "united kingdoms". Indeed, there are many similarities between these Scandanavian countries, but there also many differences to discover. Denmark, the smaller of the two, is known for its seaside holidays, while its larger neighbor features vast tracts of untouched nature.

The most bizarre but perhaps fitting travel recommendation for Denmark came from the royal mouth of its very popular and friendly Queen Margrethe II: "There is no other country in the world that is as much like Denmark as Denmark itself." But what is Denmark? Initially it was an island kingdom comprising the divided Jutland Peninsula, the larger islands of Fünen, Seeland, Falster, Møn, Lolland and Bornholm, and about four hundred smaller islands, of which not even one hundred are inhabited.

Denmark is also a small country that you can cover easily in one day, if you so desire. It is also particularly well suited to those who love the sea. Where else can you choose from 7,400 km (4,598 mi) of largely unspoiled and easily accessible coastlines, from the shimmering blue Kattegat strait and the mild Baltic Sea to the rigged Skagerrak and the tidal North Sea? Denmark's interior, characterized by lakes, fields, forests and moors, is actually quite hilly. The towns and villages, with their whitewashed

Blå Jungfrun National Park west of Öland.

and often slightly dilapidated half-timbered houses, are what the Danes refer to as "hyggelig", meaning cozy. Denmark's cultural assets range from Bronze Age and Viking era archaeological monuments to magnificent manor houses, castles, ground-breaking modern architecture and world-famous museums and art collections.

Beyond the Kattegat strait, the Baltic Sea and the Strait of Öresund, the Kingdom of Sweden – ten times larger than Denmark – offers a breathtaking diversity of landscapes and tranquil expanses. But it also attracts tourists accordingly. The southern part of the country, where little Nils Holgersson's wonderful journeys to the Sápmi region (Lapland) began, will remind travelers a bit of Denmark's meadow and field landscape. North of Gothernburg (Göteborg), however, the

Runn near Falun.

Changing of the guard in front of Amalienborg Palace in the Danish capital, Copenhagen.

Stockholm: Riddarholmskyrka on Riddarholmen. The Swedish church is the final resting place of Swedish kings.

scenery becomes typically Swedish and is more reminiscent of the film adaptations of books by Astrid Lindgren, a Swedish author best known for creating *Pippi Longstocking*. Swedish houses painted "ox blood red" stand in the middle of lush green meadows surrounded by miles of birch and conifer woodlands. Vänern and Vättern, the country's two largest lakes, almost feel like massive inland seas and are also found in this region.

North of Stockholm, nature takes on an increasingly primal feel. Population decreases, the rivers run more wildly and the forests become denser. Sweden's Sápmi region, the northernmost third of the country, is shaped by almost melancholy beauty and pure tranquility. Only the reindeer herds of the Saami people are able to find enough food in the bleak realm of the midnight sun.

Visitors here should do as the outdoor enthusiastic Swedes do and stay a few summer days in a remote *stuga* as part of their adventures in the countryside. They may even encounter one of the 500,000 Swedish moose along the way. There is no need to fear the moose, but you should always be on the lookout for trolls lurking in the forests – Sweden is a land of legends, myths and fairy tales.

This popular cultural strain is also expressed in the numerous festivals and customs here that are unknown in other parts of Europe. The nicest of these is the "magic" midsummer night's festival held all over the country in June. Along with Christmas, this longest day (shortest night) is the most popular holiday in Sweden, when people meet for an evening meal of herring and drink aquavit and "öl" (Swedish for beer).

Egeskov Castle is one of the most beautiful Renaissance water castles in Denmark.

Detour

Bornholm

Bornholm, also known as the "Pearl of the Baltic" for its mild climate, is an island about 40 km (25 mi) off the south coast of Sweden, quite far from the Danish mainland. Ferries

Bornholm is popular for sailing

to the island run from Copenhagen and the Swedish town of Ystad. Roughly 600-sq-km (2312 sq mi) in size, Bornholm is a virtual "Scandinavia in miniature", with miles of sandy beaches, lakes, moors, deciduous and coniferous forests, heaths, dunes and a rocky subsoil not found anywhere else in mainland Denmark.

There are numerous remnants of former settlements on the island. The Hammerhus brick castle from 1260, for example, is the largest and most spectacular ruin in all of Denmark, sitting majestically atop a granite cliff. It makes for a unique experience. Rønne is the largest town on the island and is home to many beautiful old houses, including some charming half-timbered buildings. The whitewashed smokehouses for herring are typical of the picturesque coastal villages.

This tour of southern Scandinavia first heads along the southern Swedish Baltic Sea coast to Stockholm, then passes by numerous lakes and through seemingly endless forests to Göteborg. In Denmark, a fairy-tale journey leads through Jutland, Fyn and Seeland with picturesque ports and trading towns before reaching Copenhagen.

① Copenhagen (see page 69) You can get to Malmö from Copenhagen by ferry or via the Öresund Bridge.

② Malmö Canals run through the picturesque Old Town here, which can be discovered either on foot or by boat. The Stortorget is lined with some wonderful buildings. The route then continues to Lund, a picturesque

Öresund Bridge

Since 2000, Denmark and Sweden have been connected by the Öresund Bridge. All in all, the project comprises a 4-km (2.5-mi) tunnel from Copenhagen Airport, the 4-km (2.5-mi) offshore island of Peberholm and an 8-km (5-mi) bridge to Malmö, a city on the Swedish mainland. Traveling time across the strait has been reduced from 60 to 15 minutes.

university town where the cathedral is the oldest Romanesque church in Sweden.

③ Ystad Many imposing half-timbered buildings make Ystad one of the most beautiful cities in Scania. The herring catch brought wealth to the monastery and fishing town back in the Hanseatic era.

After Ystad, it is worth making a detour at Tomelilla to Sweden's only castle complex still to be preserved in its original condition from 1499. Ramparts and yard-thick walls meant it had been previously impregnable. Regular ferries depart Ystad to the Danish island of Bornholm.

④ Karlskrona Many building complexes in this city were designed for military purposes in the late 17th century and are listed as UNESCO World Heritage Sites. The Karlskrona's Stortorget is among the largest squares in

northern Europe; the admiralty church, built in 1685, and the Trinity church from 1714 are also worth visiting.

⑤ Kalmar The Kalmar Union of 1397 united the kingdoms of Denmark, Norway and Sweden. The castle and cathedral of this

1 The Kalmar Union, which united the kingdoms of Sweden, Denmark and Norway, was signed at Kalmar Castle in 1397. The castle was rebuilt in the Renaissance style by Wasa kings Erik XIV and Johann III in the 16th century.

2 The cathedral in Lund, Sweden, was begun in 1103. with the help of stonemasons from the Rhineland (Germany). The crypt was completed in 1123, and the cathedral was consecrated in 1145.

3 The baroque Kalmar Cathedral was constructed between 1660 and 1703. The "Domkyrka" is one of the most important examples of Swedish baroque church archictecture.

Travel information

Route profile
Length: approx. 2,500 km (1,550 mi) without detours
Time required: 4 weeks
Start and end: Copenhagen
Route (main locations): Copenhagen, Malmö, Karlskrona, Stockholm, Falun, Göteborg, Århus, Odense, Copenhagen

Traffic information:
The Green Insurance Card is recommended. "Shark teeth" on the road replace "Yield" signs in Denmark. The Öresund and Storebælt bridges have tolls of up to 50 euros each way for passenger cars. Watch out for deer crossings in Sweden. They are quite common. Low-beam headlights are automatic in both Sweden and Denmark.

When to go:
May to October (Denmark), June to September (Sweden).

Accommodation:
All price categories are available and in demand Scandinavia, particularly holiday homes.
Typically Danish: "Kros" – royally licenced regional guesthouses/hotels (www.dansk-kroferie.dk).

Information:
Denmark:
www.dt.dk
www.visitdenmark.com
Sweden:
Sveriges Rese- och Turistråd,
Box 3030, Kungsgatan 36,
S-103 61 Stockholm,
www.visit-sweden.com and
www.sweden.se

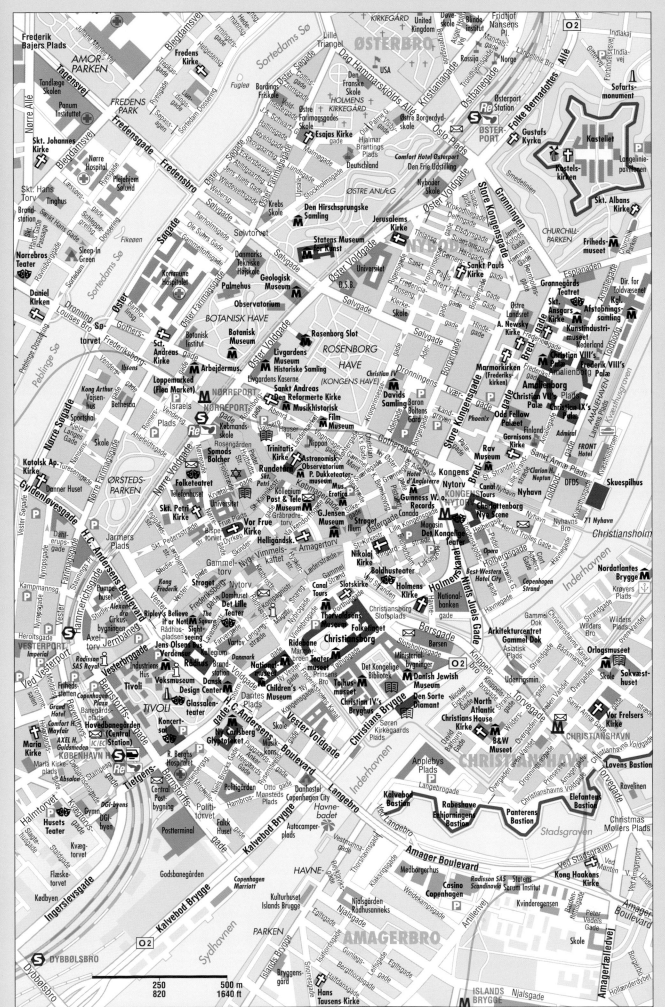

Copenhagen

History and tradition greet travelers at every turn here, the Danish capital and royal residence on the Strait of Öresund. The atmosphere is relaxed and open-minded yet pleasantly introspective, and most tourist attractions can be easily reached on foot.

The city on the Strait of Öresund, which has been the capital of Denmark since 1443, experienced its first heyday in the late Middle Ages as a trading port, and a second boom in the 16th and 17th centuries, particularly under King Christian IV, who greatly expanded and developed the city.

Sights of note here include: the Tivoli Gardens amusement park; the harbor promenade at Nyhavn Canal, lined with old wooden sailing ships and cafés; the canal and harbor tours and boat excursions from here to the popular Little Mermaid statue (Lille Havfrue) on the Langelinie pier promenade are pleasant; the rococo royal residence, Amalienborg Palace; the Zoological Gardens, the green oasis of the city; Slotsholm island with Christiansborg Castle; Thorvaldsenmuseum, with works by famous Danish sculptors; the antique collection of the Ny Carlsberg Glytotek; Rådhus Pladsen, in the heart of the in-

Top: The Little Mermaid.
Middle: Nyhavn, today the oldest port in the city, was constructed from 1671 to 1673.
Bottom: The Tivoli amusement park.

ner city with the town hall (which offers a spectacular view from its tower); the landmark portion of the Carlsberg brewery; the Nationalmuseet with historical and ethnographic collections and a number of exhibitions.

Detour

Öland and Gotland

Sweden's largest islands were all settled as early as Viking times. During the era of the Hanseatic

Öland: Stone Age cemetery, with a typical windmill in the background

cities, Gotland's capital, Visby, was an important trading hub – briefly even the most important in the entire Baltic region, and much more so than it is today. The cathedral and the mile-long 13th-century city

Top: Rock formations on Fårø beach, Gotland island.
Bottom: The walled town of Visby.

wall, which completely surrounds the UNESCO World Heritage Site, are particularly impressive.
Much praise is given to Gotland's mild climate and landscape, which features lush meadows, forests, beaches and steep coastlines with extremely peculiar rock formations that look like human creations.
Öland, the second-largest island in Sweden, is connected to Småland by a bridge and is the summer residence of the Swedish royal family. As the limestone in the subsoil drains off rainfall, vast areas of the island are stark grassy with dune steppes, a paradise for many rare species of animals and orchids. Öland also has large deciduous forests and is known for its beautiful beaches and some four hundred windmills.

city on the Kalmarsund is worth seeing, as are the baroque and Renaissance harbor and the buildings in the Old Town. A 6-km (4-mi) bridge spans the sound from Kalmar to the island of Öland.
Your route then follows the coastal road E22 toward Norrköping. Along the way there are ferry connections to Gotland from Oskarshamn and Västervik. If you have time, be sure to make a detour to the Swedish skerry coast at Västervik, or at Valdemarsvik/Fyrudden or St Anna south of Norrköping.
At Norrköping, the road continues north past the Hjälmaren to the intersection with the E20, where you follow the E20 to Gripsholm, 20 km (12 mi) beyond Strängnäs.

6 Gripsholm Castle Kurt Tucholsky created a literary monument out of this castle at Lake Mälaren. He is buried at the nearby village of Mariefred.
From Gripsholm Castle, the road follows the south-east bank of Lake Mälaren to the Swedish capital, Stockholm.

7 Stockholm (see page 71)

8 Uppsala This city is famous for having the oldest university in northern Sweden, founded in 1477, and Scandinavia's largest cathedral, the Domkyrka, which houses the remains of national heroes, kings Erik and Gustav Wasa. The 16th-century castle and the Carolina Redviva, the largest library in Sweden, are other worthwhile sights in this city on the Frysån River.
To the north is Gamla Uppsala with royal burial mounds and an 11th-century church. It was the country's political center until the 13th century.
From Uppsala, your route leads north to the harbor town of Gävle, marking the start of Highway 80, which you will take west to Falun.

9 Falun The Vikings allegedly mined copper in Falun, but the town's heyday as a center for copper processing ended in disaster: The mine collapse here in 1687 created Stora Stöten, said to be the largest hole in the world at 65 m (213 ft) deep, 370 m (1,214 ft) long and 220 m (722 ft) wide. The town's historic copper mine is a UNESCO World Heritage Site.
On Highway 70, you now head north-west to Lake Siljan, which you will almost completely circumnavigate on your trip.

10 Siljansee Dalarna is a densely forested province known for the carved wooden Dalarna horses. When travelling around the lake, it is worth stopping in Mora on the northern shore.
The town marks the end of the Wasa Track (86 km/53 mi). The "Zorngaarden", a museum by artist Anders Zorn, and the "Zorns Gammelgaarden" open-air museum is worth a visit. From Leksand at the southern end of the lake, you initially follow Highway 70 to Borlänge, where you change to Highway 60 towards Örebro.

11 Örebro In addition to the beautiful sculptures and monuments in this old city in central Sweden, it is also worth paying a visit to the 800-year-old castle on an island in the river, the 13th-century St Nicholas church and the more modern Svampen water tower.
From Örebro, the route now follows the E4 to Vättern via the town of Askersund.

12 Vättern Vättern is Sweden's second-largest lake. Plan a stop at the Göta Canal in Motala, which connects Vättern and Vänern, and in the garden city of Vadstena with its interesting minster and castle.
At the southern end of the lake is Jönköping. From there the route heads directly west to the port city of Göteborg.

13 Göteborg Sweden's second-largest city has a charming Old Town lined with canals. Highly recommended are a stroll down Kungsportsavenyn boulevard, a visit to Lieseberg amusement park and the futuristic new opera, and a boat ride through the ports, canals and islets.
From Gothenburg, it is not far to Bohuslän. Ferries depart Göteborg for Frederikshavn on the Danish Jutland peninsula via the Kattegat. Travel time is around three hours.

14 Frederikshavn The largest city in northern Jutland, Freder-

ikshavn is famous for the Krudttårnet, a 17th-century powder tower with a weapons collection spanning three centuries.
Before your journey continues south, it is worth making a small detour to the northern tip of the peninsula in Skagen.

15 Skagen About 150 years ago, a number of artists settled here on the northernmost tip of Jutland, formed an artists' colony and began creating what

1 View of Gripsholm Castle from the beach in Mariefred in Södermanland province. The castle has housed the National Portrait Collection since 1822.

2 Drottningholm Castle (1699) on the island of Lovø in Lake Mälar was modelled on Versailles and has been the residence of the royal family since 1981.

3 A village near Göteborg on the western Swedish coast in Västergötland.

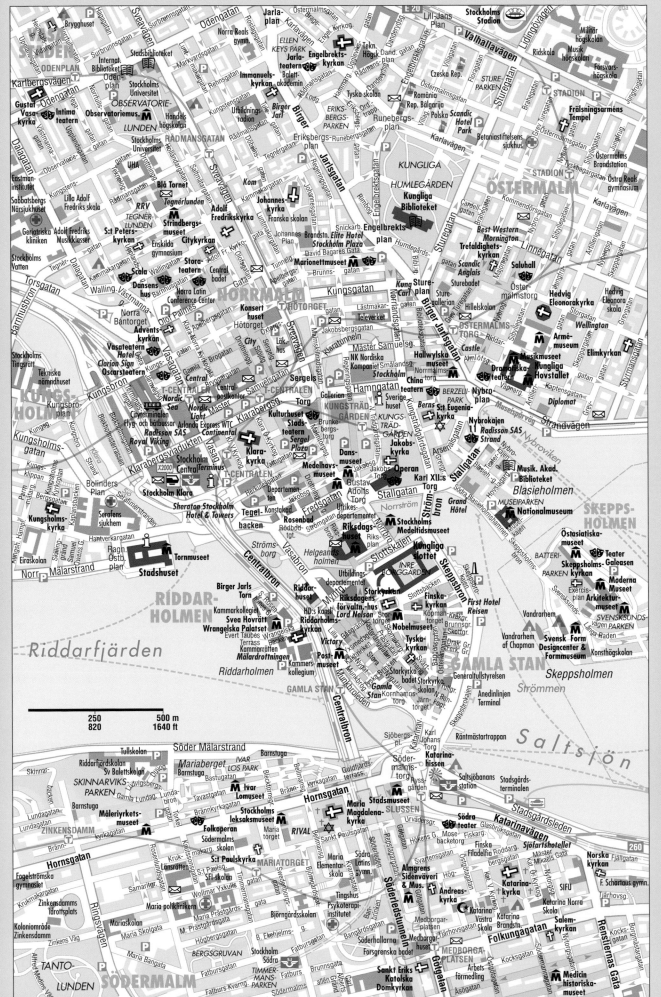

Stockholm

This metropolis, which is home to 1.6 million people, is spread out over fourteen islands at the southern end of Lake Mälar, on the skerry-rich Baltic Sea coast between fresh- and saltwater zones. Founded in 1252 and capital since 1634, Stockholm has developed into a cosmopolitan city, pulsating with diversity. Magnificent buildings, parks, rivers and bridges make it unique among its peers.

Particularly worth seeing in the Swedish capital are: the Royal City Castle (Kungliga Slottet), with around six hundred rooms one of the largest residences in the world; Storkyrkan, Stockholm's oldest church, with Gothic interior; Tyska Kyrkan, church of the German community with an impressive altar; Riddarholmkyrkan, royal burial site since the Thirty Years War; the baroque Reich Chamber of Corporations Riddarhuset; the picturesque harbor quarter between Österlanggatan and Skeppsbron; Stadshus (1911–1923), an icon of the city with a stunning view from the tower; Konserthuset, annual venue of the Nobel Prize ceremony. Some worthwhile museums include: the Nationalmuseet and Moderna Museet (modern

Top: Stockholm in winter.
Bottom: 17th-century row houses.

art); Skansen, the oldest open-air museum in the world; Vasamuseet with the flagship of Gustav II Adolf Vasa, sunk during its launch in 1628. Also worth seeing are the subway stations with artistic decoration ("the longest gallery in the world"); the magnificent Strandvägen boulevard; Stockholm's skerry garden and the residence of the royal family, Drottningholm Castle, with fully functional rococo theater.

Detour

Bohuslän

The region north of Göteborg was named after the 13th-century Bohus Fort ruins near Kungälv. The Bohuslän coast is rich in fjords and skerries and often compared to the coast of southern France because of its picturesque fishing villages and exclusive spa resorts.

One of the most beautiful routes in all of Sweden is the trip to Tjörn and Orust, Bohuslän's largest islands, connected to each other and the mainland by bridges. Animal lovers will enjoy Sweden's largest sea aquarium, Havets Hus in Lysekil, and the Nordens Ark zoo near Smögen, which specializes in Nordic species. The rock drawings near Tanums-

Top: Coastal landscape near Malmö.
Bottom: Prehistoric rock paintings at Tanumö.

hede are impressive; the only one of Bohuslän's many Bronze Age discovery sites to be included in the UNESCO World Heritage list. The engravings were done between 1800 and 800 BC, and their present-day enhanced tints allow them to be identified more easily.

The climax of the approximately 200-km (124-mi) excursion is the boat-shaped Viking formation near Blomsholm and the 420-m-long (460-yd), 60-m-high (67-yd) Svinesund Bridge near the border with Norway.

would become icons of Danish painting. Their collective works can be seen in the Skagen Museum and in the Michael and Anna Ancher House. Don't miss the Tilsandede Church, which was ultimately abandoned in 1795 due to the incessant sand that blew onshore here.

16 Sæby The half-timbered fishing houses, cutter port and minster with 15th-century frescos, this spa town is a quaint little bit of paradise. The Saeby-gaard Manor (the oldest part of which dates back to 1576) is also worth seeing. The nearby Voergaard Renaissance castle houses a world-class art and porcelain collection.

17 Aalborg The Limfjord and Aalborg are best viewed from the 105-m (345-ft) Aalborgtår-net tower. The Budolfi Cathedral is dedicated to the patron saint of sailors. Jens Bang's Stenhus, the home of a rich merchant built in 1624, and the North Jutland Art Museum should also not be missed.

18 Viborg The cathedral in Denmark's oldest city had to be completely rebuilt in the 19th century. Its ceiling frescos and the medieval quarter are worth seeing, as are the limestone mines, which were shut down in the 1950s after nearly one thousand years of mining. They are in front of the city gates.

19 Århus Denmark's second-largest city was built on a former Viking settlement. The St Clements church, begun in 1200, is Denmark's largest cathedral. The Den Gamle By is the first open-air museum for non-royal Danish culture. Architect, Arne Jacobsen, helped design the Raad-huset, completed in 1942. A 2,000-year-old preserved body

found in the marshland is the main attraction of the Moesgård Museum.

20 Vejle This "mountain town" has a spectacular location on the fjord of the same name. St Nicolai Church is the oldest building in the town and is home to something creepy: a 2,500-year-old preserved body found in the marshland and the walled-in skulls of 23 robbers. The graphic art in the museum and the city's landmark, a wind-mill, are worth seeing. North-west of Vejle is the UNESCO World Heritage Site of Jelling, with impressive burial mounds and two royal rune stones from the 10th century, which are considered to be "Denmark's baptismal certificates".
The Jutland mainland is connected to Fyn island with a railway road bridge and a highway bridge (Storebæltsbro). The island's capital is the next stop.

21 Odense Hans Christian Andersen made this island capital world famous. His childhood home and museum are dedi-

cated to him, while the Carl Nielsen Museum, the Old Town and the Gothic St Knuds Church are other attractions.
From Odense, Highway 9 leads to the next stop, Egeskov.

22 Egeskov This little 16th-century castle with its cemetery and drawbridge is one of the best-known moated castles in Europe. It has an interesting park with baroque landscaping and a nice vintage car museum. From the south of the island it's on to Nyborg on the east coast, where the 18-km (11-mi) Store-bæltbro bridge spans the Great Belt between Fyn and Sjælland.

23 Trælleborg Not far from Slagelse is the Viking fort of Trælleborg, built according to strict geometric theory and dedicated to King Harald Bluetooth (10th century).

24 Roskilde This city's cathedral is a UNESCO World Heritage Site. Thirty-eight Danish regents were buried here. The five preserved Viking ships, discovered in the adjacent Roskilde fjord,

are worth seeing and are presented in the modern Vikinge-skibs Museet.
Finally, you pass Frederiksborg castle to Helsingör at the northern end of Sjælland.

25 Helsingør The main attraction of this city located on the Strait of Öresund is Kronborg castle. Another 50 km (31 mi) or so along the coast and you arrive back in Copenhagen, the end of your journey.

1 The Renaissance Kronborg castle near Helsingør on the strait between Denmark and Sweden.

2 A walk through the open-air museum Den Gamle By in Århus shows you the old Denmark.

3 Roskilde was the summer residence of the Danish kings from the 11th to the 15th centuries. Many Danish rulers are buried in the Romanesque-Gothic cathedral.

4 Frederiksborg castle near Hille-rød, north of Copenhagen, houses the National Historic Museum.

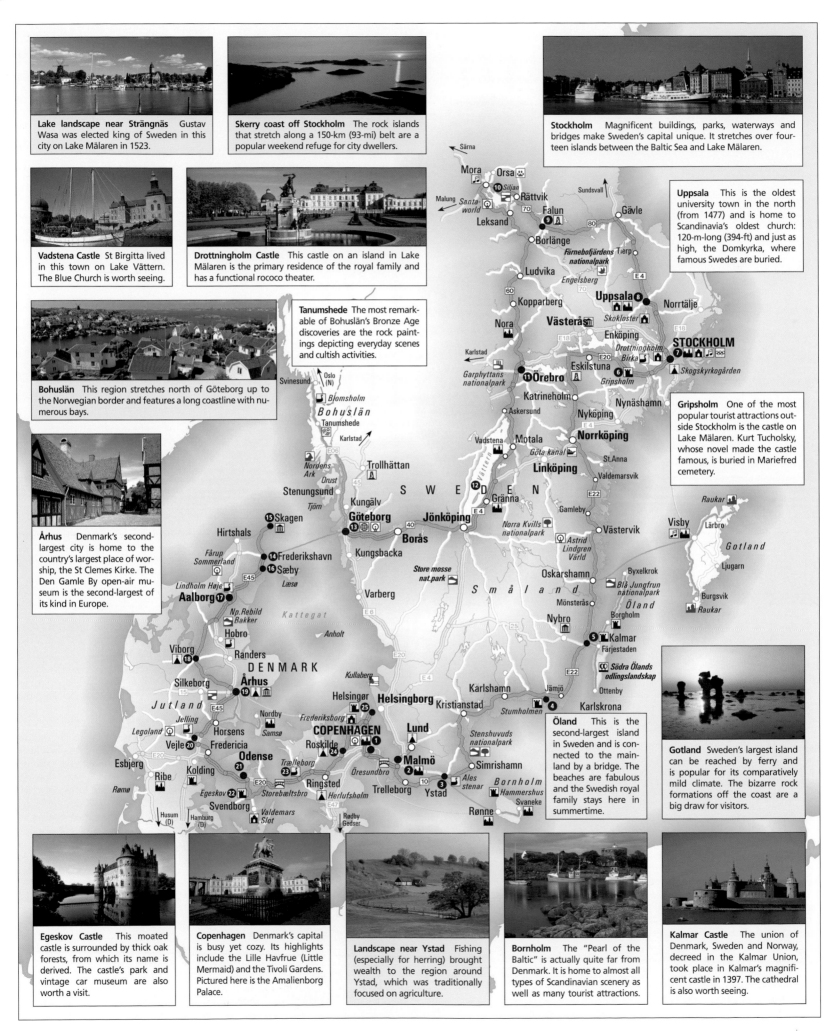

Lake landscape near Strängnäs Gustav Wasa was elected king of Sweden in this city on Lake Mälaren in 1523.

Skerry coast off Stockholm The rock islands that stretch along a 150-km (93-mi) belt are a popular weekend refuge for city dwellers.

Stockholm Magnificent buildings, parks, waterways and bridges make Sweden's capital unique. It stretches over fourteen islands between the Baltic Sea and Lake Mälaren.

Vadstena Castle St Birgitta lived in this town on Lake Vättern. The Blue Church is worth seeing.

Drottningholm Castle This castle on an island in Lake Mälaren is the primary residence of the royal family and has a functional rococo theater.

Uppsala This is the oldest university town in the north (from 1477) and is home to Scandinavia's oldest church: 120-m-long (394-ft) and just as high, the Domkyrka, where famous Swedes are buried.

Tanumshede The most remarkable of Bohuslän's Bronze Age discoveries are the rock paintings depicting everyday scenes and cultish activities.

Bohuslän This region stretches north of Göteborg up to the Norwegian border and features a long coastline with numerous bays.

Gripsholm One of the most popular tourist attractions outside Stockholm is the castle on Lake Mälaren. Kurt Tucholsky, whose novel made the castle famous, is buried in Mariefred cemetery.

Århus Denmark's second-largest city is home to the country's largest place of worship, the St Clemes Kirke. The Den Gamle By open-air museum is the second-largest of its kind in Europe.

Öland This is the second-largest island in Sweden and is connected to the mainland by a bridge. The beaches are fabulous and the Swedish royal family stays here in summertime.

Gotland Sweden's largest island can be reached by ferry and is popular for its comparatively mild climate. The bizarre rock formations off the coast are a big draw for visitors.

Egeskov Castle This moated castle is surrounded by thick oak forests, from which its name is derived. The castle's park and vintage car museum are also worth a visit.

Copenhagen Denmark's capital is busy yet cozy. Its highlights include the Lille Havfrue (Little Mermaid) and the Tivoli Gardens. Pictured here is the Amalienborg Palace.

Landscape near Ystad Fishing (especially for herring) brought wealth to the region around Ystad, which was traditionally focused on agriculture.

Bornholm The "Pearl of the Baltic" is actually quite far from Denmark. It is home to almost all types of Scandinavian scenery as well as many tourist attractions.

Kalmar Castle The union of Denmark, Sweden and Norway, decreed in the Kalmar Union, took place in Kalmar's magnificent castle in 1397. The cathedral is also worth seeing.

St Petersburg: Smolni Cathedral and Resurrection Monastery.

Finland and Russia

From the empire of the Czars to the land of a thousand lakes

Finland is a quiet country with countless lakes and seemingly endless forests. It is ideal for visitors looking for a bit of peace and seclusion. From Finland's capital, Helsinki, you can also make a detour to St Petersburg, Russia, just a few hours away.

The iconic animal of the Arctic far north, the moose, is very common in Finland. In fact, the very shape of the country is similar to the head of a female elk, and a look at any map of Finland will make it obvious why the "Elk Head" is considered the "Land of a Thousand Lakes": the complex maze of roughly 50,000 to 60,000 bodies of inland water dominates the entire southern half of the country. Approximately 12 percent of "Suomi", the Finnish name for Finland, is covered by freshwater, and nearly 70 percent by forest. The ever-changing landscape of breathtaking waterways, lakes and vast forests make Finland a dream destination for anyone seeking a quiet, relaxing holiday. Having said that, however, the Finnish Baltic Sea coast along the Gulf of Bothnia and the Gulf of Finland is also a very impressive landscape, with offshore skerry (rock) islands, innumerable bays and long, sandy beaches, picturesque villages perfect for bathing and fishing, and a verdant green hinterland. In addition to that are the slightly more melancholy fjell and tundra regions north of the Arctic Circle.

Finland offers ideal conditions for winter sports between the months of November

19th-century icons of Konevitsa in Kuopio.

and May, but the icy-cold temperatures and the somewhat bleak darkness of the long polar nights may deter. They are also the reason why the Finns are often considered a rather serious and quiet folk. In reality, however, they are a fun-loving and relaxed people who place great value on family and, as soon as summer starts, spend much of their free time outside picking berries, gathering mushrooms, fishing, swimming, boating or just lounging around. They also use the time to "tank up" on light and warmth for the long winters, forgetting time and space and simply enjoying the relief from winter. For 1.5 million music, film, literature, jazz, choir, theater and dance enthusiasts from all over the world, the summer festivals in Finland are the highlight of the year. No other country boasts as many festivals per capita.

St Petersburg: the magnificent baroque building of the Nicholas Naval Cathedral on the Griboyedov canal.

Above: the 150-year-old cathedral behind the statue of Czar Alexander II at Senate Square in Helsinki. An imposing staircase leads to the cathedral, whose interior includes a statue of Agricola, Finland's reformer.

Nearly everyone who visits Finland is there for its natural scenic charm, and less so for its cities. But that is not to say they are without their own charms. And this does not just apply to the neoclassical capital, Helsinki, or Turku, the former capital on the Gulf of Bothnia. Finland's coast is home to plenty of picturesque fishing and holiday towns where, not surprisingly, Swedish culture and language are also widespread. Meanwhile, there is a distinct Russian feel in Karelia, Finland's "Wild East". The Sami settlements beyond the Arctic Circle, like the one on Lake Inari, are also fascinating. Even Finland's unique language should not represent a hindrance as far as pronunciation. Finnish is the one of the few languages in the world to have largely solved the exasperating problem of one sound, one letter. This means you can read "suomalainen" and say it correctly without any overly complex pronunciation rules. Most Finns understand a bit of English and German as well, and only one little Finnish term is actually truly essential: "sauna". Only those who have enjoyed this 2,000-year-old Finnish body wellness ritual have experienced the "true" Finland.

From Helsinki, or one of the coastal towns on the Gulf of Finland, it is also worth taking a trip to the Russian cities of St Petersburg and Novgorod to the south, especially during the "White Nights". Both are Hanseatic cities with unique architectural and cultural treasures. The historic center of St Petersburg, with its beautiful churches, magnificent palaces, museums, canals and bridges, is listed as a UNESCO World Heritage Site, as are the churches of Novgorod.

Most of Finland's lakes are in the south of the country and are connected by rivers and canals.

Helsinki's modern architecture

The fact that Helsinki has a wealth of world-famous modern architecture is mainly due to the devastating blazes that continuously destroyed the city, which was once built of wood: in 1812, after Helsinki was elevated to the status of capital, Czar Alexander I commissioned architect Carl Ludwig Engel (Berlin, 1778–1840), to build stone reconstructions in a neoclassical style, including the cathedral and the university on Senate Square. In the early 20th century, a Finnish version of Art Nouveau architecture known as "National Romanticism" (national museum, main train station) developed. Alvar Aalto's (1898–1976) archi-

Top: National Opera in Helsinki.
Center: Underground rock church.
Bottom: Finlandia Hall, one of Alva Aalto's main works.

tectural style was rational in the 1920s (the parliament buildings) and evolved into aesthetical functionalism during the 1930s. His Finlandia Hall, from 1970, and other buildings throughout the world have indeed influenced entire generations of architects, including the Suomalainen brothers (rock church, 1996). Aalto's principle of "organic" construction, which involves the extensive use of natural materials and shapes, continues to characterize Finnish architecture even today.

The Finlandia Route: the wonders of Finland, St Petersburg and the North Cape on one, albeit long journey. Follow our route through the diversity of southern Finland (Route I) and Lake Saimaa before connecting with Route II, which takes you through Karelia's wild forests toward the northern tip of Europe.

Route I – Southern Finland

❶ Helsinki (see page 77) Your journey through southern Finland begins in the capital.

❷ St Petersburg For more details, look in the Travel Information box and on pages 78–79.

❸ Ekenäs/Tammisaari The "City of Oaks" is known for the national park just off the coast that features picturesque skerry, or rock, islands. Wooden houses from the 17th and 18th century can be found in the historic center of Ekenäs, while Alvar Aalto's bank building showcases more modern architecture. Raasepori Castle, located outside of town, is a curious place: At the time of its construction in the 14th century, it could only be reached by boat; now it is located in the country's interior.

❹ Hangö/Hanko The Hangö headland sits at the foothills of the Salpausselkä mountains and is mostly covered in dense forest. Finland's southernmost mainland point is a sailing, swimming and fishing paradise for Finns looking to take it easy amidst the skerry gardens or on the

many sandy beaches. The Art Nouveau villas in the park were built at the turn of the 20th century.
Back in Ekenäs, Road 184 leads to Salo on the Lappdalsfjärden. From there it heads back to the unique skerry coast.

❺ Turku/Åbo The skerry garden off the coast of Turku has over 20,000 islands of varying sizes and is one of the Finland's most popular attractions. Only a few buildings in the former capital survived what proved to be Scandinavia's largest fire in 1827: Turunlinna Castle, a solid stone building (built in the late 13th century), and Turku's brick cathedral, consecrated in 1290.

❻ Naantali This town has managed to preserve its late 18th- and early 19th-century architectural charm, the main attraction being the Old Town, the Minster, and the Kultarnata

1 The Uspensky Cathedral towers over the harbor in Helsinki.

2 The skerry gardens off the Finnish coast near Tammisaari.

Travel information

Route profile
Length:
Route I: 1,350 km (839 mi),
Route II (from Juva):
1,400 km (870 mi)
Time required: at least two weeks; do not underestimate the return journey!
Start and end: Helsinki

Traffic information:
The green insurance card is recommended. Video devices must be declared. Vehicle nationality labels are required and low-beam lights during the day are compulsory. Watch out for deer crossings.

When to go:
Route I: June–September
Route II: July–end of August

Accommodation:
Holiday homes, or "mökkis", with sauna facilities are popular of Finland.

Information:
Here are some websites to help you prepare for your trip:
www.visitfinland.com
www.alltravelfinland.com

St Petersburg and Nizhny Novgorod:
The best way to arrive in St Petersurg is to take a ferry from Helsinki or other Finnish port towns, or take a bus from Lappeenranta. There are also good bus or rail connections to Russia from other towns in Finland.

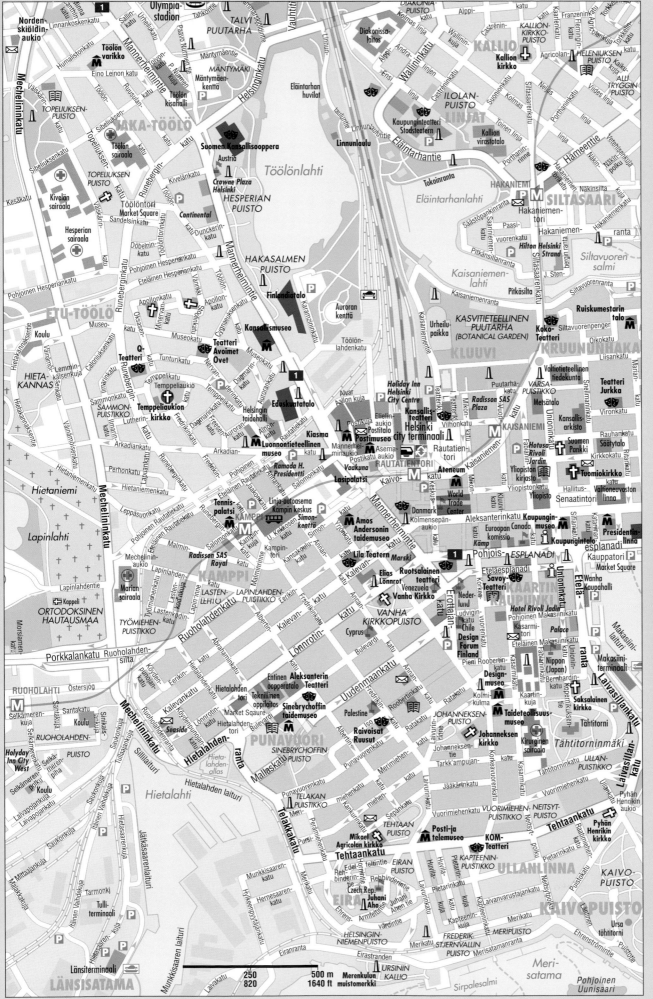

Helsinki

Roughly 500,000 people live in Helsinki, Finland's compact capital, which was founded in 1550 by Swedish King Gustav Vasa. Following devastating fires, Czar Alexander II commissioned Berlin architect, Carl Ludwig Engel, to rebuild Helsinki in the popular neo-classical style of the time. Twenty of the monuments erected between 1820 and 1850 still stand today. Combined with well-known Art Nouveau buildings and other contemporary edifices, the metropolis on the Gulf of Finland offers a unique and enjoyable cityscape.

Amond the attractions in Helsinki, Engel's Senate Square is considered one of the most beautiful plazas in the world. It includes the cathedral, the government palace, the main university campus and the university library. At its center is the statue of Czar Alexander II. The market square and historic market halls at the southern harbor has ferry piers for ships to Suomenlinna, an old Swedish island fort and UNESCO World Heritage Site, and to the skerry islands. The Katajanokka Peninsula has the best panoramic view of the capital. The

View of the cathedral from the harbor.

beautiful Orthodox Uspenski Cathedral (1868) has a lavish interior. Luotsikatu, one of the most magnificent streets in Helsinki has numerous Art Nouveau buildings. The Esplanade, Helsinki's pedestrian zone, is home to Stockmann department store, the largest in Scandinavia.

Museums include the Ateneum (Finnish), the Kiasma (modern) and the Sinebrychoff (foreign). Take a look at the central station with a 48-m-high (158-ft) clock tower, the Suomalainen brothers' rock church (1969), Alvar Aalto's Finlandia Hall (1970), where the last stage of the CSCE act was signed in 1975. The tower at the Olympic stadium provides a fantastic view over Helsinki.

Detour

St Petersburg

Czar Peter the Great planned his city down to the finest detail. First founded in 1703, St Petersburg was meant to be the Russian "window to the West" and it was here on the banks of the Neva that his vision of progress was realized. The entire city was to be built of stone, an innovation in and of itself, and since then, it has developed into one of Russia's most important cultural, political and economic centers. Since its founding, the city's name has changed three times: Petrograd, Leningrad and finally back to St Petersburg, where the October Revolution began. It is well worth paying a visit during the "White Nights" in June when it is still light at midnight. The square with the mighty Alexander Column (1832) in front of the Winter Palace is a sight along with the mag-

nificently decorated Czars' residence, which has been extended many times. The Hermitage Museum in the Winter Palace is worth a visit including the adjoining buildings. It has a renowned art collection.

Around the palace square you'll find Alexander Park with the architecturally unique Admiralty (UNESCO World Heritage Site), whose golden spire is one of the city's landmarks; Senate Square with the Peter the Great monument; St Isaac's Cathedral (19th century), the largest and most lavishly decorated church in Russia with its golden cupola; Yussupov Palace on the banks of the Moika; St Nicholas' Naval Cathedral with its shiny gold domes (18th century); and the Mariinsky Theater, the world-famous opera and ballet playhouse.

The historic city center (UNESCO World Heritage Site) includes the Peter and Paul Fortress (18th century) with Peter's Gate; the burial site of the czars in the Peter and Paul Cathedral; the crownwork with artillery museum; the Central Naval Museum in the former stock exchange; the art chamber with the rarities collection of Peter the Great and the Lomonossov Museum; the 18th-century science academy; the red and white complex of the twelve councils (1721), today a university; and the baroque Menshikov Palace with a museum on the culture at the time of Peter the Great.

Around the majestic boulevard of Nevsky Prospekt you will find: Kasaner Cathedral; Resurrection Church (1907); Stroganov Palace (1754); Arts Square with the Michaelmas Palace and the Russian Museum; the Ethnography Museum; Anitshkov Palace with Anitshkov Bridge; and the baroque Belosselsky-Belosersky Palace.

Also worth seeing are: the Summer Garden, the city's oldest park with the Summer Palace from 1710, and the Marble Palace; Alexander Nevsky Monastery with its neoclassical Trinity Cathedral; Tilchvin and Lazarus cemetery and Smolni Resurrection Monastery with the baroque Resurrection Cathedral; Pushkin Theater and Pushkin Museum, Dostoyevsky Museum; Sheremetev Palace with the Anna Achmatova Museum.

Don't miss the UNESCO World Heritage Site of Novogorod while you are here. The "New City" is some 200 km (124 mi) south-west on Lake Ilmen, on the main road to Moscow. Despite its name, Novgorod is one of Russia's oldest cities, founded in the 9th century with close ties to the Hanseatic League, which had a branch office in Novgorod. The walled Kremlin of the former city state, which existed from the 12th to the 17th centuries and is protected by nine towers, is indeed imposing. Novgorod's churches, built between the 12th and 14th centuries in a great variety of styles, are also famous. At the time, almost every residential street and guild had its own ornate church.

1 The Winter Palace: a masterpiece of Russian baroque.

2 St Isaac's Cathedral is the largest and most magnificent church in St Petersburg.

3 The Grand Palace, summer residence of the czars, is in Pushkin (Tsarskoe Selo) near St Petersburg and was built in 1724, for Catherine the Great, wife of Peter III.

4 The lavishly fanciful focal point of Peter I's summer residence is the great baroque palace near St Petersburg.

Savonlinna

Savonlinna is located at the heart of a complex maze of a thousand lakes in what is known as the Saimaa lake district. The main attractions of this charming area include the provincial museum, located in a former granary on Riihisaari Island in front of the castle gates; the Mikko, Savonlinna and Salama museum ships, the market square with a pier for boat excursions into the Saimaa lake district, and the 100-year-old Rauhalinna wooden villa, which is just outside of town.

The Olavinlinna fort, built in 1475, and reached via a pontoon bridge, is considered one of Finland's most beautifully preserved medieval castle complexes and has hosted the

Olavinlinna was the first Finnish castle to be built during the time of firearms.

Savonlinna opera festivals for more than thirty years. This festival is the largest regular cultural event in Finland. The town of Savonlinna, located about 330 km (205 mi) from Helsinki, is also happily known as the "Bayreuth of the North", a German city with a lovely Old Town and a very popular opera and music festival. The event is also often likened to the Salzburg Festival.
Many performances are held in the castle's inner courtyard under a canvas tent or in the Savonlinna concert hall, famous for its wonderful acoustics. The festival takes place from July to early August. For more detailed information, visit the official Internet site at: www.operafestival.fi

Castle, which is the summer residence of Finland's president. Anyone wishing to experience the skerry garden up close can follow a small access road to Pulkkalla. The N8 leads to Rauma at the Gulf of Bothnia.

7 **Rauma** Finland's third-oldest city is an important center for top bobbin lace making. The historic Old Town, which has been completely unaffected by any fires over the last 320 years, has been declared a World Heritage Site: 600 wooden buildings form the largest inner city complex of this kind in all of Scandinavia. From Pori take the N8 to the N2, which leads to Forssa and from there head to Hämeenlinna.

8 **Hämeenlinna** The birth house of composer Jean Sibelius (1865–1957), the Häme brick castle from the 13th century, and Aulanko Park are all among the attractions here.

9 **Lahti** This famous winter sports town is situated on an impressive moraine tuffet with two lakes. It impresses visitors with its six ski jumps and a small ski museum. The Church of the Cross (built in 1978, designed by Alvar Aalto) and the Sibelius Hall are considered architectural gems. Lahti is also the gateway to Finland's lake region, while the Salpausselkä mountains and Vesijärvi and Päijänne lakes offer a variety of leisure options.
The landscape along the N5 to Mikkeli affords visitors everything they would expect of the "Land of a Thousand Lakes".

10 **Mikkeli** This city is situated in a rolling hills landscape and was built on orders from Czar Nicholas I in 1838. It had already become an important center in eastern Finland during the Middle Ages. A small stone chapel from 1320 in the market square dates back to this time as well. The largest wooden vicarage in Finland – Kenkävero — is in the town center. Roughly 700 lakes and ponds surround the city, and marshlands stretch off toward the north. Dark-green forests, shimmering lakes, a few villages and some remote summer homes are scattered along the way to Savonlinna and Kerimäki. Those wanting to travel up to the North Cape must initially stay on the N5 and not turn off toward Savonlinna.

11 **Kerimäki** The world's largest wooden church is located in the small town of Kerimäki, north of

Savonlinna. Its benefactor – an emigrant who found wealth in America – provided the building plans in feet, but the Finnish architect built it in metres, hence its unintended dimensions (27 m (89 ft) high with a capacity of 5,000). The tiny village only has about 6,000 people!

12 **Retretti and Punkaharju** Beyond Savonlinna, it is worth making a stop at the Retretti art center – partly above ground and partly in caves – and at the mile-long moraine hill Punkaharju, which stretches between Lakes Pihlajavesi and Puruvesi. The rest of the journey on the N6 from Sääkjsalmi runs between the lake district and the Russian border.

13 **Imatra on Lake Saimaa** Imatra, a lively garden city on the Russian border, is located in the main basin of Lake Saimaa, the largest in Finland. The "Lake of a Thousand Islands" is known for its ringed seal population living in freshwater. In Imatra, it is worth visiting the community center, designed by Alvar Aalto, in the Vuoksennista district, and the Vuoksa waterfalls, mostly "subdued" for a power plant.

14 **Lappeenranta** This old garrison city is located on the Saimaa canal, which runs for 50-km (31-mi) from the lake district past the Russian border to the Gulf of Finland. All kinds of

cruises are available on Lake Saimaa and they depart from Finland's largest inland port. Most of the city's attractions are located outside the old fortress section of Lappeenranta, whose ramparts have been partially reconstructed.
The Orthodox church is the oldest in the country (1785) and is worth a visit. Near Luumäki, Route 25 takes you to Haminia on the Gulf of Finland.

15 **Hamina/Vehkalahti** The Swedish ramparts here from the early 18th century are worth seeing. They were designed to replace the Vyborg fort that fell to the Russians, but they were again seized by the Russians before their completion. Hamina's charming octagonal market square, in the center of which is the town hall from 1789, is an urban gem.

16 **Kotka** The main attractions in Finland's largest export harbor are the Orthodox St Nicholas' Church (1795), a simple edifice with an ornately decorated wall, and the grand buildings from the 19th century (trade union house, town hall, savings bank). The coastal road to Porvoo affords breathtaking views of the deep fjords and the skerry coastline.

17 **Porvoo/Borgå** This town has two old quarters: the Old Town plastered in header brick

with a Gothic brick cathedral, and a "younger" Old Town with neoclassical stone buildings. The red warehouse sheds on the shores of the Porvoonjoki are from the 18th and 19th centuries and worth seeing. The best view of the country's second-oldest city is from the old bridge. Helsinki, the final stop on the Route I section, is another 51 km (32 mi) from here.

Route II Juva – North Cape
18 **Kuopio** The city's Orthodox Church Museum shows you how deeply Russian Orthodox beliefs are rooted in the Karelian community. It has one of the most famous collections of its kind in Western Europe.
Not far from the museum, a trailhead leads you up to the Puijo at 232 m (761 ft), where you get a spectacular view of the university town and the lakes and forests of Karelia from the 75-m-high (246-ft-) tower.

19 **Kajaani** This industrial city on the Oulujärvi is particularly worth seeing for its Kajaaninlinna Castle (17th to 20th centuries) and the minuscule town

1 The historic center of Rauma, declared a UNESCO World Heritage Site in 1991.

2 An attractive rapeseed field on the way through southern Finland.

Looking out over the lake district near Kuopio in the province of Savo. Finland's nickname, "Land of a Thousand Lakes", is rather an understatement around here: more than 50,000 lakes, of all sizes and often connected to each other, cover approximately one-tenth of the country.

The Sami

Around half a million people live in Lapland, an area that spans much of the northern reaches of Scandinavia and part of Russia. One-tenth of the local population are Sami, who call themselves Samek and are often incorrectly referred to as Laps. Some 4,000 years ago, the Sami probably lived in the southern regions of the Scandinavian Peninsula as nomads, primarily subsisting on fishing and hunting, before being pushed further toward the Arctic Circle by other peoples starting in the 10th century. Even in these early times, the wild reindeer of the region supplied them with food and numerous materials to fashion basic commodities. It was not until the 17th century that the Sami actually began breeding reindeer as domesticated animals. According to historic contracts, they had to follow the tracks of their semi-wild reindeer herds, but conflicts always seemed to arise with private pasture land-owners. In 1956, Sami from Finland, Norway and Sweden founded the Nordic Sami Council to jointly represent their interests.

Depending on the source, between 5,000 and 17,000 Sami live in the Finnish part of Lapland, which means the degree of assimilation with the Finns seems to vary statistically. Around half the Finnish Sami speak their own Finno Ugric language, which is now being increasingly encouraged by the State. Our romantic image of the Sami has long become just that, imagination, as many have

The Sami domesticated the reindeer.

already chosen to renounce the nomadic life, and those who continue to breed reindeer as semi-nomads now carry out their work with four-wheel-drive vehicles and motorized sleds. Hardly any Sami now live in tents, and the colorful clothes and hats are mostly only worn for folklore events and tourism. However, the traditional legends and songs – such as the unrhymed, mostly improvised *joika* songs – are happily passed on to the young people, and the artistic working of elk fur, wood and horns has been proudly preserved.

hall. It is also worth taking a detour to see the frescoes in the wooden church (1725) in nearby Paltaniemi.

The road then continues around the Oulujärvi. A vast marshland known as the Käinuunselkä begins on the north side of the road and stretches well into Finland's northern reaches. In the Rokua district, dunes soar 80 m (262 ft) above the plains of northern Finland.

20 Oulu Like so many other Finnish cities, Oulu's medieval townscape was also destroyed by a terrible fire. The main attractions in Northern Europe's second-most important export harbor on the Gulf of Bothnia are the cathedral and the museums, including the Tietomaa science center. Off the coast of Oulu is the holiday island of Hailuoto, with quaint fishing villages, reed-roof houses, windmills, sandy beaches and an impressively large bird population. In peak summer in the Oulu region, the sun rises at three o'clock in the morning and does not set until after one o'clock at night. As a result, there is plenty of time to observe, for example, the Lapland titmouse or the Arctic diver with its rather eerie call.

21 Kemi Lapland's seaport at the mouth of the Kemijoki is an important lumber trading hub with tourist attractions such as the Sampo ice-breaker and the Isohaara power plant.

22 Rovaniemi The administrative center of Lapland is located just south of the Arctic Circle. After the city was razed to the ground in 1944, Alvar Aalto was given the job of designing its reconstruction. He had the main roads laid out in the shape of reindeer antlers, and also created the "Lappia House". The Jätkänkynttilä Bridge extends 320 m (.2 mi) and is the icon of this university town. The 172-m (564-ft) glassed-in Arcticum with the Arctic Center and the Lapland Provincial Museum are worth seeing.

23 Sodankylä This village is famous for the oldest wooden church in Lapland (1689) and also has the reputation of being the coldest place in Finland. In mid-June, the "Midnight Sun Film Festival" is held here during the long midsummer nights.

24 Vuotso und Tankavaara You can learn a bit about the handicrafts and reindeer breeding of the Sami people in the Sami settlement of Vuotso. A

museum in Tankavaara recalls the gold rush of the 1940s.

In the nearby Urho-Kekkonen National Park, you can go on some wonderful hikes. It is Finland's second-largest nature reserve. Be aware of bears and wolves here.

25 Inari It is predominantly the Sami who choose to live through more than 200 days a year with temperatures below zero. The open-air Sami Museum here provides information on their ancient culture. A nice hiking trail leads to the Pielpajärvi Wilderness Church (1760). The Inari region is dominated by Lake Inari, which is 80 km (50 mi) long and 40 km (25 mi) wide. The "Holy Lake of the Sami" is Finland's third-largest lake and is only free of ice for three months a year.

26 Karigasniemi After another 100 km (62 mi) through the stark wilderness, you reach the Norwegian border at Karigasniemi. The Ailigas rises to 620 m (2,034 ft) in the north-east, and

not far off is the start of the Kevo Nature Reserve with Finland's mightiest spring, Sulaoja.

27 North Cape The North Cape is another 261 km (162 mi) away across the severe landscape and the dark-grey cliff soaring 307 m (1,007 ft) out of the Arctic Sea is often shrouded in dense fog. The northernmost point of the European mainland is actually Cape Knivskjellodden. From the North Cape, it is now another 2,600 km (1,616 mi) by car along the E4 through Sweden along the Gulf of Bothnia to Hamburg or Berlin (see Route 5).

1 Shore landscape at Lake Inari, Finland's third-largest lake with over 3,000 islands.

2 The densest brown bear population in Finland is the east and south-east.

3 According to estimations, more than 140,000 elks live in Finland.

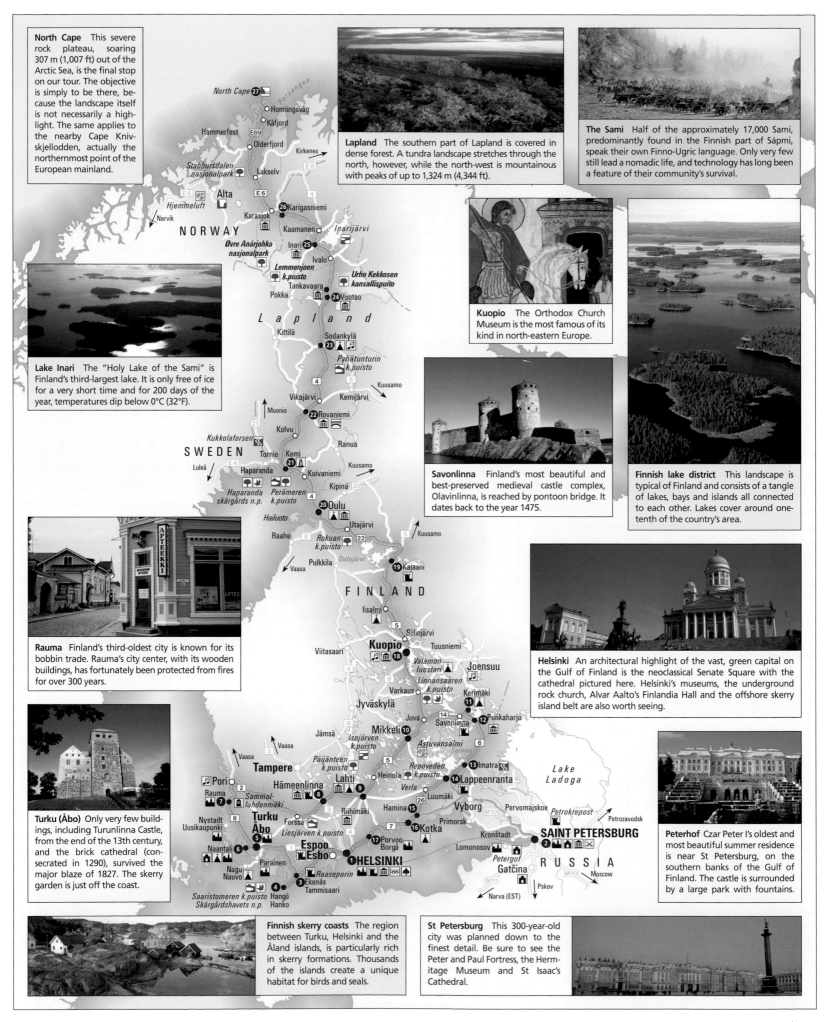

North Cape This severe rock plateau, soaring 307 m (1,007 ft) out of the Arctic Sea, is the final stop on our tour. The objective is simply to be there, because the landscape itself is not necessarily a highlight. The same applies to the nearby Cape Knivskjellodden, actually the northernmost point of the European mainland.

Lapland The southern part of Lapland is covered in dense forest. A tundra landscape stretches through the north, however, while the north-west is mountainous with peaks of up to 1,324 m (4,344 ft).

The Sami Half of the approximately 17,000 Sami, predominantly found in the Finnish part of Sápmi, speak their own Finno-Ugric language. Only very few still lead a nomadic life, and technology has long been a feature of their community's survival.

Lake Inari The "Holy Lake of the Sami" is Finland's third-largest lake. It is only free of ice for a very short time and for 200 days of the year, temperatures dip below 0°C (32°F).

Kuopio The Orthodox Church Museum is the most famous of its kind in north-eastern Europe.

Savonlinna Finland's most beautiful and best-preserved medieval castle complex, Olavinlinna, is reached by pontoon bridge. It dates back to the year 1475.

Finnish lake district This landscape is typical of Finland and consists of a tangle of lakes, bays and islands all connected to each other. Lakes cover around one-tenth of the country's area.

Rauma Finland's third-oldest city is known for its bobbin trade. Rauma's city center, with its wooden buildings, has fortunately been protected from fires for over 300 years.

Helsinki An architectural highlight of the vast, green capital on the Gulf of Finland is the neoclassical Senate Square with the cathedral pictured here. Helsinki's museums, the underground rock church, Alvar Aalto's Finlandia Hall and the offshore skerry island belt are also worth seeing.

Turku (Åbo) Only very few buildings, including Turunlinna Castle, from the end of the 13th century, and the brick cathedral (consecrated in 1290), survived the major blaze of 1827. The skerry garden is just off the coast.

Peterhof Czar Peter I's oldest and most beautiful summer residence is near St Petersburg, on the southern banks of the Gulf of Finland. The castle is surrounded by a large park with fountains.

Finnish skerry coasts The region between Turku, Helsinki and the Åland islands, is particularly rich in skerry formations. Thousands of the islands create a unique habitat for birds and seals.

St Petersburg This 300-year-old city was planned down to the finest detail. Be sure to see the Peter and Paul Fortress, the Hermitage Museum and St Isaac's Cathedral.

The old trading city of Nizhny Novgorod and its port on the ice-covered Volga River.

Russia

Moscow and the Golden Ring

The Golden Ring is really a must-see for enthusiasts of Russian art and architecture. The name itself actually refers to a ring of charming old towns north of Moscow – gems of Old Russia. They are localities that could easily be the setting for Russian novels, and the historic monasteries and churches are indeed testimony to a bygone era.

The term Golden Ring, which was first coined in Russia at the start of the 1970s, refers to a series of Old Russian towns north of Moscow, the main ones being Vladimir, Suzdal, Yaroslavl, Rostov Velikiy, Sergiev Posad, Pereslavl-Zalessky and Kostroma. Moscow itself is also included. These Old Russian centers originally evolved from former medieval fortresses built as protection against the Mongolians. Their mighty kremlins – defensive complexes – monasteries and churches were endowed with magnificent mosaics,

icons and valuable treasures and represented a stark contrast to the misery of everyday life in these rural towns. While the term "Golden" refers to the striking, gilded domes of the medieval churches, the word "Ring" denotes the close cultural and historical links between the individual towns. Today they still stand as testimony to the "Old Russia" that existed until the October Revolution and which was a deeply religious nation.

The towns of the Golden Ring are spread out across the broad, undulating plains

The New Virgin Convent in Moscow

which, shaped by the forces of multiple ice ages, extend to the south-east from the Gulf of Finland. The predominantly continental climate is characterized by warm summers and cold winters. Average temperatures in January are -11 °C (14 °F), while July reaches an average of about 19 °C (65 °F). Annual rainfall measures roughly 530 mm (209 in). The landscape along the upper reaches of the Volga and its tributaries, the Oka and Kama, is dominated by sizable rivers and lakes.

What most people would consider Russian history begins in the 10th century on the banks of the Dnepr, in Kiev, home to the Slavic tribes who traded with the passing Varangians from the north. It was only in the mid-11th century that the Russian heartland shifted towards the north-east, to the Golden Ring. The relatively mild climate, navigable rivers and

Red Square is Moscow's largest and most famous square. St Basil's Cathedral at the southern end draws everybody's attention.

Moscow: the Kremlin with the Great Kremlin Palace, the Cathedral of the Dormition and "Ivan the Great" bell tower.

existing trade routes that traversed the region led settlers to establish a series of towns during this period (9th–11th centuries). The population quickly rose to between 10,000 and 20,000.

With the collapse of the first Russian Empire, Vladimir became the successor to Kiev in the mid-12th century. During the same period, many residents of Kiev left the city for the Golden Ring region. The towns there became the capitals of powerful principalities. Rostov, Suzdal and Vladimir, for example, had already become trading centers as well as hubs of secular and religious power even before the founding and rise of mighty Moscow. At that time, Moscow was part of the principality of Vladimir-Suzdal. In the 13th century, the Mongolians subordinated the Russian Empire and forced substantial tributes from its inhabitants.

Moscow, at that time of minimal significance, eventually spearheaded the battle against the "Golden Horde", leaving the other principalities of the Ring to sink into obscurity after the end of the 14th century. Although chased out of the European zone, the Mongolians continued to leave their mark on Russia's Asian territories until the late 15th century.

An important ally of the Russian state at this time was the Orthodox Church, whose churches, monasteries and monasticism created a unified front.

A trip around the Golden Ring usually begins in Moscow, then continues through the large towns described on the following pages. However, there are also other interesting small towns to be found off the beaten track, such as Pushkino, Bratovscina, Rachmanowa, Muranovo or Abramtsevo.

Rostov Velikiy: A mighty wall encloses the kremlin and its picturesque churches.

The Kremlin

The word "kremlin" actually refers to the fortified sections of Old Russian towns. At the end of the 15th century, Italian architects built a 2-km-long (1.2-mi) wall around Moscow's Kremlin. It was between 15 and 20 meters (49 and 66 ft) in height and crowned with 19 towers. The wall forms a scalene triangle with one side running along the Moskva River. The Kremlin served as the residence of the Czars

The Moscow Kremlin complex covers around 28 hectares (69 acres).

and the Patriarchs of the Russian Orthodox Church until the 18th century. Its most important buildings include the Grand Kremlin Palace, the Armory Chamber housing Czarist treasures, the Patriarch's Palace, the Terem Palace, the Faceted Chamber, the Senate, the Arsenal and the barracks with the stables. The magnificent churches include the Annunciation, the Assumption and the Saviour's Cathedrals, as well as Ivan Veliky's bell tower dating from 1600.

Moscow and the Golden Ring: This poignant journey through the history of Old Russia begins in Moscow, continues via Rostov northwards as far as Kostroma, and then brings you back to Moscow via Ivanovo. During the trip you will be constantly confronted with the feeling that time has indeed stood still.

① Moscow (see pages 88–89) Your route begins in Moscow before heading north towards Sergiev Posad, known as Zagorsk between 1931 and 1991.

② Sergiev Posad The Monastery of the Holy Trinity and St Sergius (1340) is without doubt one of Russia's most important religious sites and serves as a pilgrimage destination for Orthodox Christians. It is encircled by a 1,600-m-long (1750 yard) wall that was breached once, albiet ultimately in vain, by Polish troops for sixteen months from 1608–1610.

Sergiev Posad was a national sanctuary even during the Czarist era and enjoyed unfettered support from the ruling class, who had their own residence in the complex, the Chertogi Palace (17th century). Large enough to accommodate a royal entourage of several hundred during official visits, the state converted the monastery into a museum in 1920 and it became a UNESCO World Heritage Site in 1993.

The Monastery of the Holy Trinity and St Sergius contains wonderful examples of paintings from Old Russia. The iconostase in the cathedral, for example, is decorated with works done by famous icon master Andrei Rublov and his assistants. The Holy Trinity was finished by the master himself.

The complex also displays outstanding examples of Russian architecture from the 14th to the 18th centuries. These defensive monasteries originally had several functions, as hospital wards, poorhouses, orphanages and schools. For a long time they were in fact the only institutions of their kind in all of Russia. The hospital building dates from the early 17th century, as do the adjoining churches St Zosima and St Sabbatius.

③ Pereslavl-Zalessky This Old Russian trading town is actually one of the oldest towns in the country and has a wealth of lovely churches and wooden houses. Located on the shores of Lake Pleshcheyevo, the town was founded in the 10th/11th centuries, and its ramparts also date from this time.

The outer walls of the white cathedral from 1152, on the Red Square behind the walls of the town's kremlin, are decorated with semicircular ornaments called "zakomaras", important stylistic features typical in Old Russian architecture.

A few of the older remaining kremlin buildings include: the Church of the Metropolitan Peter from 1585; the 17th-century Annunciation Church with its spacious nave; the Goritsky Monastery dating from the first half of the 14th century; and the Danilov Monastery, located in the lower-lying south-western part of the town, which is from the 16th century.

Travel information

Route profile
Route length: 760 km (472 mi)
Time required: 8–10 days
Start and end: Moscow
Route (main locations): Moscow, Sergiev Posad, Pereslavl-Zalessky, Rostov Veliky, Yaroslavl, Kostroma, Suzdal, Vladimir, Moscow

Special note:
There is a range of operators offering organized tours along the Golden Ring route. If you prefer to travel according to your own schedule, however, you have the option of hiring a car with a driver from Moscow.

Traffic information:
Entering Russia by car is possible, in theory, but it can be very complicated and time-consuming.
Entry visas require a passport, application and passport photograph.

Visiting the monasteries:
There are strict rules of conduct that apply in the various monasteries. Women need to wear a headscarf and a skirt; shorts and bare shoulders are taboo.
A film and photography permit is also required.

Further information:
Here are some websites to help you plan your trip:
www.thewaytorussia.net
www.russia-travel.com
www.geographia.com/russia
www.visitrussia.com
www.moscowcity.com

Starting with Ivan IV (16th century), Russian rulers bore the title Czar, derived not from the Latin "Caesar" but from the oriental "Sar" (prince). For a long time it was the Rurikids who occupied the Czarist throne, but they were eventually succeeded by the Romanov family in the early 17th century.

Czar Peter the Great, who ruled from 1689–1725, was intent on reviving the Russian nation by means of sweeping reforms and wanted to bring the country more in line with its Western European counterparts. He also liked to refer to himself as "Emperor and Absolute Ruler". Following Peter's death, Russia was

Top: Catherine II lays trophies from the Russian-Turkish War (1787–1792) at the tomb of Peter the Great. Below: The last Russian Czar, Nicholas II, and Czarina Alexandra Fyodorovna, were crowned in the Church of the Assumption in Moscow in May 1896.

④ Pereslavsky National Park This national park protects Lake Pleshcheyevo, the surrounding forest areas and wetlands, and the churches and cathedrals of Pereslavl-Zalessky. The lake is a breeding ground for 180 indigenous and thirty migratory bird species, and is home to brown bears as well. There is also a museum detailing the history of the Russian fleet and it was here that Czar Peter the Great built the first small battleships for mock warfare. It is the birthplace of the Russian navy.

⑤ Rostov Velikiy This city affords a panorama of stunning beauty, with its cathedral of seven silver roofs, a kremlin and

the towers of the Monastery of Our Savior and St Jacob rising up beyond picturesque Lake Nero. The name Rostov Velikiy has special historical significance here: In Czarist Russia, only Novgorod and Rostov were entitled to use the adjunct "Velikiy", meaning great. The town, founded in 862, had already developed into a flourishing trading center by the Middle Ages.

The large kremlin in Rostov Velikiy is protected by a wall over 1 km (0.6 mi) long with eleven towers. Silver and gold domes crown the palace here. When Prince Andrei Bogolyubsky conquered the town in the 12th century, it became the largest and most beautiful town

in his principality. He had the Cathedral of the Dormition built in 1162. Only fragments of the 12th-century frescoes survived. The five domes of the Church of the Assumption rise opposite the cathedral. The lovely Church of St John (17th century) on the banks of the Ishna River is also worth a visit as it is one of the very few surviving wooden churches in the region.

⑥ Yaroslavl Prince Yaroslav founded this fortified town at the confluence of the Kotorosl and the Volga rivers in the year 1010, and many of the original historical buildings have been preserved despite the ravages of war. The town enjoyed its gold-

en age in the 17th century and the buildings from this era are among the loveliest in Russia.

1 Moscow's St Basil's Cathedral comprises eight small chapels, each with a tower, grouped around the central church tower.

2 The Monastery of the Holy Trinity and St Sergius in Sergiev Posad is considered a unique gem among Russian monasteries.

3 One of the loveliest monasteries in Pereslavl Zalessky is the Gorizky Monastery founded in 1328.

4 Rostov is one of the smallest towns along the Golden Ring.

ruled by a numbers of Czarinas, or female Czars including Czarina Elizabeth and Czarina Catherine. Czar Alexander I was elemental in the victory over Napoleon in 1812/13, while his successor Nicholas I ultimately lost the Crimean War of 1853–1856. His successor Alexander II, however, was a reformist who put an end to Russia's serf-based society in 1861. Nicholas II, who reigned from 1894 to 1917, led Russia in World War I.

Of the last six Czars, three of them met with violent deaths: Paul I was strangled in 1801; Alexander II was killed by a terrorist bomb in 1881; and Nicholas II was shot together with his entire family in 1918 by the Bolsheviks. His death brought an end to the reign of the Russian Czars.

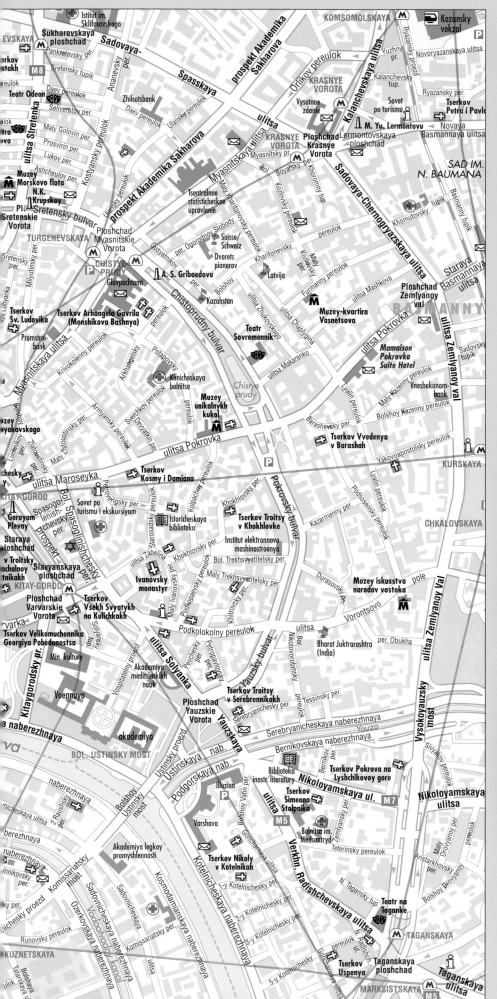

Moscow

Russia's capital lies on the Moskva River, which is a tributary of the mighty Volga. Mention was first made of Moscow in 1147, and it became the residence of the Grand Prince in 1325. In 1713, under Czar Peter the Great, Moscow lost its capital city status to the newly founded St Petersburg. In 1918, it was the Bolsheviks who once again made Moscow the political center of Russia's massive realm.

Moscow has been plundered repeatedly during its history, and has suffered a number of major fires. At the beginning of the 20th century, Moscow had 450 churches and twenty-five monasteries as well as 800 charitable institutions. Even after the decline of the Soviet Union, this city of 10 million still boasts impressive cultural statistics. Indeed, with roughly sixty theaters, seventy-five museums, over 100 colleges and 2,300 listed buildings, it is one of the world's top-ranking cities. The sights near Red Square include the enchanting St Basil's Cathedral (begun in 1555 under Ivan the Terrible in memory of the conquest of Kasan, consecrated in 1557, and completed in 1679), the Kremlin (citadel, former coronation venue, seat of power, and a

Vladimir Ilyich Lenin (1870–1924), as well as the tombs of numerous political figures and artists, the former artisan district of Kitaigorod and the GUM department store (1889–1893). Other attractions around Red Square include the Yelisseyev deli, the Duma, and the Bolshoi Theater.

Interesting sights near Arbatskaja Vorota Square include the seat of the Russian government (the "White House"), the Church of Christ the Savior (rebuilt 1994–1997), and the "Stalin high-rise buildings".

Other sights worth visiting include: the palatial Moscow subway stations (begun in the 1930s), the Tretyakov Gallery (Russian and Soviet art), the museums and the former artists' district of Arbat, the Pushkin Museum

Top: One of seven gingerbread style high-rises.
Bottom: Evening on the Moskva in the historic city center.

former prison) with twenty towers, the Great Stone Bridge, the Kremlin cathedrals (including the Uspenski Cathedral), the Alexander Garden, the remains of the Manege (former indoor riding arena that almost completely burned down in 2004) and the History Museum, the Kremlin Wall, the mausoleum with the mummified body of

of Fine Arts (also includes Western European art, the Priamos Treasure), the New Virgin Monastery including the "Celebrity Cemetery", the Lomonosov University (the oldest in Russia), Gorky Park with its sculpture garden and the lovely Kolomenskoye Church of the Ascension (southern outskirts of the city).

Nizhny Novgorod

This old trading center is situated roughly 400 km (249 miles) to the east of Moscow on the picturesque right bank of the Oka River, at its confluence with the Volga. It is surrounded by forests and swampy moorlands.

It was here that Yuri Vsevolodovich, the Grand Prince of Vladimir, built his frontier stronghold against the Mordvinians in 1221. Following a major victory over the Mongolians in 1380, the town was incorporated into the principality of Moscow in 1390, and was often visited by German merchants of the Hanseatic

Nizhny Novgorod: the cathedral in winter.

League over the course of the 14th and 15th centuries.

The upper city on the right bank of the Volga is home to the kremlin and other government buildings, as well as the Archangel Cathedral from 1227. The lower city on the right bank of the Oka, which today is Nizhny Novgorod's trading and transportation center, is home to the Stroganov Church from 1719. Nizhny Novgorod has long been the seat of a Greek-Catholic bishop and has had its own university since 1918.

As the largest industrial and trading hub in the Volga region, Nizhny Novgorod has an important river port and is also a central railway junction. The surrounding region is predominantly used for agriculture. the grain fields extend as far as the eye can see and the famously fertile Black Earth region begins south of here.

The Monastery of Our Savior (12th century) houses the Cathedral of the Resurrection of Christ (16th century). Approaching from the south you will get a lovely view of the town, with the gold-decorated domes of the cathedral and its masterful frescoes which, together with the Church of the Epiphany (17th century), is the town's most important building. The town's most magnificent church bears the name of the Prophet Elijah (17th century) and is on the central town square, from which the roads radiate out in a star shape. The church is decorated with frescoes. The famous Tolchkovo Church with its many towers and domes stands on the other side of the Volga.

7 Kostroma Kostroma marks the northernmost point of the Golden Ring and is a classic textbook town. Its current form took shape after a devastating fire in 1773. A number of significant monasteries, such as the Ipatiev Monastery, and the Resurrection Church, are among the very few surviving relics of the era before the fire. A collection of wooden buildings typical of the region are on display in the Museum of Wooden Architecture, including a windmill, a farmhouse and some churches. The museum is in the Monastery of St Hypathius, which is dominated by the Holy Trinity Cathedral with its golden towers.

8 Suzdal This unique museum town with over 100 historical buildings is the best-preserved Old Russian town. The mona-

stery town became the religious center of medieval Russia after the fall of Kiev. In the 11th century, the small town was the seat of the most powerful principality in Russia. The Mongolians destriyed it in 1238.

Suzdal, a UNESCO World Heritage Site since 1992, is on the Kamenka River. If you take an early summer morning walk among the whitewashed buildings of this unique monastery landscape, you will gain insight into the very soul of Russia.

The kremlin, the marketplace, the open-air museum, the traditional wooden houses and the monasteries stand out among the many attractions here. Some of the 18th- and 19th-century structures are decorated with woodcarvings. The 600-year-old Spaso-Yevfimiev Monastery in the east of town is the largest in Suzdal and is enclosed by a solid stone wall and crowned with

twenty towers. Many of Suzdal's churches stand in pairs next to one another: the summer church windows were larger while those of the winter church were smaller. Parts of the winter church were even heated. Some of the churches have since lost their counterparts, such as the elegant Our Lady of Smolensk Church.

9 Vladimir This town on the Klyazma River was founded in 1108, by Vladimir Monomakh, the Grand Prince of Kiev and named after himself. The earthen walls and the Golden Gate form part of the 12th-century fortifications that still remain. The town boasts wonderful churches whose magnificence and wealth of treasures compete even with the churches and monasteries of Kiev. Prince Andrei Bogolyubsky built the town's landmark, the Assump-

tion Cathedral, in 1160, with three domes. A two-floor gallery, crowned with four golden domes, was erected around the main building. The St Demetrius Cathedral is also worth a visit. Both cathedrals and the Church of the Intercession have been declared World Heritage Sites. One of the oldest Russian churches, the white Church of the Intercession of the Virgin on the Nerl (1165), is located east of Vladimir.

From Vladimir it is worth taking the detour to Nizhny Novgorod, about 250 km (155 miles) east.

1 One of several wooden churches in the open-air Museum of Wooden Architecture in Suzdal.

2 The Resurrection Church in the forest around Kostroma, the northernmost town on the Golden Ring.

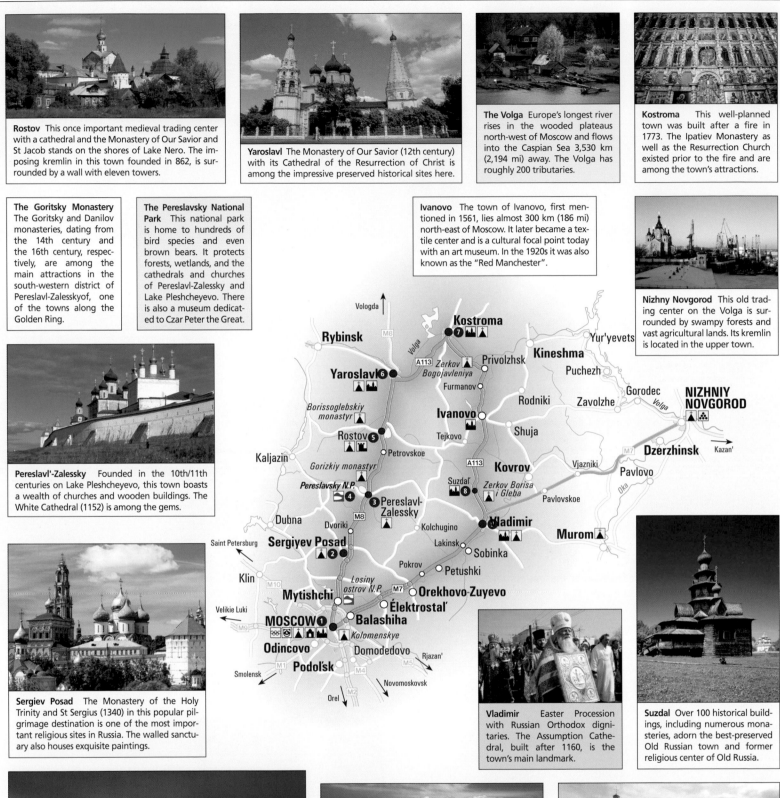

Rostov This once important medieval trading center with a cathedral and the Monastery of Our Savior and St Jacob stands on the shores of Lake Nero. The imposing kremlin in this town founded in 862, is surrounded by a wall with eleven towers.

Yaroslavl The Monastery of Our Savior (12th century) with its Cathedral of the Resurrection of Christ is among the impressive preserved historical sites here.

The Volga Europe's longest river rises in the wooded plateaus north-west of Moscow and flows into the Caspian Sea 3,530 km (2,194 mi) away. The Volga has roughly 200 tributaries.

Kostroma This well-planned town was built after a fire in 1773. The Ipatiev Monastery as well as the Resurrection Church existed prior to the fire and are among the town's attractions.

The Goritsky Monastery The Goritsky and Danilov monasteries, dating from the 14th century and the 16th century, respectively, are among the main attractions in the south-western district of Pereslavl-Zalesskyof, one of the towns along the Golden Ring.

The Pereslavsky National Park This national park is home to hundreds of bird species and even brown bears. It protects forests, wetlands, and the cathedrals and churches of Pereslavl-Zalessky and Lake Pleshcheyevo. There is also a museum dedicated to Czar Peter the Great.

Ivanovo The town of Ivanovo, first mentioned in 1561, lies almost 300 km (186 mi) north-east of Moscow. It later became a textile center and is a cultural focal point today with an art museum. In the 1920s it was also known as the "Red Manchester".

Nizhny Novgorod This old trading center on the Volga is surrounded by swampy forests and vast agricultural lands. Its kremlin is located in the upper town.

Pereslavl'-Zalessky Founded in the 10th/11th centuries on Lake Pleshcheyevo, this town boasts a wealth of churches and wooden buildings. The White Cathedral (1152) is among the gems.

Sergiev Posad The Monastery of the Holy Trinity and St Sergius (1340) in this popular pilgrimage destination is one of the most important religious sites in Russia. The walled sanctuary also houses exquisite paintings.

Vladimir Easter Procession with Russian Orthodox dignitaries. The Assumption Cathedral, built after 1160, is the town's main landmark.

Suzdal Over 100 historical buildings, including numerous monasteries, adorn the best-preserved Old Russian town and former religious center of Old Russia.

The Moscow Kremlin The most important buildings in the former residence of the Czars and patriarchs include the Great Kremlin Palace, the Armory Chamber, the Patriarch's Palace, the Terem Palace, the Faceted Chamber, the Senate, the Arsenal, the Annunciation, the Assumption and the Savior's Cathedrals as well as Ivan Veliky's bell tower.

Moscow There are 2,300 listed buildings in Russia's capital. Attractions include: Red Square, St Basil's Cathedral, the Kremlin, the Lenin Mausoleum, the GUM department store, the Bolshoi Theater, the Tretyakov Gallery, and the Pushkin Museum.

Kolomenskoye This 16th-century town, situated high above the Moskva River south-east of Moscow, used to be the Czars' summer residence. The cathedral's tent-like roof is a special attraction.

The twin towers of the Holsten Gate in Lübeck

Germany, Poland, Baltic States

In the footsteps of the Hanseatic League

The Hanseatic route along the Baltic Sea from northern Germany through Poland and into the Baltic States is unique for its tranquility, impressive scenery and dreamy qualities. Time seems to stand still here, creating a magic that is singular to this coast and the villages and cities that line it.

During the last ice age, the Baltic Sea and the Baltic states were actually buried under a thick sheet of ice. After it melted away, the land, now free from the pressure of the ice, slowly began to rise. The Baltic land ridge – a hilly moraine landscape filled with lakes on the southern coast of the Baltic Sea – is a glacial rockfill region from this last ice age, and the Baltic Sea of course has added its own features to the coastal outline. It created impressive spits, the Courland Spit being one of the most beautiful, and carved out lagoons with tranquil inland bodies of water like the Szczecin or Vistula lakes. The famous white chalk cliff coasts, owe their current appearance to the surging, post-ice age Baltic Sea.

The Baltic Sea is often known by its Latin name of Mare Balticum. "Balticum" is derived from "baltas", meaning "white" in Lithuanian and Latvian. Indeed, the beaches, dunes and craggy coastal cliffs practically sparkle in brilliant white. The Vorpommersche Boddenlandschaft, Jasmund, Slowinsky and Courland Spit national parks protect some of the most beautiful stretches of the Baltic coast.

Old Town alleyways in Estonia's capital, Tallinn.

Because the coastlines in Poland and the Baltic states are only sparsely populated, there is still enough room in the forests and marshlands for animals that have long been extinct in other parts of Europe: elks, bears, lynxes and wolves still have a natural habitat here. Storks nest in the countless church towers, while cranes brood in the marshlands.

Your journey passes through six of the countries lining the Baltic Sea. In addition to Germany and Poland, these include Lithuania, Latvia, Estonia and Russia – more specifically, Kaliningrad, a Russian exclave actually separated from Russia proper. The histories of these countries are closely intertwined with the Teutonic Order, and many of the castles and cities in the region were also members of the Hanseatic League. Since the collapse of the Soviet Union, the Baltic States have

The Dornbusch lighthouse is located at the northern tip of the sprawling Baltic Sea island of Hiddensee. It is much sandier than Rügen in the east and has no steep banks.

were built in the mid-15th century and modelled on Flemish bridge gates.

gained independence and are once again asserting their own cultural traditions.

A journey along the Baltic Sea coast is therefore in some ways a journey through time: back to before World War II – a period that is still tangible in the countryside – and the time of the Hanseatic League.

The League was an association of merchants established in the 12th century as a Germans response to the increasing risk of Baltic Sea trade. It quickly developed into a mighty urban and trading league that eventually ruled northern Europe economically for over 300 years. Many cities received their town charters in the 13th century, and the revolutionary Lübeck Law was adopted by over 100 Hanseatic cities. The Hanseatic League owes much of its success to its organization and vast capital, but also to the design of efficient ships such as the cog.

It had a wide hull, was initially oarless and intended as a sailing ship, and had high superstructural parts that allowed it to transport loads over 550 tons. Confident merchants and municipal rulers then built magnificent churches, palaces and town halls in the brick Gothic style now typical of the Baltic Sea region, and their robust Hanseatic ships used the church towers as orientation points along the coast. Many churches in the various Hanseatic cities are dedicated to St Nicholas, the patron saint of sailors and fishermen, or the pilgrims' patron saint, St James the Elder.

The decline of the Hanseatic League began in the 15th century as decreasing numbers of Germans chose to migrate east, and the Hanseatic League finally lost its supremacy to the increasingly powerful kingdom of Poland and Lithuania.

Sunrise over Gdańsk: The brick building of St Mary's Church towers over the Rechtstadt area.

The Roland Column (1360)

The Roland Column on Bremen's market square is the port city's oldest monument. The 5.5-m-tall (18-ft) figure represents freedom from market and import tariffs as well as high court jurisdiction and municipal law. Originally, a wooden statue stood at this site but it was set ablaze in 1366 by soldiers loyal to Archbishop Adalbert II. The second Roland, once again made of wood, was eventually replaced by the current stone version in 1404.

In 1513, the dais was added along with the two-headed eagle plaque and transcript, which urges the good

Roland in Bremen's market square.

citizens of Bremen to thank God for the freedom that Emperor Karl gave the city.

Over the centuries, the Roland Column has become a general symbol of freedom and can actually be found in a number of northern German cities, particularly in those with the Magdeburg city charter. Roland is usually depicted as a warrior holding a shiny sword but not wearing helmet.

Roland is the hero of the *Song of Roland* in which, in 778, as margrave of Brittany and in conjunction with Emperor Charlemagne, he fought against the Muslim Moors who had conquered the Iberian Peninsula during the early 8th century. Roland was killed that same year in the Battle of Roncesvalles in the Pyrenees. The *Song of Roland*, which made the protagonist into one of the emperor's nephews, and which enjoyed a huge revival in popularity in the 13th century, keeps the memory of his heroic feats alive.

The Hanseatic route: Passing through the lowlands of northern Germany, along the Bay of Mecklenburg and the Baltic Sea coasts of Poland, Lithuania, Latvia and Estonia, your path mirrors the trading routes of the Hanseatic League, where ports and merchant cities characterized by traditional brick architecture line the road like pearls on a necklace.

① Bremen (see page 96)
The journey begins in the Free Hanseatic City of Bremen which, with Bremerhaven 50 km (31 mi) north, forms the smallest of the federal German states. On the way to Stade, the B74 leads past Teufelsmoor, north-west of Bremen.

② Stade This small town on the lower Elbe was an important trading port more than 1,000 years ago, but Vikings destroyed the castle in 994. Stade became a Hanseatic League member in the mid-13th century, but nearby Hamburg soon challenged its dominance.
On the way to Hamburg, the road passes through the Altes Land (Old Country). In Germany's largest fruit production region, it is worth seeing the traditional farming villages, particularly in spring when the trees are in bloom. It was not until the 12th and 13th centuries that an elaborate drainage system allowed the once marshy lower Elbe to be cultivated.
South of Hamburg you can take some interesting detours to Lüneburg and the Lüneburger Heide (see margin on page 95).

③ Hamburg (see page 97)
Those not wishing to drive into Hamburg's city center should take the A1 to the port city of Lübeck.

④ Lübeck This merchant settlement founded in the 12th cen-

tury was given the status of Free Imperial City by Emperor Friedrich II in 1226. The city became the voice of "foreign affairs" for the German Hanseatic League when it was founded, and the first General Hanseatic Day was held in Lübeck in 1356. At the end of the 13th century, Lübeck was the most densely populated city in Germany after Cologne and, with 25,000 inhabitants by 1500, it was one of the largest cities in Europe.
Some of Lübeck's most important attractions are in the medieval Old Town, which was extensively rebuilt after the destruction of World War II and which is completely surrounded by moats and the Trave River. It was declared a UNESCO World Heritage Site as a main location for German Gothic brick buildings.
A series of churches have been preserved or renovated including the cathedral, begun in 1173 and completed in the 13th century, St Mary's parish church, built by the people of Lübeck, St Catherine's Basilica and the brick Gothic churches of Saints Jakobi and Petri. The city's main landmark, however, is the 15th-century Holstentor gate, part of the once-mighty fortifications. The Gothic town hall is evidence of the city's wealth and the confidence of its sponsors. A highlight of any stroll through the Old Town are the medieval burgher houses, the most attractive of which are located on Mengstraße (also home to the

Buddenbrookhaus of the Mann family), Königstraße, the Große Petersgrube and on Holsten Harbour. Your journey continues east from the city on the Trave through the Klützer Winkel to Wismar on the Bay of Wismar.

⑤ Wismar The picturesque old port in this merchant settlement

and Hanseatic town is just a fishing port these days. As an international port, Wismar was of national significance for Baltic Sea trading for over 750 years, and the walled city has largely been able to preserve its beautiful medieval look. Wismar has numerous gabled houses from the Renaissance and baroque peri-

Travel information

Route profile
Route length: approx. 1,700 km (1,056 mi)
Time required: 3–4 weeks
Route (main locations): Bremen, Hamburg, Rostock, Rügen, Sczeczin, Gdańsk, Olsztyn, Kaliningrad, Klaipèda, Riga, Tallinn

Traffic in formation:
Check the validity of the vehicle's liability insurance before driving into any of these countries!

Visas:
Russia: You need your visa, international driver's licence, vehicle registration, and an

international green insurance card.
EU countries: All you need for the EU are a valid passport or ID card.

Information:
Here are some websites to help you plan your trip.
Poland:
www.polen.travel/en
Russia:
www.waytorussia.net
Estonia:
www.visitestonia.com
Latvia:
www.latviatourism.lv
Lithuania:
www.tourism.lt

Detour

Lüneburg and the Lüneburger Heide

The foundation of Lüneburg's wealth and the reason for the city's acceptance in the Hanseatic League was the Lüneburg salt mines, which contained one of Germany's strongest and most effective natural healing sols. In the days of the League, salt was a highly sought-after commodity across the entire Baltic Sea region. Lüneburg, still very much intact today, has a wealth of northern German brick architecture and was one of Ger-

ods (16th to 18th centuries) and a Gothic residential home from 1380. The oldest burgher house in the city, the "Old Swede", is located on the market square where you will also find the fountain house, the "Wasserkunst" (1602), in Dutch Renaissance style. The fountain provided the city with water until the end of the 19th century. The royal court from 1555 is modelled on Italian styles and the sculptures can be traced back to Dutch influences. The Gothic St Mary's Church, with its slender tower, was modeled on the church of the same name in Lübeck.

A 30-km (19-mi) detour takes you south to Schwerin, capital of Mecklenburg-Vorpommern.

6 Schwerin Slavic tribes built a castle here in the "City of Seven Lakes" on the shores of Lake Schwerin in the 11th century. As a royal residence town of the Mecklenburg dukes, the castle, situated beautifully on an island, and large parts of the Old Town were given their current look back in the 15th century by royal architect, Georg Demmler.

He used Chambord Castle in the Loire Valley as a model and created one of the most famous works of historicism. The cathedral, which dates back to the 13th–15th centuries, is a masterpiece of German brick Gothic. From Schwerin, a road leads back to Wismar through Cambs, and then the B105 follows the old trading route between Lübeck and Gdańsk. On the way to Rostock you can make detours to the Cistercian monasteries of Sonnenkampf (13th century) and Bad Doberan (14th century).

7 Rostock This city was established by German merchants and craftsmen at the end of the 12th century, and experienced its heyday as part of the Hanseatic League in the 14th and 15th centuries. The University of Rostock (est. 1419) is one of the oldest in the Baltic Sea region. Today, the metropolis on the Lower Warnow River mostly survives off its lively port. The Thirty Years War left Rostock in ruins, as did heavy bombing during World War II, and most of its late-Gothic, baroque and classicist homes were destroyed, but

many have been carefully restored or rebuilt. The late-Gothic town hall, which actually comprises three buildings, is unique, and the city's two parish churches are dedicated to St Peter and St Nicholas. St Mary's Church, with its famous astronomical clock, towers over the north-west corner of the central market square.

From Rostock there are numerous possible detours to Warnemünde on the coast or to the beautiful Mecklenburg lake district farther inland.

The Rostock Heath (Rostocker Heide), east of the city, is a pristine moor and woodland. The western part was felled to build "cog" ships during the time of the Hanseatic League, while the eastern section was kept as a ducal hunting reserve.

Nature lovers should visit the fishing town of Wustrow on Fischland, the narrow spit that leads over to the Darss Peninsula in the Vorpommersche Boddenlandschaft National Park.

A lovely road between Bodstedter Bodden and Barther Bodden goes to Barth via Zingst and back to the B105 at Löbnitz.

8 Stralsund This city's former significance as Hanseatic League member is still reflected in the buildings today. It has a network of medieval streets, primarily with brick Gothic architecture, and many of the burgher houses originate from the 15th–19th centuries. This "Venice of the North" is located on the Strelasund, a strait between the mainland and Rügen. In the center of the city, which is a UNESCO World Heritage Site, the town hall towers over the Old Market, while just next door is a late-

1 View of the St Pauli piers on the dry docks in the internationally sigifi-cant Port of Hamburg.

2 The town hall and St Peter's Cathedral on Bremen's market square.

3 Merchant houses and sailing ships at Holsten Harbour in Lübeck.

4 A baroque garden surrounds Schwerin Castle on an island in Lake Schwerin.

5 The "Wasserkunst" fountain house on Wismar's market square.

Top: Reed-covered houses in the Lüneburg Heath.
Center: The Old Crane, Lüneburg.
Bottom: 14th-century court alcove in the Lüneburg town hall.

many's richest cities in the 15th and 16th centuries. Many half-timbered houses testify to this dazzling era. The main attractions of the city on the Ilmenau include the Gothic complex around the Platz Am Sande, the town hall and the Old Crane at the Stintmarkt.

Vast oak, birch and pine forests west of the city were felled to exploit the Lüneburg salt mines (956-1980), leaving behind a unique heath landscape.

The Free Hanseatic City of Bremen

The name Bremen probably derives from "on the edge" (of the water). The mighty fishing and merchant city on the Weser River was founded in the early Middle Ages, and Bremen's bishop's see and cathedral have stood close to the Weser on the fortified dune hill since 787.

Bremen's economic significance originally emerged due to its location on the Weser and proximity to the sea just 60 km (37 miles) away. The city had a port and a ford, and was also an important diocesan town. In the mid-12th century, Bremen came into conflict with Duke Heinrich the Lion,

Beautiful view over patrician houses and Bremen's Roland Column.

who seized the city on two occasions. The wealth from foreign trade during the 13th century financed the town hall, important religious buildings and a city wall (1129) enclosing residential towers built by wealthy merchants. It was not until 1358 that the city became a Hanseatic League member, and in the 17th century it became a Free City. The plagues that began in the mid-14th century haunted Bremen several times. In the 15th century, the city was a booming commercial center, but large parts of the old town were destroyed in World War II. Attractions here include: the market square with the Roland Column (1404); Schüttung, the merchants' guild house (16th century); the town hall (15th century) with its renaissance façade; the Gothic Church of Our Lady (13th century); the hall church of St Martin on the Weser; St Peter's Cathedral (begun in the 11th century) with its cathedral museum; Böttcherstraße with the Roseliushaus museum and the Paula Becker Modersohn House with works by the artist; the Schnoorviertel, formerly a residential quarter for fishermen and craftsmen; and the wall complex with a moat. Museums: Overseas Museum with folklore collection; the art gallery with its famous graphic design collection; and the Universum Science Center Bremen.

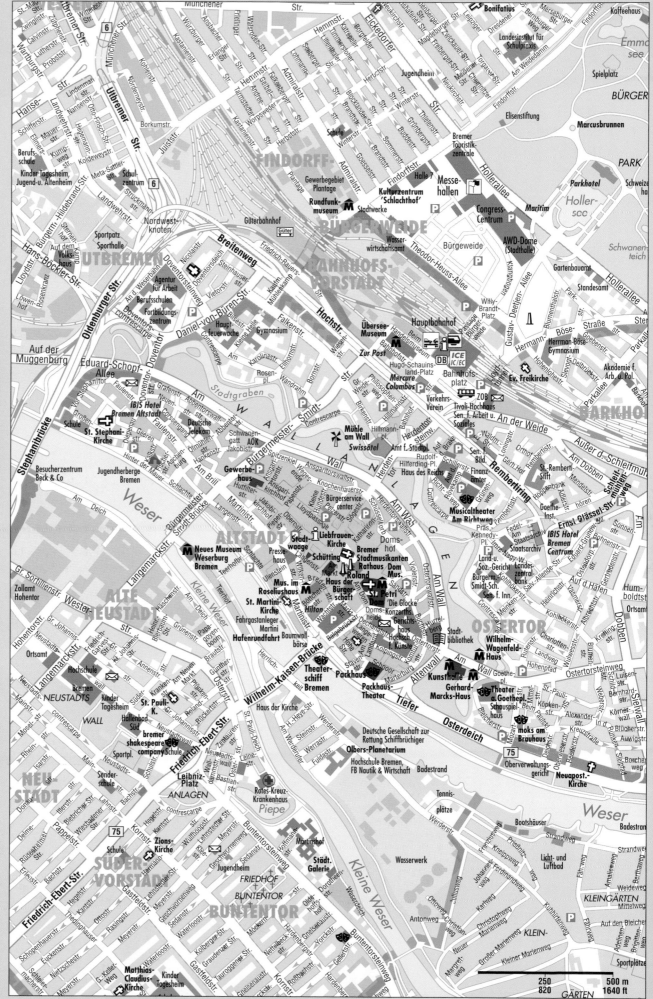

The Free Hanseatic City of Hamburg

Thanks to its location on the Elbe River and its proximity to the North Sea, Hamburg rose to significance as a trading and port town in the 12th century. The most important German port city is now a cosmopolitan metropolis.

Hamburg was an early member of the Hanseatic League and in the 14th century became the most important transshipment center between the North and Baltic Seas. The old and new town were united in 1216, and just sixty years later Hamburg was ravaged by fire. The same happened again in 1842, and large parts of the city were destroyed in World War II.

Attractions here include: St Michael's Church with Michel, symbol of the city; St James (14th century); St Catherine (14th/15th century); St Peter (14th century); St Nicholas; the homes of the Shopkeepers' Guild (17th century); the stock exchange (19th century); the old town with town hall (19th century) and town houses (17th/18th century); Inner Alster Lake with the Jungfern-

Top: St Nicholas Church and the town hall from the Lombard Bridge on the Jungfernstieg promenade.
Bottom: The Gruner+Jahr publishing house and "Michel".

stieg promenade; the warehouse district of the Old Free Harbour; St Nicholas Fleet (17th/18th century); St Paul's pier (1907-1909); the Kontorhaus district with the Chile House (UNESCO). The Ethnology Museum, the Hamburg Art Gallery, the Planten un Blomen Park, and the zoo are worth visiting too.

Vorpommersche Boddenlandschaft National Park

The Darss and Zingst peninsulas, the islands of Bock, Hiddensee and West-rügen, the continental shelf areas, and the Bodden (or bay) itself all form part of this national park established in 1990. The term "bodden" is derived from the lower German word "bod-dem" meaning sea floor, and is used to describe a bay with a beach that is separated from the sea by islands or headlands (spits). The bay typically only has one narrow opening to the open sea.

The Boddenlandschaft (or "bay land-scape") was created after the last ice age. When the ice thawed, the water

Top: Sailboats in a port at the Bostedter Bodden.
Bottom: Scenery in the narrow moor-land with a Baltic Sea Bodden.

level of the Baltic Sea rose and sea-water flooded into the relatively flat moraine landscape. The present-day is-lands are actually the peaks of former mountain ranges.

The comparatively low salt content of the Baltic ultimately gave rise to the uniquely brackish water that supports an ideal natural environment for nesting bird species as well as migratory birds. In autumn, approxi-mately 60,000 cranes come to roost on the Darss peninsula.

The Boddenlandschaft is in constant flux due to its exposure to wind and sea. Sand quickly shifts from one site to another, enlarging or reforming shallow spits and changing the shape of lagoons.

Gothic alcove. Not far away is the St Nicholas patrician church, considered one of the most beautiful on the Baltic. The late-Gothic St Mary's Church was built after 1384. The St James' Church was completed in the first half of the 14th century.

⑨ Rügen Germany's largest island owes much of its popu-larity to Caspar David Friedrich, whose painting of the Stubben-kammer chalk cliffs on the Jas-mund Peninsula is a classic of German Romanticism. The old beech trees on Jasmund (Stub-nitz) and the vast fields of color-ful spring flowers in the island's south-west make it a stunning area for hiking. Botanists are fas-cinated by the rare flora, while the pagan antiquities and burial mounds catch the attention of history enthusiasts.

A trip to Cape Arkone on the Wittow promontory, a chalk cliff with lighthouses and a Slavic fort 46 m (151 ft) in height, is a must-see. From there, go across the 8-km (5-mi) Schaabe Spit to

the Jasmund promontory. The Stubbenkammer, with its 117-m (384-ft) peak, the Königsstuhl, and the surrounding beech forests are protected within the Jasmund Nature Reserve.

From Sassnitz, a road leads along the densely forested Schmale Heide (Narrow Heath) between the Small Jasmunder Bodden and Prorer Wiek out to the Baltic Sea spa town of Binz, with its

Rügen Dam

The Rügen Dam was opened in 1937, and connects Rügen with the mainland via the island of Dänholm. The "Ziegelgraben" bascule bridge, between Strelasund and Dänholm, still renders Rügen an island for a few hours each day – but also causes traffic jams. From Dänholm, a 500-m-long (0.3-mi) bridge connects the island with Rügen.

romantic seaside resort architec-ture dating back to the 19th cen-tury. In 1994, a 370-m (0.2-mi) bridge was built, and this area also marks the start of some very nice daytrips to the chalk cliffs along the coast. From Binz, the route heads through Rügen's

"capital", Bergen, and the fertile Mutland meadows back toward Strelasund, and from there it continues on to Greifswald.

⑩ Greifswald This city on the Ryck was built on its salt trade and obtained its town charter in 1250. Salt was an important trading commodity for centuries as it was needed to preserve fish and other foodstuffs in the

Middle Ages. The St Mary's Church, a hall church from the first half of the 14th century, towers over the Greifswald Old Town. The brick Gothic cathedral of St Nicholas is one of the most beautiful in the entire state of Mecklenburg-Vorpommern, and

many late-Gothic homes still attest to the former wealth of the patrician families who once lived here. The town's most famous icon is the 30-m-long (33-yds) wooden bascule bridge in Wieck. The monastery ruins of Eldena (12th century), depicted in a number of Caspar David Friedrich paintings, became a symbol of Romanticism. The complex has housed parts of the university since 1535.

⑪ Usedom An attractive de-tour takes you through the royal Pomeranian residence town of Wolgast to Usedom, which is connected to the mainland by two bridges. The island is sepa-rated from the mainland by the Peene River and from the Polish island of Wolin by the Swina River. The eastern corner, which features the mouths of the river, is part of Poland. The famous Wilhelminian seaside resort towns of Zinnowitz, Bansin, Her-ingsdorf and Ahlbeck are inter-spersed with stunning, long sandy beaches along a 40-km

4

Mecklenburg lake district

Water as far as the eye can see. That is what one sees during a visit to the undulating landscape of Germany's largest continuous lake district. The area includes Germany's second-largest inland body of water, Lake Müritz, as well as the Feldberg district, Lake Tollense, Lake Kölpin, Lake Fleesen and Lake Plauer. Small channels, often only 2 to 3 m (6.5 to 10 ft) wide, as well as larger canals and rivers connect the lakes to each other, allowing for a full day, or more if you want, of cruising by canoe through reed stands and moorland, and past houseboats and picturesque villages with verdant green meadows and fields. Glaciers and snowmelt streams originally created these hollows, which filled with water once the

Top: Renaissance castle Güstrow. Bottom: Basedow on Lake Malchin.

(25-mi) stretch of Baltic Sea coast. Heringsdorf and Ahlbeck are home to impressively long wharfs typical of 19th-century resort towns: they are 508-m (0.3-mi) and 280-m (0.2-mi) long, respectively.

From Ahlbeck, the route returns to the mainland at the Hanseatic city of Anklam, past the Ueckermünder Heath to Pasewalk and from there over the border to Sczezcin, Poland.

⑫ Szczecin The Hanseatic City of Szczecin is located on the western banks of the Oder, not far from where it flows into the lagoon. The former capital of Vor and Hinterpommern (West and East Pomerania), Szczecin is today a modern metropolis with an active port that owes its importance to its shipyard and the heavy industries based here. The historic buildings in the badly destroyed Old Town have been partially restored. St James' Cathedral was built in the 14th/15th centuries and the beautiful Gothic St John's

Church is from the 13th century. The late-Gothic Old Town Hall dates from the 14th century and the castle of the dukes of Pomerania is from the 16th/17th centuries. The Piastentor and Hafentor gates are reminders of the mighty belt of fortifications that once protected the city.

From Szczecin, the E28 heads toward Gdańsk. About 20 km (13 mi) into the journey, it is worth making a detour north to the island of Wolin and the Cammin lagoon.

⑬ Polish Baltic Sea coast from Karlino to Gdańsk The route continues now through vast plains where golden cornfields alternate with flowering meadows and dense forests. Those looking to return to the sea, which is lined with deserted sandy beaches, should head to Kołobrzeg or turn off towards Lazy near Koszalin. Lazy is situated between Jamno and Bukow, two lakes that are protected from the Baltic Sea by a spit of land that is often just

200 m wide (219 yds). The area is an important habitat for many breeding birds.

Darłowo has the most beautiful medieval Old Town in the region. Its main attraction is the castle of the Pomeranian dukes, while the port village of Ustka offers long beaches and a relaxing atmosphere.

A day trip into the Slowinski National Park near Leba is a must here. The "Polish Sahara" has shifting sand dunes of up to 40-m (131-ft) high that move roughly 10 m (11 yds) south-east every year.

⑭ Gdańsk Gdańsk (formerly Danzig) has a history that dates 1,000 years. In the 12th and 13th centuries, the city had close trading relations with Flanders, Russia and Byzantium. It became a Hanseatic League member in 1361, and as host to the Teutonic Order it gained valuable access to the throne of Poland in 1466. By 1945, some 95 percent of the city had been destroyed by the war, but it has now been care-

fully rebuilt into a modern European metropolis.

The most important tourist attractions in Gdańsk are located in the center, the "Rechtstadt" neighborhood. St Mary's Church is the largest medieval brick work of its kind in Europe and the pride of the city. Its most notable feature is the 82-m-high (269-ft) bell tower. The long lane and the adjacent streets form the historic focal point of Gdańsk, where influential patricians erected magnificent manors such as the 17th-century Hans von Eden House in the heart of the Rechtstadt.

The most impressive examples of northern European late-Gothic architecture include the 15th-century Artushof, the Rechtstadt Town Hall, the Golden House and the Torture Chamber. The Crane Gate, which was once a medieval gate to the city, was rebuilt into a port crane. Still in the Old Town, but north of the Rechtstadt area, it is worth visiting a number of the quaint churches, the old town hall, the

1 The 280-m (0.2-mi) sea bridge from Ahlbeck (1998) on Usedom.

2 The St Mary's Church towers over Rostock's old town was also used by sailors as a landmark.

3 The Stralsund marina, with the St Mary's Church in the background.

4 The famous chalk cliffs in Jasmund National Park on the island of Rügen.

ice melted. Between Güstrow and Neustrelitz are some interesting towns and villages with Gothic churches and ornate manors. Güstrow itself, an old trading route junction, is also still home to numerous neoclassical buildings and imperial-style houses. Passing by meadows and fields, you continue on to Teterow, a city with medieval tower gates that was founded around 1270. South-east of Waren, parts of Lake Müritz are strictly protected by the Müritz National Park. The layout of the late-baroque town of Neustrelitz is unique: a star formation of eight roads radiate from a square marketplace, and you can get a very good view of this from the tower of the city church.

In about 1818, Caspar David Friedrich immortalized the Wissower Klinken formations with his painting "The Chalk Cliffs of Rügen". Seen here from the Victoria viewpoint, the plateau, which is over 100-m (328-ft) high in parts, falls away steeply into the Baltic Sea on the eastern side of island of Rügen. During the

Cretaceous period, some seventy million years ago, lime platelets were deposited in a deep strait and developed into a 100-m (109-yds) solid layer of chalk. Since 1990, the Jasmund National Park in northern Germany has protected this geological outcrop as well as the Stubnitz beech forests.

Cammin Lagoon and the Wollin Island

Although the southern Baltic Sea coast is pretty flat, it is full of pockets and peninsulas. Over the millennia, spits (long strips of sand often covered in vegetation) have isolated the numerous bays from the open sea, creating Stettin and Cammin Lagoons, for example, in

Top: Fishermen on the beach at the Miedzywodzie resort on Wollin.
Center: The cathedral of Kamien Pomorski (built 1176–1385).
Bottom: Sunset over the Cammin Lagoon.

the delta region of the Oder River. Holiday resorts on the lagoon include the Hanseatic city of Kamień Pomorski and Miedzywodzie on the island of Wollin. Parts of the island are protected as part of a national park.

big and little mills as well as the old castle. A detour to the northern edge of Gdańsk brings you to the lovely Cathedral of Oliva, with its baroque interior, as well as to Sopot, once the most glamorous seaside resort on the Baltic Sea coast.

South of Gdańsk is the Gdańsk River Isle, the northernmost part of the Vistula Delta. This landscape, which is partly submerged in the sea, was partially dried out in the 15th century and then reclaimed in the 17th century. Crossing the river island heading south-east you will soon arrive in Malbork.

⓯ Malbork St Mary's Castle, destroyed in World War II and rebuilt starting in 1961, is on the right bank of the Nogat, which flows north-east at this point. The mighty castle complex comprises two parts separated by a trench and protected by a common moat. Malbork's old German name – Marienburg – refers to its Christian founders: In the second half of the 13th century, the grand master of the Teutonic Order moved his seat of government here from Venice. South-west of the castle is the late-13th-century city of Marienburg, whose center is dominated by the impressive

town hall. St John's Church is just to the north.

Heading north-east from Malbork you arrive in yet another Hanseatic city.

⓰ Elbląg When the Teutonic Order began its fight against the "heathen" Prussians, it established a Hanseatic city here in 1237 to help their cause. Until 1370, it was of greater importance in the area than even Gdańsk. When the medieval Old Town became too small, a new town was designed.

The Elbląg River connects the city to the Gdańsk bay and therefore to the Baltic Sea, and wheat and wood exports originally made the city rich. Some of the many burgher homes from the 16th and 17th centuries have been restored and attest to the former wealth of Elbląg, which was a Free Imperial City starting in the early 16th century. In January 1945, shortly before the end of World War II, it was heavily bombed.

Attractions include the Market Gate, the Gothic Dominican church, the St Nicholas Church with its 96-m (315-ft) tower, and the Ordensburg ruins.

From Elbląg a detour south on the E77 leads to the important medieval city of Olsztyn.

⓱ Vistula Lagoon Route 503 heads north-eastward along the Vistula Lagoon to the town of Frombork. The road, which closely skirts the lagoon, is surprisingly diverse, with sudden climbs to the highlands near

Suchacz followed by stretches of forest before the road falls dramatically back down to the lagoon. Further along you'll see impressive green of the Vistula Spit. This headland stretches north-east, parallel to

The Masuria lake district

Very few visitors can resist the charming landscape of the Masuria lake district. Whether on foot, on bicycle or in a canoe, the roughly 30,000 lakes in this area are loosely connected with each other by creeks, rivers and canals flowing through stunning forests. Gnarled trees shade the cobblestone lanes where horses and carts still ride, while storks build their nests high up in the church spires. A visit to Masuria is a journey through time to the early 20th century.

Top: A birch grove in Masuria.
Center: A "Panjewagen" or small horse-drawn cart.
Bottom: Copernicus is buried in the Gothic cathedral of Frombork.

Old Town between the castle and the Pregel River; Löbenicht in the east; and the Kneipphof (1327) on Pregel Island in the south. The city became a member of the Hanseatic League in 1340. Kaliningrad is the former capital of East Prussia and the home of Imannuel Kant. He taught at the university from 1755 to 1796. Today, the Königsberg Cathedral glistens in its new splendor after being renovated in the 1990s – mostly with German money. Other worthwhile sights include the old German city manor houses on Thälmann and Kutusow Streets, while parts of the warehouse district have also remained intact. The New University, constructed from 1844 to 1862, has been rebuilt as well.

The coast near Kaliningrad is known for its amber deposits. If you are luck, you may even be

the coast, and is home to villages whose former names included Vogelsang and Schottland (German for birdsong and Scotland). The town of Tolkmicko, back on the 503 to the west, is at the northern end of Butter Mountain, the highest peak in the Elbląg Highlands: 197 m (646 ft). It has a pretty beach with fine, white-grey sand and a cute little marina with sailboats.

The onward journey takes you down some splendid avenues; gnarled old trees line the road and provide shade from the glaring sunlight. Some of the lanes have such dense treetops

that the road even stays dry in light rain.

The town of Frombork is culturally the most interesting city in the Ermland region because of the historic hilltop cathedral complex. The museum, as well as the cathedral itself, is dedicated to the works of Copernicus, who studied astronomy here. The water tower affords a wonderful view over the lagoon and port. The route continues along the lagoon to the Hanseatic city of Braniewo, former residence of a prince-bishop.

The St Catherine's Church, which was only rebuilt a few years ago,

dates back to the 14th century. The Polish-Russian (Kaliningrad) border is just a few miles further north-east.

You'll cross a few borders before arriving in Lithuania, since the Russian exclave, Kaliningrad, lies between the new EU states.

18 Kaliningrad Kaliningrad was the last major city founded by the Teutonic Order, in 1255. Having already been a refuge for Slavic Prussians, with whom the crusading German Catholics had long been in conflict, the newly designed city comprised three central components: the

Olsztyn is the capital of Masuria. From the capital, it is worth going to see some of the sights in the area. Lidzbark Warminskj, with its impressive castle, was once the residence of the Ermland bishops. The castle of Reszel dates back to the 13th century. The Teutonic Order built a fort in Ketrzyn in 1329. Beyond Ketrzyn, a sign will direct to the north-west to the "Wolfsschanze" or "Wolf's Hole", a bunker Hitler built in 1939 that became one of his favorite hideaways towards the end of the war. The pilgrimage church of Święta Lipka is a baroque gem.

1 The Crane Gate on the Mottlau in Gdańsk was both a city gate and a port crane.

2 The Renaissance castle of the dukes of Pomerania in Stettin.

3 The famous astronomer, Copernicus, is buried in the Gothic brick cathedral of Frombork.

Mighty walls and bastions surround the fort complex of Malbork, residence of the grand master of the Teutonic Order from 1309 to 1457. The middle castle with its grand master palace (left half), is a unique architectural gem of the northern German brick Gothic style. The high castle (center) contained meeting, living,

dining and sleeping quarters as well as a church (the highest tower of the complex in the background). The Dankertsturm tower (front, right) was both a watch-tower and an outhouse. The fort, half of which was destroyed in 1945, was restored and declared a UNESCO World Heritage Site in 1998.

Teutonic Order

In 1190, during the third crusade, some citizens of Bremen and Lübeck who were temporarily based in the Holy Land established the Teutonic Order, also known as the Order of the Brothers of the German House of St Mary in Jerusalem, or the Order of German Knights, German Masters and Crusaders. It has always been symbolized by a straight, symmetric black cross on a white background. After the emperor and the Pope had guaranteed that successfully evangelized regions would be assigned to the Order, what had originally been a hospice order became an military order of knights beginning in 1198. It then shifted its range and region of activities from Palestine to the non-

Once a base of the Teutonic Order, today a UNESCO World Heritage Site: the Marienburg.

Christian Baltic. Numerous forts and roughly 100 cities, including the exclave of Kaliningrad, were founded during this period. Gdańsk and Pomerelia were also conquered. In 1231, the Order established its own clerical state in eastern Prussia, but its land was never a contiguous territory, but rather a conglomeration of scattered land possessions. By 1309, the eastern Prussian city of Malbork became the Order's capital, and the Marienburg defence complex built there was the residence of the grand masters of the Order for nearly 150 years. In 1466, the western lands of the Order were lost to the Prussians and the Order's headquarters were relocated to Kaliningrad. As of the 16th century, the Order's numbers began to decline, but it resumed clerical activities in 1929 (in Germany it restarted in 1945). The approximately 1,000 members primarily work in the pastoral and care-giving fields. The grand master's residence is now in Vienna.

able to find a piece of this beautiful stone for yourself!

19 Courland Spit National Park "The Courland Spit is a narrow strip of land between Memel and Königsberg (now Klaipèda and Kaliningrad), between the Courland Lagoon and the Baltic Sea. The lagoon contains fresh water, which is unaffected by the small connection to the Baltic Sea near Memel, and is home to freshwater fish." These were the words of author Thomas Mann, who owned a house in this area in the 1930s that is now open to the public, to describe the unique natural paradise here that has been declared a UNESCO World Natural Heritage Site.

The Courland Spit National Park protects the forests rustling in the sea breeze, the dreamy towns with their traditional wooden houses, and the pristine dune and beach landscape along the Baltic Sea and the lagoon. The southernmost town in the Lithuanian part of the Courland Spit is Nida. The dune landscape, with dunes up to 60 m (197 ft) high, is also jokingly known as the "Lithuanian Sahara".

20 Klaipèda A series of seaside resorts make this coast the most attractive holiday spot in Lithuania. The Baltic town of Klaipèda, located at the mouth of the lagoon and which appeared to still be in slumber until just a few decades ago, is today one of the country's important industrial centers. Its history also began with the Teutonic Order, and Klaipèda adopted the Lübeck city charter in 1254.

Just a few miles further north is the popular spa resort of

Palanga, with its fine white-sand beaches, dunes and vast pine forests. With a bit of luck, you can experience some spectacular sunsets here after visiting the botanical garden and the interesting amber museum.

From Klaipèda, the A1 takes you through Kaunas to Vilnius, the capital of Lithuania, 300 km (186.5 mi) away. If you would rather head to Riga, Latvia, take the A12 east for 100 km (62 mi).

21 Rīga The Latvian capital on the mouth of the Daugava became a member of the Hanseatic League in 1282, and is one of the most beautiful cities in the Baltic region. The Old Town itself was declared a UNESCO

World Heritage Site. Within its walls are buildings dating back to numerous eras in European architecture including medieval patrician homes, twenty-four warehouses in the Old Town, and some art nouveau houses, which in some cases line entire residential streets. Apart from the former palace of Czar Peter the Great, it is also worth visiting St John's Church (14th century), which is on the ruins of a diocesan town and was burned to the ground in 1234. The castle of the Teutonic Order, built in 1330, features the Sweden Gate and is home to many museums. The Saints Peter and Paul Cathedral was built at the end of the 18th century.

German merchants began unifying here in what was called the Great Guild back in the mid-14th century and even constructed their own Great Guild building. The locals were excluded here and in the Small Guild, where German craftsmen held secret meetings in the Small Guild building. The Schwarzhäupterhaus, or House of the Black Heads, built by merchants from Riga in 1341, is one of the most beautiful buildings in the city. The red brick construction has several storage levels.

Rīga's icon is the 137-m (450-ft) wooden tower of St Peter's. The Latvian parliament building is a replica of the Palazzo Strozzi in Florence. The Arsenal, Rīga's old

Amber – the "Gold of the Baltic Sea"

The Baltic Sea region has always been an important source of amber, a fossil resin that originates in ancient pine trees and hardens due to lack of oxygen. By flooding ancient amber forests, the 30- and 50-million-year-old amber was dug out of the earth and transported to the Samland coast of Kaliningrad.

The world's largest source of amber is still found on the Baltic Sea coast of Samland, and the amber from here often has interesting fossil imprints (entombments) of animals, typically insects, and parts of plants. The stone is extracted through a process of open-cast mining or it is fished out using nets.

Amber was extremely popular as jewelry and in amulets as early as the Stone Age, but has also been traditionally used in medicine. In the Hanseatic territory, it played an important role as a trading commodity, and was distributed as far afield as the Islamic world. The collection of amber on the coast became the fran-

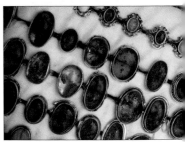

Top: Amber with an embedded insect.
Bottom: Amber, cut and mounted into jewelry.

customs house (1828–32), is also worth seeing. For those interested in architecture and rural lifestyles of the 16th to 19th centuries, be sure to visit the open-air museum.

West of Rīga is the spa resort of Jūrmala, on a headland in the Gulf of Rīga. Fine sandy beaches stretch over 30 km (19 mi) and a handy railway connects the capital with the town.

From Riga, it is worth making a small detour to Sigulda, located in the idyllic Ganja National Park about 50 km (31 mi) to the north-east. The main attractions in the park include a toboggan run, Turaida Castle, and the numerous interesting caves and wells that can be discovered along the hiking routes.

From Rīga , the E67 leads north along the Gulf of Rīga to the Estonian capital, Tallinn. You'll cross the border at Ainazi.

22 Pärnu The Estonian west coast is similarly appealing, with picturesque forests, shimmering water, simple thatched houses, stout castles and old ruins. About 180 km (112 mi) north of Riga is Pärnu, located on the

river of the same name. This quaint old city, which dates back to the 13th century, is an important Estonian port city but is also famous as a health resort because of the healing mud from the area. Homes from the 16th and 17th centuries, as well as the Orthodox St Catherine's Church and the baroque St Elizabeth Church, are also worth seeing. The last stop on your journey along the Baltic Sea coast is the Hanseatic city of Tallinn.

23 Tallinn In the 13th century, the knights of the Teutonic Order advanced as far as the northern reaches of the Baltic territories, right up to the entrance of the Gulf of Finland. Tallinn itself was first documented in 1154. Its Hanseatic League membership, which began in 1284, indeed inspired the city's rapid economic rise, but the collapse of the Order in the 16th and 17th centuries marked the start of a decline for Tallinn. After 1945, the capital became Estonia's most important industrial city.

The many churches on cathedral mountain and in the lower part of town, as well as the Gothic church spires soaring toward the heavens like giant needles, all make Tallinn a fantastic architectural destination. The towers of the city wall and the baroque domes on the patrician houses are also interesting relics of a world gone by. Many of the quiet, narrow lanes are still paved with cobblestones.

The Gothic Old Town is a UNESCO World Heritage Site and has the oldest town hall in northern Europe (14th/15th centuries). The nearly intact city walls are adorned with twenty-six towers. Cathedral mountain, which falls dramatically toward the sea, is the site of the cathedral and Toompea Castle. The view over the rooftops to the historic Old Town is magnificent. The 13th-century Cathedral of the Virgin Mary is one of the oldest churches in Estonia, while the baroque Kadriorg Palace, with its beautiful park, was designed by Nicolo Michetti for Czar Peter the Great in 1718. The Dominican monastery was built in 1246, and is the oldest existing monastery in Estonia.

1 The Courland Spit is 98 km (61 mi) long and in parts only 400 m (0.25 mi) wide. It lies between the Baltic Sea and the Courland Lagoon.

2 Looking out over the distinctive skyline of Rīga's Old Town.

3 Rīga: The tower of the 13th-century St Peter's Church.

4 With its imposing city walls and watchtowers, Tallinn had one of the best northern European defense complexes of the 16th century.

5 The cathedral – the main church of Kaliningrad – was completely destroyed in 1944, and was not rebuilt until the 1990s.

chise of the sovereign princes, initially controlled by the dukes of Pomerelia and later by the Teutonic Order. The latter also created the post of amber master within the organization and held onto a monopoly of the trade from the High Middle Ages. Amber collectors had to surrender their findings to this master, and even in the late 19th century it was not easy for outsiders to gather amber on Baltic Sea beaches. Following the collapse of the Hanseatic League, Gdańsk and Kaliningrad became centers for amber mounting.

Detour

Kaunas and Vilnius

Kaunas was the capital of Lithuania between the world wars. The old city center and the castle are located on a peninsula at the confluence of the Nemunas and Neris Rivers. The Hanseatic League had a branch office here from 1441 until 1532, before the fire of 1537 destroyed large parts of the Old Town.

From Kaunas it is roughly 100 km (62 mi) to Vilnius, the current capital on the Vilnia river. That city's landmarks are the many watchtowers scattered through the picturesque Old Town. The "Rome of the Baltic", as this picture-book town used to be called, still contains remnants of its former masters, the Jesuits, champions of the Counter-Reformation in the kingdom of Poland and Lithuania. Vilnius was first documented in 1323, and even then it was already a prosperous trading and merchant settlement. Vilnius surprises most visitors with its magnificent baroque churches and buildings. The narrow, picturesque cobblestone lanes zig-zag through the Old Town, at the center of which is the university, a Renaissance building with a number of courtyards influenced by Italian styles. The Vilnius cathedral was rebuilt several times before being given its current classicist makeover in the 18th century. The city's main road is formed by the Gediminas Prospekt, lined with lime trees. Extensive baroque and classicist palaces attest to the wealth that once flowed through the city.

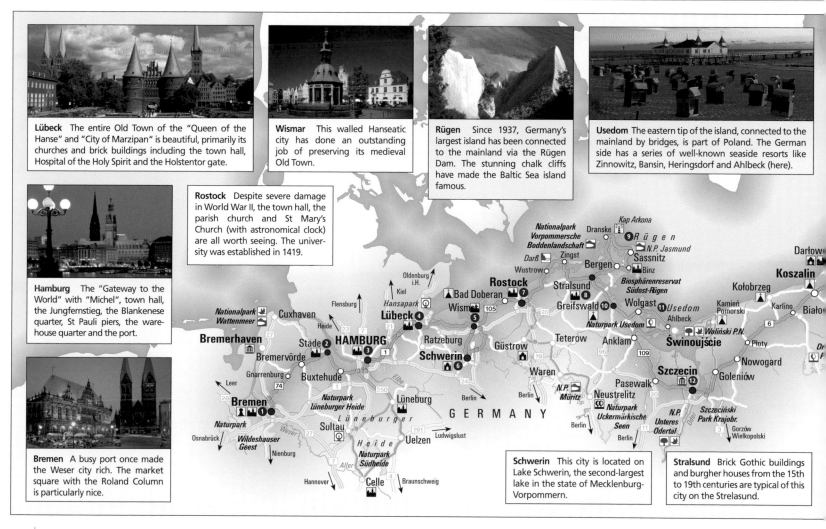

Lübeck The entire Old Town of the "Queen of the Hanse" and "City of Marzipan" is beautiful, primarily its churches and brick buildings including the town hall, Hospital of the Holy Spirit and the Holstentor gate.

Wismar This walled Hanseatic city has done an outstanding job of preserving its medieval Old Town.

Rügen Since 1937, Germany's largest island has been connected to the mainland via the Rügen Dam. The stunning chalk cliffs have made the Baltic Sea island famous.

Usedom The eastern tip of the island, connected to the mainland by bridges, is part of Poland. The German side has a series of well-known seaside resorts like Zinnowitz, Bansin, Heringsdorf and Ahlbeck (here).

Rostock Despite severe damage in World War II, the town hall, the parish church and St Mary's Church (with astronomical clock) are all worth seeing. The university was established in 1419.

Hamburg The "Gateway to the World" with "Michel", town hall, the Jungfernstieg, the Blankenese quarter, St Pauli piers, the warehouse quarter and the port.

Bremen A busy port once made the Weser city rich. The market square with the Roland Column is particularly nice.

Schwerin This city is located on Lake Schwerin, the second-largest lake in the state of Mecklenburg-Vorpommern.

Stralsund Brick Gothic buildings and burgher houses from the 15th to 19th centuries are typical of this city on the Strelasund.

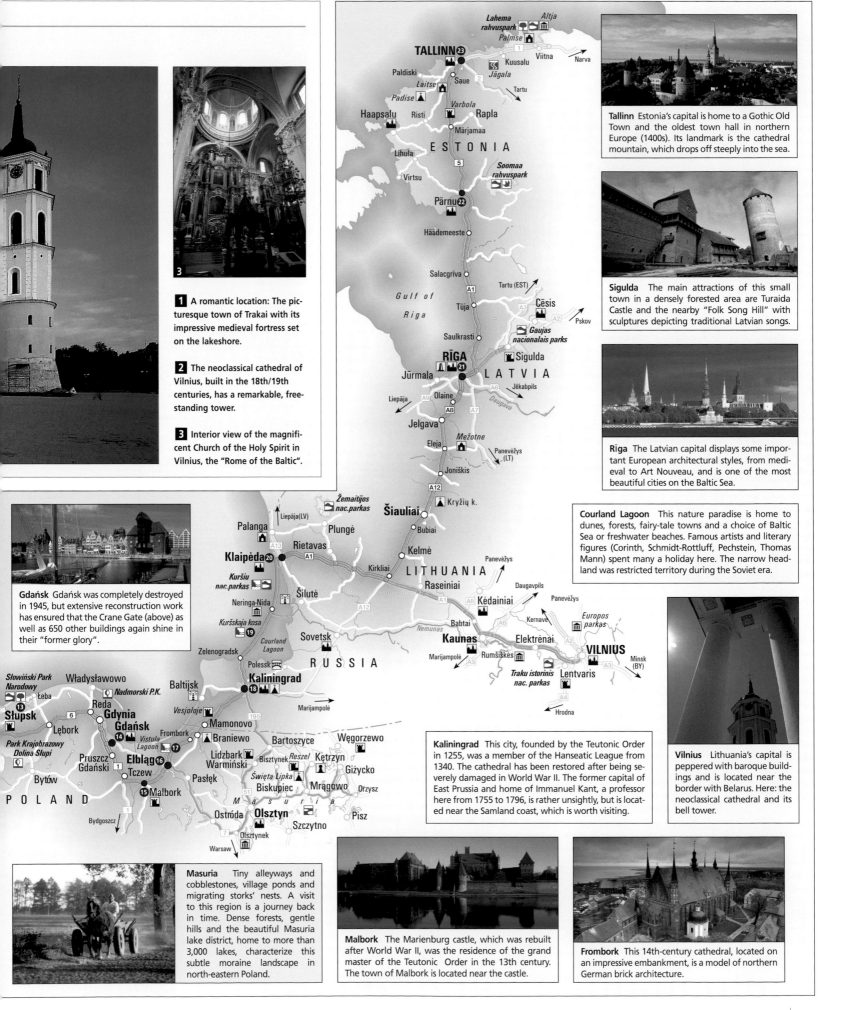

1 A romantic location: The picturesque town of Trakai with its impressive medieval fortress set on the lakeshore.

2 The neoclassical cathedral of Vilnius, built in the 18th/19th centuries, has a remarkable, free-standing tower.

3 Interior view of the magnificent Church of the Holy Spirit in Vilnius, the "Rome of the Baltic".

Tallinn Estonia's capital is home to a Gothic Old Town and the oldest town hall in northern Europe (1400s). Its landmark is the cathedral mountain, which drops off steeply into the sea.

Sigulda The main attractions of this small town in a densely forested area are Turaida Castle and the nearby "Folk Song Hill" with sculptures depicting traditional Latvian songs.

Rīga The Latvian capital displays some important European architectural styles, from medieval to Art Nouveau, and is one of the most beautiful cities on the Baltic Sea.

Courland Lagoon This nature paradise is home to dunes, forests, fairy-tale towns and a choice of Baltic Sea or freshwater beaches. Famous artists and literary figures (Corinth, Schmidt-Rottluff, Pechstein, Thomas Mann) spent many a holiday here. The narrow headland was restricted territory during the Soviet era.

Gdańsk Gdańsk was completely destroyed in 1945, but extensive reconstruction work has ensured that the Crane Gate (above) as well as 650 other buildings again shine in their "former glory".

Kaliningrad This city, founded by the Teutonic Order in 1255, was a member of the Hanseatic League from 1340. The cathedral has been restored after being severely damaged in World War II. The former capital of East Prussia and home of Immanuel Kant, a professor here from 1755 to 1796, is rather unsightly, but is located near the Samland coast, which is worth visiting.

Vilnius Lithuania's capital is peppered with baroque buildings and is located near the border with Belarus. Here: the neoclassical cathedral and its bell tower.

Masuria Tiny alleyways and cobblestones, village ponds and migrating storks' nests. A visit to this region is a journey back in time. Dense forests, gentle hills and the beautiful Masuria lake district, home to more than 3,000 lakes, characterize this subtle moraine landscape in north-eastern Poland.

Malbork The Marienburg castle, which was rebuilt after World War II, was the residence of the grand master of the Teutonic Order in the 13th century. The town of Malbork is located near the castle.

Frombork This 14th-century cathedral, located on an impressive embankment, is a model of northern German brick architecture.

The vineyard town of Löf. The tall hills of the Upper Mosel Valley taper off a bit just before the

Germany

Wine, culture and the rolling hills of the Rhine, Mosel and Neckar

The Rhine is the subject of countless songs, the "most German of all rivers" and without doubt one of the most beautiful rivers in Europe. The Mosel, which flows into the Rhine at Koblenz, is smaller but no less alluring. The Neckar, which joins the Rhine from the east at Mannheim, is a worthy rival on all counts. All three rivers boast enchanting valleys bound by lovely hills dotted with castles, vineyards and quaint villages.

The Rhine, known as Rhenus by the Celts and the Romans, is 1,320 km (820 mi) long, making it one of the longest rivers in Europe, and one of the most important waterways on the continent.

The Rhine originates in the canton of Graubünden (Grisons), Switzerland, flows into and out of Lake Constance, nips over the Rhine Falls at Schaffhausen, then continues on toward Basel as the Upper Rhine. The Upper Rhine then turns northward across the Upper Rhine Plain where

Ladenburg on the Neckar.

it enters its most familiar "German" manifestation. The Neckar joins the Rhine at Mannheim where the latter becomes the Middle Rhine, which cuts spectacularly through the low mountains of central western Germany, accompanied on the left bank by the "peaks" of the Hunsrück and on the right by the Taunus foothills. The Mosel flows into what is now the Lower Rhine at Koblenz and enters the Lower Rhine Basin near Bonn. After passing through Cologne, Düsseldorf and Duisburg, it leaves Germany just after Kleve and flows into the North Sea in the Netherlands a few river miles later.

In 2002, the Middle Rhine from Bingen to Koblenz was declared a UNESCO World Heritage Site, in recognition not only of its natural beauty but also the cultural, historical and, not least, economic significance of this stretch of the river.

This stretch of the valley is inextricably linked with the "Rhine Gold" of Wagner fame and epic Nibelung legend, and on both sides of the meandering river are steep hillsides with exquisite vineyards and defiant medieval castles.

It seems every castle and every rock formation on the Rhine is linked with a myth or a legend, whether it is of the beautiful Loreley, who is said to have lured many a boatsman to his untimely death with her songs, or of the two estranged brothers in Burg Katz (Cat) and Burg Maus (Mouse).

But perhaps all of these myths and legends were merely inspired by centuries of delectable Rhine wine, whose vineyards are as much a part of the culture here as the numerous castles that line the river's banks. Whatever the case, the wine is most certainly influential in creating the

One of Germany's most famous picture-postcard views: Heidelberg on the Neckar.

river converges with the Rhine.

View over the Rhine of the much fêted Loreley rock, which rises 132 m (433 ft) above the river.

conviviality of the people in the region, which reaches its climax during Carnival, especially in Cologne. A more recent festivity on the Rhine is the spectacle "Rhein in Flammen" (Rhine in flames): five times a year, fireworks soar over the river between Rüdesheim and Bonn.

Wine also plays an important role along the longest and largest of the Rhine's tributaries, the Mosel. Known for its romantic meandering course, the Mosel originates in the southern Vosges Mountains in France and flows into the Rhine at Koblenz after 545 km (339 mi). With the exception of Trier, which is located on a comparatively broad section of the Mosel, no other large cities have developed on its banks because the river's valley is so narrow. This makes the surrounding countryside, especially between Bernkastel-Kues and Cochem, particularly

charming with its vineyards, wine-growing towns and medieval castles. The Mosel Valley is a unique cultural landscape with thousands of years of history started by Celtic and Roman settlers.

Farther upstream from where the Mosel joins in, "Father Rhine" has already collected one of his other sons: the Neckar, yet another of the German "wine rivers". The Necker originates at 706 m (2,316 ft) in the Schwenninger Moos and flows into the Rhine 367 km (228 mi) later at Mannheim. Along its course, it twists and turns through steep valleys like the one at Rottweil, or meanders through broad meadows like the ones where Stuttgart and Heilbronn are now located.

Below Neckarelz, the river cuts through the red sandstone formations of the Odenwald, and from Heidelberg it passes through the Upper Rhine Plain.

The Reichsburg above Cochem on the Mosel is one of Germany's most attractive castles.

The Romans in Trier

Emperor Augustus founded Trier, Germany's oldest town, back in 16 BC, and gave it the name Augusta Treverorum. Augustus built the town on a strategically clever location where the Mosel River valley (in Latin Mosella) widens, the same spot where Caesar had defeated the Celtic Treverers – another reason for the Treverorum name.

In about 100 AD, an amphitheater with capacity for 20,000 spectators was built here. Its ruins can still be visited today. In 117 AD, Augusta Treverorum became the capital of the Roman province of Belgica prima,

Top: Imperial baths (ca. 360 AD).
Bottom: Porta Nigra Roman gate.

administrative seat of the prefecture for the provinces of Gallia, Britannia and Spain as well as the emperor's residence.

During the 3rd and 4th centuries, Trier was a sort of ancient world metropolis, with remarkable 70,000 inhabitants. Today, in addition to the amphitheater ruins, the Aula Palatina (once the residence of Constantine the Great), the imperial baths and the Barbara thermal hot springs still bear witness to Trier's ancient Roman heyday. The icon of the city, however, is the Porta Nigra, the 2nd-century Roman gate that was never quite completed. (The gate was remodeled as St Simeon's Church under Frankish rule in the 11th century.) The Franks had conquered the city in 475, and for centuries defended it against attempts at recapture. By the 6th century, Trier had become an archbishopric.

Your route along Germany's enchanting rivers begins in Trier and follows the course of the Mosel down to its confluence with the Rhine at Koblenz. It then heads back up through the Middle Rhine Valley past countless castles and vineyards to Mannheim. From there you will travel parallel to the Neckar River to Tübingen.

❶ Trier Framed in by the forested hills of the Hunsrück and Eifel, Trier sits in one of the few broad valleys along the Mosel. It is a city of superlatives: North east of the Roman Porta Nigra is the church of St Paulin (18th C.), designed by Balthasar Neumann and the region's most significant baroque structure. The Cathedral of St Peter was begun in the 4th century, making it the oldest cathedral in Germany. The Liebfrauenkirche next door (13th C.) is one of the oldest Gothic churches in the country. And the Hauptmarkt with its Marian cross and the St Peter's Fountain is one of Germany's most attractive fairy-tale squares.

From Trier to Koblenz you skirt both sides of the Mosel among the enchanting hillside vineyard towns.

❷ Bernkastel-Kues The half-timbered houses and the Marktplatz here are dominated by the

Travel information

Route profile
Length: approx. 550 km (342 mi)
Time required: 6–7 days
Start: Trier
End: Tübingen
Route (main locations):
Trier, Koblenz, Bingen, Mainz, Frankfurt, Darmstadt, Mannheim, Heidelberg, Heilbronn, Stuttgart, Tübingen, Lake Constance

Traffic information:
Roads in Germany are well maintained and signposted. There are no toll roads. After passing on the autobahn, return to the slow lane.

When to go:
The best time to visit Germany is from April/May to September/October. And don't forget a rain jacket!

Information:
Here are just a few of the many websites for Germany.
Mosel region:
www.mosellandtouristik.de
Rhine region:
www.e-heidelberg.com
Heidelberg region:
www.wikitravel.org/en/Heidelberg
Lake Constance area:
www.bodensee-tourismus. com

Maria Laach and the Southern Eifel

The Southern Eifel, part of the Rhenish Slate Mountains, is bordered on the south by the Mosel River. Its highest peak is the basalt hilltop of the Hohe Acht at 746 m (2,448 ft). Typical features of the Southern Eifel are its maars, small crater lakes of volcanic origin. The largest of these is Laacher Lake, which reaches a depth of 53 m (174 ft) and covers 3.3 sq km (1.3 sq mi). A strong groundwater current feeds the lake, and rising gas bubbles are indicative of the fact that the volcanic activity in the area has not entirely stopped. Other well-known maars in the area are the Dauner Maare, the so-called "blue eyes of the Eifel".

The mighty Benedictine Maria Laach Monastery

The famous Benedictine Monastery of Maria Laach, dating from the 12th century, is situated near Mendig on the shores of Laacher Lake. The monastery (consecrated in 1156), has a total of six church steeples and is considered a gem of Romanesque architecture for its strict geometric lines and extraordinary beauty. It was the last monastery in the Rhineland to be founded by the Benedictine order. The most fascinating sights inside the complex include the tomb of Heinrich II (11th century), the canopied high altar, the crypt, the arched portal and especially the famous "Laacher Paradies", a stonemason's work on the west façade's balcony that symbolizes the Garden of Eden.

---

ruins of Landshut Castle, with vineyards climbing up to its stone walls. A bridge connects Bernkastel with Kues, the birthplace of philosopher Nikolaus von Kues (1401–1464).

3 Traben-Trarbach This charming vineyard town straddling the Mosel is distinguished by attractive half-timbered houses and patrician villas. Fans of Art Nouveau architecture will find some unique specimens here, including the Brückentor, the Huesgen Villa, the small Sonora Villa and the Hotel Bellevue, all reminders of a golden age in the wine trade at the turn of the 20th century.
Towering above the small town is Grevenburg Castle. On Mont

Royal, enclosed by a wide loop in the river, are the ruins of a fortress planned by Vauban.

4 Zell This vineyard town on the right bank of the Mosel boasts remnants of very old town walls, the church of St Peter and a former electors' palace.
On the road to Bremm you can take a scenic detour to Arras Castle (9th C.) near Alf.

5 Mosel Loop at Bremm Among the most famous of the Mosel's many hairpin turns is the one around the wine village of Bremm, whose vineyards on the Bremmer Calmont are among the steepest Riesling vineyards in Europe. The village itself is lovely, with picturesque narrow

alleyways and the usual half-timbered houses. Heading downstream, take a trip to legendary Burg Eltz castle.

6 Cochem This town is one of the most attractive in the Mosel Valley. It is dominated by the Reichsburg, built in 1070, destroyed in 1688 and built once again in the 19th century in neo-Gothic style. The Marktplatz is surrounded by lovely old row houses and the town hall from 1739. Before the vineyard town of Kobern-Gondorf you will see the ruins of Ehrenburg castle near Löf-Hatzenport and in Alken the twin towers of Thuant Castle rise above the Mosel.
From Kobern, it is worth taking the time to visit Maria Laach (see

box to the right), culturally perhaps the most important sight in the southern Eifel mountains.

1 View from Calmont of the wide arch in the Mosel near Bremm.

2 The main square in Trier with Gangolf, the market cross and Steipe, which also functioned as the town hall until the 18th century.

3 Bernkastel-Kues, a medieval vineyard town on the Middle Mosel.

4 View across the Mosel towards Cochem and the Reichsburg castle.

5 Burg Landshut, nestled among the vineyards above Bernkastel-Kues, has been a ruin since 1692.

Burg Eltz is one of Germany's most beautiful medieval castles. Built on top of a 70-m-high (230-ft) rock formation and enclosed on three sides by the Elz River, the castle was damaged in battle. In 1268, it became a "Ganerben" castle, meaning it was in the possession of three lines of the same family dynasty living under

the same roof. In the course of 500 years of construction, a fortified castle complex was created with eight residential towers grouped around a small central inner courtyard. Thanks to the centuries of construction, architectural styles from romanticism to baroque can be seen here.

Rhine Wine

It was the Romans who first brought wine to the Mosel and Rhine valleys. Between Koblenz and Bingen and in the Rheingau region you will find all of the grape varieties that have made Rhine wines famous: Riesling, Müller-Thurgau, Kerner and Spätburgunder. The conditions here are ideal: the hill-

Riesling grapevines

sides alongside the Rhine provide an optimal angle of exposure to sunlight, and after sunset the rocky ground radiates back the heat that has been stored there during the day. The surrounding low central German range also shelters the vines from exposure to cold winds and the vineyards are protected from dangerous night frosts by the warm air rising from the river that sweeps across the valley's slopes like a gentle blanket. The mild climate allows the Rhine grapes to mature well into autumn, and after the harvest the maturing process continues in the barrel.

7 Koblenz This town on a spit of land at the confluence of the Mosel and the Rhine was of great strategic importance even in Roman times, and in the 11th century it became the residence of the archbishops and electors of Trier. The location is known as the Deutsches Eck (German Corner) and is home to the stately Kaiser Wilhelm Memorial.
Aside from the St Castor Basilica, sights worth seeing in Koblenz include the medieval Alte Burg castle, the Münzplatz, the birthplace of Prince Metternich, the Liebfrauenkirche (12th–15th C.) and the church of St Florin (12th–14th C.) as well as the vast Electors' Castle (16th C.) down by the Rhine. On the eastern bank of the Rhine you'll find Ehrenbreitstein Fortress, one of the largest fortified complexes in Europe.
From Koblenz, follow the B9 up the left bank to Bingen.

8 Boppard This idyllic town is tucked into a sweeping curve on the left bank of the Rhine. On the way there, you pass Stolzenfels Castle (13th C.), Lahneck Castle and Marksburg Castle. The latter is the only hilltop castle on the Rhine that was never destroyed. In Boppard itself, the remains of the medieval town walls, relics from the Roman Castellum Bodobriga and the church of St Severus (12th/13th C.) are worth a visit.

9 St Goar and St Goarshausen These two vineyard towns are dominated by Rheinfels Castle, once the mightiest fortress on the Rhine. St Goar is on the left bank while St Goarshausen is on the right, and they are linked by ferry. From the latter you can see the ruins of Burg Katz and Burg Maus castles, built by two estranged brothers in the 14th century.

10 Loreley Just a few bends downstream, this famous rock rises 133 m (436 ft) above the Rhine, just 133 m (145 yds) wide at this point. It was an historic-

ally dangerous strait for boats. Poet Heinrich Heine wrote a romantic song about the rock.

11 Kaub A ferry takes you over to this romantic village encircled by a splendid medieval wall. It is one of the most important wine-growing areas on the Rhine. Towering over Kaub is the Gutenfels Castle (13th C.), and on a small rock island in the middle of the river is the former toll tower Pfalzgrafenstein, the so-called Pfalz bei Kaub.

12 Bacharach This idyllic vineyard town on the west bank of

the Rhine is inside a wall with a number of towers and dominated by Stahleck Castle, which is now a youth hostel. Down by the river near town is Sooneck Castle. Heading now towards Bingen you will pass the castles of Reichenstein and Rheinstein, both on the west bank.

13 Bingen The icon of this town at the confluence of the Nahe and Rhine rivers is Klopp Castle, the foundations of which date back to Roman times. At the Binger Loch, the Rhine makes a dramatic entrance into the Rhenish Slate Mountains. On the left

Near Bingen-Bingerbrück, on a tiny rocky island in the middle of the Rhine, stands a former watch and toll tower dating from the 13th century. The origin of its name, Mäuseturm (Mouse Tower), likely does not come from the legend of Archbishop Hatto and the mice, but rather from the muta, or toll, that was once collected here.

In Roman times, a small fortress stood on this location, as a defense against the Teutons. The legend of the wicked Archbishop Hatto II (died in 970) tells of a devastating famine during which he provided no help or food to the

Since the 13th century, the Mouse Tower has stood in the Binger Loch.

people, and tortured them for their begging. An army of mice heard the screams and invaded the small tower. He fled, but the rodents swam after him and ate him alive.

The tower was rebuilt in the 13th century by the archbishops of Mainz. From 1298, together with Ehrenfels Castle, it served as a sentry and toll tower for ships passing on the Rhine. Tolls from the Rhine generated vital income for the archbishops of Mainz. It was mostly destroyed in the Thirty Years War and burned to the ground in 1689.

In the 18th century it was again used as a watchtower on the most dangerous narrow strait of the Rhine. The tower was given its current styling in around 1855, when Prussian king Friedrich Wilhelm IV had the tower built as a border marking. It fulfilled this function until 1974, when the rocks that had made navigation on the Rhine so dangerous were mostly blasted away.

bank is majestic Ehrenfels Castle (13th C.). In the middle of the river is the Binger Mäuseturm (Mouse Tower), a watch and toll tower along with Ehrenfels Castle. Car ferries cross the Rhine to Rüdesheim here.

⑭ Rüdesheim This vineyard town is mainly famous for the Drosselgasse, a street lined with wine bars, but old patrician estates like the Brömserhof and the ruins of the Boosenburg, Vorderburg and Brömserburg (10th C.) castles are impressive as well. The latter is home to the Rheingau Wine Museum.

Above town is the Niederwald Memorial, a statue of Germania erected in 1883 to observe the founding of the German empire in 1871.

⑮ Eltville The journey continues past a number of castles to Eltville, in a similarly picturesque location among vineyards and mountains. The ruins of a castle from the 14th century overlook the Old Town, which has some lovely old manor houses and the church of Saints Peter and Paul (14th C.). Take a short detour to the former Cistercian monastery of Eberbach, where wine has been made for 850 years.

⑯ Mainz This town dates back to Moguntiacum, a Roman fort built in 38 BC, and is one of Germany's oldest cities. St Boniface made Mainz an archbishopric in 742, and the university was founded in 1476.

In the 15th century, one of the modern world's most important

technological innovations took place here when Johann Gutenberg invented moveable metal type printing. Of the 200 bibles he ultimately printed, 48 copies are still around. One of these "Gutenberg Bibles" is on the north-eastern side of the Domplatz at the Gutenberg Museum along with a reconstruction of his workshop.

The reddish Mainz Cathedral of Saints Martin and Stephen dominates the city center with its six towers. It is a masterpiece of Romanesque architecture. The market fountain on the north side of the Domplatz is one of the most attractive Renaissance fountains in Germany. The former electors' palace down on the Rhine is now the Central Roman-Germanic Museum.

South-east of the university are the Römersteine, remains of an aqueduct built in the 1st century. Fans of Marc Chagall enjoy the Gothic church of St Stephen,

1 The picturesque "Pfalz" near Kaub stands on an island in the Rhine. It once served as a toll station. High above towers Gutenfels Castle.

2 Famous poets like Heinrich Heine, Victor Hugo and Clemens Brentano extolled the charms of the vineyard town Bacharach am Rhein.

3 Romantic Rheinstein Castle, built as a toll stronghold, is at the beginning of the Middle Rhine near Bingen, opposite the popular red wine vineyard town of Assmannshausen.

Mathildenhöhe Artists' Colony in Darmstadt

In the eastern part of Darmstadt lies Mathildenhöhe, a park created by Grand Duke Ernst Ludwig in 1899, that became the Darmstadt Artists' Colony until 1914. At the time, Art Nouveau was the style in fashion,

Top: Mathildenhöhe with exhibition building and tower.
Bottom: Mosaic in Wedding Tower.

and the grand duke became its most enthusiastic patron. Initially he invited seven young architects, painters and sculptors to the city, and on the Mathildenhöhe he encouraged them to pursue and realize their ideals, which were considered revolutionary at the time. The 48-m-high (157-ft) Wedding Tower by Joseph Maria Olbrich stands out among the Art Nouveau edifices here. Anyone wishing to explore Art Nouveau more thoroughly should pay a visit to the artists' colony museum in the Ernst-Ludwig-Haus.

An odd contrast to these buildings is the nearby Russian-Orthodox chapel with its gilded domes and lavish decorations. It was built for Czar Nicholas.

which has nine glass windows painted by the artist between 1978 and 1985, depicting scenes from the Bible.

⑰ Wiesbaden The capital of the state of Hesse is located at the foot of the wooded Taunus Mountains. Thanks to its twenty thermal hot springs here, Wiesbaden has been a popular spa resort since the Romans built a fort here in the year 6 AD. The main thoroughfare in town is the stately Wilhelmstrasse, at the northern end of which is the spa district with the imposing neoclassical Kurhaus (1907) and the Kurhauskolonnade, the longest colonnade in Europe. Diagonally opposite the Kurhaus is the impressive Hessian State Library. West of the spa district you come to the Kochbrunnen, a fountain combining fifteen of a total of twenty hot springs,

as well as the Kaiser Friedrich Baths, beautifully decorated in Art Nouveau style.
In the center of the city is the Stadtschloss (municipal palace), completed in 1841, and the seat of the Hessian Landtag (regional government) since 1946. Opposite that is the impressive old town hall from 1610, and the square is dominated by the red neo-Gothic Marktkirche church from 1862.

⑱ Frankfurt am Main (see pages 120–121)

⑲ Darmstadt This former Hessian imperial residence town is distinguished by remnants of life at the royal court. In the city center is the ducal palace, which was built over the course of more than six centuries. The last extensions were added in the 18th century.

Up on the Mathildenhöhe, evidence of the regional rulers' passion for hunting is on display in the Kranichstein Hunting Lodge. The market square and the old town hall from 1598 testify to the fact that bourgeois life has always played an influential role here. A weekly market takes place on the square around the 18th-century fountain. If you want to go for a stroll, head to the Herrngarten, formerly a park for the regional counts that was transformed into an English-style landscape garden in the 18th century and finally opened to the public in the 19th century.
From Darmstadt, the detour to Lorsch is a must. The Königshalle, or royal hall, is a jewel of Carolingian architecture and one of the oldest completely preserved medieval structures in the country. A slightly longer de-

tour goes to the former imperial city of Worms (see page 119).

⑳ Heidelberg This idyllically situated university town on the Neckar is considered one of the birthplaces of German romanticism. Towering over the Old Town are the famous castle ruins. The expansive grounds, which are laid out in terraces, were remodeled and extended several times between the 13th and the 16th centuries. To the modern eye it is a fascinating jumble of castle and chateau, with Gothic as well as Renaissance elements, the latter of which are of particular interest, especially the Ottheinrichsbau from 1566) and the Friedrichsbau from 1607. Superb views of the Old Town below unfold as you make your way around.
At the heart of the Old Town, directly on the market square

The Imperial Cathedrals of Worms and Speyer

For centuries, the icon of the imperial city of Worms has been the late-gothic St Peter's Cathedral from the 11th/12th centuries. With four spires, two domes and five ornate sandstone reliefs in the northern nave, it is a highlight of Romanesque architecture.

Over the years, the cathedral has undergone a series of internal transformations, during which it received a baroque high altar by Balthazar Neumann as well as

**Top: The cathedral in Worms.
Bottom: The Staufer crypt in the cathedral in Speyer.**

magnificent choir stalls (both from the 18th century).

The old imperial city of Speyer is also on the west side of the Rhine and, like Worms, likewise enjoys a long history. Witness to this is the six-towered, triple-naved and exceptionally tall cathedral of Saints Martin and Stephan. At the time of its consecration in the year 1061, it was the largest place of worship in the world. It houses the tombs of eight German emperors, among other figures of note. The large stone dish on the square, the so-called cathedral bowl (1490), was filled with wine whenever a new bishop was being chosen.

---

with its historic fountain, is the late-Gothic Heiliggeistkirche (Church of the Holy Spirit), which houses the tombs of the regional electors.

The Old Bridge, with its lovingly preserved medieval bridge gate, is another of the city's most recognizable icons. Once you get to the other side, it's just a short stroll to the famous Philosophers' Walk on the slopes of the Michelsberg. It is from here that you get the most attractive views of the Old Town, the Neckar and the castle.

We recommend another detour while in Heidelberg: the former imperial city of Speyer.

After returning, continue along the B37 through the Neckar Valley. From Neckargemünd, the road runs through the narrow valley via Hirschhorn up to Bad Wimpfen past picturesque villages and stout castles.

21 Bad Wimpfen This town is divided into two parts: Wimpfen im Tal (lower) and Wimpfen am Berg (upper). In the former, enclosed by old city walls, sights include the early-Romanesque Ritterstiftskirche (13th C.) and its adjacent monastery.

The landmark of Wimpfen am Berg are the Staufen towers of the Kaiserpfalz (imperial palace). Half-timbered houses such as the Bügeleisenhaus, a former bourgeois hospital, the Krone Inn, the Riesenhaus, (the manor house of the lords of Ehrenberg) all combine to create a charming medieval atmosphere in the upper town. Also worth a visit are the sumptuously decorated municipal church and the Parish Church of the Holy Cross. The best views of the old town and the Neckar Valley are from the western donjon of the former imperial palace.

22 Heilbronn This town is best known as the center of one of Germany's largest wine-growing regions. The Renaissance-style town hall on the market square has an astronomical clock from the 16th century. Construction of the nearby St Kilian's Church began back in 1278. South-west of the market square you'll find the Deutschhof, former headquarters of the knights of the Teutonic Order.

23 Ludwigsburg This city's founder, Duke Eberhard Ludwig, felt most cities lacked creativity. This inspired him in 1704, to fashion one according to his own personal designs.

Ludwigsburg's most lavish building, the Residenzschloss (palace), is still the focal point of the city today. The "Swabian Versailles" is one of the largest baroque chateaus in Germany, further enhanced by the magnificent gardens, for which Ludwigsburg is famous. During the annual Blossoming Baroque festival, thousands of visitors flock to the 30 ha (74 acres) of beautifully

1 "Mainhattan": the impressive skyline of Frankfurt am Main.

2 The royal hall of Lorsch Monastery, a "jewel of the Carolingian Renaissance".

3 Hirschhorn: the "Pearl of the Neckar Valley" is just east of Heidelberg.

4 The Kaiserpfalz palace in Bad Wimpfen was built in the 12th century by the Staufer.

5 Ludwigsburg Palace is one of the largest baroque palaces in all of Europe.

Frankfurt

"Mainhattan" or "Bankfurt" are nicknames often used to refer to Germany's metropolis on the Main. It is not entirely without reason, for the city's numerous skyscrapers do indeed resemble its North American counterpart.

Frankfurt is not just Germany's financial center, but second only to London in European finance. The 258-m-tall (846-ft) Commerzbank skyscraper is Europe's tallest office building, and Frankfurt's airport is one of the largest on the continent. The city is also a major international trade fair and publishing center. As the birthplace of Goethe, it is not unjustifiably the host of the world's largest book fair.

Indeed, Frankfurt has played an important role throughout Germany's history. Its Kaiserpfalz (imperial palace) was first mentioned in 794. In 876, it became the capital of the Ostrogoth empire. From 1356 to 1802, German kings and emperors were chosen and crowned here. In 1848/49, the German National Assembly met at St Paul's Church to defend the merits of democracy before the German court.

As "Mainhattan", Frankfurt has often had a dubious reputation – but unjust-

Sights in the Old Town include: Römerberg with the Römer Old Town hall (with corbie gables from the 15th–18th centuries); the imperial hall, once a venue for coronation banquets; the Ostzeile, opposite the town hall, featuring six half-timbered patrician houses; the old St Nicholas Church (consecrated in 1290); the Domplatz and the Kaiserdom cathedral from the 13th–15th centuries, a coronation church from 1562; Paulsplatz and the neoclassical church of St Paul (1796–1833), where the Goethe Prize and the Peace Prize of the German Book Trade are awarded by the City of Frankfurt; the baroque Hauptwache (1729/30); Goethe's birthplace and the Goethe Museum; the neoclassical Börse (stock exchange, 1879) building; the Eschenheimer Tower (with remains of the old town walls); and the late-neoclassical Old Opera House from 1880.

Past and present in close vicinity: view of the Römer, the Paulskirche and the Frankfurt skyline

ly so. Despite widespread destruction during World War II, and booming construction since, the city has managed to preserve much of its Hessian charm. This is especially evident in the historic Old Town around the Römerberg. On the other side of the Main River are half a dozen museums of world renown as well as the Sachsenhausen nightlife district.

Important museums in Frankfurt include: Kunsthalle Schirn (German painting from the Renaissance on); Museum for Modern Art; the Jewish Museum in the former Rothschild mansion; Nature Museum Senckenberg; the German Architecture Museum; Städelsches Art Institut with paintings from the 14th century to the present.

Lake Constance

Lake Constance is the second-largest lake in the Alps, and the largest in Germany. In the northern half, the Überlinger Lake, is Mainau, the "Island of Flowers", with its almost subtropical vegetation. Between Unter Lake and Zeller Lake is Reichenau, the "Island of Vegetables". From the Hoher Pfänder (1,063 m/3,488 ft) between Lindau and Bregenz, superb views unfold across the "Swabian Sea", the Old Town of Lindau, on an island in the lake, and the pictur-

Top: The Old Castle in Meersburg.
Center: Pilgrimage church of Birnau.
Bottom: View of Wasserburg.

esque villages of Wasserburg and Langenargen.

Friedrichshafen, on the German northern shore, is associated with zeppelins. In Meersburg stands the oldest lived-in castle in Germany. Near Unteruhldingen you can go visit two reconstructed prehistoric Pfahlbauten, or pile dwelling villages, which remind us of the early settlers in the area. Nearby in Birnau is one of the most beautiful baroque churches of the Lake Constance region.

landscaped gardens, which also boast an attraction for kids – the fairytale garden. Everyone from Hansel and Gretel to the witch, Sleeping Beauty, Snow White and the frog prince reside in this charming little park.

There are a number of other castles in Ludwigsburg as well. Not far from the imperial palace, in the middle of a vast nature and wildlife park, is Favorite, a baroque hunting lodge and maison de plaisance. It was constructed on the orders of Duke Eberhard Ludwig between 1713 and 1723. The Monrepos Palace on the lake was completed in 1768, a rococo building that features an attractive Empire interior and is often used as a venue for concerts, for example during the Ludwigsburg Castle Festival. From Ludwigsburg, a detour to the north-west to the Maulbronn monastery is worthwhile. This Cistercian monastery is the most completely preserved medieval monastic complex north of the Alps and has been a declared a UNESCO World Heritage Site. The triple-naved basilica was consecrated in 1178, while the chapter house dates from the 14th century.

24 Stuttgart The capital of Baden-Württemberg is charmingly nestled into a valley that opens out towards the Neckar. The historic city center and the rows of houses seem to climb up the often steep slopes.

Originally built around a 13th-century moated castle on the Neckar, Stuttgart quickly developed into a very important trad-

ing city. The magnificent Königstraße runs from the impressive, 58-m-high (190-ft) tower of the Stuttgart central station to the grand Schlossplatz. In the middle of the square are the Jubilee Column (1842) and some modern sculptures by Alexander Calder and Alfred Hrdlicka. The square is dominated by the Neues Schloss (new castle, 1807) with three separate wings, expansive gardens and the neo-classical Königsbau (1860) opposite, which houses the Stuttgart Stock Exchange.

The Altes Schloss (old castle) was completed in the Renaissance style in 1578. Today, it houses the renowned Württembergisches Landesmuseum (state museum). Also on Schillerplatz, one of Stuttgart's most attractive squares, is the Gothic collegiate church with two towers (12th–15th centuries), the old chancellery, completed in 1544, and the "Fruchtkasten" (fruit box), an old grain silo from the 16th century.

Other interesting sights include the Akademiegarten next to the new castle, the Staatstheater (state theater) and the Staatsgalerie (state gallery). Roughly 10 km (6 mi) south-west of the city center is Solitude, an extravagant rococo palace built on a hill in 1767, on the orders of Duke Karl Eugen.

North of the city center, not far from the Killesberg with its 217-m-high (712-ft) television tower, is the Weissenhof artists' colony, designed by renowned architects including Le Corbusier, Mies van der Rohe, Walter

Gropius and Hans Scharoun. In the present district of Bad Cannstadt stands the Wilhelma, one of the most attractive and diverse botanical and zoological gardens in Germany.

25 Tübingen A university town since 1477, the "Athens on the Neckar" is still defined by the overwhelming student culture and the accompanying vibrant bar scene. Tübingen's picturesque and meticulously maintained Old Town, which climbs up in terraces from the banks of the Neckar, has a number of half-timbered houses surrounding a charming market square. From the 16-century Schloss Hohentubingen, which you can reach via the delightfully scenic Burgsteige lane, you get magnificent views of the Old Town and the Hölderlin Tower on the opposite side of the river. The famous poet lived here from 1807 until 1843.

Other sights worth visiting include the nearby Alte Burse

(1478–1482), Tübingen's oldest university building, as well as the Evangelisches Stift (1536). From Alte Burse you will also be able to see the Collegiate Church, built around 1470, the old auditorium and the town hall, dating back to the 15th century. Tübingen has always had a hint of Venice about it, especially when the "Stocherer" (pokers) punt on the Neckar with their longboats.

From Tübingen, a detour to Lake Constance brings you back to the Rhine, which flows into the lake west of Bregenz, Austria, and leaves it again near Stein, where it is referred to as the Upper Rhine.

1 View across the Neckar to Tübingen and its Stiftskirche with the remarkable spire.

2 Villa Solitude in Stuttgart was built between 1763 and 1767 on the orders of Duke Carl Eugen.

Mosel Loop at Bremm The slopes on the loop are the steepest Riesling vineyards in Europe. Bremm delights visitors with its alleyways and half-timbered houses.

Cochem To see the main feature of this town on the Lower Mosel you have to look up: Reichsburg Castle was built in 1070 and renovated in the 19th century.

Eltz Castle This picturesque fortified castle with fairy-tale towers and decorative balconies was built back in 1160.

The Rhine near Kaub This small romantic town on the right bank of the Rhine is surrounded by a medieval town wall and is one of the most important wine-growing villages on the Middle Rhine. Kaub is dominated by Gutenfels Castle from the 13th century. On an island in the river is the former Pfalzgrafenstein toll tower from 1326.

Trier Germany's oldest city boasts buildings dating from Roman times to the present. The market square is a charming centerpiece.

Mainz This bishops' town was founded by the Romans and is one of Germany's oldest cities. Sights include the Gutenberg Museum, the cathedral and the half-timbered houses in the Old Town.

Bacharach Situated on the left bank of the Rhine, this little half-timbered wine village is enclosed by turreted town walls from the 16th century and dominated by Stahleck Castle.

Bingen Among the sights here at the confluence of the Nahe and the Rhine are Klopp Castle and the Mouse Tower.

Frankfurt Europe's tallest office building distinguishs the skyline of "Mainhattan". The airport is one of the largest on the continent too. Goethe's birthplace is also importance for its international trade fairs and many banks. In addition, it boasts a very attractive Old Town.

Heidelberg This venerable university town is the epitome of German romanticism. The castle ruins (13th–16th centuries) rising high above the beautiful Old Town and the Old Bridge (1786–1788) are the most recognizable icons of Heidelberg. The best views are from the Philosophenweg.

Tübingen This old university town (since 1477) boasts a picturesque and almost entirely preserved Old Town.

Speyer Located on the high banks of the Rhine, Speyer Cathedral was begun in the year 1025. It is Germany's largest Romanesque building. This is a view of the crypt, built in 1041.

Ludwigsburg This county seat is known for its ducal palace, the largest baroque palace complex in Germany, also known as the "Swabian Versailles".

Stuttgart Baden-Württemberg's capital city is situated at the bottom of the Neckar River valley. The elegant Königstraße leads up to Schlossplatz and the New Palace. Also worth seeing are the Königsbau and the Old Palace.

Lake Constance With an area of 538 sq km (207 sq mi), Constance is the second-largest lake in the Alps. Romantic villages, orchards and vineyards thrive on its shores. The mild climate even supports subtropical plant life on Mainau. Constance, Meersburg and Lindau are cultural gems.

Germany

A fairy-tale journey – the Romantic Road

Four city gates and fourteen towers surround the medieval fortress town of Dinkelsbühl.

From the vineyards of Mainfranken through the charming Tauber Valley, to the geologically unique meteor-crater landscape of Ries and along the Danube, into the foothills of the Alps and the limestone mountains of Bavaria, the Romantic Road leads past myriad cultural sites from different centuries while giving you a glimpse of Germany's diverse natural landscape.

For the millions of visitors who travel the Romantic Road each year, it is a route that makes the cliché of charming and sociable Germany a reality. The stress of modern living seems to have had no effect in towns like Rothenburg ob der Tauber, Dinkelsbühl or Nördlingen, where the Middle Ages are still very much a part of the atmosphere. Yet they are dynamic towns that have understood the value of preserving the relics of their great past and carefully rebuilding those that were destroyed in World War II.

Plenty of culture awaits the traveller along this route. Alongside the well-known highlights there are numerous architectural gems that are also worth viewing if time permits. Some examples of these are Weikersheim Castle, the small church in Detwang with its Riemenschneider altar, Schillingsfürst Castle, the old town and castle at Oettingen, Harburg high above the Wörnitz Valley, the convent in Mönchsdeggingen, the churches in Steingaden and Ilgen, the little church of St Koloman near Füssen and other

King Ludwig II by Ferdinand von Piloty.

treasures along the way that have – perhaps luckily – not yet been discovered by the tourist hordes.

And yet the natural highlights should not be forgotten either as you cruise the Romantic Road to places like Würzburg, Rothenburg, Dinkelsbühl, Nördlingen, Donauwörth, Augsburg, Landsberg, the Wieskirche or Füssen, whose unique beauty is underscored by their rustic settings in romantic valleys, enchanting forests or impressive mountains.

Two of the most visited buildings on the route have been classified as UNESCO World Heritage Sites: the Würzburger Residenz and the Wieskirche, important baroque and rococo works. A trip to Munich, the charming and cosmopolitan capital of Bavaria, or to the Werdenfels region with its famous sights such as Oberammergau, Linderhof Castle, Ettal

Donauwörth with its Gothic parish church and 15th-century Tanzhaus. The once 'free city' has an incredible medieval old town.

The St Koloman Pilgrimage Church stands in a field against the backdrop of the Schwangauer Mountains.

Monastery and the twin villages of Garmisch-Partenkirchen enhances this aspect of your German experience.

For those who have the time, a visit to one of the numerous festivals that take place along the Romantic Road is highly recommended. Some are based around regional history like the Meistertrunk in Rothenburg ob der Tauber, a re-enactment of a drinking contest from the 17th century, or the Kinderzeche in Dinkelsbühl, a children's festival originating in the 17th-century Thirty Years War.

Classical music lovers should try to obtain tickets for the Mozart Festival in Würzburg, the Jeunesses Musicales concerts in Weikersheim, the Mozart Summer in Augsburg or the Richard Strauss Days in Garmisch. The Cloister Theater performances in Feuchtwangen are staged before a magnificent backdrop.

In addition to all this, there are festivals where anybody can participate, like the Free Town Festival in Rothenburg ob der Tauber or the Peace Festival in Augsburg. All these events take place in summer. Then of course there is the world-famous Oktoberfest in Munich, unmatched on the entire planet in its degree of debauchery and its sheer size. In winter the Christmas markets set up stalls that invite you to stroll, shop and drink a mulled wine with gingerbread cookies and other delicacies.

To sum it up, the Romantic Road has myriad attractions throughout the entire year, and takes you through the prettiest regions of Bavaria and Baden-Württemberg. Like no other road in Germany, it connects regional history with broad cultural landscapes, and brings the country's rich past to life.

The majestic throne room in Neuschwanstein Castle.

Johann Balthasar Neumann and Giambattista Tiepolo

Johann Balthasar Neumann was born in 1687 in Eger. Following an apprenticeship as a cannon founder, he went to Würzburg in 1711 to work in this trade. But his passion lay in architecture and he took every possible opportunity to learn more, supported by Prince-Bishop Johann Philipp Franz of Schönborn.

In 1720 he began his greatest work as royal architect of the Würzburger Residenz. Other important works by Neumann include the Würzburg Chapel, the pilgrimage churches in Vierzehnheiligen and Gößweinstein, Weißenstein Castle in Pommersfelden, Augustusburg Castle in Brühl and the Bruchsal Castle. When the master builder died in 1753 in Würzburg he was buried with military honours.

Top: Staircase in the Würzburger Residenz.
Bottom: Self-portrait of Tiepolo in the ceiling fresco over the staircase.

Most of the works of the Venice-born painter and etcher Giambattista Tiepolo can be found in Italy and in the royal castle in Madrid. Yet his principal works were the ceiling frescoes in the staircase and emperor's rooms of the Würzburger Residenz.
Tiepolo died in 1770 in Madrid. In the ceiling fresco of the staircase in Würzburg the painter immortalized himself and Neumann. Neumann is sitting upon a cannon.

The Romantic Road – The fascinating route between Würzburg and Füssen is lined with picturesque towns, forts, castles and priceless works of art. The road starts in the Main River Valley on its way through the charming Tauber Valley into the Wörnitz Valley and then crosses the Danube to follow the Lech towards the impressive Alps.

① Würzburg The Romantic Road begins with a sensation: the majestic Würzburger Residenz (1720), a baroque masterpiece. Despite the devastating bombings of 16 March 1945, which left even the most optimistic people with little to be optimistic about, this city on the Main offers many sights: the late-Gothic chapel of Mary and the rococo Haus zum Falken blend nicely on the market square.
The cathedral, which was consecrated in 1188, has unfortunately lost some of its character due to war damage. Near the baroque Neumünster lies the tranquil Lusamgärtlein, where the minstrel Walther von der Vogelweide lies buried. And all of this is dominated by the mighty fortress (13–18th centuries) on the Marienberg with its Main-Franconia Museum containing many works by Tilman Riemenschneider.

② Tauberbischofsheim This town in the Tauber Valley is famous for its history in the sport of fencing. It is distinguished by the Kurmainzisch Castle, whose storm tower is a masterpiece from the turn of the 16th century. The Riemenschneider School altar in St Martin's Parish Church is also worth seeing.

③ Bad Mergentheim The Old Town in this health resort is dominated by the Castle of the German Knights (16th century). Don't miss the baroque castle church designed by B. Neumann and François Cuvilliés. A small detour to see 'The Madonna' by Matthias Grünewald in Stuppach Parish Church is worth it.

④ Weikersheim Continuing through the Tauber Valley, Weikersheim invites you to visit its Ren-aissance castle and baroque gardens, which are among Germany's prettiest. The small former royal capital is surrounded by numerous vineyards.

⑤ Creglingen The Tauber Valley houses many of the works of the wood sculptor Tilman

Travel information

Route profile
Length: approx. 350 km (217 miles), excluding detours
Time required: 7–10 days
Start: Würzburg
End: Füssen
Route (main locations): Würzburg, Tauberbischofsheim, Bad Mergentheim, Rothenburg ob der Tauber, Dinkelsbühl, Nördlingen, Donauwörth, Augsburg, Landsberg, Schongau, Füssen

Traffic information: Drive on the right in Germany. There is a 420-km (261-mile) cycle path that runs parallel to the Romantic Road. More information about this route can be found on the

Internet at:
www.bayerninfo.de.

Information:
There is a lot of information available on the Romantic Road but no definitive site for the entire route. The following sites might help you get an idea of how to organize your trip.

General:
www.romantischestrasse.de
en.wikipedia.org/wiki/Romantic_Road

Town sites:
www.rothenburg.de
www.dinkelsbuehl.de
www2.augsburg.de
www.fuessen.de

Jakob Fugger, known in his day as simply 'the Rich', lived from 1459 to 1525. As financier and creditor to Habsburg emperors Maximilian I and Charles V, he almost had more power than the rulers themselves since they were dependent on him for capital. But as a man of faith Jakob Fugger also wanted to do something for his salvation, so with his brothers he founded the Fuggerei in 1516, the world's first social housing project.

People who found themselves in need through no fault of their own were provided with accommodation in one of the 67 buildings containing 147 apartments. The 'town within the

the triple-nave St Jakob Basilika houses his Holy Blood Altar. Further along the route heading south you'll cross the Frankenhöhe, the European watershed between the Rhine and Danube.

7 Feuchtwangen This one-time collegiate church, part Romantic, part Gothic, is worth a visit any time of the year. The marketplace has an attractive mix of bourgeois town houses.

8 Dinkelsbühl The main attraction of this town in the idyllic Wörnitz Valley is the perfect medieval town center with its town walls. Other highlights include the Deutsches Haus, a fabulous half-timbered house, and the St Georg Parish Church (second half of the 15th century). The town is more than 1,000-years-old.

9 Nördlingen Ideally you would approach fabulous Nördlingen from above in order to fully appreciate the nearly perfectly circular city center. Its original town walls have been masterfully preserved and its five town gates are still in use today. St Georg is one of the largest late-Gothic German hall churches, its icon being 'Daniel', the 90-m (295-ft) bell tower. On a clear day from the tower you can make out the rim of the Ries crater, espe-

cially towards the south-west, the south and the east.

10 Donauwörth This 'free town' developed from a fishing village on the Wörnitz island of 'Ried' at the confluence of the Wörnitz and the Danube. Most of its attractions are located along the main road, the Reichsstrasse: the Fuggerhaus from 1536, the late-Gothic Maria Himmelfahrt Parish Church, the Tanzhaus from around 1400, the town hall and the baroque Deutschordenshaus. The baroque church of the old Benedictine monastery Heiligkreuz is also worth visiting.

11 Augsburg 'Augusta Vindelicorum' was the original name given to Augsburg by its Roman founders. By the 16th century the 'free town' was one of the most important cultural and financial metropolises north of the Alps. The town hall was

1 View of the Würzburger Residenz from Residenzplatz with the Franconia Fountain (1894).

2 The town hall in Augsburg with its remarkably symmetrical facade and 78-m (256-ft) Perlach Tower.

3 View from 'Daniel' over the Nördlingen market square.

Riemenschneider. The altar in the Creglingen Herrgottskirche is among the most beautiful. The Old Town here is a lovely mix of half-timbered houses and medieval fortresses.

6 Rothenburg ob der Tauber This small town is synonymous around the world with German

medieval Romanticism. A walk along the well-preserved town walls offers an overview of the place and great views across the Tauber Valley. The market square is dominated by the town hall, which has Gothic and Renaissance wings. You can also view more works of Tilman Riemenschneider here. In fact,

Top: The apartment blocks of the Fuggerei, the oldest low-income housing estate in the world.
Bottom: The Fuggerei Museum, showing an original sleeping area.

town' even had its own church and a well. Indeed, the flats in the Fuggerei are still available to Augsburgers in need. And the rent is still one Rhine Taler as it was when it was built – the equivalent of 0.88 euros.

House rules still oblige the daily recital of the Lord's Prayer, Hail Mary and 'believe in God for the founder'. The site is run by the Royal Fugger Foundation. It is impressive that people in the 21st century profit from Fugger's prosperity in the 16th century.

The former imperial city of Rothenburg ob der Tauber has what is considered one of the best-preserved medieval Old Towns. Its countless half-timbered houses and labyrinthine alleyways are encircled by a 3-km-long (2-mi) city wall with forty-three towers and tower gates that transport visitors back to 14th-century

Germany. One of the most romantic spots in the city is the fork in the road at the Plönlein, near the Siebersturm tower and the low-lying Kobolzeller Gate from around 1360, on the south side of town.

1

Beer gardens

The Munich beer gardens were born from the need to store the beer in a cool place. To do this the brewers built large cellars, usually right next to their breweries. In order to protect them from the heat, they planted the area with chestnut trees. And because a rest in the shade of the trees

Beer garden at the Chinese Tower in the Englischer Garten.

became popular, they set up tables and benches.

King Ludwig I allowed them to serve beer there but the breweries were forbidden to sell food. And so it came about that the citizens brought their own snacks with them – often meatloaf, cheese, radishes and pretzels. This custom has survived to this day, although now many beer gardens serve snacks or even full meals alongside their beer.

So, Cheers!

Detour

Munich

There are many ways to discover Munich – by bike through the different quarters, a museum tour or shopping in Old Town. Or you can do it by theme.

The Munich of artists

Important paintings and sculptures are on display in the large and impressive Munich museums: the Alte and Neue Pinakothek, Pinakothek der Moderne and Haus der Kunst. The Lenbachhaus and the Villa Stuck show how successful artists lived in Munich at the end of the 19th century. The Lenbachhaus was designed by the architect Gabriel von Seidl in 1887 for the painter Franz von Lenbach and is a fantastic little museum with a wonderful variety of art and photography.

Today it is home to a municipal gallery and contains major works by the Blaue Reiter group. The Villa Stuck was designed by the aristocratic painter Franz von Stuck in 1897–98 and hosts a variety of exhibits. A wander into the heart of Schwabing is also part of any trip on the trail of artists – at the beginning of the 20th century, 'bohemian Munich' used to gather near Nikolaiplatz. Schwabing has been able to preserve some of its old flair.

Green Munich

For those who have had enough of the city it is also easy to find a bit of nature in this wonderful city. The first and foremost of the green oases is of course the Englischer Garten. At 4 sq km (1.5 sq mi) it is the world's

largest city park – even larger than Central Park in New York. Beyond the vast lawns and brooks that flow through this wonderful park there are a few architectural highlights as well: the Chinese Tower, the Monopteros and the Japanese teahouse. The best way to explore the Englischer Garten – and Munich in general – is by bike. Take a break along the way at one of the beer gardens.

The Isar River runs straight through Munich and on a summer day can be a nice way to cool down. To get there just walk to the Deutsches Museum. There are stony riverbanks to stroll and dip your feet in the water, and even a few places to jump right in!

In the center of town, just a few steps from Karlsplatz (also known as Stachus), is the old botanical gardens park. The of Nymphenburg porcelain statues spread around the park are beautiful. Take a tram to Nymphenburger Park, another oasis of relaxation where you'll find landscaped gardens and a baroque castle.

Munich theater town

For theater lovers, Munich offers interesting shows and fantastic theater architecture. The majestic Cuvilliés Theater is part of the former royal Residenz. François Cuvilliés designed the fabulously ornate rococo structure. A second building that attracts theater lovers and architecture enthusiasts is the Kammerspiele in the Maximilianstrasse. Architects Richard Riemerschmid and Max Littmann allowed their art-nouveau fantasies

2

3

free rein here in 1900–01. A lengthy restoration was finished recently.

Another building with a bit of history is the Prinzregenten Theater, which was badly damaged during World War II and not reopened until the renovation was completed in 1996. It was built in 1901 to celebrate the works of Richard Wagner. You can see international operas in the Prinzregenten Theater and in the classical National Theater. Munich also has a lively free theater scene, some of which moves around regularly.

1 Munich by night: View over the Frauenkirche with its imposing spires and the neo-Gothic town hall tower. To the far right is the Olympia Tower.

2 The Siegestor gate in Schwabing separates the two great avenues of Leopoldstrasse and Ludwigstrasse.

3 The Cuvilliés Theater is the city's oldest surviving opera house. Only the interior remains of the original building.

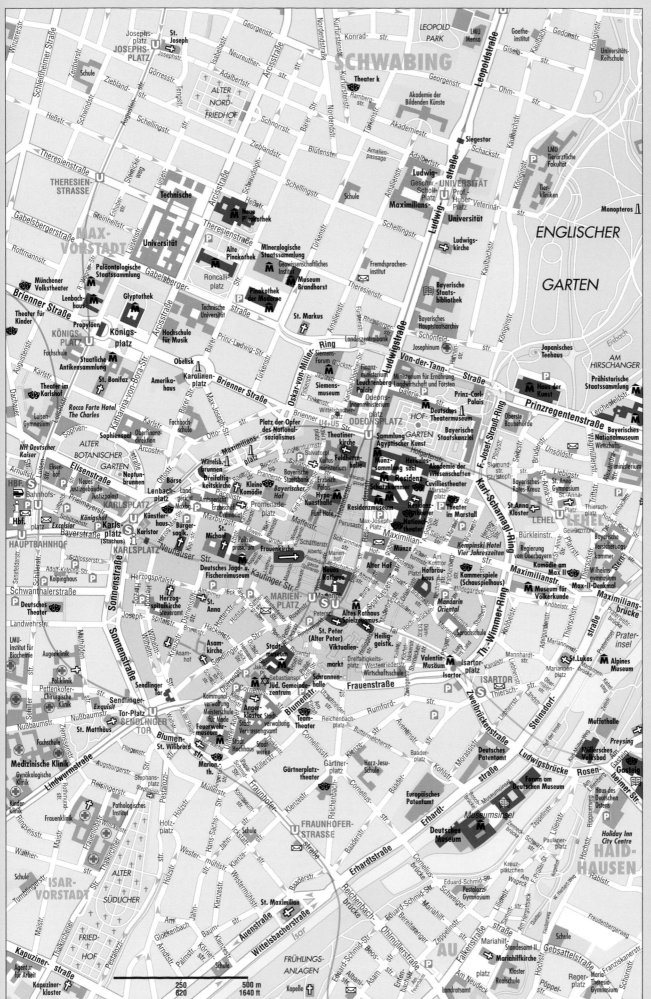

Munich

Munich exudes the magic of an old city that still manages to remain youthful, multicultural and very much itself.

Munich was originally founded by Guelph Heinrich the Lion, but the royal Wittelsbacher family controlled the city until 1918 and played a much greater role in its history. They are to be thanked for most of the city's monuments and works of art and the prettiest stretches of road. Ludwig I was particularly energetic, claiming that he wanted to build 'Athens on the Isar'. The Old Town lies between the Isartor, Sendlinger Tor, Karlstor and the Feldherrnhalle. Schwabing, the university and museum district, gives Munich its reputation for being a fun-loving and cultured city of the arts.

Attractions in the historic city center include Marienplatz with the new town hall from the 19th century, the old town hall from the 15th century and the baroque Mariensäule; the late-Gothic Frauenkirche with its two iconic spires; Asamkirche, a rococo masterpiece; the Residenz with the treasure chamber, Residenz theater (rococo) and court garden, which was expanded during the Renaissance; the National Theater; the baroque Theatinerkirche; the Renaissance church of St Michael's; the

Top: National Museum, on Max-Joseph-Platz.
Bottom: Nymphenburg Castle.

Hofbräuhaus and Viktualienmarkt and the bronze Bavaria on the Theresienwiese.
There is also the Nymphenburg Castle and Park and the Olympic Park from 1972. Don't miss the museums: Deutsches Museum, the Alte Pinakothek, the Neue Pinakothek, the Pinakothek der Moderne, Lenbachhaus, Glyptothek, Bayerisches Nationalmuseum; Stadtmuseum in the old Zeughaus and the Villa Stuck.

King Ludwig II

In 1864 Ludwig II ascended to the Bavarian throne. He soon withdrew into a dream world, where fantasies of Louis XIV's palace took over and Richard Wagner's operas influenced the architecture of the Linderhof, Neuschwanstein and Herrenchiemsee

King Ludwig II's *Night time Sled Ride*, by Rudolf Wenig.

castles. Wagner would not have been able to create the Bayreuther Festival had it not been for financial support from Ludwig. Yet the king's passions tore great holes in the state's finances and so he was certified insane in 1886. A few days later he drowned in mysterious circumstances in Lake Starnberg and thus became a popular myth.

built between 1615 and 1620 and was designed by Elias Holl, as was the Zeughaus of 1607. Stained-glass windows depicting the five prophets in St Maria Cathedral are among the oldest in the world. The streets are lined with many patrician houses like the Schaezler and Gignoux palaces. A few towers and gates (such as the Red Gate) are left over from the old town defenses. From Augsburg it is a quick half-hour drive to Munich (see pp. 130-131). From there you can take the Lindau motorway straight to Landsberg.

12 Klosterlechfeld This monastery was built on the site of an historic battlefield from the year 955. Elias Holl was the architect of this pilgrimage church, which was erected in 1603. It was based on the Pantheon in Rome.

13 Landsberg am Lech The first wall surrounding the Old Town between the Lech River and the Lech bluff was built in the 13th century. It included the Schmalzturm at the top end of the triangular main plaza, which is dominated by the town hall. The stucco facade of the

townhall was designed by Dominikus Zimmermann in 1719. The Bayer Gate, built in 1425, is part of the third wall and is one of the most beautiful of its kind in southern Germany. The four churches in Landsberg am Lech are especially noteworthy: the Gothic, late-baroque Maria Himmelfahrt; the Johannis-kirche by Dominikus Zimmermann; the Ursuline Convent Church by J.B. Gunetzrhainer (begun in 1740) and the Heiligkreuz Monastery church. Portions of the 15th-century Landsberg town wall are also quite well-preserved.

14 Altenstadt St Michael's is one of Upper Bavaria's most significant Romantic churches. It was built in the early part of the 13th century and is surrounded by a mighty protective wall. It houses frescoes from the 14th and 15th centuries as well as the 'Grosser Gott von Altenstadt', a Romanesque crucifix from around 1200. Because of its enormous size, it is one of the most important works of art of its type, radiating an expressive calm in the church.

15 Schongau The drive to Schongau follows the Lech

River through Claudia Augusta. The Gothic Ballenhaus of 1515 bears witness to its previous importance as a trading town.
The town walls with their battlements are still conserved in part, as are five towers and the Frauen Gate to the west (14th century). The Maria Himmel-fahrt Parish Church, which was remodelled by Dominikus Zimmermann in 1748, has frescoes by Matthäus Günter and is well worth a visit.If time permits, you can continue from here into the Werdenfels area to enjoy some

wonderful mountain scenery (see Detour, p. 134).

16 Rottenbuch The old Augustine canonical church in Rottenbuch was remodelled between 1737 and 1742 and now

shines with baroque cheerfulness. Stucco artist Joseph Schmuzer and painter Matthäus Günter were responsible for the wonderful interior. In this area it isn't hard to stumble over one charming baroque church after

another. Add the natural environment of the area and you've got a delightfully attractive combination for walks such as the one leading through the Ammerschlucht to Wieskirche.

17 Wieskirche One of this route's best highlights is the Wieskirche, built by Dominikus Zimmermann in 1745. Against the backdrop of the Trauchberge Mountains, the ceiling frescoes and a large part of the stucco here were done by Johann Baptist Zimmermann. The white and gold interior appears light and cheerful, as if music had been turned to stone. The Wieskirche near Steingaden is visited by hundreds of thousands of tourists every year. It is considered to be a complete work of art.

18 Hohenschwangau and Neuschwanstein These two royal castles are picturesquely set in a striking mountain scene. Crown Prince Maximilian gave Castle Hohenschwangau (12th century) a neo-Gothic facelift in 1833 – Ludwig II, the man behind nearby Castle Neuschwanstein, had spent part of his youth here in Hohenschwan-

gau. Neuschwanstein is the idealized image of a medieval castle with towers, battlements and majestic rooms.

19 Füssen The Romantic Road comes to an end in this small town on the Lech River. Don't miss the St Mang Monastery or the baroque St Magnus Parish Church. The medieval edifice here was also given a generous baroque remodel. The trompe l'oeil on the facade of the Hohen Schloss castle courtyard is particularly noteworthy. The facade of the Heilig-Geist-Spital Church (1748–1749) is sumptuously painted. To finish off the trip, how about a wild nature experience: take a gander at the nearby Lechfall.

1 Neuschwanstein Castle with the Allgäuer Alps as a backdrop.

2 The pilgrimage church of the Gegeißelter Heiland auf der Wies lies in the Pfaffenwinkel and is a UNESCO World Heritage Site.

3 The two-tiered choir in the Wieskirche with the painting of Christ in the center.

Dominikus Zimmermann

Born in 1685 in Wessobrun, this trained carpenter actually reached his masterful heights as a builder and stucco artist. He became rich and famous thanks to his trade and even became mayor of Landsberg am Lech

View from the ornate pulpit above the choir stalls in the Wieskirche.

from 1749 to 1754. In 1756 he moved into the house he had built next to his masterpiece, the Wieskirche near Steingaden, and lived there until his death in 1766. His other works include the Steinhausen Pilgrimage Church and the Frauenkirche in Günzburg.

The Oberammergau Passion Play

In 1633 a plague epidemic occurred during the Thirty Years War that inspired the people of Oberammergau to inaugurate this 'play of suffering, death and the resurrection of our Lord Jesus Christ', which they would perform every ten years.

The play was enacted for the first time in 1634 at the cemetery where the victims of the plague had been buried. This location was then used until 1820. In 1830 it was moved to its current venue where, in the year 2000, the play was performed for the 40th time.

Over 2,000 people from Oberammergau – all amateurs – took part in the most recent Passion Play, as actors, musicians, singers or stagehands. The story lasts around six hours and the text has been modified numerous times over the years. It is a regular source of dispute.

The people of Oberammergau are not always in agreement when it comes to the Passion Play. For example, the decision as to whether or not to allow married or older women to participate had

Top: Backdrop of the Passion Play in 2000.

Bottom: Crucifixion scene in Oberammergau.

to be decided by the Upper Regional Court. The result was that they are allowed to participate.

The current open-air stage was originally built in 1930 but was fully renovated between 1997 and 1999. As the theater was brought up to date with technology, the town can now host other events, such as operas, in the years between the Passion Plays.

Detour

Werdenfelser Land

A small detour from the Romantic Road takes you into the Werdenfelser Land, a magnificent mountain landscape with numerous romantic towns and villages. To take this detour, do not continue on to Füssen from the Wieskirche. Instead turn east towards Unterammergau and Oberammergau.

Oberammergau

The prettiest house in this picture-book village is the so-called Pilatushaus, which is richly decorated with paintings by Franz Seraph Zwink. The outside wall on the garden side of the house depicts the Judgement of Jesus by Pilate, hence the name of the house. Today Pilatushaus is home to a gallery and 'live-work studio' where you can watch local wood-carvers ply their trade. Oberammergau has been renowned for its wood-carving tradition since the Middle Ages and there are around 120 of them here. When the Passion Play is not scheduled you can take a tour of the theater.

Linderhof

After a short drive through the romantic Graswang Valley you reach Linderhof Castle, the only castle built by Ludwig II that was actually finished during his lifetime. The baroque construction is surrounded by large grounds containing other odd and interesting buildings, for example the Venus grotto, which was built to resemble the Hörselberg grotto in Wagner's *Tannhäuser*. Other sites include a Moorish Kiosk, a Prussian pavilion from the 1867 World Exhibition, which Ludwig II had majestically redecorated to his tastes, and the Hundinghütte, a perfect Germanic log cabin based on Wagner's Valkyrie.

Ettal Monastery

Standing in front of the majestic church of Ettal Monastery, you have the feeling of having stumbled across a little piece of Italy in the middle of the Bavarian Werdenfelser Land. The painting of Christ, the centerpiece of

the church, was donated in 1330 by Emperor Ludwig of Bavaria. There was initially a Gothic abbey here that was remodelled in 1710 in a majestic baroque style. The building, erected by the Italian Enrico Zucalli, was decorated with stucco by artists J.B. Zimmermann and J.G. Ueblherr, and a magnificent ceiling painting by J.J. Zeiller and M. Knoller. The layout, a twelve-sided central construction is unique in Germany and was actually necessary for the facade. The Benedictine monks had not only God in mind when they built their monestary, but also the awe it would inspire in its visitors.

Garmisch-Partenkirchen

In 1935 the two villages of Garmisch and Partenkirchen were joined into a market town. Many houses here are decorated with frescoes. Haus zum Husaren is a particularly well-known example. In Garmisch the old Gothic parish church of St Martin, with its

well-preserved frescoes, and the new baroque parish church of St Martin are worth visiting. In Partenkirchen the pilgrimage church St Anton, built on the Wank, the local mountain, dates back to the middle of the 18th century. Music lovers should head for the Richard Strauss Institute and the Strauss Villa, where the composer spent a large part of his life.

You shouldn't miss taking the gondola up to the Zugspitze (2,962 m/9,718 ft), Germany's highest mountain.

1 The golden cross marks the eastern peak of the Zugspitze, which offers a great panoramic view.

2 The north facade of Linderhof Castle reflected in the lake.

3 The town of Garmisch-Partenkirchen, one of the most renowned health resorts at the base of the Wetterstein Mountains.

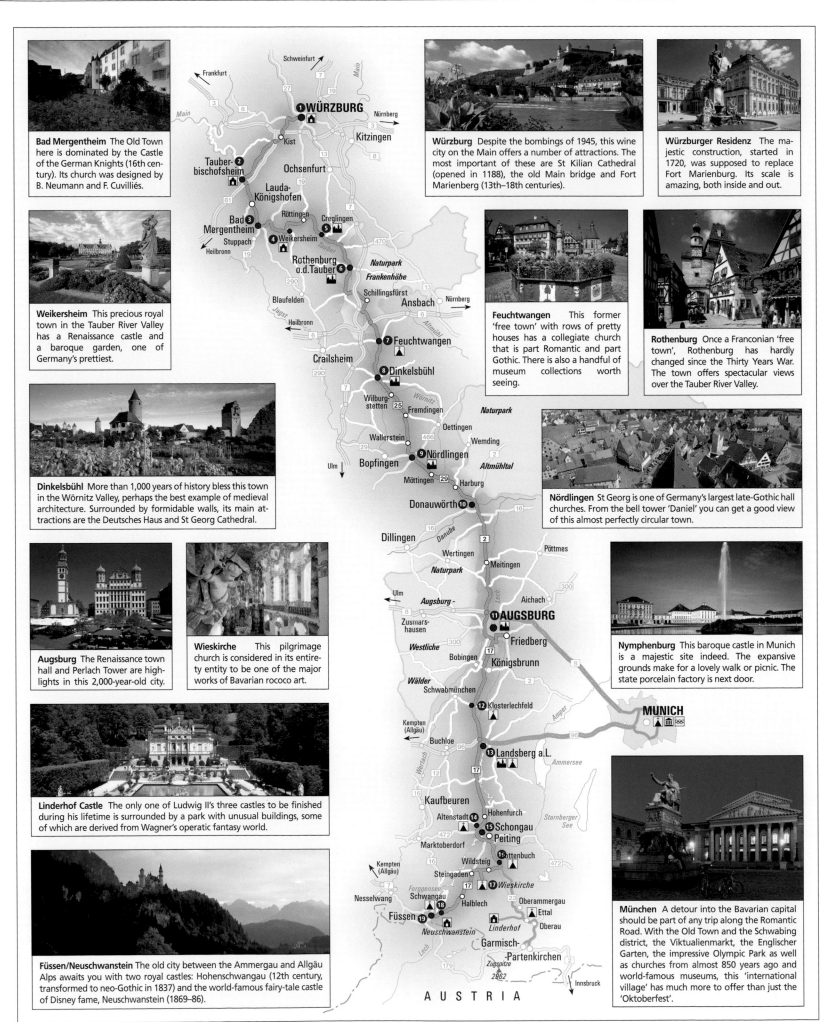

Bad Mergentheim The Old Town here is dominated by the Castle of the German Knights (16th century). Its church was designed by B. Neumann and F. Cuvilliés.

Weikersheim This precious royal town in the Tauber River Valley has a Renaissance castle and a baroque garden, one of Germany's prettiest.

Dinkelsbühl More than 1,000 years of history bless this town in the Wörnitz Valley, perhaps the best example of medieval architecture. Surrounded by formidable walls, its main attractions are the Deutsches Haus and St Georg Cathedral.

Augsburg The Renaissance town hall and Perlach Tower are highlights in this 2,000-year-old city.

Wieskirche This pilgrimage church is considered in its entirety to be one of the major works of Bavarian rococo art.

Linderhof Castle The only one of Ludwig II's three castles to be finished during his lifetime is surrounded by a park with unusual buildings, some of which are derived from Wagner's operatic fantasy world.

Füssen/Neuschwanstein The old city between the Ammergau and Allgäu Alps awaits you with two royal castles: Hohenschwangau (12th century, transformed to neo-Gothic in 1837) and the world-famous fairy-tale castle of Disney fame, Neuschwanstein (1869–86).

Würzburg Despite the bombings of 1945, this wine city on the Main offers a number of attractions. The most important of these are St Kilian Cathedral (opened in 1188), the old Main bridge and Fort Marienberg (13th–18th centuries).

Würzburger Residenz The majestic construction, started in 1720, was supposed to replace Fort Marienburg. Its scale is amazing, both inside and out.

Feuchtwangen This former 'free town' with rows of pretty houses has a collegiate church that is part Romantic and part Gothic. There is also a handful of museum collections worth seeing.

Rothenburg Once a Franconian 'free town', Rothenburg has hardly changed since the Thirty Years War. The town offers spectacular views over the Tauber River Valley.

Nördlingen St Georg is one of Germany's largest late-Gothic hall churches. From the bell tower 'Daniel' you can get a good view of this almost perfectly circular town.

Nymphenburg This baroque castle in Munich is a majestic site indeed. The expansive grounds make for a lovely walk or picnic. The state porcelain factory is next door.

München A detour into the Bavarian capital should be part of any trip along the Romantic Road. With the Old Town and the Schwabing district, the Viktualienmarkt, the Englischer Garten, the impressive Olympic Park as well as churches from almost 850 years ago and world-famous museums, this 'international village' has much more to offer than just the 'Oktoberfest'.

In the heart of Europe

Schönbrunn Palace in Vienna – a former Habsburg summer palace with

The Route of the Emperors: Berlin – Prague – Vienna – Budapest

On this journey along the ancient European transport and trade arteries of the Elbe, Vltava and Danube rivers, Europe presents itself in all its historical and cultural diversity. On the various riverbanks, cities like Dresden, Prague, Vienna and Budapest show off their abundant monuments of art, and everywhere along the route are palaces, castles and urban gems surrounded by unique natural scenery.

No emperor could ever have imagined that at the beginning of the 21st century you would be able to travel all the way from the Spree River (Berlin) to the Danube without any complicated border checks, particularly after the centuries of mini-states in the region and the tragic rift of the 20th century. What happened to the days when autocratic despots jealously erected border checkpoints and threw up 'iron curtains' to protect their territories? When the Viennese

knew nothing of Budweis or Bratislava, and to the people of West Berlin, Dresden might as well have been further away than the Dominican Republic? Gone indeed are those days. These days, the road is free to explore what is so close and yet still quite unfamiliar, and there really is a lot to discover.

Berlin, Germany's old and new capital, is its very own unique tourist cosmos. It would take weeks to see even a fraction of its museum treasures, its continuously

The landmark of Vienna: St Stephen's Cathedral.

changing skyline with so much contemporary architecture, an art and restaurant scene that is just as dynamic as that of any other cosmopolitan city, and its large green parks. On this route, however, Berlin is but the starting point of a fascinating journey across Europe.

In Brandenburg and Saxony, both core regions of German intellectual history, one highlight seems to follow the next. Potsdam, the royal residence of the Prussian kings, provides a magnificent overture to the Lutheran town of Wittenberg, to Weimar, the focal point of German classicism, and to the porcelain metropolis of Meissen, your next stops. Dresden is simply irresistible as a tourist destination. The capital of Saxony, which rose like the proverbial phoenix from the ashes (and from the floodwaters in 2002), enchants with its baroque and rococo

extensive gardens.

Charlottenburg Palace in Berlin, the summer residence of Sophie Charlotte, wife of Frederick I.

Hradčany Castle above the Charles Bridge, Prague's most famous bridge, on the Vltava River.

buildings and its art galleries. Music lovers flock to highlights like the Semper Opera, the Staatskapelle orchestra and the famous Kreuzchor choir.

Attempting to describe in words the exquisite beauty of Prague is often an exercise in futility. The views across the Vltava River towards Hradčany Castle are some of the most unforgettable city sights anywhere on earth. And just like one of Mozart's melodies, the magic hovering above the picturesque alleyways in the Small Quarter and around the Old Town Square will leave no soul untouched.

From the splendidly restored spa towns of Karlovy Vary and Mariánské Lázně, to Litoměřice, Hrad Karlštejn, České Budějovice and Český Krumlov – the number of five-star attractions in Bohemia is just incredible.

There are just as many amazing sights on the journey through Upper and Lower Austria – Freistadt, Linz, Enns, Grein and Krems, not to mention the Melk and Klosterneuburg monasteries.

Away from urban attractions, nature will also spoil you along the route – the heathlands of lower Fläming and Lower Lausitz, the sandstone mountains on the River Elbe, the Vltava Valley, the Bohemian Forest, the Mühl Quarter, Wachau and the Viennese Forest. Between city tours and museums you can tank up on oxygen everywhere on this trip. On top of that, you can always sample the tasty delicacies that the local cuisine has to offer.

An almost exotic piece of scenery awaits you at the end of your tour, east of Budapest across the River Tisza – the Hortobágy National Park, a real piece of the idyllic Hungarian Puszta.

East of Budapest's Matthias Church is the Halászbástya, the Fisherman's Bastion.

Detour

Following in Luther's footsteps

Wittenberg, the town of Luther and one of the focal points of German intellectual history, is located 30 km (18 miles) west of the impressive medieval town of Jüterbog. To get there, take the B187.

As a university town, the cradle of the Reformation and the 'workshop' of seminal humanists, Wittenberg was one of the intellectual centers not only of Germany in the 16th century, but of Central Europe. It was here that the influential scholar Martin Luther came in 1508 to hang his famous ninety-five Theses fulminating against the clerics on the Castle Church door, thereby kicking off the Reformation. Memories of him and of the theologian Philipp Melanchthon are still very much alive. In the house where

Wartburg Castle near Eisenach.

Martin Luther lived from 1508 to 1546, there is a museum on the history of the Reformation. The house where Melanchthon lived, studied and died is also open to the public, and is also the only private home remaining from the 16th century. The town church of St Mary where Luther used to give his sermons is also worth seeing.

Despite it being off your route, a visit to Wartburg castle is highly recommended. About 250 km (160 miles) from Dresden you'll find Eisenach, where Luther went to school. Southwest of Eisenach, atop the Wart Mountain, in the middle of the Thuringian Forest, is the medieval Wartburg Castle, built in 1150. It was in this castle that Luther translated the New Testament from Greek into what was then the first-ever German version of the bible in 1521–22. The rest, as they say, is history.

From the Spree in Berlin to the Danube in Budapest – a journey through the European heartland of old empires is now possible without border checks, through five countries from the German capital to the Hungarian capital. It will give you a comprehensive overview of its cultural depth and scenic beauty.

① Berlin (see pp. 140–141).

② Potsdam Our first stop outside the city limits of Berlin is Potsdam, the state capital of Brandenburg. It is famous mainly for the beautiful baroque and neoclassical buildings and its magnificent parks dating from the era of the Prussian kings. The best-known attraction of this town, which is 1,000 years old and has been partially declared a UNESCO World Heritage Site, is Frederick III's pompously decorated summer palace. Its park covers 300 ha (740 acres) and was designed by Lenné. It is an architectural gem in itself, full of statues and monuments such as the neighbouring park of Charlottenhof.

In Potsdam's Old Town, the Old Market with the St Nicholas Church and the former town hall, the Marstall stables, the Dutch Quarter and the old Russian colony of Alexandrowka are all worth a visit. Another must-see is the New Garden with its Marble Palace and Cecilienhof Castle.

From Potsdam, drive to the old town of Beelitz, and from there east to the B101 south towards Luckenwalde.

③ Luckenwalde At first glance, this medieval market town may seem dull and industrial, but its interesting historical center has been well preserved. Its landmark is the steeple of St Johannskirche with its Gothic frescoes and important altar statues. A former hat factory, built at the beginning of the 1920s by Erich Mendelsohn, is also remarkable.

④ Jüterbog This town, located 15 km (9 miles) further south at the edge of the lower Fläming heathlands, still has most of its original fortifications, including three beautiful gates. Sites here include the Liebfrauenkirche, the Nikolaikirche and the town hall, but the main attraction is really 5 km (3 miles) to the north: the ruins of the Cistercian monastery of Zinna, with important Gothic wall paintings.

Driving along the edge of the Lower Lausitz heathlands for

Travel information

Route profile
Length: approx. 1,100 km (700 miles), excluding detours
Time required: at least 2 weeks
Start: Berlin, Germany
End: Budapest, Hungary
Route (main locations): Berlin, Potsdam, Dresden, Prague, České Budějovice, Linz, Krems, Vienna, Bratislava, Komárno (Komárom), Budapest

Traffic information:
Drive on the right in all the countries on this trip. Speed limits are signposted. If not, 50 km/h (35 mph) in built-up areas, 90–100 km/h (55–60 mph) outside of towns. Autobahns in Germany have no speed limit un-

less otherwise indicated. In the other countries, 130 km/h (80 mph) is usually the limit. Roads are typically good in all five countries.

When to go:
Central Europe is typically quite warm in summer, cold in winter, and inconsistent in spring and autumn. Always have a rain jacket, regardless of season.

General travel information:
Here are some sites that may help get you started with planning:
wikitravel.org/en/Berlin
www.saxonytourism.com
www.czech.cz
www.aboutaustria.org
www.oberoesterreich.at
www.hungary.com

about 100 km (62 miles) on the B101, you will pass Elsterwerda and Großenhain before you reach the Elbe River and the porcelain center of Meissen.

5 **Meissen** In the 12th century, this 'Cradle of Saxony', where the German emperors founded the first settlement on Slavic soil, was a royal residence of the House of Wettin. Until the devastations of World War II it was able to preserve its medieval imprint, with the Gothic cathedral and Albrecht Castle representing both religious and worldly power. These are still visible from the historic Old Town with its market square and half-timbered buildings.

Today the town is more famous for its 'white gold' than for its 1,000 years of history. Home of Europe's first hard porcelain, Meissen has produced this valuable product since Augustus the

Strong founded the factory in 1710. It continues to be exported all over the world.

Past Radebeul, the route along the B26 takes us to Dresden, the Saxon state capital 25 km (16 miles) away.

6 **Dresden** This former elector's residence, which has also been praised as the 'Florence of Germany' or the 'Baroque Pearl', is doubtless one of Europe's major cultural centers. In 1485 it became the seat of the Albertinian government, and during the 17th and 18th centuries, Augustus the Strong and his successors turned it into one of the most magnificent baroque residence cities in all of Germany.

The devastating bomb raids in February 1945 were unfortunately fatal for the city, destroying the Old Town almost beyond recognition. However, many of the famous buildings have either

already been restored or are still works in progress, chief among them being the Zwinger, housing the 'Old Masters' art gallery; the Semper Opera; the castle; the Frauenkirche; the Japanese Palace; the Albertinum, housing the 'New Masters' art gallery; the Green Vault; and the Brühl Terraces high above the riverbank. You should definitely visit the important attractions in the surrounding area, above all Pillnitz Castle, Moritzburg Castle and the so-called Elbe Castles.

If you are not intending to do the detour to Weimar and Wartburg Castle, you now follow the B172 upriver from Dresden. You'll pass Pirna, with its picturesque center and the interesting Großsedlitz baroque gardens, and enter the spectacular Elbe Sandstone Mountains.

7 **Elbe Sandstone Mountains** In order to get the best possible

views of these bizarre sandstone rock formations, you would really have to do a boat trip on the meandering river. Barring that, you can get some magnificent views from the road. Most of the area is now included in the 'Saxon Switzerland' National Park, with its monumental plateaus. Königstein Castle and the bastion in the spa town of Rathen are quite popular. Bad Schandau is the starting point for hiking and climbing tours to

1 Dresden owes its nickname, the 'Florence of Germany', to its baroque cityscape, which includes the Semper Opera and the Frauenkirche Church.

2 View of Sanssouci Palace, Friedrich II's summer residence, considered a rival to Versailles.

3 Moritzburg Castle was used by the Elector Friedrich August II of Saxony as a hunting lodge.

Top: Goethe and Schiller in front of the National Theater in Weimar.
Middle: Weimar Castle, home to the state art collection.
Bottom: Lucas Cranach House on Weimar Market.

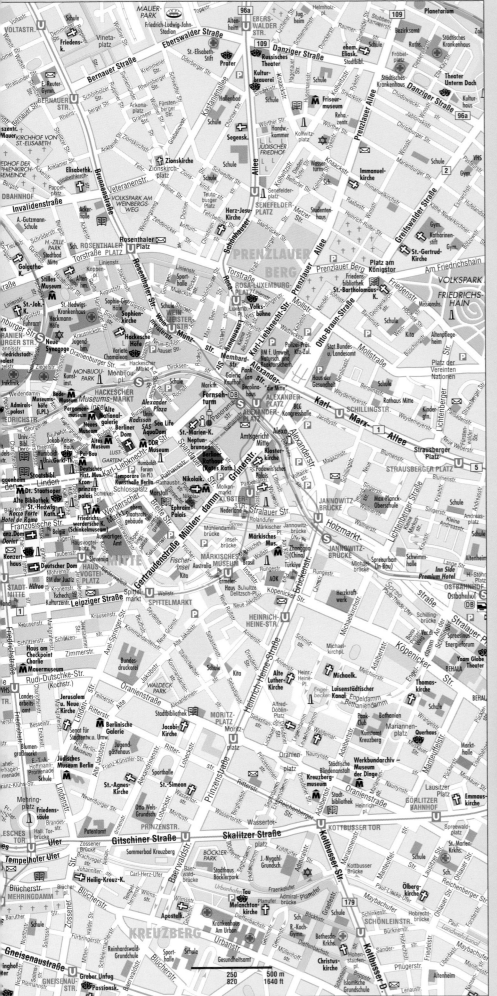

Berlin

Things have been changing incredibly rapidly in Berlin since the Berlin Wall came down in 1989. Now it seems the whole world knows that the lively German capital on the rivers Spree and Havel is a cosmopolitan city on a par with the likes of New York, Tokyo and London.

Berlin, whose history began in the 13th century, is not one of Germany's older cities. It was Prussia's rise to a great European power in the 18th century that made the capital significant. Berlin then became larger and more beautiful, finally being named the capital of the German Empire in 1871.

Under the National Socialists, terror and annihilation spread from the capital, but in 1945 it was reduced to rubble. After being divided in 1961, it went on to inspire the reunification of East and West Germany in 1989 with the opening of the Berlin Wall. Since then it has changed dramatically. Today, Berlin is still not one entity but rather a grouping of districts. In a way, however, this is a blessing – for it is the city's variety and its contrasts that define this metropolis.

In the Charlottenburg district visit: Kurfürstendamm, the city's principal shopping boulevard, the ruins of the Emperor William Memorial Church and the Zoological Gardens.

Outside the city center visit the Charlottenburg Castle and Park, the 'German Versailles', palace of the Prussian kings (built 1695–1746); the Egyptian Museum with Nefertiti; and the Museum Berggruen with great modern art. In the Tiergarten district check out Berlin's largest city park with Bellevue Castle and Park, the residence of the

tween Brandenburg Gate and Ernst-Reuter-Square.

West of city center go to Grunewald, Berlin's forest, the Wannsee, and the Dahlem Museum with an outstanding collection of ethnological exhibits.

In Kreuzberg see the ruins of Anhalt Station, the Martin Gropius Building, the Jewish Museum by Daniel Liebeskind, the German Technology Museum, and Victoria Park with Kreuzberg Memorial.

Berlin 'Mitte' (center): the Brandenburg Gate (1791); 'Unter den Linden' historic boulevard with a memorial of Frederick the Great; the New Guard by Schinkel; St Hedwig's Cathedral from the 18th century; the neoclassical public opera house, the baroque Zeughaus with the German Historical Museum; the Crown Prince's Palace (18th century); Humboldt University; the Gendarmes Market; the French and German Cathedral (18th century); the Schinkel Theater (1821); the Reichstag (Parliament) with glass dome by Sir Norman Foster; Potsdam Square's modern architecture, Museum Island with Pergamon Museum, the Old Museum (antiquities), the New Museum, the Old National Gallery, the Bode Museum and Lustgarten. Beyond that is the Berlin Cathedral (late 19th century), 'Alex' TV tower (365 m/1,198 ft), old Checkpoint Charlie with the Berlin

Brandenburg Gate, built in the late 18th century, is considered the most important landmark of Berlin and of the German Reunification.

German president; the Cultural Forum with the Philharmonic, the Museum of Musical Instruments, the Arts and Crafts Museum, a gallery with European paintings to the 19th century, the New National Gallery with 20th century art, the memorial to the German Resistance in the former Wehrmacht headquarters; the Road of 17 June with Victory Column (67 m/220 ft) be-

Wall museum; St Mary's Church (13th century); historic Nikolai Quarter; Märkisches Museum of the city.

In the Scheunenviertel go to the Hamburger Bahnhof Gallery (modern art), the New Synagogue with its center on the history of Berlin's Jewish community, and the Hackesche Höfe from 1906, once the largest working and living compound in Europe.

Detour

Karlovy Vary and Mariánské Lázně

Just over 40 km (25 miles) south of the German-Czech border, near Ústí nad Labem, follow the N13 west via Most and Chomutov to the Karlovy Vary, formerly the German Karlsbad ('Charles Bath'). Legend has it that it was actually Emperor Charles IV himself who found the hot salty springs in the area when he was out hunting deer in the 14th century.

Top: Town center of Karlovy Vary.
Bottom: Health spa facilities at Mariánské Lázně.

Over the next 500 years, Bohemia's most famous and most glamorous spa town developed around these springs, with European elites from politics, art and society all making their way here to see and be seen. After fifty years of drabness during the Communist era, a glittering re-birth followed in 1989. Most of the Wilhelminian buildings, including the Mühlbrunn Colonnades, the town theater and the Grandhotel Pupp, now radiate again with all their former glory.

From the densely settled banks of the Tepla River, take the turnoff on-to the N21 just outside Cheb and drive just 60 km (37 miles) to the second legendary spa town of Mariánské Lázně ('Mary's Bath'), where Goethe wrote his 'Marien-bad Elegies' in 1823. Its stucco fa-cades were completely restored in the original Schönbrunn imperial yellow. Especially magnificent are the 120 m (131 yds) of cast-iron colonnades.

the Schrammsteine rocks and through Kirnitz Valley up to the Lichtenhain waterfalls.

8 Děčín The rocky sandstone scenery continues in all its grandeur here on the Czech side of the border. From the town of Hřensko, for example, there is a beautiful 4-km (2.5-mile) walk to the spectacular Pravčická Gate stone formation. An ideal start-ing point for trips into the park area is Děčín, where the famous 'Shepherd's Wall' towers 150 m (492 ft) over the river.

On the way to the Ústí nad Labem region you'll find another magnificent rock formation, crowned by the ruins of Strekov castle. From here you can take a detour heading west on the N13 via Most and Chomutov to the renowned spa towns of Karlovy Vary and Mariánské Lázně.

9 Litoměřice At the conflu-ence of the Eger and the Elbe (Labe), where the Bohemian hills flatten out towards the plains, is the ancient town of Litomûfiice surrounded by vineyards and or-chards. Its Old Town is among the most beautiful in Bohemia. At its center is the market square, which is around 2 ha (5 acres) in size. Don't miss the 'Kelchhaus', the town hall and St Stephen's Cathedral on Cathedral Hill.

About 4 km (2.5 miles) to the south, Terezín invokes memories of darker times. In World War II, the German occupation was not

good to this town, which was originally built by Joseph II as a fortification against Prussia. There was a large concentration camp here.

10 Mělník High above the junc-tion of the Vltava and Elbe Rivers is the much-visited town of Mělník, with its market square surrounded by beautiful stately houses. The town's most eye-catching sight, however, is its castle, a cherished possession of the local nobility for more than 1,100 years. The terrace of the castle restaurant has some fantastic views over the idyllic river valley.

From Mělník it is 40 km (25 miles) to Prague, the fairy-tale city on the Vltava River, and only 30 km (18 miles) to what is considered Bohemia's most famous castle.

11 Prague For detailed infor-mation see p. 143.

12 Karlštejn After 16 km (10 miles) on the R4, you head westbound at Dobřichovice for around 40 km (25 miles) until you get to this monumental castle perched majestically on a limestone rock 72 m (236 ft) above the Berounka Valley. It was built in the mid 14th centu-ry by Emperor Charles IV as his royal residence and a depository for the treasures. Its highlight in terms of art history is the Chapel of the Cross in the Great Tower with its gold-plated arches.

Back on the R4, you go to Příbram, which is located 50 km (31 miles) south-west of Prague, just off the main road.

13 Příbram This industrial and mining town, where silver has been mined since the 14th cen-tury and uranium since 1945, would not be worth mentioning if it were not for one of the Czech Republic's most visited

pilgrimage destinations at its south-eastern edge – the Church of Our Lady of Svatá Hora with its baroque additions.

South-east of Příbram, not far from the B4, are two imposing castles on the bank of the Vltava River, which actually forms a reservoir more than 100 km (62 miles) long in this area. One of them is Zvíkov Castle, built in the 13th century on a tower-ing rock outcrop; this former royal residence is worth a visit for its Chapel of St Wenceslas and the late-Gothic frescoes in its Great Hall. Orlík Castle, owned by the Schwarzenberg family for

1 View over Prague's Charles Bridge with the Old Town bridge tower and the church of St Franciscus in the background.

2 Hrad Karlštejn was used as a summer residence by Charles IV.

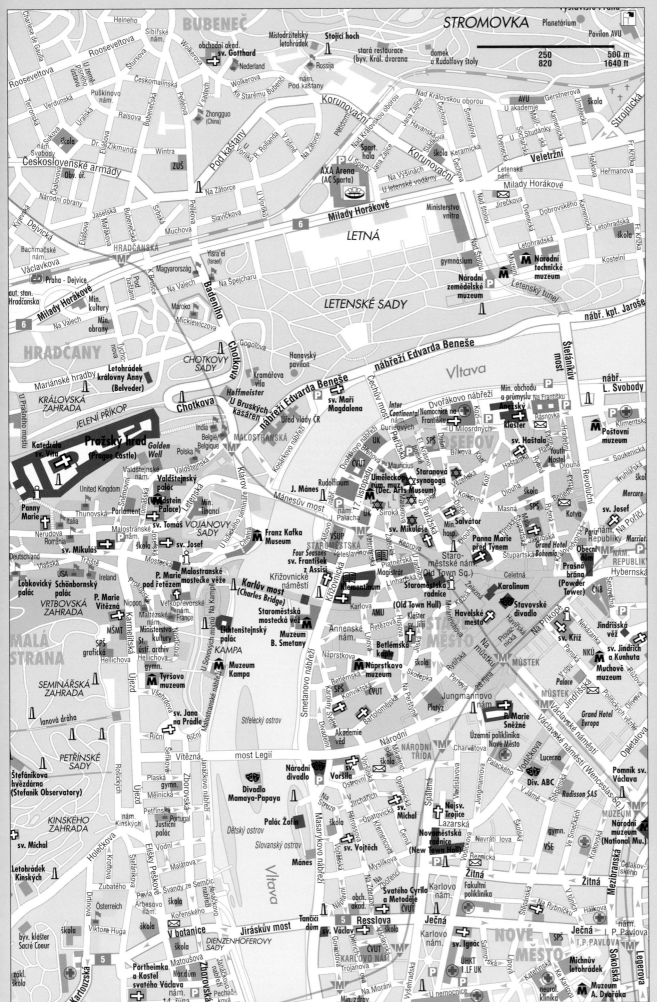

Prague

For centuries, the 'Golden City' has been an important intellectual and cultural center, characterized by unique and beautiful architecture throughout the entire city.

Although Prague escaped destruction in World War II, time has still taken its toll on the city's buildings over the centuries. Thanks to an expertly managed restoration, however, Prague can once again show off the magnificence of more than 1,000 years of history.

The Czech people can be proud of their capital, which is the former residence of Bohemian kings and Habsburg Emperors. Hradčany Castle, where they used to reside, provides you with the best views of this masterpiece of historical urban architecture – the entire city is designated a UNESCO World Heritage Site.

In the Old Town go see the Altstädter Ring with rows of historic houses; the baroque Týn Church and Jan Hus Memorial; the art-nouveau Representation House; St Wenceslas Square with buildings from the 19th and 20th centuries; the Gothic town hall with its astronomical clock; and the late-Gothic gunpowder tower.

In the Castle Quarter on the Hradčany visit the castle (royal residence since the 10th century); the Golden Alleyway; the King's Palace with Renaissance Hall; the St Veit's Cathedral, with relics from

Town hall and Týn Church, Prague.

St Wenceslas, the national saint; St George's Basilica (12th century).
In the Josefov district see the Old Jewish cemetery, the Old New Synagogue, and the Pinkas Synagogue.
In the Lesser Quarter visit the Charles Bridge (14th century); St Nicholas Church, Prague's most important baroque church and the Waldstein Palace of the commander Wallenstein.

The castle of Český Krumlov

There are many good reasons why the castle of Český Krumlov, located high above the Vltava River, is a UNESCO World Heritage Site – it comprises forty buildings and palaces with a total of 320 rooms and halls, as well as five courtyards and castle gardens measuring 7 ha (17 acres), with some very interesting detailing.

The castle buildings, erected on different rock formations, are connected by a three-storey viaduct with a canopied three-level walkway. The entrance is dominated by the tower, painted in 1590. The rococo castle theater dating from 1767 still has its original, and still functional, stage engineering. This open-air stage in the castle park is unique because it is the audience – not the stage – that turns when there is a change of scene.

The gigantic castle of Český Krumlov rises up high above the city.

The Masque Hall is also worth seeing. It is painted with figures from polite society and the *Commedia dell'Arte* (completed by J. Lederer in 1748). Also worth mentioning are the four bears guarding the entrance to the compound.

more than 700 years and reconstructed in neo-Gothic style in the 19th century, captivates with its richly decorated interior.

⑭ Písek On your way south on Road 20 you'll cross the Otava River after 50 km (31 miles). The well-manicured center of this little town used to be an important stopping point on the so-called Golden Path, the trade route between Prague and Passau. Deer Bridge recalls the town's importance as an ancient traffic hub. The bridge, which was built in the second half of the 13th century, is Bohemia's oldest stone bridge.

⑮ České Budějovice Another 50 km (31 miles) on, you come to České Budějovice, which is world-famous for its breweries. Since Ottokar II founded the town in 1265, its center has been the market square. The most dramatic sight on this huge square, which covers an area of 133 by 133 m (145 by 145 yds) and is surrounded by arcades on all sides, is the Samson Fountain. From the viewing platform of the steeple (72 m/236 ft), you can easily spot the other sights of the town – the baroque cathedral of St Nicholas, the town hall, the Dominican Monastery and the Church of Our Lady, as well as the Salt House.

Around 10 km (6 miles) to the north, the battlements of Hluboká Castle appear on the horizon. Considered 'Bohemia's Neuschwanstein', this lavishly furnished castle was also owned by the Schwarzenberg family until 1939.

⑯ Český Krumlov Upriver from České Budějovice, it is another fifteen minutes by car along the Vltava River to the famous town of Český Krumlov. UNESCO certainly had its reasons for declaring this gem of more than 700 years as a World Heritage Site. Its location on both sides of a narrow hook in the river is incredibly scenic, and the labyrinthine alleyways of the Old Town and the Latrán with its shingled roofs are almost unsurpassably quaint. Highlights of every city tour are the Gothic St Vitus Church and the Schiele Center. The painter Egon Schiele worked and lived in Český Krumlov in 1911.

The defining attraction of the town, however, is its castle. It is Bohemia's second-largest, and is surpassed only by the Hradčany in Prague. It was originally owned by the Rosenberg family for 300 years, then by Emperor Rudolph II before landing in the hands of the counts of Schwarzenberg in the early 18th century. A guided tour of the castle shows you the living quarters, gallery, chapel, the Masque Hall with frescoes and a fine rococo open-air theater. It has been a designated UNESCO World Heritage Site since 1992.

Your next stop is Linz, the capital of Upper Austria, and from there our route follows the northern banks of the Danube (B3) towards Vienna.

18 **Linz** (see sidebar on the right).

19 **Enns** This attractive town near the Danube dates back to a Roman fort called Lauriacum and is one of the most ancient towns in Austria. Its landmark is the city's free-standing tower, which measures 60 m (197 ft). Antiquity is brought to life in the Museum Lauriacum, which is located on the town square. On the left bank of the Danube, some miles north of Enns, lies the market town of Mauthausen. A monument in the local granite quarries commemorates the fact that the Germans ran a concentration camp here, where

1 View of Český Krumlov castle and the Old Town.

2 Samson Fountain on the square in České Budějovice, also known as Budweis of Budweiser fame.

3 The old cathedral on Linz's central square.

Linz

In the last couple of decades, Linz, which had long endured a bad reputation as an unattractive industrial town, has radically polished up its image. Contemporary art, using the most modern media and technology available, now defines Linz's cultural identity.

The Lentos Museum of Modern Art, the Ars Electronica Festival and the Design Center all pay their tribute to modern times. Every year, the bigwigs of computer art turn up for the Ars Electronica Festival, and a multimedia wave of sound and light descends on the city.

Beyond all this modernism is also the neatly restored historic center around the town square, which includes the Renaissance Landhaus (house of the provincial government), the castle, the Church of St Martin, the parish church and the old and new cathedrals, as well as a number of interesting galleries and museums.

An integral part of any sightseeing trip should also be a boat ride on the Danube with the Linz City Express, or a journey up the Pöstlingberg mountain on the ancient mountain railway.

17 **Freistadt** Right across the border in Austria you'll come to the next delightful example of medieval town planning. The center of the northern Mühl District, developed under the Babenberg Dynasty, quickly

became the most important trading post between Bohemia and the Danube. To this day it has kept its 14th-century fortifications. Take a stroll through the narrow alleyways between the Linz Gate and the Bohemia Gate,

past the town's handsome mansions and the huge town square to the church. Make sure not to miss the Mühl District House in the castle, which has a superb collection of reverse glass painting.

The Melk Abbey – a spiritual center on the Danube

As far back as AD 976, Margrave Leopold I had established Melk Castle as his residence. Over the years, his successors equipped it with valuable treasures and relics. Then, in 1089, Margrave Leopold II handed the castle over to the Benedictine monks of the nearby Lambach Abbey. To this day, the monks continue to live at

The monastery library, decorated in shades of brown and gold, houses roughly 100,000 books.

the abbey according to the Rule of St Benedict.

Over the course of centuries, the monks not only collected but also produced valuable manuscripts for the abbey's vast library. In many areas of the natural and social sciences, as well as in music, the members of the Melk Abbey have chalked up some outstanding achievements during the establishment's illustrious history.

To this day, the monks continue to be active in the areas of counselling, economy, culture and tourism. Ever since it was founded, Melk Abbey has been an important spiritual and religious center in Austria.

around 100,000 people lost their lives.

Around 30 km (18 miles) down-river, at the start of the 'Struden-gau', a stretch of river that is feared for its strong currents and dangerous sandbanks, is the little town of Grein. It originally became wealthy because local mariners would guide voyagers through the dangerous waters. It also has a very delightful rococo theater. Close by, the castle ruins of Klam are also worth seeing.

20 Ybbs This traditional market and toll location marks the beginning of the next section of the valley, the so-called 'Nibelungengau'. North of the power station (1958), the historic castle of Persenbeug keeps vigil over the valley. The castle remains the property of the Habsburg family and can only be viewed from outside.

A little further east, there are two reasons for a short excursion up to Maria Taferl, a Lower Austrian market town with no more than a thousand inhabitants. In addition to the baroque pilgrimage church, whose exuberant hues and shapes are truly beguiling, it is mainly the view from the terrace that is so captivating – the entire Nibelungen-gau of Burgundian legend sprawled out at your feet. In

good weather, you can even see large parts of the Eastern Alps.

21 Melk A real baroque icon salutes us from a rock outcrop 60 m (197 ft) above the south bank across the river, around 10 km (6 miles) east of the pilgrimage church. It's the Benedictine abbey of Melk with a church, two steeples and a facade of more than 360 m (393 yds) – undoubtedly one of the most magnificent of its kind in the world. This religious fortification, which was built in the

early 18th century, impressively symbolizes the euphoria among the clerics and the nobility after their dual triumph – over the Reformation and over the Turks. There is exuberant splendour everywhere in the edifice: in the Emperor's Wing with the Emperor's Gallery, which is nearly 200 m (219 yds) long; in the marble hall with its frescoes by Paul Troger; in the vast library with approximately 100,000 volumes; and also in the church, with ceiling frescoes by Johann Michael Rottmayr.

Back on the northern riverbank, the B3 takes us past the Jauerling Nature Park via Aggsbach, Spitz, Weißenkirchen and Dürnstein to the spectacular transverse valley of the Wachau River. Many of these places have an interesting history, like the Aggstein Castle on a rock outcrop high above the Danube. It is said that a series of unscrupulous men abused the castle's position on the river to rob passing Danube boats and charge exorbitant tolls. The ruin of Dürnstein tells the tale of the

Wachau

The transverse valley of the Danube, between Melk and Mautern and Emmersdorf and Krems, is the very image of a central European cultural landscape. No surprise, then, that it has been listed as a UNESCO World Heritage Site.

Blessed with a sunny climate and surrounded by picturesque, painstakingly terraced vineyards, it is just as famous for its good wines and fruit, especially its apricots, as for its history and stone memorials.

Danube, it takes just under thirty minutes to get to Tulln.

24 Tulln This town on the Danube, which started out as a Roman fort called Comagenis, has an impressive architectural ensemble of parish churches and a former charnel house. A visit to the mighty salt tower with its Roman core is also worth doing, and can easily be combined with a stroll along the riverside promenade. A museum with around ninety original paintings commemorates Egon Schiele, the town's beloved son and groundbreaking expressionist.

1 The Melk Abbey, founded c. 1000 AD, received its distinguished baroque makeover between 1702–39.

2 The icon of Wachau – the baroque monastery at Dürnstein contains a Renaissance castle, a former Augustinian monastery and a former Clarissan nunnery, all forming a unique ensemble on the bank of the Danube.

3 High above the Danube, not far from Aggsbach, is the Schönbühel Castle dating from the 12th century.

4 Impressions of Wachau – Weißenkirchen, the local wine-growing center, with its mighty Gothic parish church.

Top: Aggstein Castle ruins, Aggsbach. Bottom: A lovely vineyard near Weißenkirchen.

In addition to the historic treasures of Krems, Stein, the old Kuenringer town of Dürnstein and the monasteries at Göttweig and Melk, the many small towns with their Gothic churches, covered arcades on the vineyards and medieval castles are among the highlights of a drive through this region 'wrapped in the silver band of the Danube'.

Must-sees along the northern river bank are Spitz with the Museum of Navigation, St Michael with its bizarrely decorated filial church, Aggsbach, the wine-growing towns of Weißenkirchen, Joching and Wösendorf, and last but not least, Dürnstein with its monastery and legendary castle.

capture of Richard the Lionheart and Blondel, the singer, who recognized him.

22 Wachau (see sidebar right).

23 Krems This town is located on the exact spot where the Danube trade route meets one of the main routes between the Alpine foothills and the Bohemian Forest, and where traders and mariners as far back as the early Middle Ages came to exchange their goods. This mercantile center at the eastern en- trance to the Wachau is not only one of the oldest, but also one of the most beautiful towns in the whole area. As a way into its re- stored alleyways, take the Steiner Tor ('Stone Gate'). From here, there is a circular walk across Corn Market to the Dominican Church, which hous- es the wine museum, and on to Gozzoburg on the High Market. From the gunpowder tower you have a beautiful view onto the more modern districts, the port and the Danube over to Gött- weig Monastery. On the way back you go along the road, past such architectural gems as the Bürgerspitalkirche, Gögl House and the town hall.

At the western end of Krems is the town of Stein. Must-sees here are the Minorite and St Nicholas Churches and a num- ber of magnificent buildings as well as a former monastery which now houses the 'House of Lower Austrian Wines'.

Driving along the Wagram, a steep slope where lovely vine- yards drop colourfully and abruptly down towards the

Detour

Lake Neusiedl

This steppe lake in the northern Burgenland region, which is 30 km (18 miles) long and a maximum of 2 m (6.5 ft) deep, is not called the 'Sea of the Viennese' for nothing. In summer, it is a paradise for water sports. For the rest of the year. It is a Mecca for amateur ornithologists who can observe a large number of rare birds in the reed belt around the lake that is 1–3-km wide (0.6–2-miles). From Illmitz, you can take regular guided tours through the national park by bike, horse-drawn carriage or on horseback.

The areas in the west, north and south of Lake Neusiedl (its south-eastern corner is part of Hungary)

Top: Rust, a famous wine-growing town on Lake Neusiedl.
Bottom: Burgenland farmhouse.

are among Austria's most famous wine-growing regions. Villages in the area like Rust, Mörbisch, Donnerskirchen, Breitenbrunn or Podersdorf are worth seeing because of their picturesque town centers and neat farmhouses with stork's nests crowning their chimneys. From mid July to late August, operettas are regularly performed on the open-air stage in Mörbisch as part of the Lake Festival.

You definitely should not miss the 'excursion within the excursion' here to Eisenstadt, where you can visit the palace of the Esterházy princes and the mausoleum of Joseph Haydn in the Bergkirche church.

25 Klosterneuburg This small town right outside Vienna on the southern bank of the Danube is world-famous thanks to its Augustinian monastery. The monumental building was built in the early 12th century by the Babenberg Duke Leopold III and soon after donated to the order. For centuries, it was the scientific center of the country. The dazzling emperor's rooms, the emperor's staircase and the marble hall are the primary attractions. Don't miss the enamel Verdun Altar by Nicholas of Verdun in Leopold's Chapel. The monastery also houses the largest religious library in the country, a museum and a treasury.

26 Vienna (see p. 149). After ample time in Vienna, the capital of Austria, you can take an interesting excursion to Lake Neusiedl. Your best option is the A4 to Neusiedl on the lake's northern shore. Alternatively, carry on along the Danube.

27 Carnuntum Around 35 km (22 miles) east of Vienna, where the 'Amber Road' (between the Baltic Sea and the Mediterranean) and the East-West Route along the Danube meet, are the Roman remains of Carnuntum, south of the river. Nowhere else in Austria have archaeologists found such rich ancient heritage. The excavation site, officially made into an 'archaeological park' in 1996, comprises the whole of the civilian town with its network of ancient walls and streets, a reconstructed Diana Temple and a long piece of the original Roman Limes Road (Border Road). A little further away are the ruins of a palace, baths, an amphitheater and the Heathen's Gate. Many of the rich findings are on display in the Museum Carnuntinum in Bad Deutsch-Altenburg.

28 Bratislava When the Turks conquered Budapest in the middle of the 16th century and kept it for nearly 150 years, Bratislava, now the capital of Slovakia, was called Pozsony and was the capital of free Hungary until 1848. In modern times it was behind the Iron Curtain until 1989. Since then, it has not only forged closer ties to the Western world, but also undergone a radical beautification and rejuvenation.

The sins of socialist town planning cannot be undone, and the prefabricated tower blocks in Petržalka on the southern bank of the Danube, for example, will continue to be an eyesore for quite some time. Staré Mesto, by contrast, the largely car-free Old Town, has done itself up rather nicely. Its most important sights are St Martin's Cathedral, the archbishop's palace, the Slovak National Gallery, the National Theater and Museum and the castle residing above the river. East of Bratislava, Road 63 (E575) takes you down into the Danube Plains (Podunajsko), which are completely flat and extremely fertile. During the summer months fresh fruit and vegetable stands are everywhere.

During World War II, this region was particularly hard hit. Reconstruction led to local towns looking very much alike. This route, however, now takes us away from the Danube to the south – back through Austria to Fertőd in Hungary.

29 Fertőd/Esterházy Palace Around 5 km (3 miles) east of Fertő-tó (the Hungarian name of Lake Neusiedl), we come to Fertőd and Esterházy Palace. The Esterházys are an old Hungarian dynasty from which many politicians and military men have come.

30 Győr This large city has an important port on the Danube and is worth seeing for its 12th-century cathedral which was given a baroque makeover in the 17th century.

31 Komárno/Komárom Located where the River Váh meets the Danube, the town has always been of the utmost strategic importance. The Romans even had a fort here called Brigetio. In the course of the 19th century, the Habsburg Dynasty turned the town into

1 The classical Austrian Parliament Building in Vienna (1874–84) with the Pallas-Athene Fountain.

2 The ceremonial hall, the main hall of Vienna's National Library, was begun by Johann Bernhard Fischer von Erlach in 1719; his son finished it.

3 Esterházy Castle in Fertőd was the royal residence of the Esterházy princes and the workplace of the composer Joseph Haydn.

Vienna

Located on the 'beautiful blue Danube', the Austrian capital has a uniquely charming atmosphere and seems still to radiate the Old World feel of the Dual Monarchy.

Vienna, the old royal city and former center of the 'multicultural' Habsburg Empire, has architecture and art treasures from all eras of its long history. As a result, you will need some time to explore this city, especially if you want to catch a bit of its famous atmosphere, which is largely communicated through the pleasures of food and drink. Your best bet is in the 'Heurigen' wine taverns, in the coffee houses or on the traditional 'Naschmarkt' (literally 'Nibbles Market').

Definitely visit the Stephansdom with Romanesque, Gothic and late-Gothic sections, a richly ornate facade and precious interior; the Hofburg, until 1918 the imperial residence with treasure chamber, emperor's rooms and palace chapel; the Art History Museum with its collection of European paintings; and the baroque Josefsplatz with National Library; the Gothic Augustinerkirche with its baroque Capuchin crypt of the Habsburg emperors; the Spanish Riding School; the Karlskirche, the most beautiful baroque building in Vienna; the Museum of Applied Art; Belvedere

Top: View over Vienna's sea of houses and the Stephansdom cathedral (right). Bottom: Karlskirche by Fischer von Erlach.

Castle with Lower Belvedere (baroque museum) and Upper Belvedere (19th- and 20th-century paintings); Schönbrunn, a baroque Versailles imitation with park, Gloriette classical arcades with a beautiful view of the castle and town. The historic center and Schönbrunn Palace are UNESCO World Heritage Sites.

Budapest by night – Left: The west side of the city is dominated by the castle district with the palace (a domed structure rebuilt in 1945), St. Matthew's Church (rebuilt 1874–1896), and the Fisherman's Bastion from 1905. Foreground: The Elisabeth Bridge was the longest bridge in the world when

1897–1903. Center: The most famous Danube bridge of the city, however, is the suspension bridge built between 1839–1849. Two towers support the 380-m-long

Puszta – the central European steppe

Driving east from Budapest on the M3 motorway and then from Füzesabony on the N33, you reach Hortobágy, Hungary's oldest national park. Here, ancient prairie lands stretch out between the Tisza and Debrecen Rivers, the last vestige of the puszta landscape that once covered the entire steppe.

Crossing this grassland by car (it was designated a UNESCO World Heritage Site in 1999), you can hardly see anything but flat, monotonous

Top: The Puszta's landmarks are draw wells and herdsmen's huts. Bottom: Field of sunflowers in the Puszta.

countryside. Therefore, in order to see it in all its beauty you need to go exploring on foot, by bike, by boat or by horse-drawn carriage. Right next to the famous Bridge of Nine Arches in Hortobágy Village, a museum takes you back to the everyday life of the Puszta herdsmen, a lifestyle that has all but disappeared. You can encounter old animal breeds in this area such as grey cattle, woolly boars and Raczka sheep.

Riding performances and bird watching or a visit to a pottery and a meal of the local savoury pancakes round off your visit.

a 'city of fortifications' like no other in the monarchy. After Ferenc I, King of Hungary, had found shelter from Napoleon's army in Komárno in 1809, it was made the central defense post of the Habsburg Empire.

Ever since the Treaty of Trianon (1920) marking the Danube as the border of the realm, the city has been divided into two parts. The former Old Town on the northern shore is now part of the Slovakian town of Komárno. On the Hungarian side, three fortifications are an interesting attraction for military history enthusiasts.

Monostor, the largest of the forts with 640 rooms and 4 km (2.5 miles) of underground shelters, is sometimes nicknamed 'Gibraltar of the Danube' and there are guided tours around it. The Igmánd fort, which is significantly smaller, houses a museum with findings from Roman times.

32 Tata This spa town at the bottom of Gerecse Hill gives off an atmosphere of cosiness and charm with its lakes and complex labyrinth of rivers and canals. But its location and its history have not been kind to the 'City of Water' – for 150 years it was situated on the border between the territories of the Habsburgs and the Ottoman Empire, which resulted in consistent large-scale devastation of its buildings. But every cloud has a silver lining. In around 1730, the Esterházy princes, then rulers of the town, initiated the reconstruc-

tion of the Tata, whose myriad baroque architectural ensembles shape the town to this day. Be sure to visit the ruins of the castle, built in the 14th century and later expanded into a magnificent Renaissance Palace by Matthias Corvinus. Don't miss Esterházy Castle and the former synagogue, which houses about 100 plaster-of-Paris copies of famous antique sculptures.

Halfway between Tata and Budapest – you can see it from the M1 motorway – is an apogee of Hungary's Romance architecture reaching high up into the sky. The Zsámbék Church itself actually collapsed in the middle of the 18th century, along with the adjacent Premonstratensian priory. Even as ruins, though, the colossal dimensions of the building are truly spectacular.

33 Budapest The Magyar metropolis has around two million inhabitants on a location where the Romans had already founded a town called Aquincum. Like many others, the two medieval communities of Ofen and Pest were devastated by the Mongols in 1241.

After the reconstruction, Ofen became Hungary's most important city, but was overtaken in the early 19th century by its sister town of Pest. The two cities were finally united in 1872. In the early 20th century, Budapest was considered the 'Paris of the East', a reputation it is still hoping to regain despite the devastation of World War II and more than four decades of Soviet rule.

The first thing on a long list of things to do just has to be the castle mountain. It is here on this limestone rock, nearly 1.5 km (0.9 miles) long, above the right bank of the Danube that the country's historical heart has been beating ever since the first king's castle was constructed upon it by Béla IV. Combining the Matthias Church, the Fisherman's Bastion and the castle, which houses several first-rate museums, this quarter has some of the most important sights in the city. And there are also some unforgettable panoramic views down to the city and to the river. The view from the neighbouring Gellért Mountain is just as scenic. The majority of the city's sights are located on the left bank of the Danube, in the Pest district. Once you leave behind the narrow Old Town center, the cityscape is typified by extensive Wilhelminian ring and radial roads.

You can visit St Stephen's Basilica, the National Opera, the National Museum, the Grand Synagogue and, directly by the river, the large market hall and the even larger houses of parliament. Out in the city forest are Vajdahunyad Castle, the Széchenyi Baths and the Museum of Fine Arts.

A must-see is, of course, the baroque palace in Gödöllő 30 km (18 miles) north-east of the city center, where Emperor Franz Joseph I and his wife Elizabeth ('Sisi') lived.

1 Budapest – the Houses of Parliament on the banks of the mighty Danube. In the foreground is the city's suspension bridge.

2 Hungarian grey cattle in Hortobágy National Park.

Sanssouci The rococo ensemble, whose name means 'Carefree', is the most visited attraction in Potsdam, capital of Brandenburg, where you can take a carefree stroll through the summer residence of Friedrich II.

Berlin The old and new German capital has become even more attractive since the Berlin Wall came down. Located on the Spree and Havel rivers, it has a lot of greenery, vibrant nightlife and myriad cultural highlights both in the former east and in the west. Pictured is the Charlottenburg Palace.

Meißen The center of this porcelain town and 'Cradle of Saxony' has a medieval atmosphere. Above it is the towering cathedral and the Albrecht Castle.

Wartburg Legend has it that the castle was founded in 1067. Located at the edge of the Thuringian Forest it was probably the site of the German minstrels' contest. Luther translated the bible into German here.

Dresden Bauwerke wie der Zwinger und die Semperoper sowie kostbare Sammlungen wie die Gemäldegalerie Alte Meister haben Dresden zu einer führenden europäischen Kulturmetropole gemacht.

Sächsische Schweiz Ob bei einer Wanderung oder vom Elbdampfer aus betrachtet: Die bizarren Tafelberge, Felsnasen und Schluchten des Elbsandsteingebirges nahe Dresden sind faszinierend. Das Gebiet ist zum Großteil Nationalpark.

Prague The Czech capital is located on the Vltava River and has an unusual skyline. Hradčany Castle, Charles Bridge and the art-nouveau buildings of this 'Golden City' are unique. This photograph is of Týn Church.

České Budějovice The center of this world-famous city of breweries and beer is the market square with Samson Fountain.

Karlovy Vary This spa town on the Eger River has some healing springs as well as historical and modern spa facilities.

Český Krumlov Its location on a curve in the Vltava River, its dreamy Old Town, and the huge castle on the hill make the Bohemian town of Krumlov a real gem.

Wachau The forest and wine-growing area of Wachau extends from Melk to Krems – a transverse valley of the Danube that is 30 km (18 miles) long.

Melk The Benedictine abbey high above the Danube is baroque architecture in all its perfection.

Vienna The Austrian capital is always worth a visit. The number and quality of the sights in this metropolis on the Danube is simply overwhelming. Pictured here is the Austrian Parliament Building.

Fertőd, Esterházy Palace The 'Hungarian Versailles' in Fertőd used to belong to a family of princes. There is even an opera house and a puppet theater inside.

Budapest One of the landmarks of the Hungarian capital is the mighty suspension bridge (1839–1849). The list of further sights in the metropolis on the Danube is a long one – from Fisherman's Bastion and the crown of St Stephen in the National Museum to the neo-Gothic Houses of Parliament and the terrific art-nouveau bath houses.

The Alps

Switzerland's most photographed icon: the Matterhorn, at 4,478 m (14,692 ft).

Spectacular mountain scenery between Lake Geneva and the Salzburg region

Looking at any map, it is immediately clear that the Alps form a sort of backbone for the European landmass. This route will take you on a journey of exploration through every facet of this complex terrain, from the shores of Lake Geneva to a world of rock and ice around Zermatt and Grindelwald, from glamorous winter resorts to the fairy-tale scenery of the Dolomites, and from the Grossglockner High Alpine Road to the Salzburg region and the birthplace of Mozart.

For many, the Alps are the "most beautiful mountains in the world". All told, this high Central European range covers an area of 200,000 sq km (77,200 sq mi). The western section alone is home to about fifty peaks rising over 4,000 m (13,124 ft). There are many more in the 3,000 and 2,000 m (9,843 and 6,562 ft) range – nearly 2,000 in Austria alone.

The range features the jagged limestone spikes of the Dolomites, bulky gneiss and granite massif, and lower layers made of sandstone, slate and flysch. It stretches from mighty Mont Blanc, at 4,810-m (15,782-ft) the tallest peak in the Alps, to the gentle knolls of the Wienerwald (Vienna Woods).

Famous rivers such as the Rhine and the Rhône, the Po and the Save, the Drava and the Inn originate in the Alps, and vast lakes such as Lake Constance, Lake Geneva and Lake Lucerne are all nestled in their valleys. Immense waterfalls like the ones in Krimml, Lauterbrunnen,

Salzburg: Residenzplatz with fountain.

Gastein or on the Tosa thunder down granite faces, while glistening glaciers continue to hold their own in the highest and more remote areas – though the effects of climate change can be seen.

The main charm of the area lies in the juxtaposition of contrasts; the Côte d'Azur is just a stone's throw from the foothills of the Maritime Alps, and the glaciers of the Bernese Oberland are not far from the Wallis (Valais) wine region. An hour's drive will take you from the rocky peaks of the Dolomites to the cypress-lined lanes of Lago di Garda, and it wouldn't take much longer to get from the icy cold cirque lakes of the Hohe Tauern to the warm swimming lakes of Carinthia.

The mightiest mountain ranges in the world, such as the Himalayas or the Andes, might have more exalted reputations and are more sparsely populated,

The distinctive hallmark of South Tyrol: the Three Peaks, in the Sexten Dolomites. The highest peak rises to 2,999 m (9,840 ft).

Evening ambience in Salzburg: Looking out over the Salzach to the Old Town with Hohensalzburg Fortress.

but what sets the Alps apart is indeed their human dimension. Extreme mountaineers do not need permits, visas or porters to indulge in their passion. When it comes to infrastructure, accommodation and dining, people seeking a more comfortable experience will be delighted by the ease of travel and the plethora of options. Even the desire for a more urban environment can be satisfied in cities such as Grenoble, Bolzano and Innsbruck. And yet those seeking temporary refuge from civilization will also find more than enough solitude on hikes, climbs or just relaxing in a meadow all day long – all without bumping into another single person.

However, what makes the journey along the backbone of Europe so fascinating is not just the spectacular scenery, but rather the distinctive and diverse cultural traditions that seem to change as often as the landscape, and the undeniable natural charm of the Alps. Rural architecture, customs and handicrafts form an "alpine heritage" that is once again being enthusiastically promoted in many places – without necessarily being motivated by tourism.

Aside from the dominant peaks like the Matterhorn, the Jungfrau, the Eiger, the Mönch, Bernina, Marmolada, the Tre Cime di Lavaredo and the Grossglockner, mention should certainly be made of the fruit and wine growers along the Rhône or Adige, the anonymous architects of the Engadine or East Tyrolean manors, the thousands and thousands of alpine dairy farmers and dairymaids, and the creators of all the frescos, sgraffiti, shingle roofs, and carved altars in the village churches, castles and manors.

Rustic farmhouses are still common in the high valleys of Switzerland.

Lake Geneva

Lake Geneva is the largest lake in the Alps, its elongated crescent shape covering roughly 584 sq km (225 sq mi) between the Savoy and Waadtland (Vaud) Alps and the Jura Mountains. Sixty percent of it is in Switzerland and forty percent to France. The lake is 372 m (1,221 ft) above sea level, 72 km (45 mi) long, 14 km (9 mi) across

Chillon Castle on the banks at Montreux

at its widest point, and 310 m (1,017 ft) deep. It is fed by the Rhône River, which rises at a glacier.

On northern shore are the La Côte and Lavaux territories, long known for their particular beauty. Picturesque fortresses, vineyard towns and quaint old villages abound in this very popular holiday region, set against the backdrop of gently rolling hills and steep mountains scattered with grapevine terraces.

The most famous towns on the lake, apart from the big cities of Geneva and Lausanne, are Coppet, Nyon – a garrison town going back to the time of Julius Caesar, Rolle, Morges, Cully, the upscale resort towns of Vevey and Montreux, and Villeneuve near the Rhône Delta.

The most famous towns along the French southern banks of the lake include Thonon-les-Bains and the ritzy thermal spa resort of Evian-les-Bains, internationally renowned since the end of the 18th century and the home of Evian water.

Recommended vista points for enjoying the magnificent panoramic views of the lake and landscape include Signal de Bougy (above Rolle), Signal de Sauvabelin (above Lausanne), the Grand Roc at Meillerie and, east of Lausanne, the Corniche de Lavaux, which connects a series of reputable wine-growing towns amidst the vineyards high above the lake.

A ride onboard one of the eight old paddle boats, some of which are still steam-operated, is a great way to see the lake.

Those exploring the Alps will quickly discover the charms of this historically significant and culturally diverse region: from elegant resort towns to quaint hamlets, and from the Mediterranean-like shores of Lake Geneva to remote mountain stations among the high glaciers and peaks.

1 Geneva Your journey begins at the south-westernmost point of Switzerland at the end of Lake Geneva, known by French-speaking locals as Lac Léman. Geneva is nestled among the Jura and Savoy Alps and sits on one of the lake's many bays. The city's most famous landmark is the Fontaine du Jet d'Eau, which shoots its water up to 145 m (476 ft) into the air.

The "Protestant Rome", where Jean Calvin preached his rigorous reform ideas some 450 years ago, and Henri Dunant founded the Red Cross in 1864, is today a truly international city. One-third of its residents are foreigners, and 200 international organizations, including the United Nations (UN) and the World Health Organization (WHO), are based here.

But apart from the diplomats, the expensive clocks and fancy cigars, there are also a number of other attractions: St Peter's Cathedral with its archaeological burial site, the adjacent Place du Bourg-de-Four, the ornate Museum of Art and History, the Palais des Nations – today UN headquarters – and the monument to native son, Jean-Jacques Rousseau.

Follow the A1 along the northern shores of Lake Geneva toward the next Swiss city on the lake, Lausanne.

2 Lausanne The metropolis of Vaud is a reputable university and trade fair city as well as the home of the International Olympic Committee. Tucked in among exclusive residential neighborhoods and spanning

Travel information

Route profile
Length: approx. 1,150 km (715 mi), without detours
Time required: at least 12–14 days
Start: Geneva
Finish: Salzburg
Route (main locations):
Geneva, Lausanne, Zermatt, Interlaken, Andermatt, Chur, St Moritz, Merano, Bolzano, Cortina d'Ampezzo, Lienz, Heiligenblut, Werfen, Salzburg

Traffic information:
Motorways in both Switzerland and Austria require vignettes that you can buy at most petrol stations. French motorways require tolls.

Roads in all countries are well maintained. Check weather conditions for higher passes.

Travel weather:
www.alpineroads.com
www.weatheronline.co.uk

Information:
Here are some websites to help you plan your trip.
Switzerland:
www.myswitzerland.com/en
www.graubuenden.ch/en
www.nationalpark.ch
South Tyrol:
www.suedtirol.info (top EN)
Austria:
www.austria-tourism.info
www.hohetauern.at/english
www.nationalpark.at

Detour

Bern

Just 150 years after it was founded in the late 12th century, Bern had already become the mightiest city-state north of the Alps. It has been the national capital since the Federal State of Switzerland was created in 1848.

The Old Town, situated neatly on a sandstone shelf on a bend in the Aar River, a tributary of the Rhine, continues to radiate the comfortable aura of entreched middle-class wealth. Its cobblestone lanes reflect the grid-like pattern of many medieval settlements and are lined by tightly packed, shingled guild and burgher houses. The center is a UNESCO World Heritage Site characterized by eleven historic fountains and the 6 km (4 mi) of covered arcades that invite you to

Schützenbrunnen fountain and the clock tower in Old Town Bern.

take a pleasant stroll even on rainy days among the fashionable clothing, delicacies, handicrafts and antiques shops.

Bern's most famous landmark is the Zytglogge, clock tower from the 13th century, and the late-Gothic St Vincent's Cathedral with its ornate main entrance. The Protestant Church of the Holy Spirit provides a stunning example of Baroque architecture, and the Bundeshaus, or Federal Assembly Building, from the mid-19th century, symbolizes Bern's function as the political and diplomatic center of Switzerland.

Art lovers will find the Art Museum and its Paul Klee Foundation interesting. The so-called Bärengraben, or Bear Pit, is actually inhabited by some of Bern's furry animal mascots and is a curious place indeed.

Valley through Martigny and Sion to Visp, where the road turns right into the Matter Valley. Park the car in Täsch about 30 km (19 mi) further on, as the most famous Swiss mountain town can only be reached by railway, bus or taxi.

4 Zermatt and Matterhorn
The most renowned village in the Wallis region owes its fame to the 4,478-m-high (14,692-ft) Matterhorn, the primary icon of the Swiss Alps. The region's popularity was developed predominantly by daring mountaineers from the British Isles in the mid-19th century who became the first to conquer the imposing four-sided pyramid in 1865, led by locals. Today, 3,000 people

1 Swiss mountain paradise: the Matterhorn at 4,478 m (14,692 ft) with its pyramid-shaped peak.

2 View of Geneva's boardwalk from Lake Geneva.

3 The "Top of Europe" funicular station on the Jungfraujoch at 3,445 m (11,303 ft) provides a spectacular view over the Aletsch Glacier.

4 Oberhofen Castle (12th century) was built right on Lake Thun.

several hills, the Cité, or Old Town, is best accessed by the funicular railway from the port district of Ouchy. The main attraction there is the early-Gothic cathedral with its rose window, while the most interesting of the many museums are the Art Brut Collection and the Pipe Museum.

3 Vevey and Montreux
These two resort towns form the center of the wine-indulged "Vaud Riviera" and have enjoyed international prominence since the early 19th century.

Vevey, where the first Swiss chocolate was made at the start of the 19th century, is also the home of Nestlé, the largest food-

stuffs corporation in the world. Montreux is known primarily for the annual TV awards show, the "Golden Rose", its world-famous jazz festival and the Château de Chillon, located on the shores of the lake just 3 km (2 mi) to the south-east of town. Heading away from the lake, your route follows the Rhône

Furka-Oberalp Railway

Whether you take the St Gotthard, Grimsel, Furka or Oberalp Pass, the 2,000-m-high (6,562-ft) passes are generally closed off for four to six months during the winter in every region of the Alps, which forms part of the watershed between the Rhine and Rhône. During this time, if you want to avoid masses of snow and the risk of avalanches, you can load your car

One of the many viaducts of the Furka-Oberalp-Bahn.

onto the carriages of the Furka-Oberalp Railway. While you let the breathtaking mountain scenery pass by from your compartment, the narrow-gauge locomotive handles the transport. Loading ramps are located in Oberwald-Realp for the Base Tunnel beneath the 2,431-m-high (7,976 ft) Furka Pass. To conquer the Oberalp Pass (2,044 m/6,706 ft), you will have to wheel your vehicle onto the tracks in Andermatt or Sedrun/Camischolas.

flood the "summit of all European summits" every summer. In the town itself, a number of old houses attest to the pioneer days. Particularly worth seeing are the Alpine Museum, and the 150-year-old Hotel Monte Rosa. A ride on the Gornergrat Railway, the highest cog railway on the continent, is unforgettable. In forty minutes, it climbs up to 3,089 m (10,135 ft) over a stretch of 10 km (6 mi) before you continue another 400 m (1,312 ft) by cable car. The mountain station provides a 360-degree panoramic view of twenty-nine peaks in the 4,000 m (13,124 ft) range.

5 Brig Back in the Rhône Valley, follow the river upstream to the capital of the Oberwallis region. Once an important trading hub for goods being transported over the Simplon, Furka and Grimsel passes, Brig experi-

enced its heyday in the 17th and 18th centuries.

The main attraction in Brig is Stockalper Castle, an extensive late-Renaissance complex whose imposing towers and golden onion domes can be seen from afar. In the suburb of Glis, it is worth paying a visit to the lavish St Mary's pilgrimage church.

From here, head west again along the Rhône as far as Höge Steg, then take the car on the train through the 14.6-km-long (9-mi) Lötschberg tunnel. From Kandersteg you will go through Thun, along the northern shore of Lake Thun, past Oberhofen Castle and into the town of Interlaken.

It is especially worthwhile making a detour beforehand to the Swiss capital of Bern, roughly 25 km (16 mi) from Thun. You can easily explore the perfectly preserved Old Town on foot.

6 Interlaken Situated between Lake Thun and Lake Brienz on the "Bödeli", the Aar River floodplain, Interlaken was named after the inter lacus monastery, founded in the 12th century. It has long been one of the cornerstones of Swiss alpine tourism as the starting point for excursions into the Jungfrau region. The Höhenweg, lined with hotel mansions from the turn of the 20th century, affords breathtaking panoramic views of the snow-capped peaks to the south.

7 Grindelwald A 20-km (12 mi) detour will take you to Grindelwald, even closer to the Jungfrau region, the first alpine landscape to become a UNESCO World Natural Heritage Site, in 2001, as home to forty-seven peaks over 4,000 m (13,124 ft) and the Great Aletsch Glacier.

The Grindelwald climatic spa resort is encircled by the three mighty peaks of the Eiger at 3,970 m (13,026 ft), the Wetterhorn at 3,701 m (12,143 ft) and the Schreckhorn at 4,078 m (13,380 ft). It has been the greatest tourist draw in the Bernese Oberland for over 150 years. Don't miss a ride on the Jungfrau railway from the Kleine Scheidegg pass through Eigerwand and Mönch to Europe's highest train station – the Jungfraujoch at 3,454 m (11,333 ft).

From Grindelwald, it's back to Interlaken and then south along Lake Brienz over the Grimsel Pass (2,165 m/7,103 ft) and the Furka Pass (2,431 m/7976 ft) to Andermatt.

8 Andermatt The highland resort town of Andermatt is at the junction of the north-south route between Lake Lucerne

Detour

Lower Engadine

The charm of this valley landscape lies in its originality, sprawling as it does at the feet of the Silvretta cluster. Zernez, at the confluence of the Inn and Spöl rivers, was almost completely destroyed by fire in 1872 and has barely any of its historic buildings left, but it is the starting point for many wonderful hikes into the Swiss National Park (172 sq km/66 sq mi) – the first of its kind in Europe (established in 1909) and the only one in Switzerland.

Guarda and Ardez are the most beautiful towns of the Lower Engadine. Both come under strict protection as listed historic monuments and consist of irresistibly quaint Engadine houses. Often, they are hundred-year-old estates with artistic sgraffiti gazebos, carefully paneled parlors and sleeping quarters behind walls more than a yard thick.

The valley widens after Ardez, which is also the site of a tourist center, Scuol, which is dominated by Tarasp Castle. The town was called the "Queen of the Alps Bathing Towns" until 1915 because of its twenty healing wells, but it fell into a bit of a slumber, only to be

**Top: Tarasp Castle in Scuol
Bottom: Winter in Ftan in the Lower Engadine**

and St Gotthard, where Wallis (Valais) turns into the Upper Rhine Valley region. It has a lovely rococo church and a carefully designed valley museum, and is an ideal starting point for hikes and mountain tours. For travelers, however, it is primarily a traffic hub. Continuing east, you have to cross the Oberalp Pass (2,044 m/6,706 ft), before skirting the Upper Rhine tributary to Flims. The Furka-Oberalp railway is a nice alternative to the passes.

9 Flims This spa resort, where Rhaeto-Romanic dialects are still spoken, is situated on a ledge in a sunny high valley that owes its existence to a massive landslide during prehistoric times. It comprises the old Flims-Dorf center and the new Flims-Waldhaus hotel complex. The town and its romantic surroundings offer a variety of sporting activi-

ties in summer, and in winter it joins Laax and Falera to form a vast ski area known as the "White Arena".
Before heading to the mountains of Graubünden (Grisons) take the 10-km (6-mi) detour at Reichenau to Chur.

10 Chur This cantonal capital, which obtained its Roman town charter in the 3rd century and was the first diocesan town north of the Alps in the 4th century, puts off many newcomers with its unsightly strip of high-rise buildings. But a charming Old Town with a number of historic treasures lies hidden behind this unfortunate blemish. The most important of these are the St Mary's Cathedral and museum, the Winegrowing and Rhaetian museums, the Bündner Art Museum with works by Chur painter, Angelika Kauffmann.

11 Via Mala Back in Reichenau, you route initially heads upstream along the Lower Rhine. Over the millennia, this tributary cut a 6-km-long (4 mile) and up to 600-m-deep (1,969 ft) gorge into the rock. The romantic Via Mala is best experienced from the old road built in the early 19th century (a branch off the A13 about 1 km/0.6 mi beyond Rongellen).
At the south end, in Zillis, pay a visit to St Martin's Church for its painted wooden ceiling.
Back in Thusis, the route now heads to Tiefencastel, in the Albula Valley, and then through parts of the very steep Albula Pass (2,321 m/7,615 ft) into the Upper Engadine region.

12 St Moritz This glamorous resort town in the heart of the Upper Engadine is considered the cradle of winter tourism and,

along with Davos, the most upscale address in Graubünden. It hit the world stage as the two-time host of the Winter Olympics (1928 and 1948). Located at the gateway to unique lake scenery (Lake St Moritz, Lake Silvaplana,

1 Even beginners can enjoy some impressive hikes from Grindelwald below the north face of the Eiger.

2 Schreckhorn and Finsteraarhorn, both over 4,000 m (13,000 ft), reflected in the Bachsee above Grindelwald.

3 The Kleine Scheidegg at the foot of the Jungfrau Massif is a popular ski area in winter.

4 Lake Silvaplana, at a height of approximately 1,800 m (5,906 ft), is the largest of the three Upper Engadine lakes and is a popular windsurfing spot in summer.

brought back to life in the 1990s by the opening of an ultra-modern spa and wellness resort.
Further east, the valley narrows again, and becomes wilder and more remote. A few small villages, such as Sent, Ramosch and Tschlin, nestle into the narrow terraces before the road and river cross over the Austrian border beyond Martina, near the ravine at the Finstermünz Pass.

Funes Valley is one of the most beautiful in the South Tyrol, surrounded by the impressive mountain scenery of the Geisler range, the western part of the Puez-Geisler Nature Park. At 3,025 m (9,925 ft), the Saas Rigais is the highest mountain in the Geisler cluster. The valley behind it is known by the locals as "in Berge".

Located here, at an altitude of 1,340 m (4,397 ft) above sea level, is St Magdalena, whose church, sacristan house, old schoolhouse and Obermesnerhof farm form an interesting architectural ensemble in front of the Geisler peaks. You can access the Funes Valley through the Eisack Valley north of Klausen.

Detour

Müstair Benedictine Monastery

Where the B38 from Stilfser Joch reaches the Adige Valley, a detour heads along the B40 towards the Resia Pass as far as Schluderns. From there, it climbs over the Ofen Pass back to Zernez in the Lower Engadine region.

Müstair, located just 1 km (0.6 mi) over the border at an altitude of 1,240 m (4,068 ft), welcomes its guests with a monument known throughout Europe: the St John's Benedictine Monastery. The building, which gave the town its name (Müstair means minster and is derived from the Latin monasterium), was founded by the bishop in Chur at the end of the 8th century and was subsequently expanded on several occasions. The complex's main attraction is the nearly 1,200-year-old minster.

Not very imposing on the outside, the monastery houses a treasure

The statue of Charlemagne and frescos in the Müstair Minster.

that prompted UNESCO to declare it a World Heritage Site back in 1983: around ninety frescoes from the 8th to the 12th centuries, which two art historians unearthed rather accidentally under a new painted surface at the start of the 20th century. The oldest of these date back to the time of Charlemagne and depict scenes from the life and passion of Christ, as well as the Last Judgement. They are considered the world's most extensive cluster of frescos preserved from Carolingian times. Roughly 400 years newer, but just as impressive, are the Romanesque paintings depicting the martyrdom of St Stephen and other religious themes.

and Lake Sils), it offers a wide range of outdoor sporting options in both winter and summer. The Cresta Run, or "skeleton sled run", and the bob run to Celerina are legendary.

A varied programme of nightly entertainment meets the needs of the guests, who are as famous as they are wealthy.

From St Moritz, the B27 takes you down the Inn River through Samedan and Zuoz to the Lower Engadine region – a worthwhile detour for those who appreciate the old-world charm of Graubünden villages.

The main route now heads from St Moritz over the Pontresina and Bernina Pass at 2,323 m (7,622 ft), past the dream-like panorama of the glaciated Bernina Group, into the valley of the upper Adda, the Veltlin, and into Italy. From here, the spectacular Stilfser Joch pass rises to 2,578 m (8,458 ft) at the foot of the Ortler (Ortles) peak and heads to Bormio before taking you through the Trafoi Valley down to the Etsch (Adige), where it is worth making a detour through Schludern (Sluderno) to St John's Monastery in the Val Müstair. Continue east to Merano in the Vintschgau Valley.

⓭ Merano This city on the Passer River blossomed under the rule of the counts of Tyrol until the mid-14th century. After the Habsburgs took over co-rule in South Tyrol and moved the residence to Innsbruck, Merano's significance waned. It did not return to the spotlight until the 19th century, when word spread about the healing effect of the local springs and mild climate.

Reputable figures began coming in droves from all over Europe to seek rest and recuperation.

The main sites in the Old Town, with its narrow lanes, quaint arcades and old burgher houses, include the Gothic St Nicholas Church (with the St Barbara Chapel), the Hospital Church and the sovereigns' castle with 15th-century frescos in the chapel. It is also worth taking a walk through the elegant residential area of Obermais.

Indeed, they contain the very epitome of Dolomite magnificence, the Tre Cime de Lavaredo, which come into view as you make your way toward Misurina. The next stops are Schluderbach and Toblach. You are in the Drava Valley here, but will soon cross into Austria and arrive in Lienz just under 40 km (25 mi) away.

⑯ **Lienz** The capital of East Tyrol is surrounded by splendid mountains and is home to a number of charming buildings including St Andreas Parish Church, with the tomb of the last count of Görz, and the baroque St Michael's subsidiary church. Bruck Castle has Tyrol's largest homeland museum, and the city's Roman roots are evidenced by the graveyards of its predecessor, Aguntum.

⑰ **Heiligenblut** Over the Iselsberg at 1,204 m (3,950 ft)

1 Evening ambience at the Langkofel Massif (3,181 m/10,437 ft), west of the Sella Group.

2 After the Tre Cime de Lavaredo, the Vajolet Towers are the most beautiful in the Dolomites and are part of the Rose Garden at the Karer Pass.

3 The Grossglockner High Alpine Road affords spectacular views of the Alp summits.

Merano: Tyrol Castle

Perched high above Merano and the Vinschgau is a castle that is a detailed reflection of Tyrol's eventful history and gives the entire region its name. Tyrol Castle, built by local counts in 1140–60, experienced its golden age in the 14th century under Margarethe Maultasch, when it resisted the siege

Tyrol Castle above Merano

by King Charles of Bohemia. Once the royal residence had been moved to Innsbruck, the castle began to fall into a state of disrepair. After extensive restorations, the castle, which can be reached on foot in just twenty minutes, is now home to a regional museum. The Romanesque entrances at the forecourt of the great hall and the chapel entrance are gems of art history.

row lanes between Lauben, the Kornplatz and the Obstmarkt reveals a charming Old Town that dates back to the Middle Ages. Highlights include the Dominican and Franciscan monasteries, Maretsch Castle, Runkelstein Fort, the City Museum, and the old parish church in the Gries district, with part of an altar by Michael Pacher.
South-east of Bolzano, the SS241 takes you into the dreamy landscape of the Dolomites, littered with breathtaking limestone towers and peaks. The Karer Pass (with a view of the Rose Garden), the Fassa Valley and Passo Sella are the next stops, and the jagged rock formations here never fail to impress.
The road heads along the twisting SS242 with a view of Sassolungo toward the Val Gardena through Ortisei until you reach

the vast Val d'Isarco. Continuing north, you will arrive in Klausen. From there you can take a short detour to get a stunning view of the Funes Valley. On the way back through the Isarco and Gardena valleys, turn off on SS243 after the town of Plan and head towards the Passo Gardena. A breathtaking backdrop of giant rock walls unfolds as you pass the Sella Group via Colfosco and Corvara. As you cross the Passo di Campolongo you will be further delighted by the geological wonders here before reaching the "Great Dolomite Road" which leads to Cortina d'Ampezzo.

⑮ **Cortina d'Ampezzo** This famous spa and winter sports resort is surrounded by some of the most beautiful 3,000-m-high (9,843 ft) peaks in the region.

⑭ **Bolzano** The capital of South Tyrol is located at the confluence of the Isarco and the Adige rivers and is not only the economic center of the region, but also a hub of alpine art and culture. A stroll through the nar-

Mozart

The "Master of all Masters" was born January 27, 1756, at Getreidegasse 9 in Salzburg. Today, the house is one of the most important memorials to

The Mozart House in Salzburg.

the composer. Wolfgang Amadeus Mozart received his basic musical education from his father. At the age of six, he traveled far and wide for auditions, but despite a three-year trip around Europe and journeys to Italy, Munich and Vienna, the city on the Salzach remained the center of his personal and professional life until 1781.

and through the Upper Möll Valley (B107), you arrive in the ever popular pilgrimage and mountaineering town of Heiligenblut. The church here, with its pointed tower standing against the stunning backdrop of the Grossglockner, Austria's highest peak at 3,798 m (12,461 ft), is a longtime favorite among photographers. From here, you follow one of the most impressive mountain roads in the world, the Grossglockner High Alpine Road, which has run from Carinthia through the main alpine

The Grossglockner High Alpine Road

With twenty-seven hairpin turns, this 48-km (30 mi) panoramic road runs above the Hohe Tauern National Park between Heiligenblut and Fusch. Access roads lead to Edelweiss Peak and the Kaiser-Franz Joseph's Heights, with a unique view over the Grossglockner and the 10-km (6 mi) Pasterze Glacier. Brochures at the toll booths provide information on the exact route. The road is open from the end of April until roughly early November.

ridge to the Fusch Valley near Salzburg since 1935. It is also in the Hohe Tauern National Park.

18 Werfen From the end of the valley at Bruck-Fusch (Lake Zeller is just a few miles away), follow the Salzach upstream through Lend and the Pongau to Bischofshofen and Werfen. The picturesque Hohenwerfen Fort is perched above the quaint 12th-century market place here.

Chillon This castle, located near Montreux on an island in Lake Geneva, has twenty-five interconnected buildings.

Bern The impressive "Zytglogge-turm" clock tower (15th century) is the icon of the Swiss capital.

Lake Thun Mediterranean-like vegetation characterizes the Lake Thun area, at an altitude of roughly 560 m (1,837 ft). Oberhofen Castle on the north shore is worth a visit.

Bernese Alps Eiger, Mönch and Jungfrau are the best-known mountains in the western Alps. Many peaks of the "Bernese Alps" reach heights of over 4,000 m (13,124 ft) and have impressive glaciers.

Geneva Numerous international companies and organizations are based here. The city's attractions include St Peter's Cathedral, the Museum of Art and History, the Palais des Nations and the 145-m-high (476-ft) Fontaine du Jet d'Eau.

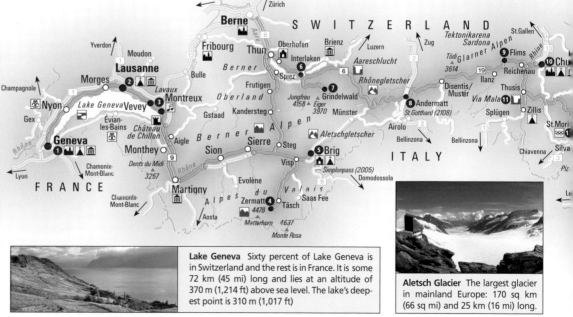

Matterhorn The 4,478-m (14,692-ft) mountain is an icon of Swiss alpinism and has few rivals when it comes to perfect proportions. It was first climbed in 1865, but its northern face was not conquered in winter until 1962. It is still a popular mountaineering challenge.

Lake Geneva Sixty percent of Lake Geneva is in Switzerland and the rest is in France. It is some 72 km (45 mi) long and lies at an altitude of 370 m (1,214 ft) above sea level. The lake's deepest point is 310 m (1,017 ft)

Aletsch Glacier The largest glacier in mainland Europe: 170 sq km (66 sq mi) and 25 km (16 mi) long.

⑲ Hallein The "small Hall", about 25 km (16 mi) down the Salzach, was a center for salt production from the 13th century to 1989. The precious substance has been mined from the Dürrnberg for 4,500 now. The Celts were specialists at this, and their culture is today documented at an open-air museum, the Celts Museum, down in the valley on the edge of this lively city with its charming Old Town. The mine has been converted into an ornate display that is open year-round.

⑳ Salzburg Finale furioso on the Salzach: You actually get the impression that the Creator and his earthly helpers wanted to demonstrate clearly to the people here that it is possible to create a beautiful harmony between the European spiritand a benevolent natural environment. The cathedral, residence, collegiate church, St Peter's Abbey, Nonnberg Monastery, the Getreidegasse and, above all, mighty Hohensalzburg Fortress certainly speak for it.
Salzburg, on the left bank of the Salzach, with its large squares and narrow lanes, myriad fountains and statues, and the vivid

The fort was erected by Archbishop Gebhard around 1077, to ensure control over the Lueg Pass. Those who climb the steep path from the parking lot into the inner ward will get a good feeling for how daunting this fortress must have once been for would-be attackers.
Another must-see here is the Eisriesenwelt or "World of the Ice Giants", the largest ice caves in the world.

marble and stucco work, all form a unique combination of urban design that continues to inspire artists from all over the world and attract admirers in their droves. Long in the shadow of the prince-bishop center on the left bank, however, is the district located on the east bank, with Mirabell Park and Castle, Mozart's home, the Marionette Theater, the St Sebastian Cemetery and the tiny alleyways at the foot of the Kapuzinerberg mountain. It offers a multitude of first-class tourist attractions, and you should not miss a visit to Hellbrunn Castle and Anif Water Castle.
Those wanting to experience another alpine gem should head along the B305 from Salzburg to Berchtesgaden and the national park of the same name, located just 20 km (12 mi) away.

1 Salzburg at sunrise with a view of the bridges and towers of the Old Town and the Hohensalzburg Fortress in the background.

2 The Anif Water Castle near Salzburg dates back to the 17th century. It can only be viewed from the outside.

Detour

The Berchtesgaden Region

This German national park is also referred to as the "Yellowstone of the German Alps", a name coined in the 19th century that is no exaggeration. The dominant feature is the 2,713-m (8,901-ft) Watzmann, a

Looking out over Berchtesgaden.

truly breathtaking peak, but the number one tourist magnet is the 8-km-long (5-mi) Königssee lake. A hike to a famous painters' enclave or a boat ride to the St Batholomä Peninsula are also worthwhile.
In Berchtesgaden, be sure to visit the salt mines and the associated museum.

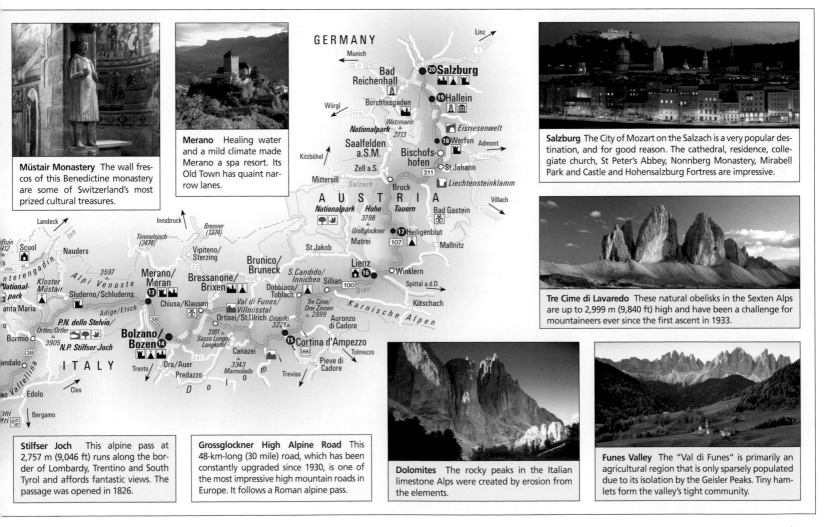

Müstair Monastery The wall frescos of this Benedictine monastery are some of Switzerland's most prized cultural treasures.

Merano Healing water and a mild climate made Merano a spa resort. Its Old Town has quaint narrow lanes.

Salzburg The City of Mozart on the Salzach is a very popular destination, and for good reason. The cathedral, residence, collegiate church, St Peter's Abbey, Nonnberg Monastery, Mirabell Park and Castle and Hohensalzburg Fortress are impressive.

Tre Cime di Lavaredo These natural obelisks in the Sexten Alps are up to 2,999 m (9,840 ft) high and have been a challenge for mountaineers ever since the first ascent in 1933.

Stilfser Joch This alpine pass at 2,757 m (9,046 ft) runs along the border of Lombardy, Trentino and South Tyrol and affords fantastic views. The passage was opened in 1826.

Grossglockner High Alpine Road This 48-km-long (30 mile) road, which has been constantly upgraded since 1930, is one of the most impressive high mountain roads in Europe. It follows a Roman alpine pass.

Dolomites The rocky peaks in the Italian limestone Alps were created by erosion from the elements.

Funes Valley The "Val di Funes" is primarily an agricultural region that is only sparsely populated due to its isolation by the Geisler Peaks. Tiny hamlets form the valley's tight community.

Netherlands, Belgium

Medieval guilds and burgher cities from Amsterdam and Bruges

The Keizersgracht canal in Amsterdam is

Flatlands, canals, dykes, windmills, clogs, and medieval houses reflected in the canals and waterways – these are all the things we associate with the Netherlands and Belgium, along with charming landscapes covered in vibrant fields of tulips, famous sea ports and bustling cities with old markets, squares and town halls.

When we think of the Netherlands, there are certain pictures that come to everyone's mind: world-famous Dutch cheeses; the stately old windmills that were once used to drain the countryside and now dot the landscape like beautiful gems; or the countless dykes that have become an essential element in protecting the country against ocean tides. For centuries, the Dutch have been trying to conquer new land from the North Sea: they build levies and embankments, pump it dry, and then settle and farm it. In fact, two-thirds of all Dutch people to-

day live in the "lower" lands, which are up to 7 m (23 ft) below sea level. This is made possible by canals and drainage ditches that are often located higher than the roads, fields or villages.

In contrast to "life on the seafloor", the sprawling metropolitan areas are home to six million people – 40 percent of the total population. However, the cities at the edge of the "Randstad" chain, which includes Amsterdam, Leiden, Haarlem, The Hague and Rotterdam, only make up a mere tenth of the country's area and are surrounded by a wonderfully

Rembrandt, self-portrait from 1669.

green landscape of croplands, marshes and moors.

In many cities, it is still easy to get a sense of how successful the Netherlands was over the centuries as a world trading power whose colonies brought great wealth to the country. That wealth is reflected in the ornate buildings of the Old Towns, which line the quaint canals. Today, more than 55,000 houses in the Netherlands are listed buildings.

The wealth of earlier times has also naturally also benefited the arts. Painters like Rembrandt, Franz Hals, Jan Vermeer and Piet Mondrian are synonymous with the Netherlands. Ultimately, this historically seafaring nation's experiences with distant lands and foreign cultures has created an atmosphere of open-mindedness that has been preserved until the present day.

The network of windmills in Kinderdijk is a listed UNESCO World Heritage Site. The successful technical innovation was developed in the 18th century.

spanned by fourteen bridges.

Ghent, with its medieval townscape of proud patrician houses on the Graslei.

There is also an extra special ambience in the land of the Flemings and Walloons, who united to form the kingdom of Belgium some 160 years ago. Although Belgium has some first-class references in men like George Simenon and Jacques Brel, and is loved for its Brussels lace, Ardennes ham and a highway that is lit up at night, it is not a classic holiday destination – but that is short-sighted.

The coastal resorts along the North Sea, the wide sandy beaches and the spectacular dune landscapes alone are worth making the trip. And it's not just romantics who go into rapture over the ornate façades and wonderful buildings that reflect off the canals and waterways, or the church spires that soar high above the historic Old Towns of Bruges and Ghent.

Brussels, which proudly calls itself the Heart of Europe, is home to one of the most beautiful market squares in the world – the Grand' Place – and the stunning Museum of Fine Art displays works by masters from Rubens to Magritte.

On an unusual note: no other country has a higher population of comics illustrators per square mile – which means that comic strips, along with Brussels lace, Antwerp diamonds and Belgian pralines, are among the most commonly exported Belgian products.

At every turn, it is apparent that Belgians know how to live. Surprising as it may seem, no other country in Europe has as many award-winning restaurants. The most popular drink in Belgium is beer, and there are almost five hundred types produced in over hundred breweries. And as far as snacks go, well, pommes frites (french fries or chips) are said to have been invented here.

Every two years in August, a spellbinding carpet of flowers covers the Grand' Place in Brussels.

Zaandam and Alkmaar

Zaandam was once the center of the Dutch shipbuilding industry and is located just 15 km (7 mi) from the city of Amsterdam. Czar Peter I (1672–1725) studied the latest in shipbuilding technologies at the time, and his house has been made into a museum.

Further to the north-west, the old mills, pretty houses and exhibits of the Zaanse Schans open-air museum display everyday village life from different eras.

Top: Windmills on the Zaan.
Bottom: Cheese market, Alkmaar.

From April to mid-September, the town of Alkmaar comes under the influence of its cheese culture. In the picturesque Old Town quarter, which is home to a number of interesting buildings, farmers sell their delicious cheese balls and cheese wheels on the open-air market.

Along the Dutch and Belgian coast: In Holland, the route heads through the "nether lands", with their seemingly endless fields of flowers, and then to the bustling metropolises. In Belgium you visit cities with charming, medieval Old Towns and priceless works of art.

1 Amsterdam (see pages 170–171) Your journey begins in Amsterdam. From there, you can initially take a day trip to Zaandam just 15 km (9 mi) north to the Zaanse Schans open-air museum and the cheese town of Alkmaar a bit further north.

2 Haarlem This city is about 20 km (12 mi) west of Amsterdam and was officially mentioned in the 10th century. It has a picturesque Old Town quarter whose Grote Markt was once a sports arena. The beautifully decorated 17th-century gabled houses are evidence of the wealth the city once achieved as the stronghold of the drapery and fabric bleaching guild.
At the south end of the square is the Grote or St Bavokerk, a late-Gothic cruciform basilica. The nursing home where painter Frans Hals spent his final years was converted into a museum in 1912, with important works by the great artist.

3 Keukenhof The Bollenstreek between Haarlem and Leiden takes you through a sea of flowers. It is home to the fields of around 8,000 nurseries that specialize in wholesale flowers.

The Tulip Route leads to the most important of these nurseries; the mecca among them for all flower lovers is the world-famous Keukenhof.
The information center was jointly founded by a community of flower growers in 1949.

4 Noordwijk aan Zee In the height of summer, this seaside resort after the turnoff at Sassenheim attracts tens of thousands of beachgoers with 13 km (8 mi) of strand and vast sandy dunes. Just like Katwijk ann Zee a few miles further south, Noordwijk has a style that is reminiscent of English seaside resorts. From here it's another 20 km (12 mi) to Leiden.

5 Leiden The oldest university town in the Netherlands was already home to 11,000 students back in the mid-17th century.

Travel information

Route profile
Length: approx. 400 km (249 mi)
Time required: at least 8–10 days
Start: Amsterdam
Finish: Bruges
Route (main locations): Amsterdam, Leiden, The Hague, Rotterdam, Breda, Antwerp, Mechelen, Brussels, Ghent, Bruges

Traffic information:
Speed limit in the city is 50 km/h (30 mph); on rural roads it's 80 km/h (50 mph) (in Belgium it is 90 km/h (56 mph)); and on highways 120 km/h (75 mph). The legal alcohol limit for drivers is 0.05, and it is strictly enforced. Remember to bring a warning triangle in case of emergencies.

When to go:
Generally from May to October. Holland is typically at its most beautiful in late spring when everything is in bloom.
From June to late August, southerly winds bring sunny and mostly dry days. At that time, the average maximum temperature is around 20°C (68°F). Only in high summer is swimming really an option.

Information:
Holland:
www.holland.com
www.traveltoholland.org
www.visitbelgium.com

The most beautiful view over the town and its canals can be seen from the Burcht or fort, a mound fortified with brick curtain walls over 1,000 years ago that was built to protect against Holland's most persistent enemy: flooding. The Pieterskerk, a Gothic cruciform basilica with five naves, is worth seeing and, of course, the city's most famous native son is Rembrandt Harmensz van Rijn, born here in 1606. A few of his works are on display in the Stedelijk Museum de Lakenhal.

6 Scheveningen The center of this North Sea coastal resort is the magnificent old Art Nouveau health spa establishment that is today a luxury hotel. The 3-km-long (2-mi) beach boardwalk and the Scheveningen Pier, which extends 400 m (437 yds) out into the North Sea, are also

well-known features of the town. The International Sand Sculptures Festival is held here every year in May.

7 The Hague The third-largest city in the Netherlands is the seat of government as well as the headquarters of the International Court of Justice with the UN War Crimes Tribunal. The city's history goes back roughly 750 years and began with a few houses built around the hunting grounds of the Count of Holland. One of these houses, the Binnenhof or "Inner Court", was built in the 13th century and is still home to the nation's politics – it is the seat of government and the Parliament. The city's most important tourist attraction is the Mauritshuis, a neoclassical building with an art gallery featuring priceless works by famous Dutch painters from

the "Golden Age" as well as Flemish Masters.
The Mesdag Panorama, a cylindrical painting created by Hendrik Willem Mesdag in 1881, is 120 m (131 yds) long and 14 m (46 ft) high and hangs in a building at Zeestraat 65. It gives visitors the impression of standing in the middle of the Scheveningen dune landscape.
The nearby Mesdag Museum has additional paintings from the Hague School of the late 19th century. Another building that constantly makes headlines is the Vredespalais in the Carnegieplein. This half neo-Gothic, half neoclassical Peace Palace is the venue for the controversial meetings of the International Court of Justice.

8 Delft Halfway between The Hague and Rotterdam is Delft, with its historic Old Town and

charming canals. It is particularly famous for its pottery.

9 Rotterdam Container terminals, trans-shipment centers, warehouses and silos all line up beside one another over 20 km (12 mi) along the Nieuwe Waterweg at the world's largest port. All kinds of goods are moved through this port at the mouth of the Maas and Rhine rivers.
It is not difficult to see that emphasis is placed on modern high-rise architecture in "Maashattan". One of the most amazing sights is the Erasmusbrug, a suspension bridge over the Nieuwe Maas constructed by Ben van Berkel in 1996.
The city museum, which has an interesting display of the history of Rotterdam, is in the Het Schielandshuis, a former administrative building that managed the 17th-century dyke systems. The Boijmans van Beuningen Museum at the Museumspark is home to a sizeable collection of Old and New Masters. A variety of

1 Around 1,300 bridges span Amsterdam's countless canals.

2 The Gravenstenenbrug bridge in Haarlem spans the Spaarne River.

3 A tulip field near Keukenhof, also known as the Garden of Europe.

4 Night view of the port city of Rotterdam.

5 The Binnenhof or "inner court" (13th century) in The Hague is seat of Parliament and other governmental institutions.

6 Beach boardwalk in Scheveningen, a seaside resort in front of the gates of The Hague.

Detour

Lake IJssel

The cities around Lake IJssel still evoke the time of the explorers. It was from Hoorn, for example, that Captain Willem Schouten set off for the southern tip of South America in 1616, now Cape Horn. Abel Tasman, the first European to discover New Zealand and Tasmania in 1642, also set sail from here. The West Frisian Museum has

Top: Hoorn with its port tower.
Bottom: Enkhuizen, spice center.

exhibits on other colonial adventures that originated from Hoorn. Enkhuizen was the spice-trading center of the East India Company. The Zuiderzee Museum, in a former warehouse in the historic center, has interesting exhibits on shipping and fishery, while an open-air complex with farmhouses and handicrafts gives you an idea of life in the old days.

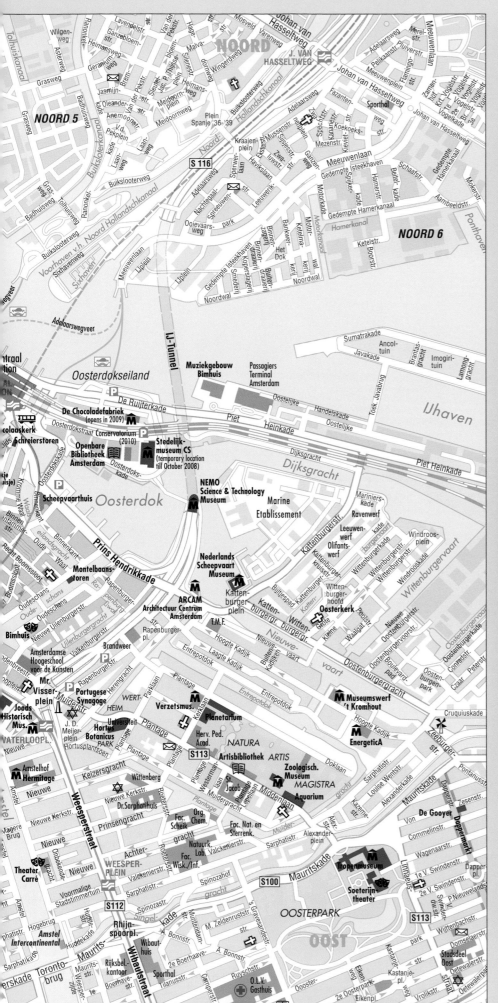

Amsterdam

The capital of the Netherlands is one of the smallest and most manageable metropolises in Europe. It is tolerant and cosmopolitan, but also characterized by a rich history, so it is no coincidence that Amsterdam, the headstrong city at the mouth of the Amstel, is a popular tourist destination.

Amsterdam is the world's largest pile-dwelling settlement. The foundations for the buildings in the entire Old Town district are formed by countless logs beaten up to 30 m (98 ft) into the ground, creating some seventy man-made islands – and the romantic flair of a city on water.

Amsterdam's Golden Century, which roughly equates to the 17th century, marked the beginning of construction on the crescent-shaped Three Canals Belt. In the historic center alone, four hundred bridges span the canals. Water levels are maintained at a constant height using a system of locks and pumps, and some goods are still transported through the city by water even today.

Hundreds of houseboats are moored at the docks of the 160 canals in the Canal Belt and are just as much part

The tourist attractions in the Old Town include: the oldest church, the Oude Kerk (14th century, rebuilt in the 16th); the late-Gothic Nieuwe Kerk where Queen Beatrix was crowned; Dam, once a market place with the Nationaal Monument; the 17th-century town hall, Koninklijk Paleis, whose façade frieze is dedicated to sea trade; Museum Amstelkring, an original canal house used by ostracized Catholics as a secret church in the 17th century; Beurs van Berlage, the 19th-century merchants' stock exchange; Montelbaanstoren, the former city tower (1512); the seven-towered Waag, formerly a city gate and part of the mighty fort; and the Rembrandt House, the master's home with a modern museum wing.

In the former Jewish quarter: the Portuguese synagogue (1675) and

Top: Patrician houses along a romantically lit canal.
Bottom: The Magere Brug is the most famous of Amsterdam's bridges.

of the townscape as the numerous cyclists, flower stands with "tulips from Amsterdam", and the beautiful barrel organs that play the world-famous popular song.

Amsterdam's cityscape resembles a bustling open-air museum, and its open-mindedness, cultural diversity, international cuisine, and the countless options for all types of accommodation suit every budget and every standard. All of this makes the capital of the Netherlands one of the most popular destionations in Europe. Amsterdam is also a very youthful and tolerant city, often leading the way in areas such as fashion and design. It is also easy to get to from just about anywhere.

Joods Historisch Museum; a museum complex housed in four former synagogues; the neo-Gothic Central Station (19th century); Amsterdam's historic museum in the complex of the former orphanage; and the Begijnhof, a former Beguine convent.

In the Canal Belt: Westerkerk (17th century); the Anne Frank House, preserved in its original state; and the historic working quarter of Jordaan with the beautifully renovated Hofjes, historic residential complexes.

In the museum quarter: The Rijks-museum, the world's most famous collection of Dutch Masters; the Van Gogh Museum; Stedelijk Museum for Modern Art; and the Vondelpark landscaped gardens.

Gouda

Gouda – this city is virtually synonymous with cheese. In actual fact, the nourishing, golden-yellow delicacy is one of the most popular varieties in the world. It comes on the market in either "natural" flavor or refined with herbs, mustard, pepper or caraway, and is brought to you by Frau Antje, a prim and proper blond woman wearing a traditional Dutch bonnet – an invention of savvy marketing specialists over forty years ago. Since then she has advertised "authentic cheese from Holland" from 700,000 tonnes (770,000 tons) of milk and seventy million cows.

The town hall in Gouda.

After a short tour of the city, it becomes clear that Gouda has more to offer than just the cheese market, which is held every Thursday morning from mid-June until the end of August on the square between the town hall and the Renaissance building of the Waag. The first thing you notice at the market place is the Gothic Stadhuis (town hall) made from grey blocks of stone. It is adorned with merlons, turrets and red-and-white shutters, and has musical figurines on its eastern façade that every half hour commemorate the granting of the town charter in 1272.

The Grote or St Janskerk at the southern end of the market is home to one of the treasures of the Old Town quarter, which is surrounded by canals. The church, built at the end of the 16th century and measuring 123 m (135 yds), is the longest church in the Netherlands. Its greatest attraction are its seventy stained glass windows from the 16th century – the most beautiful church windows in the country.

The municipal museum in the former city hospital, Het Catharina Gasthuis (14th century), provides information on the history of Gouda.

artwork is also exhibited at the Rotterdamer Kunsthal.

From Rotterdam it's roughly 20 km (12 mi) north-east to the country's most famous "cheese town", Gouda. Just a few miles south of Rotterdam, the route leads to one of the country's iconic landmarks – the windmills of Kinderdijk.

⑩ Kinderdijk It really is an impressive sight: nineteen old polder mills lined up in a tidy row along the town's drainage canals. The ingenious constructions at the confluence of the Noord and Lek rivers once drove pumping stations that regulated water levels. These days, the blades, which are covered in canvas and have a span of up to 28 m (92 ft), only rotate on

Saturday afternoons. The mills were declared a UNESCO World Heritage Site in 1997, and are particularly impressive in the second week of September when they are illuminated at night by floodlights.

⑪ Breda With its numerous barracks and military facilities, this garrison city at the confluence of the Mark and Aa rivers has a lot to offer visitors. Beautiful burgher houses on the Old Town market square, for example, date back to the 18th and 19th centuries and include the Stadhuis. And, as is often the case, the Old Town is surrounded by charming canals. The Kasteel van Breda is encircled by moats and features four corner towers. It is considered the ancestral cas-

tle of the House of Orange, the Dutch royal family. Breda is also home to another moated castle, Kasteel Bouvigne, and the city's most important building is the Gothic Onze Lieve Vrouwe Kerk (Church of Our Lady) with a spire 97 m (318 ft) tall.

Those looking to head back to the North Sea before continuing on to Belgium are advised to visit the islands of Walcheren and Beveland. They are connected to the mainland by a series of dams and bridges.

From Breda, the N263 takes you through green, flat and sparsely settled landscapes towards Antwerp, the first real metropolis on this journey.

⑫ Antwerp The port here in Belgium's second-largest metro-

politan area is the lifeblood of the city and home to a number of automotive and chemical industry companies. The port is the second-largest in Europe after Rotterdam, a fact that has created an open-minded attitude and contributed greatly to Antwerp's rise as the center of the diamond trade.

The 1993 European Capital of Culture is home to historic monuments and a vibrant cultural scene. Most of its tourist attractions are in the inner city, which forms a semicircle on the right bank of the Schelde. The most striking part of Antwerp is the Steen, the former fort complex whose oldest section dates back to the 9th century. It now houses the National Shipping Museum, with a 15th-century Flemish war-

Detour

The Schelde Estuary (Walcheren, Beveland)

North of Antwerp, the Schelde opens out into a wide delta. Although the estuary is a natural landscape, it has been politically divided between the Netherlands and Belgium since 1585. The former North Sea islands of Walcheren and Beveland provide holiday-

Kasteel Westhove near Domburg now houses a youth hostel.

makers with sand, surf and sea, charming villages and historic towns. Middelburg is one of the oldest cities in Holland, with a beautifully restored historic center that earned it the title of European Heritage City in 1975.

After the dreadful storm surge of 1953, the barrier of the Oosterschelde Dam was built north of Middelburg.

ship as its centerpiece. The fort's lookout platform provides an amazing view over the Schelde – which is 500 m (547 yds) wide at this point – the bridges, the old wharf, and the sea of countless cargo derricks along the horizon at the modern port.

The Museum of Municipal History is housed in the late-Gothic meat market, while the Diamond Museum on Lange Herentalsestraat in the Jewish Quarter lets you watch diamond polishers at work.

The Rubens House, a symbolic city palace reminiscent of an Italian palazzo, was home to Peter Paul Rubens from 1610 to 1640. The master's lavish quarters, studio and art cabinet as well as some works by the painter and his students are on display.

⓭ **Mechelen** This city south of Antwerp has a rich history. It experienced its heyday when Margarethe of Austria ruled the country from here and her statue at the Grote Markt, which marks the city center, commemorates this time. The square is encircled by the town hall, a Gothic palace and the former cloth hall from the 14th century. Mechelen aimed high throughout its history, in fact. In the second century, the 97-m-tall (318-ft) spire of the Romboutskathedraal was designed as the highest symbol of Christianity, and its carillon of forty-nine bells still charms listeners today.

From Mechelen, it's just a half-hour drive to the Belgian capital. Those wanting to head towards the North Sea after that will ini-

tially pass through Aalst, the "Gateway to Flanders", on the way to Bruges.

⓮ **Brussels** (see pages 176–177)

⓯ **Aalst** This city is heavily influenced by industry and, well, flowers. Every morning there is a flower market at the Grote Markt, and beautiful Gothic row houses line the square.

⓰ **Ghent** A center of the textile industry since the Middle Ages, Ghent has continued to remain true to this tradition even today. Fruits, vegetables and even flowers play only a supporting role. The most important attractions are found in the well-preserved historic city center between the

1 The current design of the Ooidonk water castle south-west of Ghent dates back to 1595.

2 Kasteel Bouvigne water castle near Breda in North Brabant was used as a hunting lodge in the 17th century.

3 The Onze Lieve Vrouwe Cathedral in Antwerp, with its 123-m-high (404-ft) spire, is the largest Gothic cathedral in Belgium. Construction work commenced in 1352.

4 Mechelen's Rombourtskathedraal was completed in 1546. The church is known for its beautiful glockenspiel.

5 The 88-m-high (289-ft) Belfort (city tower) in Ghent was the city's commercial center in the Middle Ages. It has forty-seven bells.

Top: The northern end of the Grand' Place in Brussels shows the Hotel de Ville (1401–1459) on the left. The middle of the picture is taken up with several guild houses; second from the left is the mariners' guild house and the last house on the right is the domed Maison des Boulangers. The right side of the picture is

dominated by the Maison du Roi (1536). Bottom: The southern end of the square is characterized by the neoclassical Maison des Ducs de Brabant in the middle of the picture, while on the left is the Maison du Roi, with the historic town hall again on the right.

Brussels

Belgium's confident metropolis awaits visitors with grandiose cultural monuments and special culinary treats. It calls itself the Capital of Europe, which is true at least as far as the institutions of the European Union.

Brussels has been a wealthy city for centuries. Between the Middle Ages and the baroque period, it was primarily the middle classes who adorned their city with majestic row houses. The 19th century saw some wonderful additions to the unique townscape, which then suffered during the construction boom of the 20th century. The EU's ambitious buildings claimed many architectural victims, for instance in the Quartier Léopold, which was razed. Luckily, numerous Art Nouveau works remained intact. At the turn of the 20th century, Brussels was one of the focal points of this architectural style, and artists such as Victor Horta, Henry van de Velde and Philippe Wolfers enriched the city with a series of unique edifices.

Brussels is Belgium's most important cultural city and scientific center, with a university, the polytechnic, the Royal Academy and numerous technical colleges and art schools. The city is at the crossroads of major transport routes and it is home to Belgium's national bank.

Although Brussels has a number of tourist attractions and gets a lot of attention as the "Capital of Europe" and the headquarters of NATO, the Belgian capital is overshadowed by metropolises like Paris, London and Amsterdam. This actually makes it a very interesting destination: slightly chaotic, not always pleasant, easy to access and never overrun. It's still an insiders' tip! Particularly worth seeing are: the Manneken Pis, the famous peeing boy statue and icon of the city from 1619; Grand' Place, one of the most beautiful squares in Europe and a World Heritage Site with the Hôtel de Ville and the Gothic town hall with its ornate façade; the Cathédrale St Michel; the Center Belge de la Bande dessinée, a comics museum in an Art Nouveau building; the "Old England" Grand Magasin, a fanciful building; Musées Royaux des Beaux Arts with an outstanding collection of old and new masters from Brueghel to Magritte; Hôtel van Eetvelde, a magnificent building from the late 19th century; Hôtel Hannon, Maison Cauchie and

Top: The Grand' Place with the Maison du Roi, home to the municipal museum.
Bottom: The Atomium was built for the 1958 World Exhibition.

Furthermore, Brussels is the second largest industrial city in the country after Antwerp. "Fine goods" such as the famous Brussels lace, woolen, cotton and silk goods, carpets and even porcelain are all produced here. And of course, world-famous culinary products such as exquisite chocolates, delectable pralines, and even beer – virtually a given in the hometown of fabled King Gambrinus – keep visitors coming back for more.

Maison St Cyr, three examples of Brussels Art Nouveau residential architecture; Musée Charlier, 20th-century art in an Art Nouveau building; Musée du Cinquantenaire (works from the Middle Ages to the 19th century); Place du Grand Sablon with galleries and antique stores, and an antiques market on weekends; and Place du Jeu de Balle in the multicultural Marolles (Dutch: Marollen) district.

Knokke

Knokke-Heist, the most elegant town on the Belgian coast along with Ostend, is located amidst a spectacular dune landscape near the Dutch border. The sandy beach is 12 km (7 mi) long.

The rise of Knokke began in 1880, when it rapidly grew from a small fishing village to one of the most glamorous coastal resorts in Europe.

On the beach in Knokke.

The walking trails are particularly lovely: "Bloemenwandeling" in the Het Zoute villa district, and the "Landelijke Knokke" and "Polderwandeling" through the beautiful dune landscape.

In Heist, the Polder- en Visserijmuseum Sincfala, with its exhibits on fishing, handicrafts and everyday life on the coast, is also worth a short visit.

Count's Castle and the St Bavo Cathedral (14th century). The cathedral is on a rise and is visible from afar. Its most valuable treasure is the *Ghent Altarpiece*, also known as the *Adoration of the Mystic Lamb*, completed by the van Eyck brothers, Hubert and Jan, in the 15th century. The cathedral tower once housed thirty-nine bells, but only seven remain now. The others were sold or destroyed.

The Belfort bell tower, opposite the cathedral, is 91 m (312 ft) high and was considered the symbol of the aspiring middle classes in the 14th century. The Belfort is 88 m high (289 ft) and has forty-seven bells. It has also served as a municipal treasure chamber and a watchtower.

The cloth hall, the Great Meat Market, the Count's Castle, and the town hall are also worth visiting while downtown.

About 15 km (9 mi) from Ghent, between Deinze and Ghent, is the 17th-century Ooidonk castle complex. The moated castle's name means "high location in a swampland", which can be traced back to an older Low Franconian word "hodonk". Both Flemish and Dutch are creations of a linguistic root dating back to the Franconian empire. On the way to Bruges, you will pass through Eeklo, where jenever (gin) is made in the historic

van Hoorebeke distillery. The jenever is spicier than its English counterpart and the oude genever, or old-style jenever, is yellower in hue.

17 Bruges With its semicircular Old Town full of canals, the capital of Western Flanders is a perfect example of medieval city architecture and, in those days, was considered the richest and most magnificent city in the known world after Venice. All major trading houses were based in Bruges, the dukes of Burgundy held court here, and art was of the utmost importance. Artists such as Jan van Eyck and Hans Memling were dedicated city painters.

The best way to discover Bruges is on a circle tour. The Grote Markt, which was the scene of lively jousting competitions in the Middle Ages, continues to form the city center, which is also home to the 83-m-high (272-ft) Belfort tower.

From the Grote Markt, Vlamingstraat heads to the "Hanseatic Bruges" with its beautiful patrician homes and trading houses from the 14th and 15th century; the Old Customs House; and then the Burgplein before continuing on to the Groeninge Museum with Belgian contemporaries; and finally the 15th-century Gruuthusepalais, a lavish

palace that was home to rich patricians who earned their money by taxing the brewery for their ingredients, the "Gruute".

The Gothic Onze Lieve Vrouwekerk, or Church of Our Lady, has a spire 122 m high (400 ft) that is in an atypical position on the left side of the church. It is home to the city's greatest artistic gem: the *Bruges Madonna* from 1503, the first of Michaelangelo's works to make it across the Alps during his lifetime.

The old sluice-house at the southern end of Wijngaardplaats is also interesting. It is used to regulate the water levels of the city's canals. The Minnewater, behind the house in a park, was the city's main dock in the Middle Ages.

After all of this journeying back in time to the Middle Ages, the charming coastal resorts on the North Sea may be calling: Knokke, Zeebruges, Blankenberge and Ostend are all just a few miles away from Bruges.

1 The historic town of Bruges takes you on a journey through time to the Middle Ages. Here: the Belfort tower reflected in the waters of the Dijver.

2 The medieval St Mary's Church, Onze Lieve Vrouwekerk, in Bruges. Located nearby are some Beguine courts, early institutions for penniless women.

Haarlem The Old Town quarter of this bulb-growing city features gabled houses and the mighty Grote Kerk church.

Alkmaar The traditional "cheese market" includes weighing and tasting down at the quaint market square. It is held every Friday in summer.

Amsterdam Despite its historic appearance, the capital of the Netherlands is a youthful city built on several islands and criss-crossed by crescent-shaped canals. It has myriad attractions including world-class museums and fantastic art collections.

Hoorn Cape Horn owes its name to a sailor from Hoorn, but this cute town on Lake IJssel is significantly less rugged than the South American headland.

The Hague The Dutch government, the International Court of Justice and the UN War Crimes Tribunal hold meetings in famous historic buildings while the museums exhibit some fine art.

Keukenhof A community of florists display their plants over an area of 28 ha (69 acres).

Edam The cheese trade has been booming in Edam since the 17th century, and a lovely cheese market is held every Wednesday from July to August. Before this small town on Lake IJssel was made famous by its cheese balls encased in red or yellow packaging, it was well known as a shipbuilding town.

Rotterdam This city in the estuary region of the Maas and Rhine rivers is characterized by modern architecture, such as the Erasmus Bridge, and the world's largest port where the facilities along the Nieuwe Waterweg stretch over 20 km (12 mi).

Gouda This city is not just worth visiting for the cheese of the same name. It is also has a picturesque Old Town with a Gothic town hall.

Delft The Grote Markt, the Nieuwe Kerk, and the Stadhuis make the city of blue-and-white porcelain tiles one of the prettiest in the Netherlands.

Kinderdijk A picture-perfect panorama unfolds at the confluence of the Lek and Noord rivers: a row of nineteen polder mills that once drove a pumping station to drain the fields for agriculture.

Mechelen The treasures of the Romboutskathedraal include a van Dyck painting and the glockenspiel. The spire is 97 m high (318 ft) and was originally supposed to reach a height of 167 m (548 ft).

Bruges The Old Town in Bruges has numerous canals, grand squares and patrician houses from the 14th and 15th centuries, as well as churches and museums that cannot be matched anywhere in Europe.

Ghent Most of Ghent's medieval attractions are found between the Count's Castle and the St Bavo Cathedral and include the Belfort tower, the cloth hall, meat market, St Nicholas Church and more.

Brussels The Belgian capital (and Capital of Europe) is known around the world for its excellent cuisine. World-famous symbols of Brussels also include the vast Grand' Place and the Atomium, the 60-cm-tall (2-ft) Manneken Pis (peeing boy), the city's Art Nouveau buildings, museums, palaces and, of course, fine Brussels lace.

Mechelen The treasures of the Romboutskathedraal include a van Dyck painting and the glockenspiel. The spire is 97 m high (318 ft) and was originally supposed to reach a height of 167 m (548 ft).

The picturesque fishing ports of Saint-Guénolé

France

Limestone and granite: natural and cultural landscapes of the French Atlantic coast

The territory extending out into the Atlantic and the English Channel in north-western France is not exactly hospitable in terms of weather, but the romantic windswept coast and the luscious green interior radiate a sense of magic that captivates even the most unsentimental visitors. Indeed, across the entire region between Le Havre and Nantes, every stone seems to have a story to tell.

Powerful Atlantic surf, jagged windy bluffs, and shimmering white limestone cliffs scattered with the long, deserted sandy beaches. These are the elements that define the coastlines of Normandy and Brittany, where dynamic forces of nature are unfettered and the aesthetic is that of an ancient world. Augmenting the scene are sleepy fishing villages and busy port cities, elegant seaside resorts and cozy holiday towns.

Thousands of years of human history here have left so much behind that the entire

Fort La Latte on the Brittany Côte d'Armor.

region could be considered an open-air museum. Castles and manors, abbeys and cathedrals, meticulously preserved Old Town centers, half-timbered row houses and stone buildings all attest to eras of power and wealth.

Stout fortifications and sentry towers are reminiscent of darker times. Normandy was ruled by the Celts, Romans and Germanic tribes until the 5th century, before the Vikings and Normans claimed the area as theirs. The war between England and France lasted for centuries before the Huguenots devastated the land. But all of this was nothing compared to the German occupation in 1940. Within four years, all of Normandy had become a battlefield until allied troops landed on Calvados and Cotentin beaches on June 6, 1944, "D-Day". The territory was eventually liberated in September of

1944, but many of the cities lay under soot and ash.

Today, Normandy is experiencing what is arguably the most peaceful era in its long history. The roughly 30,000-sq-km (11,580-sq-mi) region is primarily involved in agriculture, and is characterized by grasslands with stone walls, fields of grain and apple plantations.

The coast, which is about 600 km long (373 mi), transforms Normandy a popular holiday destination in July and August, when not only the French come to the lovely resorts and stunning beaches in droves. From here, it is possible to make interesting detours to places such as the famous rock island monastery of Mont Saint-Michel.

Before the Common Era, Brittany was home to a culture that continues to mystify the scientific world: Who were the

The impressive limestone cliffs (falaises) of the Normandy coast near Étretat, north of Le Havre. It is definitely worth seeing the Falaises d´Amont and the Falaises d´Aval not far from the city.

on the Bigouden Peninsula form the south-western tip of Brittany.

people of the megalith culture? Were the menhirs, the stone monuments from between 5000 and 2000 BC, used as solar or lunar calendars? Were they fertility symbols, cult sites or processional avenues? There are still no explanations for any of these exciting questions.

After 500 BC, the history becomes clearer. Around this time, the Celts came and settled in the area, which they called "Armor" or "Land by the Sea". Although they were evangelized around AD 500, they preserved many of their "pagan" customs and legends, as well as their Breton language. Certain Celtic elements still thrive here: fantasy and defiance are particularly defined, fuelled on by a healthy dose of pride. Brittany, which covers an area of roughly 27,200 sq km (10,499 sq mi), is one of France's most important agricultural regions. It is a fishing center and almost every sea bass (loup de mer) or monkfish you eat in Europe comes from its waters. It also specializes in early vegetable exports as well as meat and dairy processing. With its 1,200-km (746 mi) coastline, it is second only to the Côte d'Azur among tourism regions in Europe.

The wind and the stones, the green the meadows and the wild Atlantic ocean spray – Brittany is defined by all of this. That said, it did not achieve true international fame until the emergence of the comic book, *Asterix and Obelix*. Indeed, they are the best-known Bretons after King Arthur and have delighted readers around the world since the first strip by René Goscinny and Albert Uderzo appeared in 1959. The only downside is that their village unfortunately does not exist anywhere Brittany.

Saint-Malo on the northern coast of Brittany is situated on an island of granite.

Cotentin Peninsula

The Cotentin Peninsula is the most impressively primeval landscape in Normandy. The coastline here is mostly craggy and wild, but there are long, sandy beaches that occasionally stretch between the jagged rocks. In the south, for example, the peninsula separates a vast moorland area from the interior, while in the north the landscape is reminiscent of Ireland or southern England, with rolling hills, verdant green meadows and rustic stone walls.

The storming of the beaches in Normandy by Allied troops on June 6, 1944, is remembered in many local towns here. At La Madeleine, for instance, a museum commemorates the soldiers who landed at "Utah Beach". Massive fortifications, which were built by

Fishing boats in the port of Barfleur in the north of the peninsula.

the Germans as part of the Atlantic wall to protect against a British invasion of the continent, can be seen near Crisbec. A memorial skydiver hangs from the church spire of Sainte-Mére-Église, and there is also a war museum.

The most important city in the area, Cherbourg, emerged from World War II virtually unscathed, and the streets and narrow rows of houses still emanate the charming atmosphere of the 18th and 19th centuries. The umbrellas of Cherbourg, which were the inspiration in 1963 for the title of the award-winning film, *Les parapluies de Cherbourg*, are still produced.

A tour of the Norman-Breton coast takes you first from the urban jungle of Paris to the wildly romantic limestone cliffs of Normandy and the beaches where Allied forces landed in 1944. Brittany then offers a unique natural and scenic experience and confronts visitors with the mysteries of prehistoric cultures and myths.

1 Paris (see Tour No. 16) Highway N 15 is a good way to get to Normandy from Paris, and leads you along the impressive Seine River valley.

2 Rouen This Norman city is home to one of France's largest sea ports, despite its inland location. However, what really fascinates visitors is the historic Old Town, with its quaint alleyways snaking between crooked half-timbered houses, churches with extravagant ornamentation, the magnificent Notre-Dame Cathedral and the rest of the massive fortifications.

3 Fécamp This is where the road meets the Côte d'Albâtre, the Alabaster Coast, where the bizarre limestone cliffs drop more than 110 m (361 ft) down to the sea. Fécamp was once famous for two things: its booming fishing port and its tasty Bénédictine cordial. The Sainte-Trinité Church of the Benedictine abbey has been lovingly preserved.

4 Étretat This village was one of the fishing villages that was particularly popular among artists in the 19th century. It is situated in a bay enclosed on both sides by romantic cliffs. The Notre-Dame Church from the 13th century is astonishingly large for such a small town, and is well worth visiting.

5 Le Havre This city at the mouth of the Seine was occupied by the Germans in World War II and bombed by the Allies for an entire week in an attempt to win it back. The important port and center were rebuilt, but it is more modern and functional than it is picturesque. The most impressive site is Europe's longest suspension bridge, inaugurated in 1988. The art museum houses a collection of impressionist and cubist works.

6 Honfleur This port city is steeped in tradition and considered the most beautiful city on the Côte Fleurie, the Floral Coast. The architectural gems of the old port, the wharfs lined with narrow row houses, and the steep, hilly Ste Catherine quarter exude fishing village romanticism and an artistic flair.

Travel information

Route profile
Length: approx. 1,400 km (870 mi)
Duration: 10–14 days
Start: Paris
Finish: Nantes
Route course: Paris, Rouen, Le Havre, Honfleur, Caen, Brest, Quimper, Lorient, Nantes

Traffic information:
The blood-alcohol limit for drivers is 0.05 and it is strictly enforced.
The speed limit in cities is 50 km/h (30 mph), on rural roads 90 km/h (55 mph), on expressways 110 km/h (70 mph) and 130 km/h (80 mph) on the motorways. Motorways require tolls.

When to go:
Spring and autumn are ideal, because it the peak season at most resorts is in high summer. Extreme heat is not an issue in this region. Temperatures average around 15°C (59°F) in May and October, while June to September you can expect about 18-20°C (64-68°F). Regardless of the season, the weather here is very active and it can rain at any time.

Information:
Here are some websites to help you plan your trip.
www.franceguide.com
www.brittanytourism.com
www.discoverfrance.com

Dinan

Dinan, perched high above the Rance Valley, is one of the most impressive walled cities in Brittany. It is dominated by a mighty fort that contains the residential tower of Duchess Anne and dates all the way back to the 14th century. The wall, which is 3 km long (2 mi), still contains sixteen towers and gates, and to

**Top: View of Dinan with the Gothic bridge over the Rance.
Bottom: An alleyway in Dinan.**

this day completely encircles the picturesque Old Town.

The Old Town quarter itself has lovingly preserved its medieval character, with narrow alleyways, half-timbered houses, patrician row houses and quaint churches. It is clear that the city was wealthy in its day and that the trade in products like fabrics, canvas, wood and grains was lucrative, particularly in the 18th century.

The sites that are worth seeing include the St Sauveur Church, which was partially built in the 12th century and has a late-Gothic gable, and the St Malo Church, built in the 15th-century with window panes telling the history of the town. Also worth a visit is the Franciscan monastery, which today houses a school, but the Gothic cloister can also be viewed. Walkers will find rest and relaxation in the English Garden near the Tour Ste Catherine view point.

The Musée de la Marine is housed in the oldest church of St Étienne, dating back to the 14th century.

7 Deauville This town is the epitome of sophisticated seaside resorts. In the mid-19th century, the rich and famous came in droves to the expensive luxury hotel, part of which still exists today. Deauville's town center comprises the casino, which served as inspiration for Ian Fleming's *Casino Royal*, and the stylish squares include the Promenade de Planches, which is constructed of wooden planks.

8 Caen Nearly completely destroyed in World War II, Caen is now a modern city. Its historic features are the two abbeys of Abbaye-des-Dames and Abbaye-aux-Hommes.

It is worth making a detour out to the Cotentin Peninsula, which includes Cherbourg and other villages such as Barfleur. From Coutances at the south-western end of the peninsula, continue south on the D971.

9 Granville The "Monaco of the North" is today a mix of medieval city and fishing village. The impressive Old Town is perched high above the center on a cliff. As in Deauville, one of the most famous buildings is the casino, opened in 1910. Couturier, Christian Dior, spent his childhood in the pinkish house with exotic garden. Today, it is the Dior Museum.

Heading towards Avranches on the D911 you will get magnificent views of the Bay of Mont Saint-Michel, which runs right along the coast.

10 Mont Saint-Michel France's most frequently visited attraction is not necessarily a place of peace and quiet, but you can still feel the magic of this town. Its location on a conical mountain in the middle of a tidal bay renders the monadnock either isolated as an island in the ocean or as a rock island surrounded by sand. It is simply sensational. Hermits lived in the first houses of worship in the area until, according to lore, Saint Aubert was charged in the 8th century by Archangel Michael to build a sanctuary on the mountain. Further development on the structure began in the 13th century. The church of Notre-Dame-sous-Terre, the new abbey church, the three-levelled monastery complex, the cloister and the Salle de Chevaliers are the most interesting areas.

The D155 heads out of the Bay of Mont St-Michel towards the Côte d'Emeraude, the Emerald Coast, which is home to probably the most beautiful town of the Breton north coast.

11 Saint-Malo This medieval city of the corsairs was badly destroyed in World War II but was rebuilt to its original condi-

1 Six-storey row houses from the 17th century line the beautiful port of Honfleur.

2 Mont Saint-Michel, an icon of Normandy and a famous abbey, is an unrivaled synthesis of monastery and fortress architecture.

3 Looking out over the city wall of St Malo, which encloses the restored Old Town quarter.

Pointe de Saint-Mathieu is a unique complex atop a 30-m-high (98 ft) headland, approximately 20 km (12 mi) west of Brest. The complex includes a 36-m-high (118 ft) lighthouse, a square signal tower, the ruins of a former Benedictine abbey church, Notre-Dame-de-Grâce, whose western façade is from the 12th century.

(the rest was built between the 13th and 16th centuries), and the village church of Saint-Mathieu. The lighthouse itself was built in 1835, using the stones from the church ruins, and helps sailors navigate the very dangerous waters off the Côte des Abers in Brittany.

The "calvaires" of Brittany

Among Brittany's most famous tourist attractions are the ornate granite calvaries, or calvaires. Some of the most beautiful ones are found in the Elorn Valley between Morlaix and Brest, and a well-signposted "Circuit des Enclos Paroissiaux" connects the most interesting of them.

Calvaires typically depict the apostles and saints of the Passion story grouping around Christ on the cross with other biblical figures. They were primarily created by Breton artists during the time of the plague. All of the calvaires are in "enclos paroissiaux", or walled churchyards, and the faithful enter through an impos-

The calvaire of Saint-Thégonnec.

ing gate, or "porte triumphale". The church and ossuary (ossuaire) were built with the calvaires to create a grandiose church complex. Local communities actually competed with each other to design the most beautiful vicarages.

One of the most impressive is the Saint-Thégonnec village calvaire built in 1610. It portrays an enthralling version of the Passion story of Jesus Christ and includes Saint Thégonnec. According to legend, the saint had his cart drawn by a wolf after his donkey was eaten by the pack to which the wolf belonged. The pulpit in the church of Saint-Thégonnec is also worth seeing.

tion after 1945. The Ville Close, the Old Town with its granite houses from the 17th and 18th centuries, as well as the promenade along the ramparts are but a few of the highlights.

The road to Dinard heads over the 750-m-long (0.5 mile) dam cum bridge of the tidal power station over the Rance. Its lock is 65 m (213 ft) long.

12 Dinard The second-largest seaside resort in Brittany is a garden city nestled neatly into a hilly landscape. A walk along the Promenade du Clair de Lune is a must. Dinard was and still is a favorite meeting place for the international jet set.

A great detour from here takes you 22 km (14 mi) south towards Dinan, a picturesque little town perched high above the Rance River. Anyone wishing to skip this side trip can head along the scenic coastal road past Cap Fréhel to the capital of the Côte d'Armor, St-Brieuc, some 3 km (2 miles) inland.

13 St.-Brieuc This city has a nicely preserved Old Town with gorgeous half-timbered houses, including the Hôtel des Ducs de Bretagne. The twin-spired cathe-

dral from the 13th century, which was modified over the 18th and 19th centuries, looks almost like a fort.

14 Côte de Granit Rose Off the coast from the fishing port of Paimpol is the Ile-de-Bréhat, a birdlife reserve with red granite rock formations like the rest of the neighboring eighty-six islands. It is of course this stone that gave the entire coast the name Côte de Granit Rose. Also worth seeing is the fishing town of Ploumanach just a few miles

further north, as well as Plougrescant at the mouth of the Jaudy River north of Tréguier. The chapel in the small seaside resort of Perros-Guirec is also made of red granite.

From Lannion, the road continues along the coast to Finistère, the "end of the earth", and it is here that Brittany showcases its most attractive side: the Atlantic crashing along the wild, craggy cliffs, and lighthouses balancing precariously on promontories and islands surrounded by the ocean. The picturesque

fishing villages feature houses of solid stone and walled church courtyards.

15 Morlaix This port city is home to an Old Town that is well worth seeing for its carefully preserved medieval houses, but the townscape is actually dominated by a massive railway viaduct.

Those interested in the vicarages and calvaires should turn off here onto the N 12 into the Elorn Valley and head towards St.-Thégonnec (see left margin).

16 Roscoff There is a regular ferry connection to England and Ireland from this heavily frequented spa resort. The town has a number of beautiful old fishermen's houses, and the laboratory for oceanographic and marine biology research here is world renowned.

17 Brest This city was transformed into France's largest naval port by Cardinal Richelieu in the mid-17th century, and it remained so until being reduced to rubble during World War II. Since its reconstruction, it has become one of the most modern cities in the country and is once again an important naval base. The Pont de Recouvrance, with pylons 64 m (210 ft) high and a total length of 87 m (285 ft), is the longest drawbridge in

Europe. Brest's research center and Océanopolis maritime museum are located at the Moulin Blanc yacht harbor.
A short detour west takes you to the Pointe de St-Mathieu, famous for the lighthouse located within the ruins of an old monastery. From Brest, take the N165 along the Bay of Brest to Le Faou, a town with interesting medieval houses made of granite. The D791 will take you to the Crozon Peninsula with its stunning coatal cliffs.

18 Crozon The main town on the peninsula of the same name is a popular holiday destination. Gorgeous beaches are tucked between breathtaking cliffs, and you can take boats to explore the picturesque coastal grottos. Four headlands extend out into

the sea here. Perched atop one of them is Camaret-sur-Mer, at one point the most important lobster and crayfish port in France. It is worth going to see the Château Vauban, a fort built according to designs by Louis XIV's master military engineer, the Marquis de Vauban.
West of Camaret-sur-Mer are the Alignements des Lagatjar, quartzite menhirs arranged in a U-shape in three rows. You can get a spectacular view of this prehistoric wonder from the peninsula's most beautiful cape, Pointe de Penhir.

19 Douarnenez This city has an interesting Old Town and is one of the most important fishing ports in Brittany. The maritime museum displays a collection of boats and all sorts of informa-

tion on shipbuilding. Popular spa resorts in the area invite you to spend a day on the beach.

20 Pointe du Raz This cliff drops 70 m (230 ft) to the sea and is the westernmost point of France. It is also one of the most visited places in Brittany. Countless holidaymakers do the half-hour climb over the rocky ridge every day. And for good reason: the view of this rugged landscape amidst the surging waves of the Atlantic is spectacular. Offshore is the small tiny Ile de Sein. It is flat and has hardly any vegetation, but the charming white houses shimmer invitingly. Far out at sea, the mighty lighthouse of Phare d'Ar-Men, built on a ledge in 1881, helps ships navigate the dangerous waters from up to 50 km (31 mi) away.

1 View from the 72-m-high (236-ft) coastal cliffs of the Pointe du Raz in Finistère, looking out over its most striking imagery, the storm-swept lighthouses.

2 Ile-de-Bréhat on the Côte de Granit Rose, the Pink Granite Coast, far away from the holiday resorts and crowds.

3 A Breton stone house at the northern tip of Brittany near Plougrescant, not far from Tréguier.

4 The natural harbor in Brest, with the mighty Château de Brest from the 12th–17th centuries. The city is one of the most important naval bases in France.

5 A remote Breton house on the Pointe du Raz – an abode for individualists.

Detour

Quiberon

Millions of years ago, the stunning Quiberon Peninsula was an island. Now, it is connected to the mainland by a narrow isthmus and is home to an upscale holiday paradise with a wide range of spa resort and watersport options.
The Côte Sauvage is a series of craggy rock cliffs that is intermit-

Quiberon at dusk.

tently broken up by small, sandy bays. The east coast is home to wide, sandy beaches that are perfect for relaxing family holidays as well as sports like wind surfing and land sailing. Analgesic Thalasso therapies are also on offer in the town of Quiberon, and St Pierre-Quiberon has a stone formation with twenty-two menhirs.

㉑ Quimper The capital of Finistère is a pretty old town with pedestrian zones, quaint medieval row houses and towering church spires.
It is definitely worth seeing St-Correntin Cathedral with its magnificent 15th-century Gothic windows and twin 76-m-high (249 ft) spires. Local history and culture is exhibited at the Musée Départemental Breton.
Point-l'Abbé, south of Quimper, is a small town whose ornate lacework and embroidery made it famous well beyond Brittany. On the way to Quimperlé you

will pass Pont Aven, where Paul Gauguin painted and developed his unique expressionist style with Emile Bernard between 1886 and 1889. The Musée de Pont-Aven provides an insight into this time. A well signposted footpath heads from the banks of the Aven River to the painters' favorite spots.

㉒ Quimperlé This small town has a lower section as well as an upper section picturesquely situated on a headland between the Isole and Ellé rivers. It has some charming old houses and

the circular Ste-Crolx Church is also worth seeing.
Your route now heads into the southern part of Brittany. The port city of Lorient has no less than five ports, including one of the most important fishing ports

in France. In Auray, roughly 18 km (11 mi) before Vannes, you should not miss the detour to the approximately 3,000 menhirs of Carnac. From there continue along the peninsula to Quiberon.

St. Thégonnec The pulpit and calvaire of the village church here are masterpieces of 17th-century Breton art.

Côte de Granit Rose Picturesque pink and reddish rocks characterize the northernmost tip of Brittany. They have been beautifully shaped by the wind and waves.

Cap Frehel On a clear day you can see as far as Saint Malo and the Channel Islands from the reddish cliffs of the cape. You can get a panorama view of the 70-m-high (230-ft) cliffs while on a boat tour.

Brest France's largest naval port was almost completely destroyed in World War II. Today, Brest is one of the country's most modern cities.

Pointe de Saint Mathieu Looks can be deceiving: the lighthouse 20 km (12 miles) west of Brest is not on top of the old monastery walls (12th–16th centuries), but behind them.

Pointe du Raz This dramatic lighthouse is on a 70-m-high rock formation in the Atlantic. The climb takes about thirty minutes.

Quiberon This peninsula is popular among watersport enthusiasts, while families prefer the more sheltered east coast.

Carnac Now a spa resort, this location was even popular in prehistoric times: 3,000 menhirs (from 4000–2000 BC) and other stone monuments attest to human settlements.

In the realm of the menhirs

Carnac and the surrounding area are home to the largest megalith field in the world. Roughly 3,000 megaliths, also known as menhirs, are spread over several areas, all fenced in for their protection. The largest and most beautiful of them is the Alignement de Kerzhero, stony witness of a history dating back to between 4000 and 2000 BC. There are also prehistoric burial mounds, the most interesting

houses attract thousands of visitors every year.

Archaeological relics from the region are displayed in the Musée d'Árchéologie du Morbi-kau, in the 15th-century Château Gaillard. Anyone who does not want to go directly to Nantes from Vannes on the highway should take the 30-km (19 mi) detour to the French coast, for example to Le Croisic, at La Roche-Bernard.

㉔ Nantes The journey ends in Nantes, which vied for centuries with Rennes to be the capital of

㉓ Vannes The capital of Morbihan is a worthwhile destination for anyone with a romantic streak. The medieval alleyways, the partially preserved Old City wall with its quaint towers, and the charming half-timbered

Brittany, It eventually lost in the late 19th century.

This city at the mouth of the Loire River was once the most important port city on the Loire, and magnificent buildings in the Old Town attest to this. The Château des Ducs de Bretagne is an impressive fort surrounded by a moat.

In addition to the impressive cathedral, the Old Town's Art Nouveau plazas and elegant 18th-century arcades enchant visitors to Nantes.

1 The coastal landscape on the Quiberon Peninsula is breathtaking: the shimmering cliffs, electric blue-white skies and the crashing waves are conducive for a stroll.

2 Half-timbered row houses in front of St Corentin Cathedral in Quimper. This capital of the Département Finistére is also a bishop's see.

3 Hundreds of yachts bob up and down in the marina of Le Croisic on the headland west of St Nazaire. The popular holiday resort offers a wide range of watersports in summer.

Carnac: Alignement de Kerlescan.

of which is the 12-m-high (39 ft) St Michel tumulus with chapel. From above, you can get a wonderful view over the landscape of menhirs. If this doesn't satisfy your passion for prehistory, don't worry: you can also visit the dolmens (tomb chambers) in the surrounding area.

Honfleur The city on the Côte Fleurie, the Floral Coast, emanates port romanticism. The Musée de la Marine is inside Honfleur's oldest church, while the Musée Satie remembers the city's great composer.

Limestone coast near Étretat This village lined with glorious cliffs ("falaises") was a favorite among artists like Monet and Courbet in the 19th century.

Deauville This elegant seaside resort was already popular in the mid-19th century. Luxury hotels, casinos and the Promenade des Planches still prosper here.

Paris The capital of France is also the country's cultural center. If you want to explore the city's numerous museums and enjoy its special flair, make sure you allow plenty of time.

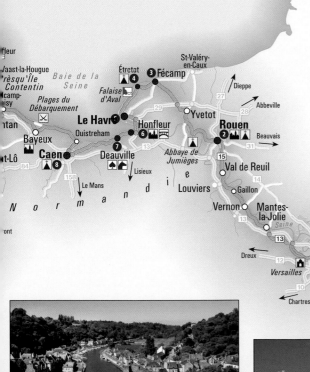

Dinan A mighty castle towers over Dinan, considered one of the most idyllic towns in Brittany. Miles of walls with sixteen gates surround the Old Town quarter on the left bank of the Rance River.

St. Malo The granite houses in the Old Town quarter and the boardwalk on the ramparts are impressive here. The city has been restored to its original state.

Mont St Michel This cone-shaped monadnock with its magical location in a tidal bay, is one of the country's most popular attractions. Additions were made in the 8th century, and again from the 13th century onwards. Three million visitors come to the small monastery island every year.

France

The old port of La Rochelle and the watchtowers of St-Nicolas and Tour de la Chaîne.

Via Turonensis – on the old pilgrimage route from Paris to Biarritz

The Via Turonensis was mainly travelled by pilgrims from the Netherlands and northern France on their way to Santiago de Compostela in Galicia, the far north-west corner of Spain. They mostly went on foot to their imminent salvation. Today, there are still pilgrims who follow the Camino de Santiago (St James' Way) and its various 'side streets' for religious purposes, but most people these days are simply interested in seeing the wonderful sights along the way.

Four different trails originally led pilgrims through France to the tomb of St James in Santiago de Compostela – the Via Tolosana from Arles through Montpellier and Toulouse to Spain; the Via Podensis from Le Puy through Conques, Cahors and Moissac to the border; the Via Lemovicensis from Vézelay through Avallon, Nevers and Limoges; and finally, the fourth route, the Via Turonensis, known as the 'magnum iter Sancti Jacobi' (the Great Route of St James).

The route's name comes from the city of Tours, through which it passed. The pilgrims started at the tomb of St Dionysius in St Denis before heading through Paris, down the Rue St-Jacques to the church of the same name, where only the tower still stands on the right bank of the Seine. The tomb of St Evurtius was the destination in Orléans, while the tomb of St Martin, who was often compared to St James, awaited pilgrims in Tours. In Poitiers, there were three churches on the

Jeanne d'Arc Arriving at Orléans, a painting by Jean Jacques Scherrer.

intinerary: St-Hilaire, Notre Dame la Grande and Ste-Radegonde. The head of John the Baptist was the object of worship in St-Jean-d'Angély, and pilgrims would pray at the tomb of St Eutropius in Saintes. Bordeaux was also the custodian of important relics like the bones of St Severin and the Horn of Roland.

The pilgrims of the Middle Ages would most certainly have been amazed and would have shaken their heads at the buildings that the modern pilgrims along the Via Turonensis today find so fascinating. While the largest and most beautiful buildings in the Middle Ages were erected to honour and praise God, modern man seems obsessed with himself and his comforts. 'Pilgrims' nowadays are most interested in visiting the castles along the Via Turonensis, drawn to the extravagance as if by magic.

Château de Chambord, in the middle of a large forest, is a structure of fairy-tale proportions.

The modern glass pyramid by I.M. Pei in front of the magnificent Louvre building has been the museum's main entrance since 1989.

Perfect examples of this absolutism are just outside Paris in the Île-de-France – the enormous palace complex of Versailles and the castle of Rambouillet which, as the summer residence of French presidents, continues to be a center of power. Many other magnificent buildings are scattered along the Loire River and its tributaries, the Indre, Cher and Vienne, including the colossal Château de Chambord, a dream realized by King Francis I, the Château de Chenonceaux, and others like Beauregard, Chaumont, Valençay, Loches, Le Lude and Langeais. The area around Bordeaux is home to a completely different kind of château. Médoc, Bordeaux and Entre-Deux-Mers are names that make the wine-lover's heart skip a beat. This region is the home of myriad great wines, in particular red wine. The wineries around Bordeaux, most of which look like real castles in the middle of vast vineyards, are referred to as châteaus and include internationally renowned names such as Mouton-Rothschild, Lafitte-Rothschild and Latour. Last but not least, today's 'car pilgrims' are attracted to destinations that are far off the beaten track and would have seemed rather absurd as a detour to the pilgrims of the Middle Ages – namely, those on the Atlantic coast. The sandy beaches and coves of the Arcachon Basin and the sections of coast further south on the Bay of Biscay provide wind and waves for windsurfers and surfers. The elegant life of the 19th century is celebrated in the charming seaside resort of Biarritz and, from here, it's not much further to the Aragonian section of the Camino de Santiago, which stretches along the northern coast of Spain.

The Médoc on the left bank of the Gironde is one of the best red wine regions in the world.

Detour

Chartres

Even from a great distance, Chartres Cathedral is an impressive edifice, soaring like a mirage above the vast expanse of cornfields in the Beauce region. Up close, any doubts of its stature vanish immediately. This masterpiece of Gothic architecture, a large portion of which was built in the second half of the 12th century, simply overwhelms with its dimensions and design.

Chartres Cathedral

The facade and, in particular, the entrance area are a dazzling sight full of lavish ornamentation, but the cathedral's greatest treasure is inside: glass paintings unsurpassed in their number and beauty anywhere else in the world. The vivid stained-glass windows depict both biblical and historical scenes, and thus provided literate and illiterate believers alike with their wealth of information.

The rose windows are also stunning, and their engraved tracery contains an extensive range of images. The southern and western rose windows illustrate the Last Judgement, while the eastern rose window is dedicated to the Virgin Mary.

Chartres Cathedral, a UNESCO World Heritage Site since 1979, should definitely not be missed.

The Via Turonensis follows one of the four major French routes of the St James' pilgrimage trail. Starting in the Île-de-France, you'll head to Orléans on the Loire, continue downstream past some of the most beautiful and famous Loire châteaus and then, from Saumur onwards, make your way south into the Gironde to Bordeaux. Prior to arriving in Biarritz, you stop in St-Jean-Pied-de-Port, the former last stop for pilgrims before crossing the Pyrenees.

1 St-Denis The actual pilgrim route begins in St-Denis, north of Paris. During the heyday of the Camino de Santiago (St James' Way) pilgrimages, this town was located north of the former city border and was the meeting place for the pilgrims coming from Paris. The French national saint, Dionysius, is buried in the city's cathedral. The basilica, where almost all of France's kings are entombed, is considered the first masterpiece of Gothic architecture.

2 Paris (see pp. 194–197). South-west of Paris is Versailles. The name of the palace is intrinsically tied to the Sun King, Louis XIV, and is a symbol of his display of absolutist power.

3 The Palace of Versailles Louis XIII first had a small hunting lodge built on the site where this magnificent building now stands. Under Louis XIV, the lodge was gradually expanded to the immense dimensions we know today, followed by some 'insignificant' extensions like the opera, built under Louis XV. During the reign of the Sun King, Versailles was the place where anyone who wanted to have any sort of influence in the State had to stay. Apart from the large, opulent reception rooms such as the Hall of Mirrors, the Venus Room, the Hercules Room or the Abundance Salon, there were also the king and queen's lavishly furnished private chambers. The opera is a real gem, completed in 1770.

Beyond the water features of the Bassin d'Apollon is the vast park complex, which is home to the Grand Trianon, Petit Trianon and Le Hameau. The Grand Trianon was built under the orders of Louis XIV – one wing for him and the other for his beloved, Madame de Maintenon. The Petit Trianon was built for

Louis XV's mistresses. Le Hameau is almost an absurdity – a small village with a homestead, dairy farm, mill and pigeon loft, where Marie Antoinette played 'peasant', a game that did not win her any fans among supporters of the revolution – she wound up under the guillotine on the Place de la Concorde.

4 Rambouillet Although the palace is the summer residence of the French president, it can be visited most of the time. The building consists of wings designed in different architectural styles including Gothic, Renaissance and baroque.

This castle only became royal property in 1783, when Louis XVI

The town revolves around its castle, where the individual building phases are very easily recognized. The oldest section is Louis XII's wing, constructed in red brick with white limestone decorations. The Francis I wing is far more lavish, built in Renaissance style with traces of French Gothic in parts. The king would often have his heraldic animal, the salamander, displayed in certain areas. What really catches your eye is the Renaissance-style staircase tower in the interior courtyard, where the royal family could attend events.

Noble palaces such as the Hôtel Sardini, the Hôtel d'Alluye and the Hôtel de Guise are proof that, apart from royalty, numerous other aristocrats also had their residences along the Loire. The St-Louis Cathedral is not Gothic and only dates back to the 17th century, the previous building having been extensively destroyed by a hurricane. An

Ludwig XIV and Absolutism

L'état c'est moi – I am the State. This statement by Louis XIV aptly characterizes his understanding of power. The 'Sun King' was born in 1638 and, following the death of his father in 1643,

Louis XIV – a painting by H. Rigaud, 1701, Louvre, Paris.

proclaimed king at the tender age of five. His reign was subsequently defined by his love of all things opulent and gaudy, and the Palace of Versailles is the most impressive and repeatedly copied example of this.

After the death of Cardinal Mazarin, Louis XIV limited the rights of parliament and the aristocracy and strengthened the army. He ruled with absolute power until his death in 1715.

acquired it as a hunting lodge. The park and the adjacent Rambouillet forest are ideal places to take a relaxing stroll. On the way to Orléans to the south of Paris, it's worth making a detour to Chartres, whose name is automatically associated with its Gothic cathedral, the largest in Europe.

⑤ Orléans This city's cathedral, Ste-Croix, is built in Gothic style, though only very small parts of it date back to the Gothic period. The original building, destroyed during the French Wars of Religion, was rebuilt under Henry VI, and the architects of the 18th and 19th centuries continued to use the Gothic style. The city's liberator lived in the house named after her – the Maison de Jeanne d'Arc. The half-timbered house, which was destroyed in World War II, was reconstructed identically to the original. Only very few of the

beautiful old houses and noble palaces were spared from the severe attacks of the war, but the Hôtel Toutin, with its gorgeous Renaissance interior courtyard, is one that was. Of course, Orléans wouldn't be complete without the statue of Jeanne d'Arc, erected on the Place du Martroi in 1855.

Before heading on to Blois, it's well worth making a detour to the beautiful moated castle of Sully-sur-Loire, some 40 km (25 miles) south-east of Orléans. From Orléans, you have two options for reaching Chambord, which is somewhat outside of the Loire Valley – either along the right bank of the Loire to Merand and across a bridge, or along the left bank of the Loire on small rural roads.

⑥ Chambord King Francis I had this château built on the site of an older hunting lodge. Lost among the vast forests, the

result was a vast dream castle with an incredible 440 rooms, seventy staircases, corner towers, a parapet and a moat. Leonardo da Vinci was apparently involved in its construction as well, designing the elaborate double-helix staircase whose two spirals are so intertwined that the people going up cannot see the people going down, and vice versa.

One of the château's real charms is its unique roof silhouette with its numerous turrets and chimneys. Francis I did not live to see the completion of his château, and work was not continued on it until the reign of Louis XIV. Louis XV gave it as a gift to the Elector of Saxony, who had it gloriously renovated. The château fell into temporary neglect after his death.

⑦ Blois In the first half of the 17th century, Blois was the center of France's political world.

1 View of the Eiffel Tower lit up at night from one of the many bridges along the Seine.

2 The Palace of Versailles – the Cour de Marbre courtyard is paved with marble slabs.

3 The oldest bridge in Paris, the Pont Neuf, spans the Seine on the north and south sides of the Île de la Cité. Despite its name 'New Bridge', the Pont Neuf was opened in 1607 and connected the city to the island in the river, its medieval center.

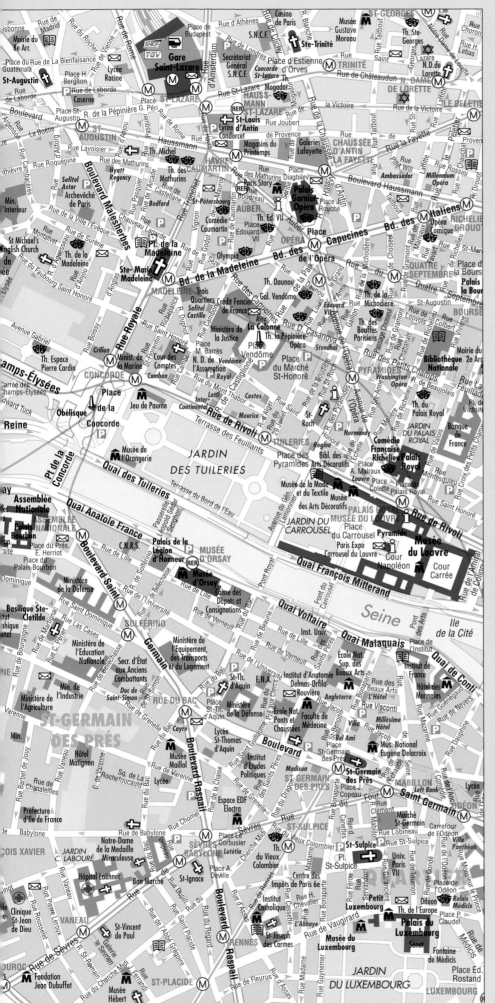

Paris

The French capital is a city of thrilling contrasts – rich in tradition and at the same time avant-garde, enormous in size and yet captivatingly charming. Paris is also a university city and the place of government, a global center for fashion and art, incredibly multicultural and yet still very much the epitome of all things French.

Throughout its long history, Paris has continually been in a state of expansion. The city always appeared to be bursting at the seams. Today, greater Paris covers an area of about 105 sq km (40 sq miles) and is home to some twelve million people – more than twenty percent of the entire population of France. This city's non-stop growth is not least due to the fact that Paris does not accept any rivals. The nation's capital has always been unchallenged in its political, economic and cultural significance.

On the south side of the Seine you won't be able to miss the Eiffel Tower, the symbol of Paris built for the World Fair in 1889. The iron construction, towering 300 m (984 ft) over the city, took engineer Gustav Eiffel just sixteen months to completed. The viewing platform, accessed by

Be sure to see the Place de la Concorde, an excellent example of wide boulevards and geometric plazas that gave the French capital its 'big city' look during its renovation in the 19th century. Also visit the park complex Jardin des Tuileries, which leads up to the Louvre; the Place Vendôme with its upmarket shopping; the Palais Garnier, an opulent 19th-century opera house; and the 17th-century Palais Royal.

Montmartre, on the north side of town, is great for exploring both day and night. Things to see include the historic Moulin de la Galette with its outdoor garden restaurant; the Sacre Coeur basilica up on the hill, with fantastic views of the city; the Père Lachaise Cemetery (east, outside city center), one of three large cemeteries built around 1800 with the graves of numerous celebrities (Oscar Wilde, Jim

Top: Place de la Concorde, one of the most magnificent plazas in Europe.
Middle: The striking Arc de Triomphe on the Champs-Elysées by night.
Bottom: The Eiffel Tower was erected in 1889 for the World Fair.

elevator, is one of the city's major attractions. The Hôtel des Invalides, a complex crowned by the Dôme des Invalides, was built by Louis XIV for the victims of his numerous wars.

North of the Seine is probably the most magnificent boulevard in the world, the Champs-Elysées, with the Arc de Triomphe providing a great view of the streets emanating from its center.

Morrison, Edith Piaf, Eugène Delacroix and Frédéric Chopin, for example). All the cemeteries have detailed maps available at the main entrance.

In the northern suburb of St-Denis you will find the early-Gothic church of St-Denis, the burial place of the French kings, and the Stade de France, a massive football stadium with capacity for 80,000, built for the 1998 World Cup.

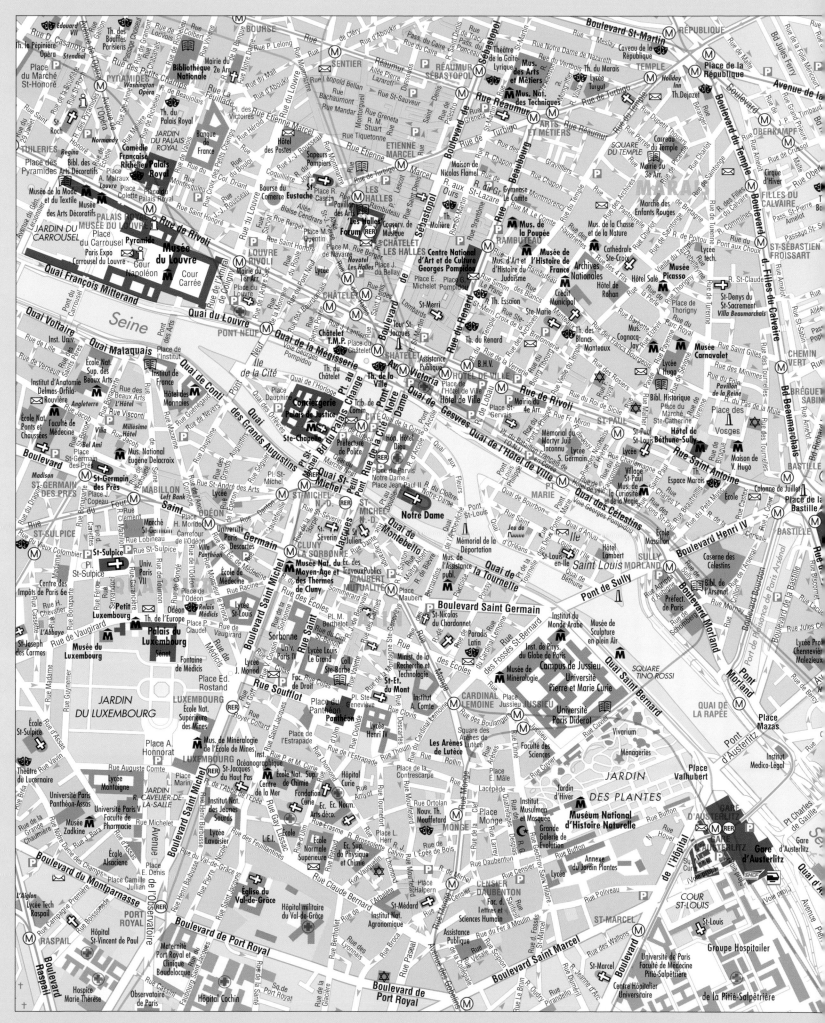

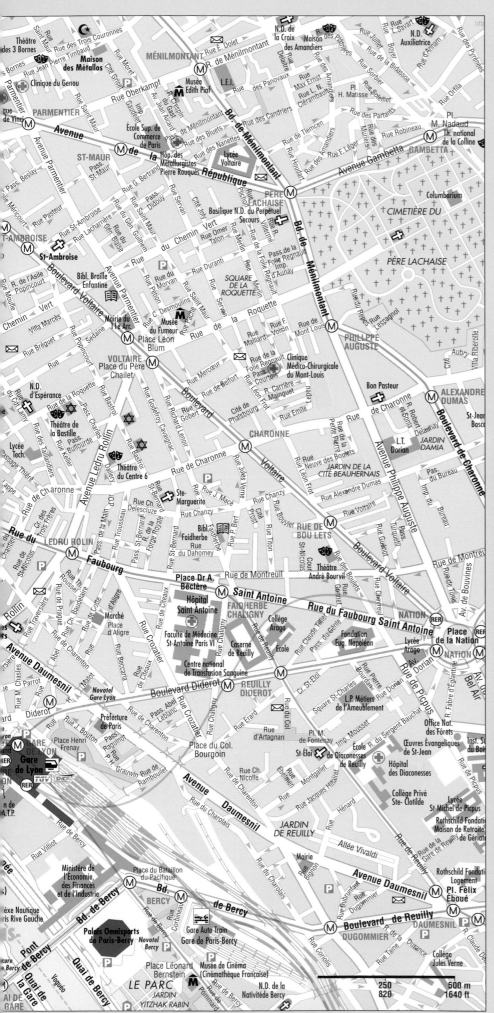

Paris

The historic center of the 'City of Light' is relatively easy to navigate, and many sights can be reached on foot. However, you should allow yourself copious amounts of time – after all, if you fancied it, you could spend days just wandering around the Louvre.

During the Middle Ages, when Paris was arguably the most important city in Europe, three factors determined the city's development and status – the church, its royalty and the university, all of which have left their mark on the historic city center. Out on the Île de la Cité – the city's oldest core settlement where the Romans, Merovingians and Carolingians based their dominions – stands one of France's most splendid cathedrals: Notre Dame.

As of 1400, medieval royalty focused their power on the northern banks of the Seine at the Louvre, which was begun in 1200 as part of a first ring of fortifications and developed into a magnificent residence over the centuries. On the other side of the river, in the Latin Quarter, professors and students united to establish the Sorbonne at the end of the 12th century. The riverbank, with its grand buildings, is a UNESCO World Heritage Site.

the former palace chapel of Ste-Chapelle, a high-Gothic masterpiece; the Conciergerie, part of the medieval royal palace; Pont Neuf, one of the most beautiful bridges on the Seine; and the idyllic Île St-Louis, south-east of the Île de la Cité, with its Renaissance buildings.

North of the Seine visit the Louvre, first a medieval castle, then the royal residence until the 17th century, then rebuilt and made into one of the largest art museums in the world; the Centre Pompidou, a cultural center with exemplary modern architecture; the Hôtel de Ville, the 19th-century town hall at the Place de Grève; the Marais quarter with the romantic Place des Vosges, the avant-garde Opéra National de Paris, the Gothic church of St-Gervais-et-St-Protais, the Picasso museum, and the Hôtel Carnavalet's museum on the city's history.

Top: The illuminated Louvre pyramid was built at the end of the 20th century as part of the costly modernization of the largest art museum in the world. Below: From the 12th to 14th centuries, the Gothic Notre Dame Cathedral was built on the Île de la Cité in the medieval city center.

On the Île de la Cité, don't miss the early-Gothic Cathédrale Notre Dame (12th/13th centuries), where you can climb both 68-m-high (223-ft) towers;

South of the Seine go to the famous Latin Quarter; the St-Germain-des-Prés and Montparnasse Quarters and the Jardin du Luxembourg park.

Jeanne d'Arc (Joan of Arc)

Jeanne d'Arc was born in 1412, the daughter of a rich farmer in Domrémy in the Lorraine region. At the time, France had been heavily involved in the Hundred Years War with England since 1337, and the English had advanced as far as the Loire.

At the age of thirteen, Jeanne began hearing voices in her head telling her to join forces with the French heir apparent, Charles VII, and expel the English from France. After she recognized him in Chinon, despite his disguise, people started believing in her divine mission. She was then given his support and went with the French army to Orléans, which was occupied by the English. With

A golden statue of Jeanne d'Arc on the Place des Pyramides in Paris.

her help, the city was liberated on 8 May 1429.

Jeanne was also able to persuade Charles VII to follow the dangerous road to Reims to be crowned. The ceremony took place in July 1420 in the Reims cathedral. However, the farmer's daughter from Lorraine, who was now France's heroine, had enemies too. In 1430, the Burgundians, who were allied with England, succeeded in imprisoning and handing Jeanne over to the English. She was accused of heresy and witchery in Rouen in 1431 and, as Charles VII thought it to be politically incorrect to help her, condemned to be burned at the stake on 30 May 1431. The conviction was overturned in 1456 and in 1920 Jeanne d'Arc was granted sainthood.

especially lovely half-timbered house, the Maison des Acrobates, is located on the cathedral square. If you are interested in Gothic churches, pay a visit to the 12th-century St-Nicolas.

⑧ Cheverny This castle, built between 1620 and 1634, is still owned by the family of the builder, Henri Hurault. It is also probably thanks to this fact that the castle still contains a large part of the original, opulent interior decor. The ceiling frescoes in the dining hall and bedroom are particularly worth inspecting.

⑨ Chenonceaux Powerful women played a large role in the history of this romantic pleasure palace. For example, Cathérine Briçonnet supervised its construction in the early 16th century while her husband was in Italy. After Thomas Bohier's death, the building fell into the hands of the king and Henry II gave it as a gift to his beloved, Diane de Poitiers, who extended it to include a bridge over the Cher. Following Henry's death, his wife, Catherine de Medici, kept the castle for herself, and it is thanks to her idea that the Florentine-style bridge was built, including its own gallery.

After Catherine de Medici, the widow of the assasinated Henry III, Louise de Lorraine, proceeded to live a life of mourning in what was actually a very

bright and cheerful-looking castle. This spirit returned in the 18th century with the arrival of middle-class Louise Dupin, who saved the castle from the destruction of the revolution. Only very little remains of the original decor, but Renaissance furnishings have been used to give an impression of what the interior may have been like.

Located on the bridge pier is the gorgeous kitchen, where copper pots and pans still hang in an orderly fashion.

⑩ Amboise Perched on a hill sloping steeply into the Loire is France's first major Renaissance château. Although only parts of the construction have been preserved, they are still very impressive in their size and grandeur.

Following an expedition to Italy in 1496, Charles VIII brought back with him Italian artists, craftsmen and works of art to decorate the palace. The interiors of the mighty towers were constructed in such a way that a rider on a horse could reach up into the storey above. The Chapelle-St-Hubert is a good example of Gothic architecture.

Not far from the château is the Le Clos-Lucé mansion, where Leonardo da Vinci spent the final years of his life. Francis I had originally arranged for the Italian universal genius to come to France, and a small museum displaying models of Leonardo's inventions pays homage to this influential man.

The small town located below the château, a row of houses,

and the clock tower all date back to the time of this region's heyday. From Amboise, a small road leads through the middle of the Loire Valley to Tours.

⑪ Tours This is the town that gave the Via Turonensis its name, and the tomb of St Martin here was an extremely important stop for St James pilgrims. Revolutionaries demolished the old St-Martin Basilica at the end of the 18th century. The new St-Martin Basilica, in neo-Byzantine style, contains the tomb of the saint, consecrated in 1890. It is an example of the monumental church architecture of the time, one that made use of many different styles.

The St-Gatien Cathedral is the city's most important historic

3

4

Romanesque church art in Poitiers and Parthenay-le-vieux

The Romanesque style of the Poitou region is typified, for the most part, by rich sculptural decorations. The facade of the former collegiate church of

Top: The western facade of the Notre Dame Cathedral in Poitiers.
Bottom: A look inside the church.

Notre Dame la Grande in Poitiers, completed in the mid 12th century, is a particularly good example of this. Above the three portals, as well as to the left and right of the large second-floor window, is an ornately sculptured series of images depicting themes from the Old and New Testament such as Adam and Eve, the prophet Moses, Jeremiah, Josiah and Daniel, the Tree of Jesse, the Annunciation, the birth of Christ, the twelve apostles and, in the gables, Christ in the Mandorla with two angels.

The church of St-Pierre in nearby Parthenay-le-Vieux was built in the late 11th century. The most striking part of this building is the eight-cornered transept tower, but the most beautiful features are the decorative figures on the facade. Samson's battle with the lion is depicted here, as well as the horseman, which is typical for the Romanesque style in Poitiers. The image of the Melusine fairy, which appears more than thirty times, is an original element.

church. The two-storey cloister provides a great view of the towers' tracery and the finely carved flying buttresses.

In some parts of the Old Town, like the Place Plumereau, you could be forgiven for thinking you were back in the Middle Ages. Charming half-timbered houses with pointed gables and often ornately carved balconies are proof of the wealth of the traders at the time. A waxworks cabinet is located in the historic rooms of the Château Royal (13th century).

⑫ Villandry The last of the great castles to be built in the Loire during the Renaissance (1536) fell into ruin in the 19th century and its Renaissance gardens were then made into an English-style park. The Spanish Carvallo family eventually bought it in 1906 and it is thanks to them that the castle has been renovated. More importantly, the gardens were re-modelled in the original Renaissance style. This explains why a lot of the people who visit the castle today are lovers of historic landscaping. Whether it be beds of flowers or vegetables, everything is laid out artistically and trees and hedges are perfectly trimmed into geometric shapes.

⑬ Azay-le-Rideau This castle on the Indre, built between 1519 and 1524, captivates visitors with the harmony of its proportions and its romantic location on an island in the river. However, it did not bring its builder, the mayor of Tours, Gilles Berthelot, much luck. Like other French kings, Francis I could not tolerate his subjects openly displaying their wealth. Without further ado, he accused the mayor of infidelity and embezzlement, and seized the castle.

⑭ Ussé The Château d'Ussé was built on the walls of a fortified castle in the second half of the 15th century. With its turrets and merlons, as well as its location at the edge of the forest, it's easy to see how it was the inspiration for authors of fairy tales. The Gothic chapel houses an important work of art from the Italian Renaissance, a terracotta Madonna by the Florentine sculptor Luca della Robbia.

⑮ Saumur Horse lovers around the world should be very familiar with the name Saumur. The cavalry school, founded in 1763, is still France's national riding school. The castle was built in the second half of the 14th century and is located on a hillside above the city.

Today, it houses two museums, an art museum and the Musée du Cheval. In the Old Town, half-timbered houses like the town hall on the Place St-Pierre, which was created in 1508 as a patrician palace, and the numerous 17th-century villas are all worth a look. In the Gothic church of Notre Dame de Nantilly, the side aisle, which Louis XI had built in a flamboyant style, is home to a prayer chapel that an inscription identifies as being the royal oratorio. On rainy days there are two interesting museums worth visiting: a mask museum (Saumur produces a large quantity of carnival masks) and a mushroom museum. These

1 After Versailles, the fantastic 16th-century water palace in Chenonceaux is the most visited château in France.

2 A stone bridge crosses the Loire in Amboise, home to the grand château of the same name.

3 Located on the left bank of the Indre, the 15th-century Château d'Ussé is like a fairy-tale castle made into reality.

4 Saumur – a view over the Loire to the Château de Saumur and the church tower of St-Pierre.

La Rochelle and Île de Ré

A detour to Île de Ré first takes you to La Rochelle, an important port town since the 11th century and considered one of France's most beautiful cities. In 1628, Cardinal Richelieu seized the town, which had for too long taken the wrong side in the political debate of the day – over 23,000 people died during the brutal occupation.

Today, its main attraction is the Atlantic port, where yachts bob up and down in a picture-perfect

Top: An aerial photo of Île de Ré.
Bottom: A view of the port at St-Martin-de-Ré.

scene. The city's best-known tourist sites are down by the Old Harbour – the Tour St-Nicolas and the Tour de la Chaîne. In times of war, an iron chain was stretched between the two towers to protect the port from enemy ships. The town hall (1595–1606) is built in Renaissance style with a gorgeous arcaded interior courtyard.

The Île de Ré – also known as the 'White Island' – is connected to the mainland by a 4-km-long (2.5-mile) bridge. Vineyards and salt marshes dominate the scene and are surrounded by pretty villages whose houses are decorated with lush flowers. The main town on the island is St-Martin-de-Ré, with a citadel that was constructed in the 17th century by the famous fort builder, Vauban.

St-Clément-des-Baleines near the north-western tip of the island is also interesting – it has two lighthouses worth seeing.

precious fungi are grown in the surrounding area in numerous limestone caves.

From Saumur, the westernmost point of the journey through the Loire, the road heads 11 km (7 miles) back towards Fontevraud-l'Abbey.

16 Fontevraud-l'Abbaye This abbey was founded in 1101 and existed as such until the 19th century. In the tall, bright church (consecrated in 1119) is the tomb of Eleonore of Aquitania. Southwest France 'wedded' England when she married Henry Plantagenet, later Henry II of England. Eleonore's husband and their son, Richard the Lionheart, are also buried in Fontevraud. The 16th-century cloister is the largest in all of France. However, the abbey's most original building is the monastery kitchen, which almost looks like a chapel with six arches.

17 Chinon This castle-like château high above the banks of the Vienne played an important role in French history. This is where Jeanne d'Arc first met Charles VII and recognized him despite his costume, his courtiers, who were hiding him, and the fact that she had never seen him before. It is for this reason that the large tower, the Tour de l'Horloge, houses a small museum dedicated to her. Other

parts of the castle, originating from the 10th to 15th centuries, are only ruins now. A highlight of any visit to the castle is the view over the Vienne valley.

18 Châtellerault This town, no longer of much significance, was once an important stop for pilgrims on the Camino de Santiago. Pilgrims would enter the town, as did Jeanne d'Arc, through Porte Ste-Cathérine. The church of St-Jacques, the destination of all pilgrims on the Camino de Santiago, was furnished with an ornate set of chimes. Some of the houses, such as the Logis Cognet, enable you to imagine what life was like in the 15th century.

19 Poitiers This old city, which was an important stop for pilgrims on the Camino de Santiago, found an important patron in Duke Jean de Berry. In the second half of the 16th century, it became a center of spiritualism and science and its churches still show evidence of this today.

20 Marais Poitevin The marshland located west of Poitiers and stretching all the way to the coast seems to have remained stuck in time. The most important and often the only means of transport in the 'Venise Verte' (Green Venice) is one of the flat-bottomed boats.

The Romanesque churches of Parthenay-le-Vieux, some 50 km (31 miles) west of Poitiers, are well worth a visit. You have to return to Poitiers before continuing on to St-Jean-d'Angély.

21 St-Jean-d'Angély Although it has now paled into insignificance, this town was once an important destination for St James pilgrims as it was here that they had the opportunity to pay their respects to John the Baptist. Only ruins remain of the Gothic church, but a row of beautiful half-timbered houses, the Tour de la Grosse Horloge (clock tower) dating from 1406, an artistic fountain (1546), and the 17th-century abbey enable modern visitors to take a trip back in time.

From here, it's worth making a detour to the port town of La Rochelle on the Atlantic, where you can make an excursion out to the Île de Ré.

22 Saintes The capital of the Saintonge looks back on a long history, traces of which can still be seen today. The Arc de Germanicus, which was originally the gateway to a bridge, dates back to Roman times. When the bridge eroded, it was saved and rebuilt on the right bank. The ruins of the amphitheater, dating back to the 1st century and today overgrown with grass, once

seated 20,000 people. There are also some impressive remains from the Middle Ages.

The Abbaye aux Dames, for example, was founded in 1047, and the Romanesque church was built in the 11th and 12th centuries. The Gothic St-Pierre Cathedral was constructed in the 13th and 14th centuries and the tower was added in the 17th century. The church of St-Eutrope, dating from the late 11th century, was one of the destinations of the St James

Château Mouton-Rothschild

In the Bordelais wine region, château does not mean castle, but rather a large vineyard. One of this region's world-famous vineyard abodes is the Château Mouton-Rothschild in Pauillac on the Gironde. Predominantly upmarket Cabernet-Sauvignon grapes are grown here, on a piece of land covering about 80 ha (198 acres).

Baron Philippe de Rothschild came up with the idea to make his wine bottles into small works of art. As a result, for over half a century artists have been creating labels for the property's top red wines. The list of contributing painters reads like a 'Who's Who' of modern art – Jean Cocteau (1947), Georges

Top: Vineyards as far as the eye can see.
Bottom: The château's wine cellar.

Braque (1955), Salvador Dalí (1958), Juan Miro (1969), Marc Chagall (1970), Pablo Picasso (1973), Andy Warhol (1975), Keith Haring (1988). You can admire these artworks, as well as many other exhibits, in the château's wine museum.

---

pilgrims. They prayed here in the spacious crypt at the tomb of the city's saint, Eutropius.

From Saintes you head south-east towards Cognac.

㉓ Cognac This town, on the banks of the Charente, today very much revolves around the drink of the same name, which expert noses will be able to catch whiffs of as they stroll through the town. The Valois Castle, from the 15th and 16th centuries, has a cognac distillery.

An exhibition at the town hall allows you to get a better understanding of the history and production of the precious brandy, which takes between five and forty years to mature. Some of the distilleries offer interesting tours of their facilities.

You head south-west from here to Pons before continuing on to Libourne.

㉔ Libourne This small town is a typical bastide, a fortified town, built at the time when

South-West France was an apple of discord between England and France (1150–1450). Every bastide is surrounded by a wall and has a grid-like layout and a large market square. Libourne was founded in 1270 and was for a long time a very important port for shipping wine out of the region. Today, it's worth taking a stroll around the Place Abel Surchamp.

㉕ St-Émilion Soaring out of the sea of vineyards that belong

to the St-Émilion appellation, which produce very high-quality wines, is the small town whose beginnings trace back to a monastery. The sizeable rock-hewn church here (9th–12th centuries), whose understated facade faces towards the pretty market place, is a special attraction. The collegiate church was built in the 12th century and its main aisle is Romanesque. By no means should you miss having a look at the very well-preserved cloister. The donjon, a relic from the royal fort, towers high above St-Émilion where the 'Jurade' wine confrèrie meets to test the new wines. Every year, from the tower platform, the members ceremoniously declare the grape harvest open.

㉖ Bordeaux This old city on the Garonne has long been dominated by trade – predominantly the wine trade. An historic event had a profound effect on the city – in 1154, Bordeaux fell under English rule

1 Storm clouds over the port of La Rochelle with its 15th-century Tour de la Lanterne.

2 With its medieval houses, squares and streets, St-Émilion is a charming little town in the middle of the lovely wine region of the same name.

Côte d'Argent and Côte des Basques

The Côte d'Argent refers to the stretch of coast between the Bassin d'Arcachon and Biarritz, where it turns into the Côte Basque, straddling the French-Spanish border. Apart from excellent swimming, the Côte d'Argent also hosts a unique natural landscape.

The Dune de Pilat is Europe's highest dune, fluctuating between 105 m and 120 m (345 ft and 394 ft), with a width of 500 m (1,640 ft), and a length of 2.7 km (2 miles). The

The romantic coast of Biarritz.

Parc Ornithologique du Teich is also worth a visit.

The Côte Basque is home to one of few swanky seaside resorts in the region – Biarritz. It experienced its heyday during the Belle Époque, when Napoleon III and his wife, Eugénie, spent their holidays here. The Rocher de la Vierge (Rock of the Virgin) and its statue of Madonna have a charming location out in the sea. A footbridge leads you out to the isolated formation. The casino and many of the hotel palaces are evidence of the glitz and glamour of Biarritz' golden age. St-Jean-de-Luz is a picturesque old town and several of its houses display the typically Basque half-timber style.

The Sun King met his bride, the Spanish Infanta Maria Theresa, for the first time here in the Maison Louis XIV. Her house, the Maison de l'Infante, is located just a little further on.

and, thanks to their huge interest in the region's wines, trade boomed. Even when Bordeaux was again part of France, it still maintained a close relationship with the British Isles.

The Place de la Comédie, with the classical columned facade of the Grand Théâtre, is an ideal place to start a stroll through the city. The Esplanade des Quinconces here is considered the largest square in Europe. You shouldn't miss seeing the city's churches. The St-André Cathedral was built between the 13th and 15th centuries and fascinates visitors with its Porte Royale, a magnificent door lavishly decorated with sculptures. Apart from the church, there is the Tour Pey-Berland, a free-standing tower. St-Michel was constructed somewhat later, in the 14th/16th centuries, and is furnished in 17th-century baroque style.

Those following in the footsteps of Camino de Santiago pilgrims should pay a visit to St-Seurin. Worshipping St-Severin (St-Seurin) was an important part of the route. The early-Romanesque crypt dates back to this time.

Bordeaux has a lot more to offer than just St James relics – the city gates of Porte de Cailhau, Porte d'Aquitaine, Porte de la Monnaie and Porte Dijeaux, for example. The Pont de Pierre (a stone bridge) and the tall, modern bridge, Pont d'Aquitaine, datingfrom 1967, are also worth a look.

Those interested in seeing the region's world-famous vineyards should make the 50-km (31-mile) journey along the Gironde to the Château Mouton-Rothschild in Pauillac.

27 Les Landes This is the name given to the landscape typical of the area south of Bordeaux – flat, sandy earth with sparse pine forests. The forests are planted by hand and are still used for their lumber by-products, predominantly for the extraction of resin.

Pont-Vieux

The small town of Orthez was already of strategic importance during the Middle Ages because of its Gothic bridge over the Gave du Pau. The medieval pilgrim bridge dates back to the 13th and 14th centuries and is home to a striking bridge tower.

The region's capital is Mont-de-Marsan, located somewhat off the beaten track in the southeast and home to some interesting Romanesque houses, the 15th-century Lacataye donjon and some very pretty parks.

28 Dax This small town on the Adour is one of France's most frequently visited thermal baths. Water at a temperature of 64°C (147°F) bubbles out of the Fontaine de la Néhé.

The 17th-century cathedral here is also worth seeing. The apostle gate from the earlier Gothic building is significant in an art-history context.

A visit to the Musée Borda in a beautiful city palace and a stroll along the banks of the Adour round off the visit.

If you want to go to the seaside, you can can drive 40 km (25 miles) from Dax to the southern end of the Côte d'Argent and then further on to the Côte des Basques around Biarritz.

On the other hand, those wanting to get a whiff of the mountain air in the Pyrenees should continue south-east along the spectacular route to Orthez.

29 St-Jean-Pied-de-Port In the Middle Ages, this mountain town was already an important stop for pilgrims – and the last before the strenuous crossing of the Pyrenees over the Roncesvalles Pass and across the Spanish border. 'Saint John at the Foot of the Pass' manages to preserve its medieval character even today. The banks of the Nive River are lined with houses from the 16th and 17th centuries and the Gothic church of Notre Dame du Bout du Pont.

30 Bayonne The capital of the Pays Basque is a densely settled area but it has managed to retain much of its charm in its center with bridges on two rivers, large squares and rows of houses packed closely together around the Gothic cathedral of Ste Marie. Its city festival is famous, held every year on the second weekend in August.

1 The Bay of Biarritz with its tiny port and the main beach.

2 The Pont du Pierre crosses the Garonne in Bordeaux, with the striking tower of the Cathédrale St-André in the background.

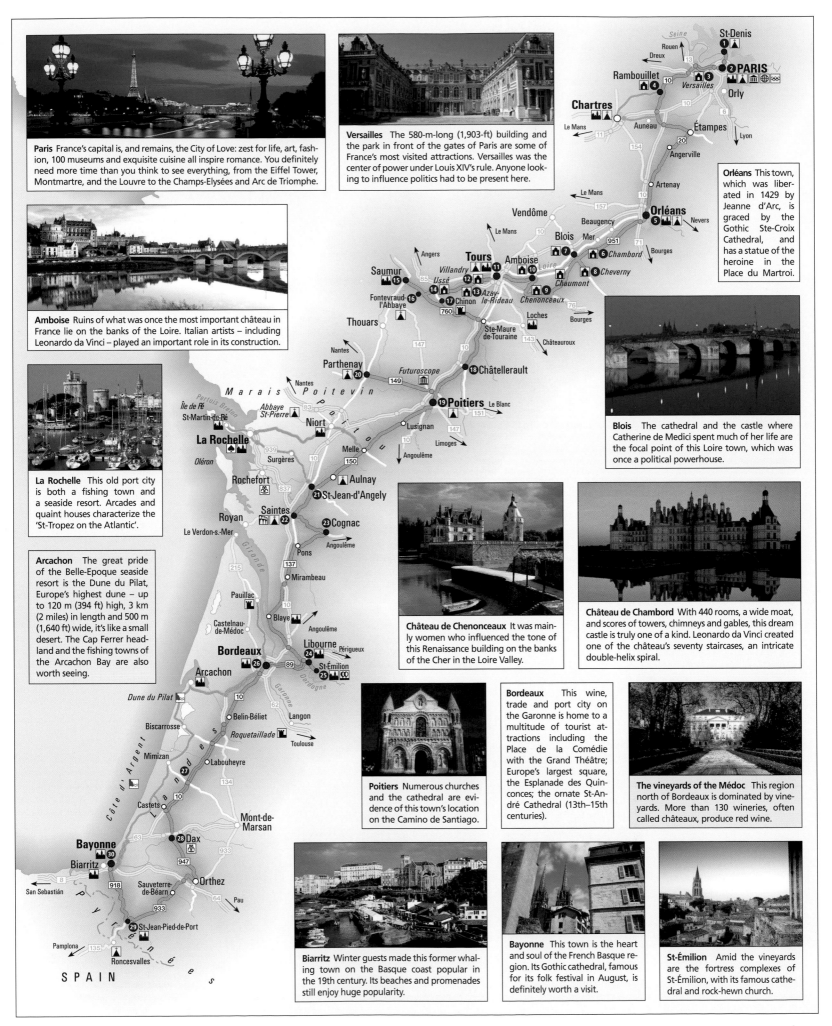

Paris France's capital is, and remains, the City of Love: zest for life, art, fashion, 100 museums and exquisite cuisine all inspire romance. You definitely need more time than you think to see everything, from the Eiffel Tower, Montmartre, and the Louvre to the Champs-Elysées and Arc de Triomphe.

Versailles The 580-m-long (1,903-ft) building and the park in front of the gates of Paris are some of France's most visited attractions. Versailles was the center of power under Louis XIV's rule. Anyone looking to influence politics had to be present here.

Amboise Ruins of what was once the most important château in France lie on the banks of the Loire. Italian artists – including Leonardo da Vinci – played an important role in its construction.

Orléans This town, which was liberated in 1429 by Jeanne d'Arc, is graced by the Gothic Ste-Croix Cathedral, and has a statue of the heroine in the Place du Martroi.

La Rochelle This old port city is both a fishing town and a seaside resort. Arcades and quaint houses characterize the 'St-Tropez on the Atlantic'.

Arcachon The great pride of the Belle-Epoque seaside resort is the Dune du Pilat, Europe's highest dune – up to 120 m (394 ft) high, 3 km (2 miles) in length and 500 m (1,640 ft) wide, it's like a small desert. The Cap Ferrer headland and the fishing towns of the Arcachon Bay are also worth seeing.

Blois The cathedral and the castle where Catherine de Medici spent much of her life are the focal point of this Loire town, which was once a political powerhouse.

Château de Chenonceaux It was mainly women who influenced the tone of this Renaissance building on the banks of the Cher in the Loire Valley.

Château de Chambord With 440 rooms, a wide moat, and scores of towers, chimneys and gables, this dream castle is truly one of a kind. Leonardo da Vinci created one of the château's seventy staircases, an intricate double-helix spiral.

Poitiers Numerous churches and the cathedral are evidence of this town's location on the Camino de Santiago.

Bordeaux This wine, trade and port city on the Garonne is home to a multitude of tourist attractions including the Place de la Comédie with the Grand Théâtre; Europe's largest square, the Esplanade des Quinconces; the ornate St-André Cathedral (13th–15th centuries).

The vineyards of the Médoc This region north of Bordeaux is dominated by vineyards. More than 130 wineries, often called châteaux, produce red wine.

Biarritz Winter guests made this former whaling town on the Basque coast popular in the 19th century. Its beaches and promenades still enjoy huge popularity.

Bayonne This town is the heart and soul of the French Basque region. Its Gothic cathedral, famous for its folk festival in August, is definitely worth a visit.

St-Émilion Amid the vineyards are the fortress complexes of St-Émilion, with its famous cathedral and rock-hewn church.

Lavender fields – a symbol of Provence. The plants are cultivated for their scented oil.

Route 17

France and Spain

The land of light between the Côte d'Azur and the Costa Brava

The coastline along the Côte d'Azur, the Golfe du Lion and the Costa Brava could hardly be more diverse or enticing. At the southern edge of the Alps, the Côte d'Azur showcases a landscape of breathtakingly unique beauty. Provence is a paradise for nature lovers and culture enthusiasts, while the Camargue is a near pristine delta landscape. The Costa Brava gets its name from the mountains which drop away steeply into the sea.

An incredibly varied stretch of coast between Menton on the Côte d'Azur and Barcelona on the Costa Brava greets visitors with all the beauty the French Midi and the north-eastern Spanish coast have to offer.

Directly behind Monte Carlo's sea of houses and apartments are the captivating mountains of the Alpes-Maritimes, which only begin to flatten out near Nice, allowing trendier cities like Cannes and Antibes to sprawl a bit. The foothills of the Massif des Maures once again

straddle the coast beyond St-Tropez where there is really only enough room for small, picturesque villages – your search for sandy beaches will be in vain. But not to worry, you'll find them again around Hyères and the offshore islands in the area.

Wine-lovers will get their money's worth between Toulon and Cassis – the wines grown between Bandol and Le Castellet are some of the best in the Midi. Marseille then presents itself as the port city with two faces. Founded by the Greeks, and

The Calanques cliffs near Cassis.

later a stronghold of the Romans, its cultural history dates back 2,500 years. At the same time, it was long the gateway to the cultures on other Mediterranean shores – Europe, North Africa and the Near East are all represented in Marseille's multicultural population.

West of Marseille, in the delta between the two mouths of the Rhône, sprawls a breathtakingly beautiful wetland of ponds, marshes, meadows and plains abundant with springs, grass, and salt fields – the Camargue. North of here is where you'll discover the heart of Provence. Cities such as Arles, Avignon and Nîmes are strongholds of European cultural history with their unique examples of Roman architecture.

The Languedoc-Roussillon region begins west of the Rhône delta and stretches to the Spanish border with a mix of long

St-Tropez: The international jet set discovered this idyllic fishing town in the 1950s and since then there have been more yachts than fishing boats anchored in the port.

Isolated bays along the rocky coast of the Costa Brava near Cadaqués.

beaches and mountainous hinterland. The Languedoc is home to the troubadours, and the Roussillon was part of Spain until the 1659 Treaty of the Pyrenees. The Catalán legacy in this region can still be seen at every turn. Even bullfights are still held here. The Languedoc was also home to the Cathars, who broke away from the Catholic Church in the 13th century.

Between Narbonne and Carcassone in the hills of Corbières, where an invitation to taste wine should never be refused, are numerous ruins of the proud castles that once stood here. With its fortress complexes, Carcassonne takes you back in time to the Middle Ages. South of Narbonne, near Leucate, marks the start of long, brilliantly white sandy beaches stretching to the Franco-Spanish border and the eastern foothills of the Pyrenees.

The last of the French villages before reaching Spain are self-assured fishing villages virtually embedded into the mountains. The Costa Brava, as this coastline is called, owes its name to the steep seaside cliffs at the eastern end of the Pyrenees. Bravo also means 'brave' or 'outstanding' in Spanish, so travellers should expect much more than just a wild coast.

The further south you go, the bigger the beaches become and the more towns and villages appear. The Catalán capital, Barcelona, is Spain's second-largest city. Carthaginians, Romans, Visigoths and Moors have all left their legacy here, making the city into a European metropolis with a special Catalán charm. The numerous art-nouveau buildings by Gaudí and Domènech i Montaner are quite spectacular. Life pulses day and night on the Ramblas, Barcelona's pedestrian zone.

The Old Town of Carcassonne enclosed by a double wall.

The Principality of Monaco

The area where the skyscrapers of 'Manhattan on the Côte d'Azur' soar above Monaco's modest 190 ha (222 acres) was first settled by the Greeks, followed by the Romans, and then later ruled by the powerful maritime city-state of Genoa.

In 1297, the coastal strip came under the rule of the mighty Grimaldi family, aristocrats from Genoa who later created the principality in 1612. The Grimaldis built their residence on a rock south of the port and have been able to retain their mini principality to this day.

Monaco owes its wealth to Prince Charles III, who built a casino on the headland north of the port in 1865. The revenues were so great that five years later the prince was able to abolish all taxes and thus lay

The Monaco casino.

the second foundation for the small state's successful history, a tax haven. In his honour, the rock on which the casino was built was given the name of Monte Carlo in 1878, a name that now applies to the entire region north of the port.

The casinos and the tax privileges guarantee Monaco's incessant growth. Nowhere else in Europe do so many Rolls Royces cruise the streets, nowhere else in the world are there so many millionaires living in such a small area, and nowhere else in the world will you find so many tax evaders. Tennis players and film stars alike ensure that the fairy tale of perpetual wealth never ends, and that the yachts in the port never get smaller.

The most important sights are the Palais de Monaco (16th–17th centuries), the houses of government; the casino, built by Charles Garnier in 1878; the Musée Océanographique, one of Europe's best aquariums; and the Jardin Exotique with a unique cactus collection.

Along the north-western Mediterranean coast – our dream route from Menton to Barcelona takes you on forays into the hinterland of Provence, leads you along impressive rocky coasts, white beaches, the Rhône delta and the foothills of the Pyrenees, and passes through famous seaside resorts on a journey that includes 2,000-year-old towns in a region with unmatched cultural history.

1 Menton Rich Englishmen discovered the pleasant climate of the Côte d'Azur quite late – around 1870. But they didn't waste any time. Villas and magnificent hotels from this Belle Époque recall the glory days of their 'winter residences' between the Alps and the sea.

The most beautiful view over Menton and the bay here can be seen from the cemetery above the city. Its attractions include the baroque Church of St-Michel, the Register Office in the town hall with frescoes by Jean Cocteau, and the Musée Cocteau in a 17th-century fort.

Just a few kilometers beyond Menton is the Principality of Monaco, where a steep street heads into the mountainous interior towards Èze.

2 Èze This tiny village sits on the top of a 427-m-high (1,401-ft) rock formation overlooking the Mediterranean Sea as if from a throne. It is one of Provence's

most beautiful medieval fortified villages, the so-called 'villages perchés'.

A thick stone wall surrounds the houses, which are clustered around a castle donjon high in the mountains. An exotic garden was created around the former fort, and the view from here reaches as far as Corsica on a clear day.

Following the N7 towards Nice, the route heads back along the sea to Villefranche-sur-Mer.

3 Cap Ferrat In the shadows of mighty pines and hidden behind high walls, the magnificent villas of millionaires cling to the coastline of Cap Ferrat, which drops steeply into the sea. The Fondation Ephrussi de Rothschild, probably the most beautiful villa on the Cap Ferrat peninsula, is even open to the public. The stately building, in gorgeous gardens, displays the furnishings bequeathed by Baroness Rothschild.

Travel information

Route profile
Length: approx. 1,300 km (808 miles), excluding detours
Time required: 2–3 weeks
Start: Menton, France
End: Barcelona, Spain
Route (main locations):
Menton, Monaco, Nice, Toulon, Marseille, Aix-en-Provence, Arles, Avignon, Orange, Nîmes, Camargue, Narbonne, Carcassonne, Perpignan, Barcelona

---

Traffic information:
Drive on the right in both countries. The speed limit for urban areas is 60 km/h (37 mph), 90 km/h (56 mph) on rural roads, and 130 km/h (80 mph) on highways (120 km/h/75 mph in Spain). In rainy conditions, the speed

limit for rural roads is 80 km/h (50 mph) and 100 km/h (62 mph) for highways.
The 'right before left' rule almost always applies in built-up areas in both France and Spain!

When to go:
Spring and autumn are the best seasons for the Mediterranean coast. Summer is often very hot, while winter can be quite cold, rainy and even snowy, particularly higher up.

Information:
France
General: *www.france.com*
Provence: *www.beyond.fr*
Spain
General: *www.spain.info*
Costa Brava:
www.costabrava.org

red rocks, cliffs, many gorges and secluded bays.

7 **Fréjus** The Roman legacy of this settlement, founded by Julius Caesar in 46 BC, is still clearly visible in the cityscape. Parts of the Roman city wall, the aqueduct and, most importantly, the amphitheater have all been very well-preserved. The area around the Cathédrale St-Léone is also worth seeing.
The fortified church and the monastery were founded in the

Antibes and Picasso

Antibes dates back to the ancient Greeks, who originally founded it as Antipolis. It has been a fortress town throughout its history, the port and Fort Carrée being creations of French architect Vauban.
Medieval towers and the beautiful Grimaldi Castle dominate the Antibes cityscape, and the old watchtower is now used as the bell tower for the Eglise de l'Immaculée Conception.

4 **Nice** The 'unofficial' capital of the Côte d'Azur is a city of contrasts – the grand boulevards try to rekindle the memories of the Belle Époque while parts of the Old Town are still like an Italian village. The Greeks founded Nikaia here, the 'Victorious City', in the 5th century BC, but the Romans preferred the hills further up for their township of Cemenelum, today Cimiez.
The most powerful icon of Nice is the Promenade des Anglais, which is directly on the sea. Wealthy British made Nice their retirement home in the mid 19th century and the most impressive mansions from that era are the famous Hotel Négresco and the Palais Masséna.
The main square in the Old Town, with its maze of small alleyways and Italian-style houses, is the Cour Saleya, with a remarkable flower and vegetable market. The castle hill provides a

great view over the Old Town and the sea.
The city's most interesting museums are the Musée d'Art Contemporain, the Musée Chagall and the Musée Matisse in Cimiez, which displays works by the artist, who moved to Nice in 1916. Some of the most impressive Roman ruins in Nice make up the 67-m-long (220-ft), 56-m-wide (184-ft) arena, which used to hold some 5,000 Romans. The city's most exotic landmark is the Cathédrale Orthodoxe Russe St-Nicolas (1912).
After passing the airport, the route now leaves the coastal road for a trip into Provence's hilly interior. For art lovers, it is worth taking the 10-km (6-mile) detour into St-Paul-de-Vence, a medieval town where the Fondation Maeght displays modern artwork. From the coast, the D2085 heads to Grasse, a perfume manufacturing center.

5 **Grasse** Perfume brought this town its early prosperity, traces of which can still be seen in the medieval alleys and streets of the Old Town. The International Perfume Museum will tell you everything you wanted to know about the manufacture of these valuable essences, and the large factories hold daily tours. From Grasse, the N85 heads back to the sea towards Cannes, one of the swankier places on the already swanky Côte d'Azur.

6 **Cannes** This city is of course known for its annual film festival, where the world's rich and famous gather on the Boulevarde la Croisette. Cap d'Antibes, with the holiday resorts of Juan-les-Pins and Antibes, is just 11 km (7 miles) from here.
The N98 heads from Cannes to Fréjus along the Corniche d'Esterel, which is one of the highlights of the journey with its

1 The marina in Menton on the eastern Côte d'Azur.

2 The famous Promenade des Anglais in Nice is 8 km (5 miles) long and separates the beach from the Old Town.

3 This view of the village of Èze shows its exposed location.

4 The château in Mandelieu-la-Napoule, a spa resort west of Cannes, dates back to the 14th century.

5 Red cliffs dominate the Corniche de l'Esterel between St-Raphaël and Agay.

6 The view of the Old Town in Cannes on the slope of Mont Chevalier.

The Old Town of Antibes.

The Château Grimaldi (12th century) was the residence of the Grimaldis of Monaco between 1385 and 1609, and the city allowed Pablo Picasso to use some rooms as his studio in the autumn of 1946, after the war, to 'free himself from the evils of civilization'. He produced 150 works in a very short time, which he then gave to what is now the Musée Picasso in return for the hospitality.

The Romans in southern France

When the Romans elected to overrun southern France, the decision was strategic in nature – after the victory over Carthage in the 2nd century BC they needed a safe land route to Spain. The hammer fell in 102 BC when Marius crushed the Teutons at the foot of the St-Victoire Massif. The resulting region was called Aquae Sextiae Saluvorium – Aix-en-Provence.

Soon after, the Greek settlements throughout the entire region were re-modelled to reflect the design of Rome. The streets were built according to an ordered grid pattern using blocks approximately 100 m (328 ft) in length. This layout can most clearly be seen in Orange and Arles.

A city's center point was its forum, a square lined with colonnades around which temples and other public buildings were grouped. Extravagant stages and large amphitheaters satis-

The Pont du Gard was built around 19 BC and towers 48 m (157 ft) over the Gard. Once part of the aqueduct between Uzès and Nîmes, today it is a UNESCO World Heritage Site.

fied the Romans' need for cultural entertainment.

The triumphal arches, public baths and aqueducts continue to provide testimony to the architectural and engineering mastery of the Roman occupation army.

12th century, and the older baptistry dates back as far as the 5th century.

8 St-Tropez Between Fréjus and Hyères, thick pine, oak and chestnut forests line the coast, and the hills drop away steeply into the sea, leaving no room for townships of any size on the Corniche des Maures. The coastal road is nothing less than spectacular here, and although it winds partly into the hills it continually provides stunning views of the sea. Small villages that were once dedicated to fishing are nestled tidily into the small bays, many of them retaining most of their original charm. St-Tropez is no exception. In this town – which first became famous after the film *And God Created Woman* (1956) with Brigitte Bardot – it's all about seeing and being seen. The image of the extravagant life in the film captivated the youth of the world and ultimately drew mass tourism to the sleepy coastal town.

9 Hyères This small town east of Toulon is the oldest seaside resort on the coast. The medieval Vieille Ville, with its

Place Massillon, is delightful. The old castle ruins provide an amazing panoramic view of the coast. Offshore from Hyères are the Iles d'Hyères, a group of islands that President Pompidou ordered the French state to make into a nature preserve in 1971. A visit to Porquerolles allows you to imagine how the entire Côte d'Azur must have looked before tourism began.

10 Toulon The capital of the Département Var owes its importance to the large natural port here, which continues to be an important marine base. Architect Vauban built Toulon into a war port in the 17th century under King Louis XIV.

11 Route de Crêtes La Ciotat is the starting point for a trip over the Route des Crêtes to Cassis. The 'Mountain Ridge Road' leads over the steep slopes of the Montagne de la Canaille and provides magnificent views of both the sea and the country. The small port town of Cassis has been able to retain much of its early charm, particularly in the old alleys directly behind the port. The shops and businesses give an insight into the

original Midi way of life. West of Cassis, white limestone walls rise straight out of the crystal blue waters. You can take a boat ride to the cliffs from Cassis.

If you take the rural road N 559 direct towards Marseille and turn left, you'll see narrow access roads leading to three bays that are worth seeing – Port Miou, Port Pin and En-Vau.

To drive into the heart of Provence, take the highway or the N559 to Aubagne and then the N96 to Aix-en-Provence.

12 Marseille (see p. 209).

13 Aix-en-Provence The Romans originally founded the colony of Aquae Sextiae Saluvorium on the former Celtic-Ligurian township of Entremont in 122 BC – what is now Aix-en-Provence. This spa and university town eventually became the capital of Provence at the end of the 12th century and remained so for hundreds of years. It also developed into a city of artists and academics.

The Old Town is tucked between the Cours Mirabeau, an avenue of sycamores with a gorgeous 18th-century city palace, and the Cathedral of St-Sauveur with

a baptistry from the Merovingian era.

Other attractions include the town hall (17th-century), the Musée des Tapisseries and the Atelier de Paul Cézanne. A popular source of inspiration of the city's most famous son was the Mont St-Victoire in the eastern section of the town, which is also worth a detour to see for yourself.

The shortest connection to Arles heads along the A8 and A7 to Salon-de-Provence and from there crosses the eastern part of the Rhône delta.

14 Arles The gateway to the Camargue was an area settled by the Celts, the Greeks and the Romans. Emperor Constantine had a splendid residence here, where he once summoned a council in AD 314.

Today, Arles is still home to impressive and important buildings from Roman times – the amphitheater, a grandiose oval

1 Les Arènes, a former Roman amphitheater in Arles.

2 The view of St-Tropez from the walls of the citadel.

Marseille

The second-largest city in France and the country's most important port town boasts a long history of 2,500 years. Its significance as an important gateway to North Africa is reflected in its multicultural population.

Marseille was originally founded as Massalia by Greeks from Asia Minor who built the city on the hill where Notre Dame de la Garde now stands. It then came under the yoke of the Romans, with Caesar eventually conquering the Greek republic in 49 BC. The port city experienced its first big boom in the 12th century when legions of crusaders embarked from here on their journeys to Jerusalem and the Holy Land. For the next few centuries, Marseille was the most important port in the entire Mediterranean.

The heart of Marseille continues to beat in the old port quarter. It marks the beginning of the city's main road, the Canebière, which connects the port with the rest of the city and was once the icon of a lively town. The entrance to the old port is flanked on the north side by the Fort St-Jean and on the south side by the Fort St-Nicolas.

The best view over the port and the city is from the Plateau de la Croix in front of the Basilica of Notre Dame de la Garde, Marseille's most visible landmark. Another good vista point is the rock peak of Château d'If, which

Notre Dame de la Garde watches over the port city of Marseille.

looks out over Marseille from across the port.

Other attractions include the Basilique St-Victor, a 5th-century church with early-Christian sarcophagi and sculptural fragments in its crypt; Basilique de Notre Dame de la Garde (19th century), a neo-Byzantine church with a gold-plated figure of Mary on the bell tower and mosaics inside and the Chateau d'If (1516–28) on the rock in front of the port, accessed from the Quai des Belges. The citadel was the state jail from 1580.

Museums include Vieille Charité, Musée des Docks Romains, Musée du Vieux Marseille, and Musée Grobet-Labadié with relics of the 19th century.

Roussillon in the Luberon range was the center for ocher mining at the end of the 19th century. Over fifteen different shades were obtained from the rock quarries near the town. Some of these old quarries can be explored on hiking trails.

Detour

Luberon and Haute Provence

East of Avignon, halfway between the Alps and the Mediterranean, is the sprawling limestone Luberon massif. The rocky region is home to lonely oak forests, small mountain villages and ancient stone huts, which all add to its natural beauty. The mountains, which reach 1,125 m (3,691 ft) in places, still contain wide swathes of uninhabited land where over 1,000 different types of plants thrive. The Parc Naturel Régional du Luberon was established in 1977 to protect the vegetation.

However, the seclusion of many parts of the Luberon today belies the fact that this tertiary limestone range has been settled by humans for thousands of years. In the Middle Ages, this place was home to villages nestled in vales and hollows, with thick-walled houses and churches that also doubled as refuges. Inhabitants of the region lived on meagre agricultural cultivation. When incomes were no longer sufficient, the villages in the northern sections were abandoned.

One of the symbols of the Luberon are some 3,000 'bories', unique one- or two-storey stone huts located seemingly randomly in the fields either on their own or in picturesque groups. The bories were made using lime slabs without mortar and were used by farmers as stalls and sheds.

During construction, each row of stones was staggered a little towards the middle so that when a height of about 3–4 m (10–13 ft) was reached, the final opening on top could be closed with a single slab. The most beautiful bories are found around Gordes, at the edge of the Plateau de Vaucluse on the north side of the Luberon.

Nestled into a hilly knoll like a picture postcard, Gordes welcomes visitors with arcaded lanes and a 16th-century castle. In the south is the Village des Bories with about twenty restored bories.

Another of the Luberon's landmarks are its ochre quarries, which are grouped around the picturesque tourist area of Roussillon. One of the most impressive is the now-closed quarry at Sentier des Ochres.

One understands the partially dry climate of the Luberon after a visit to Fontaine de Vaucluse. Here, in a grotto at the foot of a massive rock formation is the source of the Sorgue River, the largest spring in France and one of the largest karst springs in the world with up to 90,000 litres (409,090 gal) of water bubbling up from the mountains of the Luberon and the Vaucluse per second.

Hidden in a small gorge on the Plateau de Vaucluse is a very different sort of attraction – the Abbey de Sénanque. Founded in 1148 by Cistercians, the abbey had its heyday in the early 13th century and was destroyed in 1544. It wasn't until 1854 that seventy-two monks took the risk of rebuilding it. Lavender fields surround the monastery with its church and cloister.

To observe the Luberon from above, hike up the 1,125-m (3,691-ft) Mourre Nègre, east of Apt. The 1,909-m (6,263-ft) Mont Ventoux is the highest point in Provence and also provides

great views. You can get there on foot or by car. The diverse vegetation here is impressive, from lavender fields and vineyards to oak, beech and pine forests and bare rock mounds with cushion plants.

1 Lavender fields surround the 12th-century Abbaye de Sénanque.

2 An isolated homestead in Haute Provence at the foot of the Vaucluse Mountains.

3 A symbol of Provence – endless rows of blossoming lavender fields.

4 Fields of sunflowers dominate the Luberon along with vineyards and wheat fields.

Top: View from the far side of the Rhône across to Avignon, capital of the Département of Vaucluse. All that remains of the famous Pont St.-Bénézet are the arches. The medieval city is encircled by a 4.5-km-long (7-mi) city wall.

Bottom: The centerpiece of Marseille is the Vieux Port (old port), which is protected by two mighty forts: St.-Jean (here) and St.-Nicolas. The imposing new-Byzantine Cathédrale de la Major to the left of the fort dates from the 9th century. It is 140 m (460 ft) long with a 70-m-high (230-ft) dome.

The horses of the Camargue

Covering a marsh, meadow and grasslands area of roughly 140,000 ha (345,940 acres), the delta between the two main forks of the mouth of the Rhône is one of the largest wetlands in Europe. Agriculture – predominantly rice cultivation – is concentrated on the northern part of the Camargue, while salt is extracted in the flat lagoons of the south-eastern section.

The southern part, on the other hand, is a nature paradise not found anywhere else in Europe. The delta's grassy meadows are home to not only the well-known Camargue horses and Camargue bulls, but also to numerous water and marsh birds – around 10,000 pairs of flamingos breed in the marshes, the largest of which is the Etang de Vaccarés. Twice a year, more than 350 species of

Wild Camargue horses.

birds stop at the Parc Ornithologique du Pont de Grau in the Camargue's south-west.

The black Camargue bulls are distinguished by their lyre-shaped horns. The white Camargue horses, semi-white thoroughbreds found in the Solutré cave paintings, often frolic among the bulls. Their physical characteristics include a compact body, angular head and thick mane, and they are born black or dark brown in color only growing their white coat after the age of five. If the wild horses are broken in to saddles and bridles at a young age, they can be perserving riding animals and very useful to herdsmen for controlling herds of cattle. A number of guided tours offer even amateur riders the chance to go for a gallop into the marshes, to the beaches or to see the bull herds, allowing people to experience many parts of the Camargue that would be otherwise inaccessible.

structure about 137 m (446 ft) by 107 m (351 ft) wide with a capacity of 20,000; and the theater, which could fit an impressive 12,000 people into its semicircle.

The tidy Romanesque Church of St-Trophime is a masterpiece of Provencal stonemasonry, with a portal that dates back to 1190. The Romanesque-Gothic cloister adjacent to the church is considered the most beautiful in all of Provence.

From Arles, a rural road heads north-east to one of Provence's best-known villages, Les Baux.

⑮ Les Baux-de-Provence This stone village is perched on a 900-m-long (2,953-ft) by 200-m-wide (656-ft) rocky ridge that rises dramatically out of the modest Alpilles range. In the Middle Ages, troubadours performed their courtly love songs in the once proud fort of Les Baux. The fort's unique location on a rock combined with the gorgeous view over the expanses of the

Camargue and the Rhône delta draw countless visitors to this car-free town every year.

From Les Baux, the road crosses the Alpilles to St-Rémy, a 24-km-long (15-mile) mountain range between Rhône and Durance.

⑯ St-Rémy-de-Provence Nostradamus was born in this quintessential Provencal town in 1503, and van Gogh painted his picture of the cornfield and cypresses here in 1889. St-Rémy's predecessor was the old city of Glanum, about 1 km (0.6 miles) south of the present-day center. An 18-m-high (59-ft) mausoleum dates back to this time and the Arc Municipal traces back to the time of Emperor Augustus.

⑰ Avignon This former papal city dominates the left bank of the Rhône and is still surrounded by a 4.5-km-long (3-mile) city wall. The Rocher des Doms and the enormous Palais des Papes (Papal Palace) are an impressive sight even from a distance.

Seven French popes resided here between 1309 and 1377, the time of the Papal Schism. The last 'antipope' did not flee his palace until 1403. The mighty fort-like Palais des Papes was built during this century-long schism, but next to nothing remains of the once ostentatious interior decor.

The famous bridge, Pont St-Bénézet (also known as Pont d'Avignon), was built in 1177, and four of its original twenty-two arches still stand today. From Aix, the journey heads north to two more of Europe's most beautiful Roman constructions. Near Sorgues, the D17 turns off towards Châteauneuf-du-Pape. The popes of Avignon built yet another castle here in the 14th century. Today, the wine from this region is one of the best in the Côtes du Rhône region. If you have enough time, you should make a detour into the Luberon or Villeneuve-les-Avignon on the way to Orange (see p. 211).

⑱ Orange Emperor Augustus founded this location as Arausio in 35 BC. The theater was built soon after, and today it is one of the most beautiful Roman works in Provence. The large stage wall is 103 m (338 ft) wide and 38 m (125 ft) high.

On the north side of the city is the third-largest triumphal arch of its kind, with a height of 22 m (72 ft), a width of 21 m (69 ft) and a thickness of 8 m (26 ft).

Driving south-west along the A9 you reach the Pont du Gard, a famous Roman aqueduct.

⑲ Nîmes This city of temples, public baths and theaters was founded in AD 16, also by Emperor Augustus. The Romans' most impressive building is the amphitheater, with an oval arena and tiered stone benches that seated 25,000 guests. The Maison Carrée, from the second and third centuries AD, is one of Europe's best-preserved Roman temples, with columns and decorative friezes. Many public baths,

Canal du Midi

The dream of connecting the Mediterranean to the Atlantic existed for many years but wasn't made a reality until Paul Riquet, an engineer from Béziers, took on the task between 1666 and 1681. With the 240-km-long (149-mile) Canal du Midi he connected the Mediterranean port town of Sète to the industrial city of Toulouse, which he in turn connected to the Atlantic via the Garonne River, navigable from Toulouse onwards.

The canal, with its countless dams, aqueducts, bridges and locks, was an engineering masterpiece for the 17th century and, with regard to trade, became the backbone of goods transport in the Languedoc region. Today, the canal is a romantic waterway for leisure skippers for whom the French way of life is more important than a quick journey.

The Canal du Midi is a UNESCO World Heritage Site.

Houseboats can be rented in Sète, Béziers, Narbonne, Castelnaudary, Carcassonne and Toulouse, and they indeed make for some interesting excursions. The journey is done at a leisurely pace and in some parts passes beneath long avenues of sycamores, through impressive landscapes and grand vineyards, and near cultural attractions.

Along the way, there is still time for fishing, swimming or simply relaxing. A boat licence is not required to charter a boat, as all important instructions are given at the start.

24 **Narbonne** This town was once the most significant Roman port in the area. The Horreum, an underground granary built in the first century BC, is visible evidence of this time.

The Cathédrale St-Just, with its beautiful sculptures and vivid stained-glass windows, dates back to the 13th century. The Palais des Archevêques is a fort-like complex with massive towers (14th century). Some 60 km (37 miles) west of Narbonne is Carcassonne, a prime example of medieval fortress architecture.

25 **Carcassonne** This city on the steep bank of the Aude is visible from quite a distance. Its double walls with distinctive merlons and towers date back to King Louis IX, who began construction in the 13th century. Porte Narbonnaise takes you to the Old Town, where the most

1 Along with the Cathédrale St-Nazaire, the historic fort town of Carcassonne has been listed as a UNESCO World Heritage Site.

2 Some of France's best wines are grown in the mountainous hinterland of the Languedoc.

3 Visible from a distance – the Cathédrale St-Nazaire, the landmark of Béziers on the Canal du Midi. This Romanesque-Gothic church was built between the 12th and 14th centuries. In the foreground is the Pont Vieux (13th century) over the River Orb.

Pont du Gard

This 2,000-year-old bridge at 49 m (161 ft) in height is the highest bridge ever built by the Romans and probably the best example of Roman bridge construction. The 'bridge' was actually also an aqueduct carrying water from Uzès to Nîmes. It was in operation for about 500 years.

temples and a theater (today a park) are concentrated around the Jardin de la Fontaine. About 20 km (12 miles) north-east of Nîmes is the Pont du Gard.
From Nîmes, the route heads along the north-western edge of the Camargue to Aigues-Mortes.

20 **Aigues-Mortes** This town impresses visitors with the mighty walls of its fort, which are still completely intact. Aigues-Mortes, or 'Place of Dead Water', was constructed by Louis XI in the 13th century to consolidate his power on the Mediterranean coast. One part of the city wall can still be accessed. The Tour de Constance provides the best view over the city and the Camargue.

21 **Saintes-Maries-de-la-Mer** A 30-km-long (19-mile) road heads through the Camargue to the département capital, Les Saintes-Maries-de-la-Mer, well-known for the gypsy pilgrimage held every year in May. The Roman church here looks like

a medieval castle with its battlements and crenellated platform.

22 **Montpellier** The capital of the Département Hérault is home to France's oldest Botanic Garden, among other things. The focal point of the city is the Place de la Comédie, with a 19th-century opera house. Its most important attractions include the 17th-century patrician houses.

23 **Béziers** The route now heads through Montepellier to this lovely city on the Canal du Midi. The town's most recognizable landmark is the massive Cathédrale St-Nazaire (14th century), which is perched like a fort on a mountain above the city.

Barcelona

The capital of Catalonia, with its striking monuments, exciting nightlife and beautiful walks along the port and the sea, combines cosmopolitan flair with independent local tradition. Of course, it is also the city where Antoní Gaudí erected his largest and most compelling architectural feats.

Madrid's eternal competitor has a history that spans more than 2,000 years. Founded by the Romans, it was later conquered in 236 BC by the Carthaginian Hamilka Barcas, who named it Barcino. Control over this Mediterranean city changed hands between the Visigoths in 415, the Arabs in 713 and the Franks in 803.

When the kingdoms of Catalonia and Aragon were united (1137), it rose to become an important Spanish port and trading city. It unsuccessfully tried to become independent from Spain in the 17th century, and during the Spanish Civil War in the 20th century, Barcelona sided with the Republicans – against the eventual victor, Franco.

Towards the end of the 19th century, a completely new style of art and architecture developed in Barcelona – Modernism, the Catalán version of art nouveau, which has shaped the city's contemporary image like no other. Apart from Antoní Gaudí, the most important figures in this movement were architects Josep Puig i Cadalfalch and Lluís Domènech i Montaner. Many of their buildings are found in the Eixample quarter.

The best views of the city are seen from Montjuic in the south, or the 532-m-high (1745-ft) Tibidabo in the west, both of which are accessed by cable car. Particularly worth seeing are the Barri Gòtic, the oldest, elevated part of the city; the medieval square; Plaça del Rei with the palace of the Catalán and Castilian kings; Palau Real Major; the mighty Gothic cathedral; La Seu with its crypt and cloister where geese traditionally guard the tombs; Plaça del Pi, a square full of atmosphere; Las Ramblas, Catalonia's most famous pedestrian and shopping strip; the nostalgic market hall of La Boqueria (the 'gorge') with a wide range of products; Museu Nacional d'Art de Catalunya, whose collection of Romanesque frescoes and altar paintings is internationally reputed; Museu Picasso, with 3,600 works by the artist, who studied in Barcelona; and the Museu Maritim, a maritime museum in old shipbuilding halls.

The city's most magnificent building, and Antoní Gaudí's (1852–1926) masterpiece is the huge, still-incomplete church of La Sagrada Familia with its flamboyant, deeply symbolic design. Gaudí's other works include the counts' private residence of Palau Güell in the Barri Xinès; the apartment blocks of Casa Milà, with bizarre sculptural decorations and a magical roof landscape; Casa Calvet and Casa Batlló in the modernist Eixample; and the Avinguda de

Gaudí, with its wide avenues very much in keeping with the great architect's style. Palau Güell and Casa Milà are UN-ESCO World Heritage Sites.

Domènech i Montaner has various works throughout the city, including:

Top: La Sagrada Familia by Gaudí.
Middle: Palau de la Música Catalana.
Bottom: Las Ramblas, Barcelona's 'pedestrian mall'.

Casa de l'Ardiaca, Casa Lleó Morera, Palau de la Música Catalana, Fundació Antoni Tàpies, Illa de la Discòrdia, Hospital de la Santa Creu i de Sant Pa and Museo de Zoologia.

Dalí Museum

Salvador Dalí (1904–89) is without question the most popular son of the city of Figueres. The artist, a prominent ambassador of surrealism, built his own museum here in the old glass-domed city theater, which he bought

Inside the Dalí Museum in Figueres.

himself. You'll not only find numerous works from all of his different periods, but there are also portraits and busts of Dalí himself – without any false sense of modesty.

important buildings are the Château Comtal and the Basilique St-Nazaire, home to France's most beautiful stained-glass windows. The castle, a mighty fort inside a fort, was constructed in the 12th century and has five defense towers.
The next part of the journey heads towards Perpignan along the D118 as far as Quillan, and it's worth making a detour on the D117 to the Château de Peyrepertuse, probably the most impressive Cathar castle ruins in the Corbières hills.

26 Perpignan The capital of Roussillon had its heyday under the kings of Mallorca in the 13th and 14th centuries. The fortified Palais des Rois de Majorque, picturesquely built around an arcaded courtyard, is evidence of this time. The two-storey chapel, a Gothic masterpiece with

Moorish elements, is also a real dazzler. The Cathédrale de St-Jean was begun in 1324 and completed in 1509 and the houses on the palm-lined River Têt promenade are painted in vivid hues. Catalán influence is particularly noticeable in summer in Perpignan. The Place de la Loge becomes a stage for Sardana, a Catalán dance in which both young and old participate. You'll also find the most beautiful building in the city here, the Loge de Mer, built in 1397.
At the point where the Pyrenees meet the Mediterranean, the coastal road snakes along the red (vermillion) rocks of the Côte Vermeille, where ancient fishing villages are tucked into picturesque bays. The most significant of these old towns are Argelès-Plages, Cerbère and Banyuls on the French side and Portbou on the Spanish side.

27 Cadaqués One of the most beautiful fishing villages on the Costa Brava, which stretches from Empordà to Blanes, is behind the Coll de Perafita and can only be reached on a narrow side road. Cadaqués is home to tidy white houses and a stunning 16th-century baroque church. The Museu Perrot Moore has a collection of European art from the 15th to 20th centuries.
North of Cadaqués, the cape of Creus is the last of the Pyrenees foothills and also the easternmost point of the Iberian Peninsula. The Parc Natural del Cap de Creus combines nature and sea and is a vast uninhabited region. The Greeks were some of the first to recognize the beauty of the Badia de Roses with its long beaches. From here it's worth making a detour to the Dalí museum in Figueres. Continuing south, you cross a

Béziers This city, dominated by the Cathédrale St-Nazaire (14th century), has an interesting regional museum.

Pont du Gard The 49-m-high (161-ft) bridge was built by the Romans over 2,000 years ago and also served as a water channel. For 500 years it supplied the citizens of Nîmes with cool mountain water.

Arles This city, located at the gateway to the Camargue, was Vincent van Gogh's temporary place of residence and has many Roman buildings. The amphitheater has a capacity for 20,000 people.

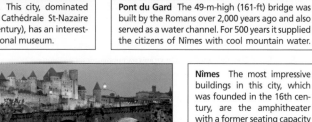

Carcassonne This city is encircled by two protective walls dating back to the 13th century. It is also home to the 12th-century Château Comtal Castle.

Nîmes The most impressive buildings in this city, which was founded in the 16th century, are the amphitheater with a former seating capacity of 25,000, and the Maison Carrée, one of Europe's best-preserved Roman temples. Other sites include the Romanesque Cathédrale Notre Dame et St-Castor and the 18th-centuryJardin de la Fontaine.

Tossa de Mar This former Roman city is located in one of the most beautiful areas on the Costa Brava. Below the town is a lovely bay and beach.

Cadaqués This fishing village on the Costa Brava captivates visitors with its white houses and a mighty baroque church.

Barcelona Catalonia's proud capital has a Gothic old town as well as numerous quarters in the characteristic Modernism style – art nouveau. Here we see the Museu Nacional d'Art de Catalunya (1929).

Avignon A mile-long wall encircles this city on the Rhône River – the city of the Papal Schism (13th–14th centuries). Behind it tower the Rocher des Doms and the enormous Palais des Papes.

Camargue Black bulls, semi-wild white horses, huge mountains of salt and flocks of flamingos and other unique birds are typical of the vast Rhône delta.

plain where there is an amazing view of the eastern Pyrenees.

28 **Costa Brava** Pals, the most beautiful village on the entire Costa Brava, is located just north and inland of Palafrugell. It enchants visitors with its quaint back alleys. Back on the coast is one holiday resort after another. Around Palamós are some isolated bays and beaches, but Platja d'Aro is lined with high-rise hotels. The medieval old town of Tossa de Mar is a great place for a stroll while the famous Botanical Gardens of Mar i Murtra rise high above the town of Blanes.

29 **Barcelona** (see pp. 216–217). Our journey ends here, in Spain's second-largest city.

1 Cadaqués an der Costa Brava: Im Ortsteil Port Llegat verbrachte Dalí viele Jahre seines Lebens.

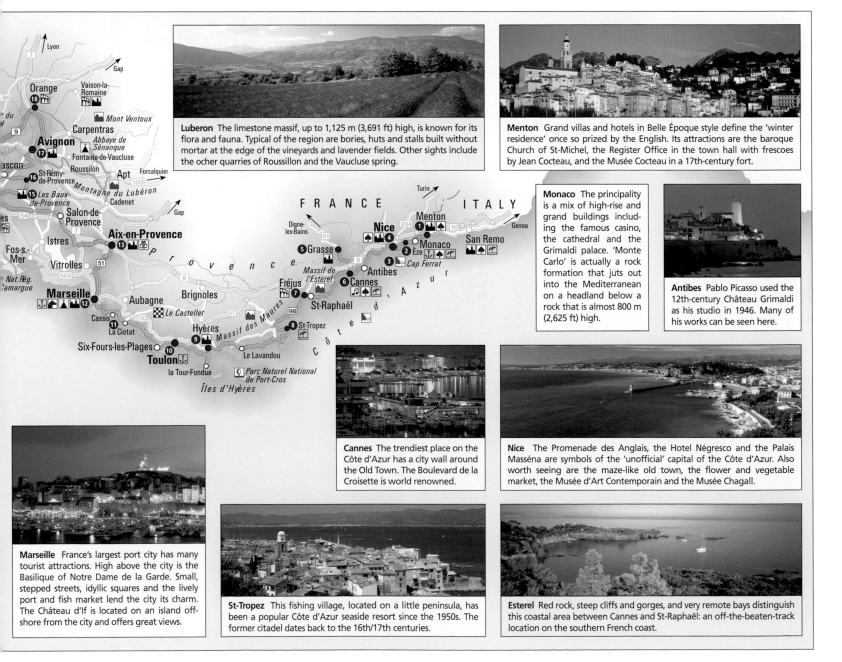

Luberon The limestone massif, up to 1,125 m (3,691 ft) high, is known for its flora and fauna. Typical of the region are bories, huts and stalls built without mortar at the edge of the vineyards and lavender fields. Other sights include the ocher quarries of Roussillon and the Vaucluse spring.

Menton Grand villas and hotels in Belle Époque style define the 'winter residence' once so prized by the English. Its attractions are the baroque Church of St-Michel, the Register Office in the town hall with frescoes by Jean Cocteau, and the Musée Cocteau in a 17th-century fort.

Monaco The principality is a mix of high-rise and grand buildings including the famous casino, the cathedral and the Grimaldi palace. 'Monte Carlo' is actually a rock formation that juts out into the Mediterranean on a headland below a rock that is almost 800 m (2,625 ft) high.

Antibes Pablo Picasso used the 12th-century Château Grimaldi as his studio in 1946. Many of his works can be seen here.

Cannes The trendiest place on the Côte d'Azur has a city wall around the Old Town. The Boulevard de la Croisette is world renowned.

Nice The Promenade des Anglais, the Hotel Négresco and the Palais Masséna are symbols of the 'unofficial' capital of the Côte d'Azur. Also worth seeing are the maze-like old town, the flower and vegetable market, the Musée d'Art Contemporain and the Musée Chagall.

Marseille France's largest port city has many tourist attractions. High above the city is the Basilique of Notre Dame de la Garde. Small, stepped streets, idyllic squares and the lively port and fish market lend the city its charm. The Château d'If is located on an island offshore from the city and offers great views.

St-Tropez This fishing village, located on a little peninsula, has been a popular Côte d'Azur seaside resort since the 1950s. The former citadel dates back to the 16th/17th centuries.

Esterel Red rock, steep cliffs and gorges, and very remote bays distinguish this coastal area between Cannes and St-Raphaël: an off-the-beaten-track location on the southern French coast.

Spain

A picturesque village crowned with a pilgrimage church along the Camino de Santiago in Galicia.

Camino de Santiago and Costa Verde – a journey through verdant Spain

Since the Middle Ages, pilgrims from all over the world have been drawn to the shrine of the apostle St James in Santiago de Compostela. Picturesque villages and towns, monasteries and castles, and the mighty cathedrals of Burgos and León line the 'Camino', which stretches from the Pyrenees on the border with France to Galicia in the north-western corner of Spain. The return journey skirts the rugged northern Spanish coast.

Legend has it that the apostle St James was beheaded in Palestine in the year AD 44 and his remains were sent by boat to the extreme north-west of Spain, where he had previously taught the gospel. It was not until much later, after the apostle's grave was discovered in the early 9th century, that the first St James' Basilica was built.

Subsequently, in 950, Gotescalco, the Bishop of Le Puy, became one of the first to make the pilgrimage to Compostela with a large entourage. Cesareo, the Abbot of Montserrat, followed suit in 959. The stream of pilgrims grew so much that in 1072 Alfonso VI suspended the toll for the Galician Trail. Just one century later, Aymeric Picaud, a priest from Poitou, wrote the first guidebook for the pilgrimage to Compostela, which was published throughout all Europe's monasteries as *Codex Calixtinus*.

Paris, Vezelay, Le Puy and Arles became the main meeting points from which the groups of pious travellers would continue on their way. Before starting their jour-

The bulls entering the arena of Pamplona.

ney, the pilgrims and their equipment – a hat and coat to protect against the weather, a gourd for water and a staff for defence – were ceremoniously blessed. The seashells that the first pilgrims brought back from Galicia quickly became the symbol for future pilgrims. Those who arrived in Santiago and could prove the pilgrimage by showing their pilgrim book to the cathedral's secretary received the 'compostela', an official pilgrim certificate. To this day, every pilgrim who travels along the Camino de Santiago for at least 100 km (62 miles) either by walking or riding a bicycle or a horse also receives such a certificate.

Picaud described the meeting points in France: the two trails over the Pyrenees and the main trail from the Puente la Reina. Pilgrims coming from Paris, Vezelay and Le Puy would go over the

Every pilgrim's goal – the Cathedral of Santiago de Compostela. According to legend, the remains of the apostle St James were brought to Galicia from Jerusalem and were later found in the city on this site.

The Cuevas del Marbei Llanes beach lies on the Costa Verde at the foot of the Sierra de Cuera.

Puerto de Ibaneta (1,057 m/3,468 ft), and those coming from Arles would go over the Puerto de Somport (1,650 m/5,414 ft). In his trail guide, Picaud even describes the townships, hospitals and accommodation options along the way in great detail – the classic pilgrim trail still follows these today.

Nowadays, the thousand-year-old trail is signposted with blue signs depicting hikers or yellow St James shells. You can also experience the beauty along the way as an 'independent pilgrim', perhaps learning even more about the country, the people, the art and the culture of this stunning area. The rugged mountains stretch from the western Pyrenees to the Cantabrian Mountains, over the plateaus of the northern Meseta, mostly moorland, to the semi-desert area of the Navarran Bardenas Reales.

While the pilgrims' destination is Santiago, you have the option of heading back along the northern Spanish coast, which partly corresponds to the Aragonian pilgrim route, and experiencing the charming interplay of mountains and sea on the rugged, craggy Atlantic coast between Galicia and the Basque country (País Vasco).

On the way to the Basque country, the tour passes through the historic province of Asturias, with its mountain pastures, and Cantabria, with its impressive Atlantic coniferous forests. The mountains then go east into the Pyrenees. Both routes also offer a multitude of art and culture, with historical relics dating back 1,500 years. From the treasures hidden in the tiniest of village churches to the lavishly filled chambers of major cathedrals, St James' Way will not disappoint.

Chaparral scenery along the Camino de Santiago, from the Pyrenees to Galicia.

Fiesta San Fermin in Pamplona

Ernest Hemingway called the Feria del Toro (Festival of the Bull) a 'damn good party' and eternalized it as 'The Running of the Bulls' in his novel Fiesta. The festival is held in honour of St Fermin and the days of the event, held every year in Pamplona from 6 to 14 July, are also known as San Fermines, when the town is reduced to a chaotic state of emergency for a long 204 hours.

People begin celebrations early in the morning and party all night until ex-

Top: Bulls run through the old town alleys of Pamplona.
Bottom: The evening bullfight.

actly 8 am, when the encierro begins – the 900-m (2,952-ft) chase through the city with the bulls hots on the tails of people. The run starts at the stalls of the Cuesta de Santo Domingo, goes through the town hall square, and ends at the entrance to the arena.

In front of, next to and behind the six bulls, thousands of people follow the same route and try not to end up on the bulls' horns. After the race comes all kinds of merrymaking, and in the evening the bulls are finally able to demonstrate their fighting strength in the arena.

Everywhere you look, peñas (circles of friends) trundle through the streets and alleys playing loud music, spurred on by free-flowing sangria and endless cerveza. The inspiration for the festival was to honour Bishop Fermin, who died as a martyr in Amiens in AD 287. In 1186, his remains were brought back to Pamplona.

The Camino de Santiago and the northern Spanish coast are home to several pilgrim trails that lead from the Pyrenees to the shrine of St James in Galicia. This particular route starts in Roncesvalles and heads through Burgos and León to Santiago de Compostela. The return trip along the Atlantic coast unleashes the beauty of the Galician, Asturian, Cantabrian and Basque coastline.

1 Roncesvalles In the year AD 778, this small village below the Ibañeta Pass decided the fate of one Marquis Roland, who in the wake of Charles the Great had tried to expel the Moors from Zaragoza. When the armies retreated, Roland led the rearguard but got caught in an ambush and was killed. The heroic sagas surrounding his death became the 'Song of Roland' in 1080.

The historic Augustine Hostel in Roncesvalles is one of the oldest along the pilgrimage route and the collegiate church dates back to 1127. The Gothic Church of Santa Maria was built in the 13th century and is home to the Madonna of Roncevalles, a silver-plated statue with a core of cedar wood.

2 Pamplona The city of the San Fermines, with the famous 'Running of the Bulls', was founded by the Roman General Pompeius in 75 BC. The Moors ruled here in the 8th century, but starting in 905 it became the capital of the Kingdom of Navarra, which transformed into the Castillian Empire in 1512. Today, the Plaza del Castillo,

with its rows of houses from the 18th and 19th centuries, is the lively center of the city. The facade of the town hall at the Plaza Consistorial is really quite impressive with its interesting Doric, Ionic and Corinthian features. Opposite the plaza is the Church of San Saturnino, once a military church, and next door is the hostel for pilgrims travelling the Camino de Santiago.

The symbol of Pamplona is, however, the Santa Maria Cathedral, with its 50-m-high (164-ft) towers. Behind its classical facade is a French-style Gothic interior. The dominating feature of the cathedral is the Virgen del Sagrario, who looks over the main altar. In the Middle Ages, the kings of Navarra were crowned here under the Romanesque statue of Mary. Make sure not to miss the Gothic cloister, built in 1472, with its numerous tomb slabs.

3 Puente la Reina This town's name traces its origins to the Puente Regina, the five-arched pedestrian bridge built in the 11th century that was a donation from Doña Mayor, the wife of the Navarran King Sancho el

Travel information

Route profile
Length: approx. 1,800 km (1,119 miles), excluding detours
Time required: at least 2 weeks
Start: Roncesvalles
End: San Sebastián
Route (main locations):
The main Camino de Santiago including Roncesvalles, Pamplona, Logroño, Burgos, León, Astorga, Ponferrada, Santiago de Compostela, then back through La Coruña, Gijón, Santander, Bilbao, San Sebastián.

Traffic information: Drive on the right in Spain. The speed limit in urban areas is 50 km/h (31 mph), 90 km/h (56 miles) on rural roads, 100–120 km/h (62–75 mph) on expressways and 120 km/h (75 mph) on freeways. Important: you must carry two

warning triangles and a set of spare bulbs for the vehicle lights in the car at all times.

Accommodation:
The pilgrim hostels along the Camino de Santiago are reserved for hiking pilgrims with an official pilgrim book. Pilgrims are only accepted on bicycles if they have vacancies. Drivers are not normally accepted. You may only stay once in each hostel, except in Santiago itself, where three nights are allowed.

Information
www.aragonguide.com
www.euskadi.net (Basque)
www.galiciaguide.com
www.turismodecantabria.com
www.visitasturias.co.uk
St James' Way:
www.caminodesantiago.me.uk

3

4

Romanesque churches on the Camino de Santiago

From approximately the 10th century onwards, church builders all over Europe began erecting structures with classic Roman features like rounded arches, columns, pillars and vaults, and uniting them in the standard Basilica shape. Originally they had flat roofs – only the crypts had arches, and in the 11th century this was also introduced over the aisle.

Not much later, however, the Mediterranean countries in particular began adopting dome vaults as well as barrel vaults. The round shape, dic-

Top: San Martín in Frómista.
Bottom: San Pedro de Tejada in Puente Arenas in the Valle de Valdivielso.

Mayor. The Romanesque pilgrim bridge over the Río Arga is the most beautiful on the entire pilgrimage route.

Right at the entrance to the town, next to the old pilgrim hospital, is the Iglesia del Crucifijo, built in the 12th century by the Knights Templar and housing a crucifix from the 14th century. This parish church has a Romanesque facade with a baroque interior and contains the interesting little carving Santiago Beltza, the 'Black James'.

4 Estella In its heyday, this old royal residence included no less than twenty churches, monasteries and chapels, the most beautiful of which is San Pedro de la Rúa (12th century). Its three Gothic naves each have Romanesque arches, and the main arch was completed in the 17th century. The most precious pieces are the figure of Mary dating from the 12th century and one of Christ from the 14th century. The finely crafted column capi-

tals in the ruins of the cloister are also interesting.

5 Logroño The most beautiful part of La Rioja's capital is its old city center around the Plaza del Mercado, where you will find the Cathedral of Santa Maria la Redonda. Its baroque towers are visible from quite a distance. The building dates back to the 15th century, and its most precious piece is an image of the crucifixion by Michelangelo.

6 Nájera This small town, which was the capital of La Rioja and Navarra until 1076, experienced its heyday under King Sancho el Mayor until 1035. The monastery of Santa María la Real also dates back to this time. The Knights Cloister in the monastery was built in the 16th century and the church of Santa Maria in the 15th century.

At the center of the golden baroque altar is a wonderful image of Mary. However, the most beautiful feature is the magnifi-

cently decorated late 15th-century choir stalls.

7 Santo Domingo de la Calzada The main attraction of the local cathedral is an ornate chicken coop where a white hen and a white rooster have been kept for centuries. According to legend, the two birds are said to have saved the life of an innocent boy who was condemned to the gallows.

The church itself was founded by St Domingo, who rendered outstanding services to the pilgrims along the Camino de Compostela in the 11th century. An impressively high altar dating back to 1540 fills the Romanesque choir of the church.

8 Burgos Over the centuries, this city was one of the most important stops on the Camino de Santiago. At the end of the 15th century it had no less than thirty-two hostels for those making their way to or from Galicia. Its importance was also due to the

cathedral, the construction of which began in 1221 under the auspices of Bishop Mauricio. Work continued on this, the third-largest cathedral in Spain, for more than three centuries – 108 m (354 ft) long and 61 m (200 ft) wide with a central arch measuring 20 m (66 ft) in height. Its Gothic towers, completed in the 15th century, soar to 80 m (262 ft) while its main, lavishly decorated facade displays eight statues of kings. All four entrances are sculptural master-

1 The Puente la Reina over the Río Agra was built as a pedestrian bridge in the 11th century.

2 The cloister in the Gothic cathedral of Pamplona.

3 The Gothic cathedral of Burgos was inaugurated in 1221.

4 San Pedro de la Rua in Estella, an important stop on the Camino de Santiago.

tated by the simple structural calculations involved in these buildings, was softened with pedestals, pilaster strips, pilasters and half columns while the cornices and mini galleries gave the plain walls a sense of elegance. Romanesque artists displayed their work on decorative friezes, portal and window soffits and, last but not least, the column capitals.

Las Médulas

This small town near Carucedo, some 25 km (16 miles) south-west of Ponferrada, sits on a throne of gold – at least this was the case during Roman times. The Romans systematically dug up so many square kilometers of land in the search for this precious metal that the bizarre land formations can still be seen today.

Cave and shaft entrances are interspersed with tombs, ancient washing systems and hills in a unique eroded landscape of gorges and rock. Everything points to the fact that this place was the site of an extremely well-organized search for gold, despite having only the most basic of means.

Contemporary sources provide evidence of the hard labour carried out by entire legions of slaves, who had to dig like moles for the prized metal while being whipped by their masters. The Lago de Carucedo, south-west of Ponferrade, is also a by-product of the search for gold. This is where the slaves

The scenery around Las Médulas

were forced to dig an artificial lake which, along with the network of canals and channels, was used to wash the millions of tonnes of rock from the surrounding hills.

The Romans eventually mined around 500 tonnes (550 tons) of the precious metal from the area. Today, the ancient gold-mine site is a UNESCO World Heritage Site accessible by a 2-km-long (1-mile) track.

The Mirador de Orellán provides the most beautiful view of the rugged, orange-red rock landscape and can be reached by car. Las Médulas itself, after which the gold-mine was named, also offers good views over the region.

pieces and the interior is similarly awe-inspiring.

Art lovers will be blown away by the nineteen chapels, thirty-eight altars and numerous sculptures, reliefs and paintings. The chapels, in particular, house many centuries' worth of individual works of art. In the center of the opulent high altar stands the silver statue of Santa Maria la Mayor, patron saint of Burgos. A visit to the 13th-century cloister and the adjacent chapels is also not to be missed.

The city's most famous son, El Cid (1043–99), who retook Valencia from the Moors in 1094 and was immortalized through the poem *El Cantar del mio Cid,* is buried in the cathedral.

Those who are short of time to see all the many interesting churches the city has to offer should at least visit the old Carthusian monastery of Cartuja de Santa María de Miraflores in the east of the city.

The Gothic minster, which was completed in 1499, contains a masterful Renaissance choir stall, a high altar decorated in gold, and the alabaster tomb of Juan II and Isabel of Portugal.

⑨ Frómista This tiny town is home to what is probably the most beautiful, stylistically sound Romanesque church on the entire Camino de Santiago. Begun in 1066, both the eight-cornered intersecting tower and the two round towers in the west look almost like defence fortifications. The eaves extending out over the walls were decorated with more than three hundred mythical creatures, animals, plants and designs.

Inside the sacred building is a 14th-century portrait of St Martin, and another of St James from the 16th century. The column capitals are also unique, ornately decorated with animal motifs and biblical scenes.

⑩ León The old royal city of León on the Río Bernesga was founded in the 1st century. It quickly became an important stop along the Camino de Santiago, and its grand churches were built accordingly. The best of these is the Gothic Cathedral of Santa María de la Regla, begun in the 13th century, with its two 65- and 68-m-high (213- and 223-ft) towers.

The lavishly decorated western facade is impressive with its rose window and three entrances adorned with exquisite relief work. The southern facade also has a large rose window and the ruins of Roman baths under glass casing.

The cathedral's main treasure, however, is its more than a hundred stained-glass windows covering an area of about 1,800 sq m (19,368 sq ft). The oldest of these dates back to the 13th century, with the most recent dating back to the 20th cen-

tury, and all of them cover a variety of themes from mythical creatures to plant motifs.

Similarly significant is the royal collegiate church of San Isidoro, tracing back to the 11th century. It is an example of Spanish Romanesque architecture and has housed the relics of St Isidor of Seville since 1063.

Next to the church is the Panteón Real (Royal Pantheon), which can be visited as a museum and is the final resting place of no fewer than twenty-three kings and queens. The ceiling was painted with unique Ro-manesque frescoes as early as 1160, which gave the Pantheon its nickname, the 'Sistine Chapel of Spain's Roman-esque Art.' Go through the cloister to get to the actual museum with its countless artistic treasures.

Catholic kings were responsible for the Monastery of San Marcos, which was founded at the start of the 16th century.

St James

The apostle St James was active on the Iberian Peninsula for seven years before being beheaded in Jerusalem in the year AD 44. His disciples allegedly transported his remains to Galicia thereafter.

The altar in the Cathedral of Santiago de Compostela.

The holy cult around James began in earnest after a monk was repeatedly guided by a group of stars back in 813 (Lat. Campus stellae = Compostela = field of stars) to the location of the present-day church, and the king saw an apparition of St James during his victorious battle against the Arabs.

Behind the monastery's ornate facade – considered one of the most impressive examples of the Spanish Renaissance style – is a hotel. If you are are interested in seeing the beautiful cloister of the old monastery you can go into the hotel hall and take the second door on the right.

11 Astorga This city's finest treasures can all be seen from the Avenida de las Murallas – the impressive city wall dating back to Roman times, the Episcopal Palace built by Antoni Gaudí, and the Santa María Cathedral. Gaudí's palace, completed in 1913, was never actually used by the bishops and today serves as an interesting Camino de Santiago museum (Museo de los Caminos).
Construction on the late-Gothic Santa María Cathedral began in 1471 but wasn't completed until the 18th century. Its main altar dates back to the mid 16th cen-

tury, as does the richly decorated choir stall.

12 Ponferrada The Knights Templar built this enormous castle with a surface area of 160 m by 90 m (525 ft by 295 ft) on the 'Pons Ferrata', an 11th-century iron bridge, to protect pilgrims travelling on the Camino de Santiago. The attractions of the old town include the Mozarabic Iglesia de Santo Tomás de las Ollas, with its horseshoe arches. It's worth taking a trip out of Ponferrada to the ancient gold-mine of Las Médulas (see sidebar left).

13 Cebreiro This tiny village is home to the oldest little church on the Camino de Santiago. It was built in the 9th century and its well-fortified walls house a painting of the Madonna from the 12th century.

14 Santiago de Compostela In the Middle Ages, the tomb of

St James was the most important Christian pilgrimage site outside of Rome and Jerusalem. In 1075, after the Moors were expelled, Bishop Diego Pelaez began building a cathedral to reflect the importance of this pilgrimage destination, although it was not completed until the mid 18th century. In fact, the two solid exterior towers were only finished in 1750.
The long construction time meant that simple Romanesque styles and opulent baroque touches existed side by side. This fusion also dominates the facade. The Pórtico de la Gloria, with its ornate sculpture work, is now within a late-baroque building placed in front of it, and the mix of styles continues inside as well. The impressive Romanesque design of the building is partially covered in the most lavish of baroque decor, and the entire structure is crowned with a golden high

altar with a 13th-century silver-plated figure of St James in the center. Under the high altar is the mausoleum of the saint, whose remains rest in a silver shrine.

1 The Cathedral at León illuminated at night.

2 San Martin de Frómista – the most beautiful Romanesque church on the Camino de Santiago.

3 A typical mountain landscape north of León.

4 The core of the Cathedral Santiago de Compostela is unchanged since the 11th century.

5 The Palace of Astorga was designed by Antoni Gaudí.

6 The Knights Templar built the Castle of Ponferrada between the 12th and 14th centuries to ensure the safety of pilgrims on the 'Camino'.

About half of the 1,600 km (1,000 mi) of Galicia's coastline comprises cliffs, some of them the highest in Europe. Rías such as this one are river deltas that are subject to tidal movements and are also typical of the wild coast. Comparable to fjords but much flatter, they are distributed throughout the

north-western Rías Baixas and northern Rías Altas regions. The majority of Galicia's population lives along the coast where fishing is still the most important commercial industry.

Detour

Picos de Europa

The 'Peaks of Europe' form the center of the national park of the same name, dominated in particular by forested mountains that range between 800 and 1,500 m in height (2,625–4,922 ft). The thick-trunked, ancient chestnut trees, oaks and yews all provide an ideal habitat for a wide range of wildlife.

Top: The Picos de Europa.
Middle: Stone bridges over the Duje River.
Bottom: San Salvador de Cantamuda near Potes.

The national park can be accessed from the towns of Unquera in the east and Cangas de Onis in the west. The most famous gorges include the Desfiladera de los Beyos and the Desfiladero del Río Cares.

A cable car from Fuente Dé takes visitors up to a 900-m-high (2,953-ft) rock plateau. On the west side are Covadonga and the grotto of the same name where Don Pelayo is buried. Just 15 km (9 miles) further up, at about 1,150 m (3,773 ft), are the glacial lakes of Enol and Ercina, which mark the start of numerous hikes in the national park.

The cathedral museum includes the treasure chamber, the chapter house and the cloister from the 16th century. The city itself practically grew around the cathedral and is today similar to an historic open-air museum. Countless churches, particularly ones built in baroque style, await the eyes of connoisseurs, while picturesque old town alleys offer recreation of all kinds to both tourists and religious pilgrims.

In addition to the journey along the historic Camino de Santiago, it is worth heading further out to the Galician coast. The road then heads back along the shores of northern Spain to the Basque town of San Sebastián back near the French border.

15 **Carnota** The 7-km-long (4-mile) sandy beach on Spain's north-west coast is a surfer's paradise. The small village itself is home to the longest (over 30 m/98 ft) and probably also the most beautiful granary in Galicia, built out of granite at the end of the 18th century. To protect the grain from mice, the granary stands on two rows of pillars, secured with a corbel.

16 **Cabo Finisterre** The *finis terrae*, the end of the world, is a peninsula that towers above the Costa da Morte. Even today, the Atlantic tides and the dangerous cliffs mean numerous ships are wrecked on this 'Coast of Death'. The westernmost point of continental Europe is further north at Cape Touriñana. Both places are hauntingly beautiful and were important cult sites for the Celts.

17 **La Coruña** The Romans built this, the second-largest city in Galicia, into an important port city. The Torre de Hércules on the western side of the peninsula dates back to those Roman times. Begun in AD 100, it is said to be the oldest lighthouse in the world. Today, the tower is 60 m (197 ft) tall and can be climbed in summer.

The Old Town of La Coruña grew out of the former pescaderia, the fishmongers' quarter. Apart from Romanesque and baroque churches, two museums are of particular interest – the Museum of Archaeological History in the San Antón Castle displays findings from Celtic and Roman times as well as medieval sculptures; and the Fine Arts Museum at the Plaza de Zalaeta exhibits works from Rubens to Picasso.

18 **Rías Altas** Those following the coastal road between La Coruña and Ribadeo will see picturesque estuaries, small holiday and fishing towns, ancient farmhouses and even older granaries. Flat coastal plains are interspersed with steep coastal mountains and striking promontories and headlands. The interior is dominated by pine and eucalypt forests and the weather is dictated by the windy and wet Atlantic.

19 **Ribadeo** This is the easternmost town in Galicia. It is situated on the Ría, the Atlantic mouth of the Río Eo, which cuts deep into the interior like a Scandinavian fjord. Old manors surround the Plaza de España, and the Convento de Santa Clara dates back to the 14th century.

20 **Luarca** This port town on the Costa Verde is undoubtedly one of the most beautiful parts of the Asturias region. The fishing port is so tightly

Altamira

The world-famous Altamira Cave is located in the hills above Santillana del Mar and was discovered in 1879. The ceiling paintings were first thought to be fakes, as no one could believe that the early civilizations were capable of such artistic talent. Only after the discovery of similiar Stone-Age caves in the area were the paintings in Altamira further researched, proved to be authentic and given more specific dates.

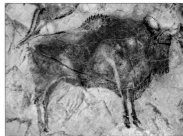

The Stone-Age drawing of a European bison.

The 270-m-long (886-ft) cave opens up from an anteroom into a large, natural hall whose walls and ceiling are covered with depictions of buffalo, deer, horses and all sorts of other game animals either lying on the ground or running.

The individual drawings can measure up to 2.2 m (7 ft) tall, are in colour and are even partially carved into the rock. Brown, yellowish and red ochre colours, black manganese soil and coal were all used in the depictions. The bison, in particular, are painted in so many different shades that the animals look plastic and realistic. The overall effect of the hall also resulted in the cave being nicknamed the 'Stone-Age Sistine Chapel'.

Using the most modern of tests, researchers have proved that the drawings dated back to the Old Stone Age (Palaeolithic times) and were thus around sixteen thousand years old, making them the most important example of pre-historic art in the world. At some point, the cave purveyors realized that visitors' breath and perspiration was starting to damage the drawings, so the original cave was closed to the general public and an authentic replica was created in the museum. Those who wish to see the original cave, in which only 25 people a day are admitted, must ask to do so at the Museo y Centro de Investigación de Altamira *(39330 Santillana del Mar)* – the waiting time is three years.

today. The town's main points of interest are, however, its picturesque alleys, the variety of lovingly tended flowerpots, and the old walls, romantically overgrown with ivy.

Hidden about 2 km (1 mile) up from the village is the world-famous Altamira Cave.

㉖ Santander Cantabria's capital, jutting out on a long peninsula, is a port city, seaside resort and secret 'Capital of Promenades'. The city grew from a small fishing port into a relatively large trading port. In 1941, however, many of its buildings went up in flames during a devastating city fire. That's why walkers are again in demand in Santander, and their main destination should be the La Magdalena Peninsula. King Alfonso XIII chose the Palacio de la Magdalena, built in English style at the start of the 20th century, to be his summer residence.

Sprawling north-west of the peninsula are the beautiful

1 The view of the port of Castro Urdiales between Santander and Bilbao.

2 Cabo Finisterre above the vast Atlantic.

3 Closely-packed fishing boats at the port of La Coruña.

4 A view of the port in Ribadesella on the Costa Verde.

jammed in between the rock faces and the rows of houses that there is only a tiny bit of room for the fishing boats to come in and out. The fish market quarter is especially picturesque, and you'll get the best view from the city hill of Atalaya.

㉑ Costa Verde The coast between Ribadeo and Santander showcases a series of spectacular, as well as very isolated, sandy bays and impressive cliffs that are only interrupted once by the long Rías. The town of Cudillero has a gorgeous fishing port, cosy pubs and, more importantly, a number of isolated and often empty beaches. Turning off from the coastal highway, there are plenty of peaceful spots for everyone. It's worth taking a detour inland at Avilés to visit Oviedo, the beautiful capital of Asturias.

㉒ Luanco North-west of the industrial city of Gijón, this beach town has its own oceanography museum. A vast beach sprawls from Banugues to the windy and exposed Cabo de Peñas. Swimming can be dangerous along some sections of this coast.

㉓ Ribadesella The Old Town at the mouth of the Río Sella and the long promenade around the fine sandy beach are what make this town so attractive. It also has a point of interest worth seeing – the cave of Tito Bustillo, which was discovered in 1968. This dripstone cave contains Stone Age rock paintings that are around twenty thousand years old depicting red and black deer and horses. For preservation purposes, the number of visitors allowed in per day has had to be limited, similar to the caves in Altamira.

㉔ Cueva del Pindal Beneath the small farming village of Pimiango, the Pindal cave also contains prehistoric rock paintings. It is best to come in the early morning, as only 200 people are admitted each day.

In Unquera it's worth taking a detour away from the coastal road to head south into the Picos de Europa. The Desfiladero de la Hermida Gorge starts after Panes, with some nearly vertical rock faces that reach 600 m (1,969 ft) in height. Potes is the main town in the eastern Picos de Europa.

㉕ Santillana del Mar This small town, located slightly away from the sea, owes its existence to the remains of St Juliana. Monks built a monastery around her remains and its Romanesque collegiate church is the area's most important building even

Bilbao: architecture old and new

To improve the image of the city, which does not have much to offer in the way of tourism, Bilbao's city planners asked a series of famous architects

Siete Calles in Bilbao.

to contribute to the city's lacklustre facade. Apart from Gehry's Museo Guggenheim, the pedestrian bridge Puente del Campo Volantin and the futuristic airport, both by Santiago Calatrava, as well as the metro stations by Norman Foster, are some of the most important additions. The most beautiful old buildings are found in the Siete Calles in the old town – seven streets of neoclassical buildings from the 19th century with lovely gazebos and wrought-iron balconies.

beaches of Primera Playa and Segunda Playa. Following the coastal road further east you will eventually come to Castro Urdiales, an attractive port town dominated by a Knights Templar castle.

27 Bilbao Now an industrial town, Bilbao originally grew out of a fishing village started back in the 11th century. Steelworks were eventually established here in the second half of the 19th century, which brought considerable wealth to the city. Only the Old Town is really worth seeing, in particular its Siete Calles, the 'Seven Streets', between the cathedral and the river. The 14th-century cathedral was completely burnt down in 1571 so its current form and its cloister date back to the 16th century. A more elegant life is reflected in the 19th-century neoclassical Plaza Nueva. North of the square you should visit the 15th-century church of San Nicolas. It has a gorgeous Gothic carved altar, as well as some interesting sculptures.

Always worth a visit is the Museum of Fine Arts with important works by El Greco, Goya and Gaugin. The gigantic Guggenheim Museum, designed by Frank O. Gehry, is an absolute must. It alone attracts over one million people a year to the city.

28 Costa Vasca The 176-km-long (109 mile) Basque coast is defined by bays and estuaries lined by numerous cliffs. The landscape of the hinterland is one of wooded hills. Travellers stumble across heavenly beaches near Algorta on the eastern coast of the Ría of Bilbao.

Far more interesting, however, is the chapel of San Juan de Gaztelugatxe, west of Cape Machichaco, perched on a protruding rock in the middle of wildly romantic, windswept cliffs. It is only accessible on foot up a uniquely beautiful set of steps formed out of the rock. The 11th-century sailors' chapel on the rock is also of interest.

Whalers set off from Bermeo towards Iceland and Labrador. The Museo del Pescador in the 16th-century Ercilla military tower has all the answers on the topic of fish.

29 Guernica This city is evidence of one of the darkest chapters in Spanish-German history. During the Spanish Civil War, an air raid by the German Condor Legion on 26 April 1937 destroyed virtually the entire city. Some two thousand people died in the inferno, but the world did not see it as a precursor to the disaster that was World War II. Only Pablo Picasso captured the horror in his world-famous *Guernica* painting, which now hangs in Madrid's Museo Nacional Centro de Arte Reina Sofía. Guernica is considered the 'holy city of the Basques' because the Basques held their regional meetings here in the Middle Ages. When the Basque region became part of Castile, the Spanish kings had to swear that they would forever respect the rights of the Basques.

Everything worth knowing about the Basques can be found in the Museo Euskal Herria.

30 San Sebastián The journey across northern Spain ends in this beautiful seaside town from the Belle Époque, which was for a long time the summer resort of the Spanish kings. Aristocracy from all over Europe would stay in the mansions from this era that still dominate the cityscape. The Monte Urgull and the Castillo de la Mota tower above the Old Town, at the center of which is the Plaza de la Constitución. Bullfights used to be held

in this square – the large number of balconies is evidence of this.

The other attractions of the Basque city include the aquarium, the Museo de San Telmo in a 16th-century monastery, and the Palacio del Mar – and of course the best tapas in Spain. On the west side is an enormous bay with two popular beaches. The view from the Monte Igueldo is by far the most beautiful.

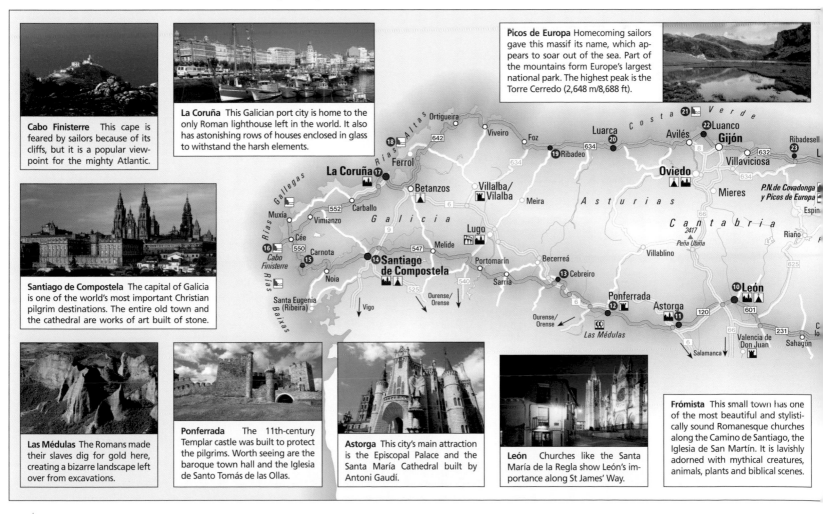

Cabo Finisterre This cape is feared by sailors because of its cliffs, but it is a popular viewpoint for the mighty Atlantic.

La Coruña This Galician port city is home to the only Roman lighthouse left in the world. It also has astonishing rows of houses enclosed in glass to withstand the harsh elements.

Picos de Europa Homecoming sailors gave this massif its name, which appears to soar out of the sea. Part of the mountains form Europe's largest national park. The highest peak is the Torre Cerredo (2,648 m/8,688 ft).

Santiago de Compostela The capital of Galicia is one of the world's most important Christian pilgrim destinations. The entire old town and the cathedral are works of art built of stone.

Las Médulas The Romans made their slaves dig for gold here, creating a bizarre landscape left over from excavations.

Ponferrada The 11th-century Templar castle was built to protect the pilgrims. Worth seeing are the baroque town hall and the Iglesia de Santo Tomás de las Ollas.

Astorga This city's main attraction is the Episcopal Palace and the Santa María Cathedral built by Antoni Gaudí.

León Churches like the Santa María de la Regla show León's importance along St James' Way.

Frómista This small town has one of the most beautiful and stylistically sound Romanesque churches along the Camino de Santiago, the Iglesia de San Martín. It is lavishly adorned with mythical creatures, animals, plants and biblical scenes.

Guggenheim Museum in Bilbao

The museum, which was designed by star architect Frank O. Gehry, opened in Bilbao in 1997 and is located on the banks of the Rio Nervion. It is a prime example of modern architecture. The structure, made of limestone, titanium and glass, cost around 100 million dollars and took four years to build. Its fusion of flat surfaces and shapes, as well as its silver exterior, are an impressive sight even from afar. The locals refer to the mighty metal roof as a 'metallic flower'. The uniquely designed parts of the building are loosely grouped around a central, glazed atrium 50 m (164 ft) high from which all parts of the building can be accessed. The entrance hall alone is 130 m (427 ft) long and 30 m (98 ft) wide and contains no obstructive pillars. Nineteen exhibition halls with a total surface area of 24,290 sq m (261,360 sq ft) provide enough space for gigantic displays.

1 The glittering facade of Gehry's Museo Guggenheim was covered in 60 tonnes (66 tons) of titanium. Its exterior shell is just 3 mm (0.1 in) thick.

2 San Sebastián is located on La Concha (shell) Bay. The sides of the semicircular bay mark the border of the rock massif of Monte Igueldo and Monte Urgull. In the entrance to the bay is the small rock island of Santa Clara.

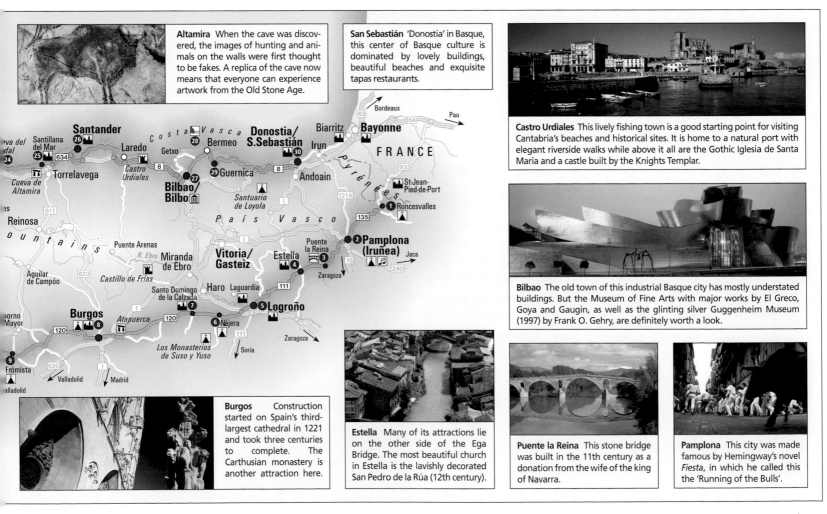

Altamira When the cave was discovered, the images of hunting and animals on the walls were first thought to be fakes. A replica of the cave now means that everyone can experience artwork from the Old Stone Age.

San Sebastián 'Donostia' in Basque, this center of Basque culture is dominated by lovely buildings, beautiful beaches and exquisite tapas restaurants.

Castro Urdiales This lively fishing town is a good starting point for visiting Cantabria's beaches and historical sites. It is home to a natural port with elegant riverside walks while above it all are the Gothic Iglesia de Santa Maria and a castle built by the Knights Templar.

Bilbao The old town of this industrial Basque city has mostly understated buildings. But the Museum of Fine Arts with major works by El Greco, Goya and Gaugin, as well as the glinting silver Guggenheim Museum (1997) by Frank O. Gehry, are definitely worth a look.

Burgos Construction started on Spain's third-largest cathedral in 1221 and took three centuries to complete. The Carthusian monastery is another attraction here.

Estella Many of its attractions lie on the other side of the Ega Bridge. The most beautiful church in Estella is the lavishly decorated San Pedro de la Rúa (12th century).

Puente la Reina This stone bridge was built in the 11th century as a donation from the wife of the king of Navarra.

Pamplona This city was made famous by Hemingway's novel *Fiesta*, in which he called this the 'Running of the Bulls'.

Spain

Castile: On the road in Don Quixote country

Palacio Real de Aranjuez, the king's summer residence south of Madrid.

Castile is not only the geographical center of Spain, but also its historical heartland and the birthplace of Castilian Spanish. Vast, ochre-colored plains, magnificent cities and monumental castles distinguish the region surrounding Madrid.

In modern-day Spain, the Castilian highlands contain two of the country's autonomous regions: Castilla y León in the north-west and Castilla-La Mancha in the south-east. This political division largely reflects the natural geography, with the Cordillera Central, or the Castilian Dividing Range, running straight through the two regions and separating them from each other.

On either side of the mountain range extends the Meseta Central, an expansive, slightly arid plateau where vegetation is sparse and only solitary pine and eucalyptus trees dot the landscape. Despite the relative aridity, however, the ground is fertile and supports the cultivation of grains, sunflowers, chickpeas (garbanzo beans) and wine grapes. In winter, the predominantly treeless landscape is more or less fully exposed to the strong winds and cooler temperatures, while in summer the sun beats down mercilessly on the hot plains.

The large La Mancha plateau to the south-east of the meseta owes its name to the Moors, people of Arab and Berber (North African) descent who conquered much of Iberia for several hundred years. They named it manxa, meaning "parched

Easter processions ("Semana Santa") in Zamora.

land", but in present-day Spanish mancha simply means "spot".

In the Middle Ages, Castile was actually still densely forested, but the former world power needed every available tree to build its extensive fleet of ships. In the bare countryside that resulted, grassland fortunately took hold in some areas and is able to sustain a modest living for goat and sheep farmers. The animals supply milk for the region's best-selling export product – savory and rich Manchego cheese. Some parts of the countryside here seem almost uninhabited. While the landscape is often monotonous at first glance, however, this is what makes it so fascinating. The sunsets are unique, the sky dowsed in a range of reddish hues.

The most important chapters of Spanish history were written in the heart of this

Iconic windmills and a castillo near Consuegra overlooking over the plains of La Mancha.

Built onto a rock, the Alcázar defiantly stands guard over the Old Town of Segovia.

region. In the 11th century, for example, it was here that the Reconquista gained momentum and Christian forces massed in order to reclaim the southern half of Iberia from the Moors. It is as such the birthplace of the Spanish nation, a fact that is reflected in the seemingly non-stop historical sites. Generals and kings erected great fortified castles that became monuments to their victories in the Christian reclamation of the area.

On a journey through Castile, it is these old cities that receive the lion's share of your attention. Some Old Towns, such as those in Ávila, Salamanca, Segovia, Cuenca and Toledo have been declared UNESCO World Heritage Sites due to their historical importance. The city of Salamanca is home to the oldest university in Spain; the charming Plaza Mayor in Valladolid became the model for similar squares in other cities. Few other cities possess such perfectly preserved medieval town walls as Ávila; and stunning Toledo awaits visitors with countless architectural treasures from the Convivencia (coexistence), a period when Jews, Christians and Muslims lived peacefully together and the city experienced a period of unrivalled prosperity.

Not only the larger cities, but in particular the smallest villages proudly celebrate their cultural treasures and landmarks, be they architectural, in the form of majestic castles, old churches or "simply" windmills, or cultural in the form of festivals. One literary figure of the region gained world-wide fame through his struggle with the windmills – Don Quixote de la Mancha. He mistook the windmills for giants, wildly flailing about, and he rode to attack them with his lance drawn.

The library of the Monasterio San Lorenzo de El Escorial, north of Madrid.

El Escorial

About 50 km (31 mi) north-west of Madrid is one of most popular sites in all of Spain, the royal residence of San Lorenzo Real de El Escorial, or El Escorial for short. In addition to the actual palace portion, the mighty complex of buildings comprises a church, a monastery and a library.

The palace was commissioned by King Felipe II, who designed it together with architect Juan Batista de Toledo, a former pupil of Michaelangelo. Toledo died before its completion in 1584, but his apprentice, Juan de Herrera, took over and is often given credit for the entire project. The Spanish empire had reached a zenith at the time, and this was to be not only a necropolis but also a place of learning that would support the king's efforts to stem the Protestant tide.

Top: The impressive El Escorial.
Bottom: Inside the palace of Felipe II.

From the outside, the light granite and inconceivable proportions (nearly two football fields long and wide) is more reminiscent of a fortress than a royal residence. The corridors, each up to 150 m (164 yds) long, cover a total length of about 16 km (10 mi). The estate has more than 2,500 windows, about half as many doors, eighty-six staircases and eighty-eight wells.

The central building is the austere and monumental basilica whose walls are decorated with impressive frescoes. Other structures, such as the royal palace, are appointed with unimaginable splendor. El Escorial is still considered the epitome of the former might and greatness of the Spanish world empire.

The 1,200-km (746-mi) journey through the high plains of Castile begins in Madrid before taking you first north-west across the Castilian Dividing Range into the Castile and León region. You return to Madrid after crossing the Sierra de Guadarrama and visiting the cultural and scenic highlights of the Castile-La Mancha Region.

① Madrid (see pages 236–237)

② El Escorial From Madrid your journey heads out towards the 500-km-long (311-mile) Castilian Dividing Range (Cordillera Central), which forms a natural border between Old and New Castile. The scenic C505 begins at Las Rozas. The water in the reservoirs along the road is used to irrigate the olive groves.

El Escorial, King Felipe II's impressive palace, lies in the Sierra de Guadarrama, which is part of the Cordillera Central.

Beyond the northern foothills of the mountains you come to Ávila at an elevation of 1,130 m (3,708 ft).

③ Ávila This tranquil town provides insight into life in Castile in the Middle Ages. With 50,000 inhabitants, Ávila rises abrupty from the plains, its stunning walls visible from afar. They are considered the most magnificent medieval fortifications in Europe and their dimensions are difficult to fathom: 2,500 m (2,734 yds) long, an average of 12 m (39 ft) high and 3 m (3 yds) thick. Some of the eighty-eight towers are open to the public and can be climbed.

Inside, the city has managed to preserve its medieval appearance. In the heart of the Old Town is the Plaza Mayor where once the bullfights took place. East of the square is the cathedral, which has been integrated into the town walls (11th–14th centuries). Other evidence of the town's heyday in the 16th century are the many aristocratic palaces and bourgeois mansions.

④ Peñaranda de Bracamonte North-west of Ávila, halfway to Salamanca, is the small town of Peñaranda de Bracamonte. On the plaza it is worth checking out the pharmacy, which has antique interior fittings.

Travel information

Route profile
Length: approx. 1,200 km (745 mi)
Time required: 8–10 days
Start and finish: Madrid
Route (main locations): Madrid, Ávila, Salamanca, Zamora, Valladolid, Cuéllar, Segovia, Guadalajara, Cuenca, Alcázar de San Juan, Toledo, Aranjuez, Madrid

Traffic information:
There is an extensive network of maintained roads throughout Spain. The motorways require tolls but are therefore also well maintained. The best seasons to visit the hot central region of Spain are spring and autumn, when temperatures are not as extreme.

Where to stay:
A Spanish specialty is the Paradores, upscale hotels in beautiful historic buildings such as castles, monasteries or palaces.
www.parador.es

Further information:
Here are a few websites to help you plan your trip.
www.spain.info
www.whatmadrid.com
www.justspain.org

The church of San Miguel features a unique high altar.

⑤ **Salamanca** Continuing over the virtually treeless plains you arrive in Salamanca, one of Castile's main cultural centers and the European Capital of Culture in 2002.

The main sights of the city – the Plaza Mayor, two cathedrals and the university – are all in the Old Town. The trapeze-shaped Plaza Mayor was created in the middle of the 18th century.

Significant buildings in the university district include the Palacio Anaya, a Renaissance palace,

and the famous Casa de las Conchas of 1514, the most prestigious example of the Queen Isabella Renaissance style.

The university was founded in 1218 by King Alfonso IX, and the ornately adorned façade of the Patio de las Escuelas is a classic example of the famous picaresque style.

Salamanca boasts not just one but two cathedrals. The Romanesque Catedral Vieja (old cathedral), which dates from the 12th century, has some priceless frescoes. If you go out the Patio Chico you can go straight over to the Catedral Nueva (new

cathedral), a mostly Gothic structure from the 16th–18th centuries that also features other architectural styles.

⑥ **Zamora** About 65 km (40 mi) north of Salamanca is Zamora, a medieval town with about 160,000 inhabitants that is considered an open-air museum of Romanesque architecture. Its heritage of buildings from this style period is unrivalled in Spain. Two very old and stylistically important bridges here span the Río Duero. One, the Puente Viejo, was built in the 14th century on Roman founda-

tions, has sixteen pointed arches, and is the more prominent. However, the undisputed architectural highlight here is the cathedral, built in just twenty-three years in the 12th century and standing on a rise in the Old Town. The cathedral museum exhibits a collection of very precious tapestries and superb goldsmiths' works.

Following the valley of the Río Valderaduey for a bit, the journey now leads to Medina de Ríoseco, the northernmost point of the trip through the highlands.

⑦ **Medina de Ríoseco** This charming little town flourished in the Middle Ages thanks to its trade in wool and features a handful of historic buildings. The most important sacral building is Santa María de Mediavilla (16th century), which boasts a beautiful star-vaulted ceiling.

⑧ **Valladolid** The capital of the Castilla y León region is spread across fertile plains on the banks of the Río Pisuerga, which flows into the Río Duero to the south-west of the town. Valladolid has 320,000 inhabitants, making it one of the largest cities in Central Spain, but only a few historic buildings have been preserved in the Old Town.

Some 500 m (547 yds) east of the Plaza Mayor, which instantly became a model for similar plazas in Madrid and other cities, is the city's cathedral. Construction began in the year 1580, but the church remains unfinished. The cathedral combines a relatively plain architectural style with sheer size: the interior is 122 m (133 yds) long and 62 m (68 yds) wide. The oldest place of worship in Valladolid is the Church of Santa María la Antigua (13th/14th centuries). Behind the cathedral is the university, which was founded in 1346, and features an attractive baroque façade. One of the gems in the city's sea of houses is the Casa de Cervantes. Another treasure is the small Casa de Colón, the house where Christopher Columbus died.

1 The Plaza de Cibeles with its enormous fountain, Fuente de Cibeles, is one of the Madrid's most attractive squares.

2 The Old Cathedral of Salamanca, built in the 12th century.

3 The Old Town of Ávila and the churches outside the town walls have all been declared UNESCO World Heritage Sites.

Madrid

The capital of Spain is not only the geographical center of the Iberian Peninsula, but was once the center of an empire upon which the "sun never set". Dynasties like the Habsburgs and the Bourbons have all had an influence on the city, and its urban landscape is accordingly very heterogeneous, even within the city center. Since the end of the Franco dictatorship in 1975, Madrid has undergone a rapid transformation and developed from a sleepy administrative center into a vibrant and pulsating metropolis.

As the capital of Spain, Madrid began attracting both artists and merchants back in the 16th century. Velazquez and Goya, for example, were called to the Spanish Court as royal painters. An extensive collection of their works as well as those of other artists can today be admired in the Museo del Prado. It is one of the most famous collections of classic works of art with more than 9,000 paintings, 5,000 etchings and 700 sculptures. Aside from the Prado, Madrid is home to other museums of world renown: the Museo Thyssen Bornemisza provides an overview of more than 700 years of European art history, with an important collection of modern classics; the Museo Nacional

Especially worth seeing: Museo del Prado; Museo Nacional Centro de Arte Reina Sofía; Monasterio de las Descalzas Reales, a Renaissance monastery with a rich collection of art treasures (16th century) that was reserved for women from the upper aristocracy; the Museo Arqueológico Nacional, with outstanding collections from early Iberian history; Museo Thyssen Bornemisza; Parque del Retiro, a green oasis in the middle of the capital fashioned in neoclassical style; Palacio Real, the royal palace built in late-baroque and neoclassical styles; Plaza Mayor (17th century), the imposing main square in the capital and the model for similar squares

Top: The Plaza Mayor in Madrid, dating back to the 17th century
Bottom: The Prado displays one of the most important collections Old Masters.

Centro de Arte Reina Sofia mainly has Spanish modern art with works by Dalí, Miró, Tàpies and Picasso, including *Guernica*.

Madrid also offers a wide variety of architecture styles, from Renaissance and "Madrid de los Austrias" (the Monasterio de las Calzas Reales) to baroque, neoclassicism, Art Deco and Postmodernism (Urbanización AZCA). With the so-called "Movida", the avant-garde art and fashion scene of the 1980s, a rich cultural scene developed after the stagnation of the Franco era, with plenty of activity in all areas of art, music, film, theater and fashion. One expression of this phenomenon is an extremely lively nightlife scene with a vibrant bar and restaurant culture.

around Spain; Rastro, the flea market that takes place every Sunday in the Old Town district of Lavapiés, the Madrid of the "little people", where 19th-century tenement blocks known as corralas have picturesque inner courtyards and wooden balconies; Real Academia de Bellas Artes de San Fernando, with works by Spanish masters (16th–19th centuries) in a baroque city palace.

No capital without a boulevard: the Gran Vía was begun in 1910, north of the center. Its splendid bourgeois villas exude a certain charm. A bit farther away, the original Madrid can be seen in the Malasaña and Chueca barrios, former artisan districts and now the lively gathering point of a more youthful scene in the evenings.

Fortified castles of Castile

Castile's name comes unsurprisingly from the numerous castles (castillos in Spanish) scattered throughout the region. The fortifications were typically built on strategically significant locations such as promontories or rocks and many often towered high above their subject cities and villages. Indeed, the mighty fortresses in central Spain are testimony to the immense wealth and power that resulted from the country's New World conquests. Castile had religious, political and social wars, battles and skirmishes like no other region on the Iberian Peninsula. The Christians fought the

Top: Castle in Medina del Campo.
Bottom: Castillo de Belmonte.

Moors, the nobility fought the monarchy, and the peasants fought their feudal landlords.

In fact, many of the castles in the area were built by the Moors, who conquered the Iberian Peninsula for over five hundred years – sometimes on the site of earlier buildings that dated back to Roman times. After their systematic expulsion during the Reconquista, the Christian generals and the Castilian nobility extended the fortresses to defend and protect the surrounding countryside from any such further invations.

A visit to the Museo Nacional de Escultura north of the city center is a must. This sculpture museum, housed in the Colegio de San Gregorio (15th century), has the most important collection of religious woodcarvings in Spain.

⑨ Medina del Campo This small town to the south-west of Valladolid on the Río Zapardiel was the royal residence of the Spanish kings in the 15th and 16th centuries. Catholic Queen Isabella I died here in 1504.
A reminder of this period is the Castillo de la Mota, originally a Moorish fortress that towers over Medina del Campo. Built in 1440, it is among the most beautiful in all of Spain.
From Medina, the C112 continues east to Cuéllar, where you can see more fascinating castle fortifications.

⑩ Cuéllar The castillo de Cuéllar (15th century) is situated on a barren hill and dominates its surroundings. The castle, which is fearsome to look at from the outside, also served as a residence for the Castilian kings. Its walls contain a magnificent palace, a Gothic chapel and a lovely Renaissance courtyard.
If you have the time before continuing on to Segovia, make a detour to the fascinating castles

in the villages north-east of Segovia. To get there, leave the N601 at Navalmanzano and continue north-east. The first stop is Turégano, home to the partial ruins of a once imposing castillo. About 14 km (9 mi) north-east, in Cantalejo, turn onto a minor road that takes you to Sepúlveda about 20 km (13 mi) away. The village, located high above a curve in the Río Duratón, has preserved the remains of Roman town walls. From there, the route heads south to the Moorish castles of Castillo Morisco and Castillo de Castilnovo. The last stop before returning to the N601 is Pedraza de la Sierra, with a monumental castle atop a prominent rock.
From Pedraza, Segovia is another 25 km (16 mi) on the N110.

⑪ Segovia Situated on a rocky promontory that is about 100 m (328 ft) wide is the provincial capital of Segovia. The heart of its Old Town is the Plaza Mayor where Segovia presents itself from its most vibrant side. The center of the square even has a music pavilion where, in the evening street entertainers of all kinds jibe for the attention of passersby.
The Roman aqueduct, which still carried the city's water supply as late as the 19th century,

counts as one of the most magnificent Roman structures in all of Spain. The cathedral, which dominates the city center with its 100-m-high (328-ft) steeple, stands on the highest point of the Old Town and is protected by a wall with eighty-six towers. Its cloisters are adorned with 17th-century Brussels tapestries and paintings by old masters.
Among the other churches in Segovia, the church of San Martín from the 12th century stands out. Its Romanesque columned hall is decorated with flower patterns and Biblical scenes. San Miguel achieved historical significance as the coronation church of Isabella II as Queen of Castile and León.
"Old Segovia" is bordered in the north by the Alcázar. The fortress, which has been altered several times, is adapted to the shape of the rock on which it stands. Dating back to the 11th century, it is an outstanding example of Old Castilian castle architecture.

⑫ Guadalajara The special jewel of Guadalajara on the Río Henares is the Palacio del Duque del Infantado. The influential Mendoza Family had this palace built between the 14th and 17th centuries, the façade of which is from the 15th century and is

richly adorned with exceptionally beautiful diamond-shaped blocks and filigreed columns. It is one of the most flawless examples of the Mudéjar Gothic style. The palacio houses the Museo de Bellas Artes, which holds a collection of valuable paintings from the 15th–17th centuries.
Aside from several churches, including the church of Santa María de la Fuente, which was erected on the remains of a

Moorish mosque, the 16th-century Convent of La Piedad is one of the most famous sights in Guadalajara. It is framed in by double arcades.

⑬ Cuenca The Old Town here was built on a steep rock that drops away suddenly on both sides to the gorges of the Río Júcar and the Río Huécar. Famous for its *casas colgadas* ("hanging houses"), Cuenca ori-

ginally achieved prosperity with the wool and fabric trade and is one of the most picturesque in the country.
In one of the *casas colgadas* is the Museo de Arte Abstracto Español. With more than seven hundred paintings, it is one of the largest collections of Spanish modern abstract art. Not far away is the Museo Arqueológico, which has valuable finds from the region.

The Old Town has largely managed to preserve its medieval character. The Gothic cathedral, built in the 12th–13th centuries on the site of a former mosque, has Norman influences and was rebuilt after collapsing in the early 20th century; the interior had been largely undamaged. The Plaza Mayor is also lined with noteworthy old mansions that feature wooden balconies and wrought-iron balustrades.

On the highest point of the rocky plateau is the Torre de Mangana, the former fortress watchtower that affords panoramic views.

⑭ Carrascosa del Campo West of Cuenca, the N400 leads to the 1,166-m-high (36,636-ft) high Puerto de Cabrejas via tight hairpin turns before continuing through several smaller towns and past the ruins of several castles to Carrascosa del Campo. This village features a Gothic church with a beautiful baroque portal as well as the remains of an old fortress.
Some steep inclines and bends have to be navigated during the onward journey to Tarancón. From Tarancón, a detour to Uclés is worthwhile for one of the most beautiful monasteries in the province of Castile-La Mancha. The Monasterio de Uclés dates back to the 16th–18th centuries, and is often jokingly called "El Escorial de la Mancha". It is known for its valuable wood carvings and the crypt contains the tomb of writer Jorge Manrique. The remarkable patio is richly adorned with a sea of plants.
If you do not wish to return to Tarancón, you can continue via Saelices (which contains the remains of a Roman aqueduct) di-

rectly to Quintanar de la Orden, some 50 km (31 mi) to the southeast.
This region, which is dominated by vineyards and fields of grain, was immortalized by Miguel de Cervantes as the backdrop for the adventures of his knight-errant Don Quixote.
From Mota del Cuervo, it is worth taking the 35-km (2-mi) detour to Belmonte.

⑮ Mota del Cuervo and Belmonte An entire hillside here is covered with the windmills that are typical for La Mancha.
On a hill above Belmonte, which was the birthplace of the poet Fray Luis de León, stands the Castillo Villena, built in the 15th century. One of its three gates is decorated with a scallop shell and a crucifix, symbols of the St James' pilgrims on their way to Santiago de Compostella.
A double ring of walls encircles the star-shaped late-Gothic complex with six round towers. The

1 Two structures tower over the Old Town of Segovia: the Gothic cathedral in the town center and the Alcázar on the westernmost edge of the city.

2 These "hanging houses" are the most recognizable icon of the picturesque Old Town of Cuenca.

The Río Tajo (Tagus River) forms a natural boundary on three sides of the Old Town of Toledo, where the Alcázar and cathedral dominate the cityscape. Like most castle palaces in central Spain, the Alcázar of Toledo is also of Moorish origin; its name goes back to the Arabic al-qasr, roughly "fortified village". Initially the

capital of Visigothic Hispania, Toledo enjoyed a long period of prosperity known as La Convivencia (the coexistence) that began in the 8th century under the rule of the Caliphate of Cordoba. The mixed Gothic and Moorish styles here date back to these periods. Toledo was also briefly the residence of the Castilian kings

Don Quijote and Sancho Panza

The two protagonists of the novel *Don Quijote de la Mancha* (1605–1615) by Miguel de Cervantes (1547–1616) are gloriously different: Don Quixote, knight-errant, driven by boundless idealism in his struggle against the windmills, which he perceives as giants, and his faithful squire and companion, Sancho Panza, slightly

The monument to Don Quixote and Sancho Panza stands on the Plaza de España in Madrid.

dim-witted at first but ultimately at least not crazy.

Cervantes' book is not only the most famous Spanish novel, but also the country's most significant contribution to world literature. Originally, the book was conceived as a parody of the chivalric novels that were so fashionable at the beginning of the 17th century, but it eventually became a fitting depiction of Spanish society.

three sections of the castle are grouped around a triangular inner courtyard.

From here, we return on the same route to Mota del Cuervo and then continue towards Alcázar de San Juan.

16 La Mancha (south-east of Toledo) To the south-west of Mota del Cuervo, a number of castle ruins can be seen on both sides of the road and in the hills of the Sierra de Molinos near Campo de Criptana, a number of windmills have small museums. The Alcázar de San Juan houses a real treasure and the Museo Arqueológico has a beautiful display of Roman mosaics. The charming church of Santa María dates back to the 13th century.

17 Consuegra From here, the journey continues to follow the road to Toledo until you reach Consuegra, about 40 km (24 mi) away. The town is also dominated by castle ruins, which afford lovely views of the southern Mancha.

Staying on the same road and passing the Montes des Consuegra and the Embalse de Finisterre, you eventually arrive in Mora, about 30 km (19 mi) away. It has the remains of some interesting Roman structures.

18 Toledo The Middle Ages still seem omnipresent in this city on the Tajo. Its location alone is absolutely superb: the Old Town is spread out over a rock promontory that is surrounded on three sides by the Río Tajo in a deep gorge. The first panoramic view from the opposite bank of the river allows visitor to admire the splendor of the cityscape. The cathedral, the

Alcázar and countless medieval buildings combine to form a magnificent urban architectural ensemble while narrow alleyways with nooks and crannies characterize the Old Town, all surrounded by a medieval wall with numerous towers.

Toledo is a veritable treasure trove of Spanish and Moorish architecture. The city's most recognizable icon is the cathedral, which dates from the 13th–15th centuries and was erected on the site of a former late-Gothic church and an even older Moorish mosque. While the exterior is pure early French Gothic, the interior is a perfect example of late Spanish Gothic. The three portals on the main façade are richly adorned with reliefs and sculptures. The interior measures a stately 110 m (120 yds) and features the Capilla Mayor, a depiction of a number of Biblical scenes using life-sized figures carved from wood that are either painted or gilded.

The Alcázar stands on the highest point of town. The façade of the virtually square building is predominantly from the 16th century. The way up to the fortress begins at the Plaza de Zocodover. This triangular plaza is the actual center of town.

Other attractions include the Franciscan Monastery San Juan de los Reyes (15th–17th centuries) and the Casa El Greco. The famous painter lived in Toledo for almost forty years and created many works here. The journey then takes you along the Río Tajo to the west, past extensive fields that are irrigated with water from the river. As a last stopping point before you return to Madrid, be sure to visit Aranjuez.

19 Aranjuez This town, which has been well-known at least since Rodrigo's Concierto de Aranjuez, is laid out on a geometric grid and is most famous for its lovely gardens.

The largest area of the park is the Jardín del Príncipe in the north-east. Inside the park, which was created by French landscape gardeners in 1763, you will find the Casa del Labrador, a small palace that is worth a look. In another building, the Casa de Marinos, you will find six royal barges on display. The Palacio Real (the royal palace) south of the gardens was rebuilt in the 17th century after two fires. Its main façade combines elements of Renaissance and baroque styles.

1 Most of the windmills in the La Mancha region south-east of Madrid (here near Consuegra) are no longer in operation.

2 The preciously appointed interior of the summer residence in Aranjuez can be admired on a guided tour.

Salamanca This town's university was founded back in 1254. Buildings in yellow stone characterize the Old Town, which can boast not just one but two beautiful medieval cathedrals.

Valladolid The most significant sight in this town is the cathedral, begun in 1580, but still an unfinished project today. Equally impressive is the baroque façade of the university.

Medina del Campo This town was the residence of the Spanish kings in the 15th and 16th centuries. The Castillo de la Mota was once a Moorish fortress.

Semana Santa Easter week here begins with a procession on Palm Sunday for which palm fronds, woven sculptures and oversized representations of the Passion of Christ are carried around town – often by fraternities wearing red hooded cloaks of repentance.

Segovia Die Provinzhauptstadt ist ein Mix aus maurisch inspirierten und mittelalterlichen Profanbauten, Türmen und Plätzen, Kirchen, einer Kathedrale, einer eindrucksvollen Stadtbefestigung und einem berühmten römischen Aquädukt mit mehr als 100 Mauerbögen. Im Norden der Altstadt liegt das Musterbeispiel einer altkastilischen Burg, die Festung Alcázar.

Madrid The highest capital in Europe is a city of extreme weather and mixed architectural styles. Churches, monasteries, palaces and breathtaking modern buildings convey a fantastic impression of old and new. The art museums of Madrid also enjoy worldwide reputations, especially the Museo del Prado and the Museo Thyssen-Bornemisza.

Guadalajara The gem of Guadalajara on the Henares River is the Palacio del Duque del Infantado (14th–17th centuries) with its ornate façade and valuable collection of paintings.

Cuenca The Old Town here is situated atop a rocky cliff that is surrounded by two rivers. The "hanging houses" cling for survival on the cliff's edge.

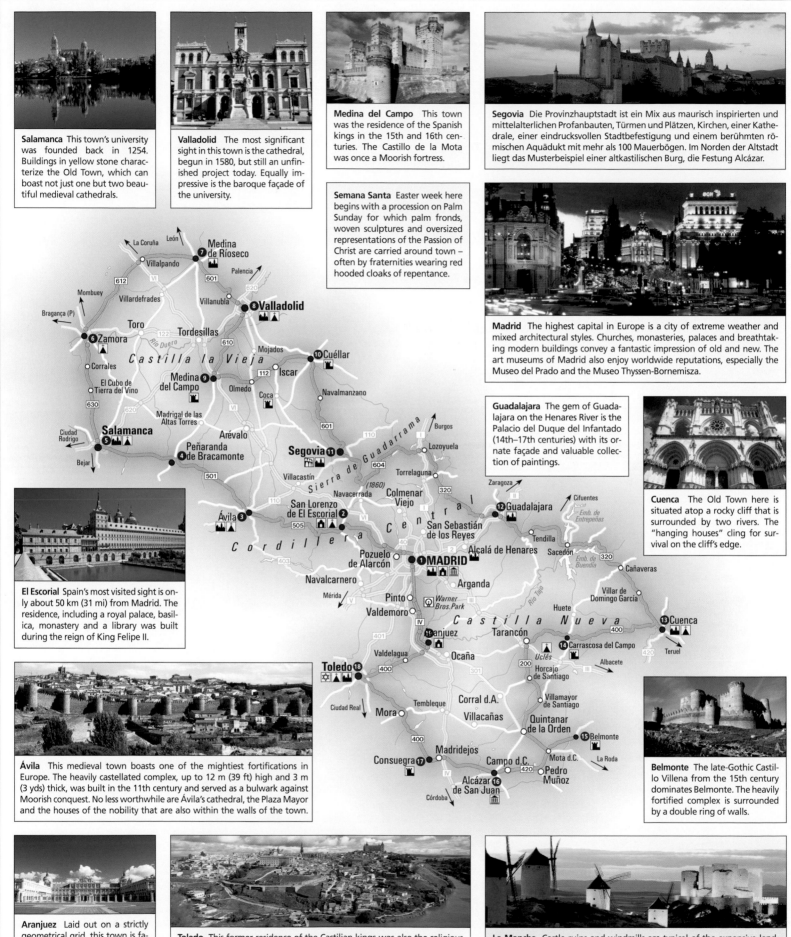

El Escorial Spain's most visited sight is only about 50 km (31 mi) from Madrid. The residence, including a royal palace, basilica, monastery and a library was built during the reign of King Felipe II.

Ávila This medieval town boasts one of the mightiest fortifications in Europe. The heavily castellated complex, up to 12 m (39 ft) high and 3 m (3 yds) thick, was built in the 11th century and served as a bulwark against Moorish conquest. No less worthwhile are Ávila's cathedral, the Plaza Mayor and the houses of the nobility that are also within the walls of the town.

Belmonte The late-Gothic Castillo Villena from the 15th century dominates Belmonte. The heavily fortified complex is surrounded by a double ring of walls.

Aranjuez Laid out on a strictly geometrical grid, this town is famous for its gardens and the splendidly appointed palace with its cabinets and galleries.

Toledo This former residence of the Castilian kings was also the religious center of the country and for a long time the home of painter El Greco. Toledo is perched a mighty promontory surrounded by the Río Tajo. The Gothic cathedral and the Alcázar look over the Old Town and its alleyways.

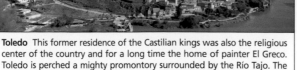

La Mancha Castle ruins and windmills are typical of the expansive landscape south-east of Toledo. Also worth visiting are the museums of Alcázar de San Juan and the castle of Consuegra. The views across the distant southern La Mancha are wonderful.

Puerto Banus near Marbella, one of the best-known yacht ports on the Costa del Sol.

Spain

Andalusia – a Moorish legacy in southern Europe

Andalusia is a region filled with passion and culture. The fertile agricultural land here is blessed with plentiful sun where olives trees grow against a backdrop of snow-covered mountains and the tidy whitewashed houses recall Moorish architectural styles. This natural setting coupled with the local aromas of leather and sherry and the rhythms of the castanets and flamenco all combine to create a truly unforgettable experience.

'Al Andaluz' – the 'Land of Light' – is what the Arabs called this sunny southern part of Spain. Interestingly, it was not meant as a metaphor. This region, where two continents and two seas meet, actually possesses a unique light that seems not to exist anywhere else in the world, and whose clarity never ceases to amaze its inspired visitors.

Andalusia covers an area of more than 87,000 sq km (33,582 sq mi). Its landscape is defined by the Sierra Morena Mountains and the Betic Cordillera Range, whose 3,481-m-high (11,421-ft) Sierra Nevada Mountains are covered in snow almost all year long.

The area is home to ancient settlements that pre-date the Romans, including Cadiz, which was first settled by the Phoenicians in around 1100 BC. Since then, Greeks, Romans, Vandals and Visigoths have taken turns settling and farming the sun-drenched land in the south of Iberia. It wasn't until the 8th century that the Arabs ended the reign of the Visigoths and took control of the area.

Flamenco – a dance and a way of life.

It turns out to have been an easy campaign for the Arabs to gain their foothold in Andalusia. When they secretly crossed the Strait of Gibraltar under Tariq ibn Ziyad, and later Musa ibn Nusair in 711, they only needed gradually to seize the already deteriorating kingdom of Roderic, the Visigoth ruler. After that, virtually no one else stood in their way and their expansion reached as far as Galicia and the Pyrenees. They were only halted by Charles Martell in 732 at the Battle of Tours in France.

In Spain, however, the Arabs reigned supreme for over half a century. Abd ar-Rahman I made Córdoba the capital of his Caliphate and adorned the city with an exquisite mosque. In Granada, Islamic culture developed with consummate splendour. Over the centuries, the Moors erected some truly magnificent buildings

The 'White Village' ('Pueblo Blanco') of Zahara de la Sierra is a national monument.

The Puente Nuevo across the rock gorge in Ronda, which is more than 100 m (328 ft) deep, is a technical masterpiece dating from the 18th century.

all throughout this region, in architectural styles that remain the defining element of Andalusia even to this day.

In the 13th century, the Christian 'Reconquista' of the Iberian Peninsula began in earnest and a huge victory was won for the Catholic monarchs Ferdinand and Isabella when Seville fell in 1248. When Granada was taken as well in 1492, the last Muslim minorities were expelled, marking the start of a new Andalusia that would not just ride the tide of good fortune that came with the discovery and conquest of the 'New World', but even dictate its development. Following the conquests of Mexico and Peru, the city of Seville became the most important trading center in all of Spain.

Today, the autonomous region of Andalusia, which enjoys 3,000 hours of sun a year and where oranges, olives, wine and almonds all flourish, is home to some seven million people and has around 760 towns and communities. Traditional festivals and religious life are of extreme importance to Andalusians, and these are celebrated with full fervour and devotion especially during the Semana Santa, or Holy Week, when numerous pilgrimages and processions take place.

Community culture is reflected in the local festival weeks, the ferias, as well as in the bullfights and diverse flamenco styles. These events show the true Andalusia, the land of bold caballeros, beautiful señoritas, formidable black bulls – the land that gets your blood pumping like no other place. And the natural landscape is breathtaking and diverse, from the glorious beaches of the Costa del Sol to the magnificent snow-covered peaks of the Sierra Nevada.

The famous stone pillars in the lion courtyard of the Alhambra in Granada.

Flamenco

Flamenco is 'the' dance of Spain, but it was actually a mix of non-spanish minorities who were responsible for its survival. The gitanos (gypsies) who travelled the area around Cádiz and Seville in the 15th century are said to have invented the 'cante andaluz' (Andalusian canto) or 'cante jondo' (deep canto). Flamenco was later used as background music in brothels until it became acceptable in the 1920s.

The musical form has been internationally renowned since Carlos Sauras'

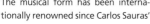
A flamenco festival in Andalusia.

sensational film *Carmen*. Flamenco is not just a dance to an exciting rhythm or a simple form of entertainment with catchy tunes, it is also a way of opening up the soul. For many, it is also the impressive reflection of a way of life – pride and passion under the torrid Andalusian sun.

Your Andalusian excursion takes you 1,600 km (994 miles) through the mountains of the Sierra Nevada Range, across the fertile plains of the Guadalquivir River and on down towards the Costa del Sol and the Costa del Luz. You'll visit the charming 'white villages' and the magnificent cities that are home to Moorish architectural masterpieces.

1 Seville For detailed information see p. 247.

2 Vega del Guadalquivir After leaving Seville on the C431 towards Córdoba you will emerge onto the flat, green and fertile plains known as the Vega del Guadalquivir. It is one of Andalusia's primary agricultural regions, with orange plantations, cornfields and sunflower fields sprawling across a wide valley formed by the river that made Seville a world power in the days of the explorers.

Small villages pop up along the route, with tidy white houses perched on top of lush hills. Most of the people in the area live off the rich agricultural bounty.

3 Palma del Río Its prime location at the confluence of the Guadalquivir and Genil is romantic enough. Add to that the verdant green surroundings and you've got two good reasons why this area is called 'Andalusia's Garden'.

The impressive 12th-century city walls have been well preserved in parts and recall the town's rich history, which goes back to the Romans who founded it. Palma del Río then played a special role in Spain's history from the 16th to 18th centuries when the Convento de San Francisco regularly sent missionaries to the New World. One of them was Brother Junípero Serra, who was responsible in large for the fabulous mission churches that can still be seen in California. But those times have long passed and the monastery has been given a new purpose now – beautifully renovated, today it is used as a hotel.

1 Weithin sichtbar ist der maurische Glockenturm La Giralda über der gotischen Kathedrale und dem Archivo General de Indias in Sevilla.

2 Die Kathedrale Santa Maria in Sevilla wurde auf den Grundmauern der Almohadenmoschee errichtet.

Travel Information

Route profile
Length: approx. 1,600 km (994 miles), excluding detours
Time required: at least 8–10 days
Start and end: Seville
Route (main locations): Seville, Córdoba, Granada, Almería, Málaga, Ronda, Olvera, Arcos de la Frontera, Cádiz, Sanlúcar, Jerez, Seville

Traffic information:
Drive on the right in Spain. The speed limit in built-up areas is 50 km/h (31 mph), 90 or 100 km/h (56 or 62 mph) outside built-up areas, and 120 km/h (75 mph) on highways (generally tolls are required).

When to go:
The recommended times to travel are spring (around 26°C/79°F) and autumn (up to 32°C/90°C in September). Summer can be brutally hot.

Accommodation:
Paradores are state-run hotels in historic buildings. Bookings and reservations are made through Ibero Hotel (*www.iberotours.de*).

Information:
www.tourspain.es
Info on Andalusia: *www.andalusien-web.com*

Seville

To experience Spain you simply have to visit Seville, the capital of Andalusia.

Seville is one of the country's most charming cities, competing directly with Granada, Andalusia's second Moorish treasure, for the position. After America was discovered, Seville had its heyday as a river port on the Guadalquivir and as an important trading center where goods from Spanish colonies overseas were unloaded and transported to the interior. This brought extreme wealth and a breath of fresh air from the New World to this old city!

Particularly worth seeing here are the 15th-century Santa María Cathedral, a complex with lavishly designed porticos, the Patio de los Naranjos, the former mosque courtyard with early medieval marble bowls, and the Giralda bell tower, built as a minaret in the 12th century; the Reales Alcázares, built in the 12th century by the Almohadas, used as a Christian royal palace from 1248 and continually expanded until the 16th century.

Highlights of any visit also include the exquisitely decorated interior courtyards around which the palace buildings are grouped, as well as the gardens (the cathedral and the Alcázares are UNESCO World Heritage Sites); the Barrio de Santa Cruz, the Jewish quarter with its narrow alleys, tiled inner courtyards and wrought-iron balconies; the Casa de Pilatos,

Ceramic works on the Plaza de España.

a rambling private palace combining a fascinating mix of styles; the Hospital de la Caridad (17th century), the most important piece of Sevillian baroque architecture; the Museo de Bellas Artes with collections focusing on Spanish baroque art; the Plaza de España, a dazzling structure with ceramic paintings in the city park, Parque de María Luisa. Outside the city are the ruins of the Roman Itálica.

Córdoba: view of the Puente Romano bridge and the Río Guadalquivir across to the Mezquita, the most important attraction in the city. The Mezquita represents 1,200 years of architecture from both Islam and Christendom. The prayer house was begun by Abd ar-Rahman I in the 8th century and was expanded in the 10th

century by caliphs al Hakam II and Al Mansur into the largest mosque in the Muslim West. In the 16th century, a cathedral was built in the middle of this unique

Moorish art

Andalusia owes its most magnificent buildings to the Arabs who once ruled the area – the Mezquita in Córdoba, the Alhambra in Granada, and the Alcázar and the Giralda in Seville. One of the outstanding features of Moorish style is its ornate attention to detail. Because Islam prohibits the depiction of any of Allah's creatures, exquisite wall patterns were created in inscriptions and by combining geometric, floral and calligraphy motifs. The grandiose ornamentation often incorporated mosaics, ceramics, Koranic proverbs sculptured in marble and glass compounds adorned with Byzantine patterns imported from the eastern end of the Mediterranean. Mosques usually contained extravagant domes and entire halls of columns.

Top: The Myrtle Courtyard.
Middle: Lion courtyard with fountain.
Bottom: Courtyard of the Alcázar.

The style of arch most frequently used are the rounded, spiked or the Moorish horseshoe arch. The most popular building material during the time of the caliphs was ashlar rock. The Almohadas used natural stone for foundations and pedestals, and fired bricks and stamped clay for other parts of the structures.

Apart from the religious buildings and the palaces, Moorish architecture is still visible in the maze of streets in many of the Old City quarters in Andalusia.

4 **Medina Azahara** Just before reaching Córdoba, a road turns off towards the ruins of Medina Azahara, the old palace city built on three terraces where the caliphs lived together with their royal suite between the mid 10th and early 11th centuries. Parts of the complex have been renovated and give you a pretty good idea of the former beauty of the 'Flower City', a masterpiece of Islamic architecture.

5 **Córdoba** This city was an important political and cultural center as early as Roman times – one of its most famous sons is the philosopher, Seneca, from the 3rd century BC. By AD 929, Córdoba had risen to become one of the Caliphate's most resplendent metropolises on Spanish soil, competing even with the likes of the former cosmopolitan city of Baghdad. Jews, Arabs and Christians lived in harmony with each other. Science and philosophy flourished like never before.
In the old city center, traces remain of this heyday when the mighty Caliphate city had over a million inhabitants. It has now become a provincial capital with a population of just 300,000, but Córdoba remains a gem indeed: the Old City's narrow little alley-ways, whitewashed houses and inner courtyards decorated with flowers all create an idyllic scene. At the center of it all is the Mezquita – previously a mosque and now a cathedral – standing strong like an old fortification. The enormous building, with the magnificent prayer hall supported by 856 ornate columns, was declared a UNESCO 'Legacy of Mankind'. Nineteen naves and thirty-eight transepts, exquisite Oriental decorations and light casting mysterious shadows on the pillars make the Mezquita a truly unforgettable sight.
Just next to the Mezquita is the Judería, the former Jewish quarter with narrow streets adorned with flowers. One of the most beautiful of these is the aptly named Calleja de las Flores. The former synagogue and the bull-fighting museum, which inci-dentally is one of the most interesting in all of Spain, are also worth a visit.
The Alcázar de los Reyes Cristianos, a royal residence built as a fort in the 14th century, has really lovely gardens. The Museo Arqueológico Provincial, located in a Renaissance palace, has a number of Roman, Visigoth and Arabic exhibits. In the quarter around the Christian churches, Córdoba has another tourist attraction in store – the Palacio de Viana, a mansion with twelve inner courtyards and spectacular gardens.
The two most important centers during Spain's Moorish period, Córdoba and Granada, are connected by the Caliphate Route. Today it is known as the N432, a slightly less romantic name, but it still passes through a hilly region with relatively little settlement, some small homesteads and a handful of well-fortified castles and towers.
At the town of Alcalá la Real, nestled in the shadow of the Moorish Castillo de la Mota, you leave the N432 for a leisurely drive through the villages of the fertile highlands of the Vega.

6 **Montefrio** This town lies in a unique mountain landscape and is known for its castle, Castillo de la Villa, which was built around 1500 on the walls of an old Moorish fort.
After some 20 km (12 miles) you come to the A9 heading towards Granada.

7 **Granada** The geographic location of this city is fascinating in itself – bordered in the west by a high plateau, in the south by the northern bank of the river Genil,

and with the snowcapped peaks of the Sierra Nevada as a background setting. However, what really gives Granada its 'One-Thousand-and-One-Nights' feel is the extensive Moorish legacy that has defined this city for more than seven hundred years now. Granada experienced its heyday between the 13th and 15th centuries, before the Moors were pushed south by the gathering armies of the Christian 'Reconquista'. At that point the city had been the capital of the independent Kingdom of the Nasrids for 250 years, and it was during this time that its most magnificent edifice was built – the Alhambra.

A total of twenty-three sultans from the Nasrid Dynasty contributed to this tour de force of Spanish-Arabic constructions.

Now the castle, at once fortress-like and elegant, is the pearl of the city of Granada.

The Alhambra, whose name 'The Red One' derives from the reddish ochre of its walls, is an enormous complex of fortifications, towers, royal residential palaces, mosques and gardens. It comprises four main sections – the defences, or Alcazaba, on the western tip of the hill; the Palacio Árabe (Alhambra Palace); the Palacio de Carlos V, a Renaissance palace with the Museum of Fine Arts in the center of the hill; and the gardens of the Generalife in the east. Apart from the gardens, which were part of a summer residence, all other buildings are surrounded by fortified walls with towers.

The Palacio de los Leones, with its arcade passage adorned with filigree work, and the lion foun-

tain are two of the most impressive parts of the Alhambra, along with the water features in the gardens, which have a real oasis feel. But the Alhambra is not all that this splendid city has to offer.

The Albaicin is also something to behold – the whitewashed Moorish quarter is an architectural gem in its own right, with tiny alleyways and the mirador, the San Nicolás lookout. In addition, there is the area around the 16th/17th-century cathedral, the Capilla Real, the late-Gothic royal chapel and the Carthusian monastery, founded in the early 16th century – each and every one of them worth a visit.

A must for poetry-lovers after all this is the small detour from Granada to Fuente Vaqueros, the birthplace of García Lorca, 17 km (11 miles) away on the

1 To get the most beautiful view of the Alhambra in Granada and the Sierra Nevada Mountains, go to the Mirador de San Nicolás in Albaicín.

2 The prayer room of the former Umayyad Mosque in Córdoba has 856 columns.

3 The churches of Iglesia de la Villa (16th century) and Iglesia de la Encarnación (18th century) tower over Montefrío.

Carretera Granada–Veleta

Europe's highest mountain road runs for 46 km (29 miles) from Granada to Pico Veleta, the second-highest peak in the Sierra Nevada at 3,392 m (2,108 ft). The mountain is normally only free of snow from August to September, meaning snow fields are quite common along the road, which has an average incline of 5.1 per cent from Granada and 6.5 per cent from the actual start of the slope. The view from the top is sensational, spanning from the mountains of the Sierra Nevada over Granada, the Mediterranean 30 km (19 miles) away and all the way to the North African coast.

Detour

Sierra Nevada

The Sierra Nevada, whose name literally means 'Snowy Range', is Spain's highest mountain range. Its name obviously says a lot about these mountains – they are often

Fields in front of the snow-covered peaks of the Sierra Nevada

snow-capped, even in summer. There are fourteen peaks here over 3,000 m (9,843 ft), in front of which are mountain ranges also reaching up to 2,000 m (6,562 ft) in height. The highest point is the Cerro de Mulhacén at 3,481 m (11,421 ft). Between the second-highest peak, the Pico Veleta, and the town of Pradollano, located at an elevation of 1,300 m (4,265 ft), is an excellent region for skiing with nineteen lifts and a total of 61 km (38 miles) of trails.

Costa del Sol

'Costa del Sol' – the Sunshine Coast – refers to a roughly 150-km-long (93-mile) stretch of the south-eastern coast of Spain. And rightly so, because this lovely area of Andalusia enjoys a pleasant, sunny climate, with mild temperatures even in winter.

Marbella's yacht port.

It is certainly one of the reasons that the Costa del Sol has become one of the most popular holiday destinations in the world. Many of the small, once poor, fishing towns like Fuengirola and Torremolinos have now become tourist hot spots with enormous hotel and apartment complexes, holiday villas, golf courses and yacht ports.

Some of the former villages have kept their Andalusian charm, including Estepona.

Even Marbella, the luxurious and glamorous city favoured by the international jetset, has preserved traditional houses, lanes, squares and gardens in its historic center.

plains. From there it is up into the mountains for a detour into the Sierra Nevada over Europe's highest pass.

As you leave Granada heading east on a small road parallel to the A92, the landscape becomes sparser and wilder. This effect is enhanced when you see the first cave dwellings dug into the rocky hillsides.

8 Guadix This truly ancient city with grand Moorish ruins and a history that dates back to Roman times also has a section with cave dwellings – some five thousand gitanos (gypsies) live here underground in the Barrio de Santiago. Their homes, painstakingly carved into the steep loess slopes and actually comprising multiple rooms, are even connected to the city water supply and electricity network. The landscape remains sparse for a while now. After Guadix, the castle of La Calahorra is worth a detour. The Gulf of Almería soon comes into view.

9 Almería This fine city has always benefited from its special geographic location. Protected from the mainland by mountain ranges, the vast Gulf of Almería fulfills all the right conditions for a nice port and a good center for trade. The Phoenicians even recognized this and built a port that became the foundation for the Roman Portus Magnus. Pirates later found it to be an ideal hideout, too.

During the time of the caliphs, Almería experienced yet another rise as an important trading center, becoming the capital of a kingdom to which the likes of Córdoba, Murcia, Jaén and even parts of Granada temporarily paid allegiance. In 1489, the city was reconquered by the Christians and from then on only played a secondary role.

Today, Almería is very much an agricultural town. The surrounding area is home to rows of enormous greenhouses where fruit and vegetables are grown for export. The nearby Andarax Valley is home to the region's orchards and vineyards.

Almería is a predominantly modern town with wide, palm-lined streets dominated by the massive alcazaba (fort), which sits on top of a hill as if on its own throne. Construction began on the alcazaba in the 10th century and it is one of the most powerful and best-preserved fort complexes in all of Andalusia.

The Old Town, with its picturesque fishing and gitano quarter on the castle hill, La Chanca, still has an undeniable Moorish feel to it. The colourful cubic houses and the cave dwellings look like relics from distant times.

For the next part of the journey there is an alternative route to the highway – the very picturesque 332/348, which take you inland through the mountains of the Sierra Nevada and then back down the coast.

Passing through Motril, the road continues towards the Costa del Sol through the fertile plains where tropical fruits are a speciality. Along the way, a good place to stop is Nerja, about 50 km (31 miles) before reaching Málaga. Perched on a ridge, this

town is home to the amazing Cueva de Nerja dripstone cave.

10 Málaga Málaga is a very important economic center, Andalusia's second-largest city with over half a million inhabitants, and the second-largest Spanish port on the Mediterranean after that of Barcelona. It is the main trading center for the agricultural products from the nearby plains, in particular wine and raisins.

In terms of tourist attractions, Málaga does not have a lot to offer. However, it is well worth climbing up to the Gibralfaro, the Moorish citadel and lighthouse that gives you a beautiful view of the semicircular expanse of land.

Today, next to nothing remains of the splendour of the alcazaba – often compared to the Alhambra in Granada – and the cathedral, whose construction started in the 16th century but was not completed: the middle section of the tower, 'La Manquita', (the missing one) is still open for all to see.

Detour

Gibraltar

The first impression is imposing: the 425-m-high (1,394-ft) limestone rock of Gibraltar suddenly soars out of the sea, connected to the mainland only by a flat alluvial plain. This is where the airfield was built, and where every visitor must pass upon presenting their passport or personal ID.

The British enclave, just 6 sq km (2.3 sq mi) in size and with a population of 30,000, controls the strait between Europe and Africa. Its name derives from Djebal al-Tarik, – Tarik's Mountain – the name of its Arab conqueror from 711.

The British originally seized the strategically important southern tip of Spain in 1713 during the War of the Spanish Succession, and at the start of the 19th century they built the Anglican Church here. Today, the British governor resides in a former Franciscan monastery dating back to the 16th century. The official language on the island is English and the most interesting

The rock of Gibraltar towers over the strait of the same name.

tourist attraction is the cable car to the top of the rock. From the top there is an amazing view of the Bay of Algeciras, the Gibraltar port and the North African coast.

The darlings of all visitors to Gibraltar, however, are the frisky Barbary apes, which can be fed without any problem. Legend has it that Britain's rule of Gibraltar will be protected as long as the apes continue to inhabit the rock.

From Málaga, the Costa del Sol continues along coastal road 340 with its large holiday resorts. After Marbella, the main road turns off into San Pedro de Alcántara. For those who want to enjoy some beautiful scenery, however, drive another 30 km (19 miles) west and take the route at Manilva that heads up into the Serranía de Ronda. If you wish to to visit Gibraltar you can do so by continuing another 40 km (25 miles) from Manilva along the coastal road.

⑪ Ronda If for nothing else, this town is worth seeing for its adventuresome location. It lies at the edge of a high plateau divided by the Río Guadalevín, which flows by in a gorge that is up to 200 m (656 ft) deep. Its houses and numerous mansions are built right up to the edge of the cliff. The 98-m-high (322-ft) Puente Nuovo, built in the 18th century, spans the gorge. Ernest Hemingway was as fascinated with the city, the deep gorge, the houses and the cliffs as was the poet Rainer Maria Rilke, who once

wrote: 'I have searched everywhere for my dream city and I have found it in Ronda.'

Ronda is divided into three sections. The oldest, La Ciudad, lies in the middle of the limestone plateau and is bordered on one side by a Moorish wall and on the other by steep terrain; sprawled at its feet is the San Francisco Quarter, with a street network lined with farms; and on the other side of the 'Tajo' gorge is the modern area El Mercadillo, where most of Ronda's 35,000 inhabitants live. One of the most important attractions here is the Casa del Rey Moro in the La Ciudad. Inside the rock, a staircase with 365 steps leads down from this Moorish palace into the gorge. The cathedral, the Palacio de Mondragón and the Casa del Gigante with their Arabic ornamentation and decorative elements are worth seeing.

Then there is the bullfighting arena. Built in 1785, it is one of the oldest in Spain. Ronda was also the place where bullfights

were given a sort of 'constitution' in the 18th century.

It is absolutely essential to do day trips around Ronda where the 'white villages' are charmingly tucked into the rugged mountains and valleys – Prado del Rey, with its neatly planned streets; Ubrique, capital of the Sierra de Cádiz, known for its leather products; Zahara or Setenil, which look like large eyries with their houses clinging to the rock; and of course Olvera, a town whose architecture is still entirely Moorish and whose walled upper city is dominated by a 12th-century castle.

⑫ Arcos de la Frontera The route now continues towards the Atlantic coast, passing by Embalse de Zahara. This town has a population of 30,000 and sits on a rocky ridge basically in the middle of the Guadelete River. Its whitewashed houses still create a Moorish atmosphere, while the church of San Pedro is most definitely worth a look, perched directly on a cliff with an impressive view of the

gorge and the plains with their seemingly endless olive groves. The route now follows Highway 328 towards the Atlantic coast, although it is worth making a detour to Cádiz beforehand.

⑬ Cádiz This city is considered the oldest in Spain; the Phoenicians were already making good use of its narrow, 10-km-long (6-mile) peninsula as a storage yard. Much later, after America

1 The view over the port city of Málaga on the Costa del Sol.

2 White houses in Ronda look out over the abyss on the high plateau.

3 Setenil, one of the 'white villages' around Ronda.

4 Casares, west of Marbella, was founded by Julius Caesar.

5 The mountain town of Arcos de la Frontera captivates visitors with its Moorish quarter.

6 An olive grove in the Sierra de Grazalema.

Coto de Doñana

This region covering 757 sq km (292 sq mi) of the Guadalquivir delta

Top: Swamps in the national park.
Bottom: An indigenous pearl lizard.

area has been a national park since 1969. Formerly a royal hunting ground, a sand dune separates the marsh from the sea. This allowed numerous biotopes to develop where rare and endangered animal species live and migratory birds make temporary stops.

was discovered, the city became extremely wealthy. Cádiz is still the second most important shipyard in Spain after El Ferrol. Fish is also an important source of revenue, as is salt, which is obtained from enormous salt refineries in the south-east of the city.

The best way to discover Cádiz is to take a taxi ride around the Old Town, which is especially picturesque with the golden cupola of the Catedral Nueva towering over the tiny square houses. The treasures of its church include the largest and most precious processional monstrance in the world. The Church of San Felipe Neri downtown is also worth a visit as the location where the Cádiz Cortes government in exile declared Spain's liberal Constitution in 1812. The Museo de Bellas Artes has some beautiful works by Spanish masters such as Francisco de Zurbarán and Murillo.

North of Cádiz on the Atlantic coast is a series of lovely resort towns – Puerto Real, Puerto de Santa Maria, Rota and Chipiona all have long, wide, fine sandy beaches.

14 Sanlúcar de Barrameda This dignified city, located at the mouth of the Guadalquivir, is

the export hub for the famous Manzanilla sherry. The Fino variety is only produced here in Sanlúcar.

The city is divided into two sections, the upper and lower city. Be sure to pay a visit to the palace of the once influential dukes of Medina-Sidonia and the superb Mudejar portico of the Church of Santa Maria. Another attraction is the royal equestrian school, the Real Escuela Andaluza de Arte Ecuestre, where you can witness Spanish dressage riding styles. This famous port saw Columbus begin his third voyage to America, and Magellan also set off from here on the trip on which his ship became the first to circumnavigate the globe.

Long before that, the Holy Virgin is said to have appeared here, hence the name Coto de Doñana (Coast of the Mistress). Today, you can take a boat to the Parque Nacional de Coto de Doñana from the quay.

From Sanlúcar the C440 'Ruta del Vino', or Wine Road, leads into the home of jerez (sherry).

15 Jerez de la Frontera A visit to one of the most wonderful bodegas – wine cellars – is a must in this charming city so rich in tradition. Many of these bodegas also have something special to offer apart from sherry. The Bodega Domecq in Calle Ildefonso, for example, enchants visitors with its Moorish interior, while the ironwork in the Bodega González Byass was

done by none other than Gustave Eiffel. Those still keen on seeing more sights after the enticing bodegas should head to the Old Town and have a look at the 17th/18th-century Church of San Salvador, the 11th-century Alcázar and the 'Cartuja', somewhat outside the city, whose Gothic church is particularly ornate. From Jerez, highway E05 then heads back to your starting point, Seville.

1 Jerez de la Frontera: in the vaults of the Bodega Pedro Domecq, sherry matures painstakingly in hundreds of barrels until it can be bottled and drunk.

2 The Catedral Nueva offers a magnificent view of the Cádiz headlands.

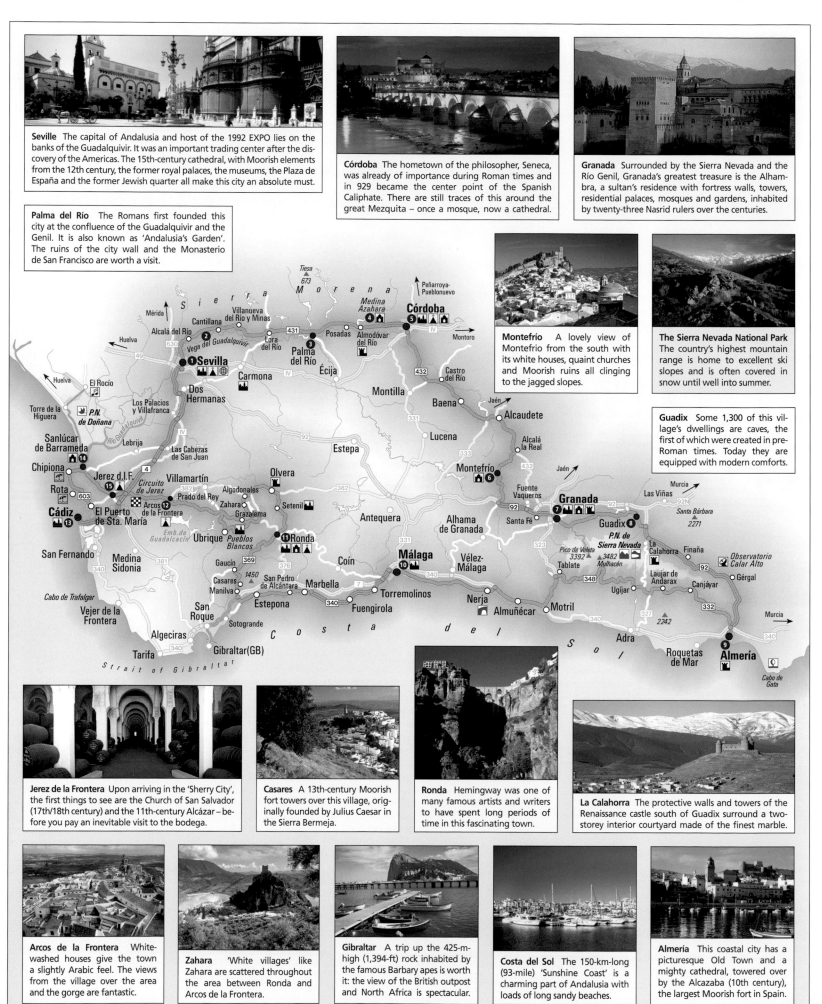

Seville The capital of Andalusia and host of the 1992 EXPO lies on the banks of the Guadalquivir. It was an important trading center after the discovery of the Americas. The 15th-century cathedral, with Moorish elements from the 12th century, the former royal palaces, the museums, the Plaza de España and the former Jewish quarter all make this city an absolute must.

Córdoba The hometown of the philosopher, Seneca, was already of importance during Roman times and in 929 became the center point of the Spanish Caliphate. There are still traces of this around the great Mezquita – once a mosque, now a cathedral.

Granada Surrounded by the Sierra Nevada and the Río Genil, Granada's greatest treasure is the Alhambra, a sultan's residence with fortress walls, towers, residential palaces, mosques and gardens, inhabited by twenty-three Nasrid rulers over the centuries.

Palma del Río The Romans first founded this city at the confluence of the Guadalquivir and the Genil. It is also known as 'Andalusia's Garden'. The ruins of the city wall and the Monasterio de San Francisco are worth a visit.

Montefrío A lovely view of Montefrio from the south with its white houses, quaint churches and Moorish ruins all clinging to the jagged slopes.

The Sierra Nevada National Park The country's highest mountain range is home to excellent ski slopes and is often covered in snow until well into summer.

Guadix Some 1,300 of this village's dwellings are caves, the first of which were created in pre-Roman times. Today they are equipped with modern comforts.

Jerez de la Frontera Upon arriving in the 'Sherry City', the first things to see are the Church of San Salvador (17th/18th century) and the 11th-century Alcázar – before you pay an inevitable visit to the bodega.

Casares A 13th-century Moorish fort towers over this village, originally founded by Julius Caesar in the Sierra Bermeja.

Ronda Hemingway was one of many famous artists and writers to have spent long periods of time in this fascinating town.

La Calahorra The protective walls and towers of the Renaissance castle south of Guadix surround a two-storey interior courtyard made of the finest marble.

Arcos de la Frontera Whitewashed houses give the town a slightly Arabic feel. The views from the village over the area and the gorge are fantastic.

Zahara 'White villages' like Zahara are scattered throughout the area between Ronda and Arcos de la Frontera.

Gibraltar A trip up the 425-m-high (1,394-ft) rock inhabited by the famous Barbary apes is worth it: the view of the British outpost and North Africa is spectacular.

Costa del Sol The 150-km-long (93-mile) 'Sunshine Coast' is a charming part of Andalusia with loads of long sandy beaches.

Almería This coastal city has a picturesque Old Town and a mighty cathedral, towered over by the Alcazaba (10th century), the largest Moorish fort in Spain.

The Santa Maria da Vitória monastery in Batalha was built partly in the Manueline style.

Portugal

The land of fado and peaceful matadors: a journey to the "edge of the world"

When it was still a province of the Roman empire, what is now Portugal was once called Lusitania. In the sixth century it was part of the Visigothic empire. In the 8th century the Moors took over, but as a result of the "Reconquista" to take back Iberia, it became a kingdom separate from Galicia and León. Portugal finally gained independence in around 1267, and takes its name from the port city of Porto (Latin: porto cale).

Portugal was known in Antiquity and in the Middle Ages as the "edge of the world" and, even in the 20th century, its location on the edge of the continent had both advantages and disadvantages. It is a relatively narrow country, roughly 150 km (93 mi) wide and 550 km (342 mi) in length, but it has 832 km (517 mi) of coastline characterized by steep cliffs and miles of glorious beaches.

The mighty Tagus River (Tejo) divides the mountainous north, the Montanhas, from the rolling south known as Planícies,

Armação de Pera beach near Albufeira.

or plains. In the north you journey through what is still largely an untouched forest and mountain landscape with abundant water resources, the Costa Verde with its pine groves, the fertile Minho region with the vineyards of the Douro Valley, and the remote "land behind the mountains", Trás-os-Montes. Central Portugal has a very different character, with the Serra da Estrela range rising to an altitude of almost 2,000 m (6,562 ft), with vineyards dotting the river valleys and the flood plains of the Tagus. Southern Portugal is dominated by Alentejo, Portugal's "breadbasket", with its vast landed estates that were dissolved after the "Carnation Revolution" of 1974. It is a flat, open region extending as far as the Serra de Monchique. Portugal's best-known region, of course, is Algarve, with its rocky cliffs and sandy beaches.

The population distribution is uneven throughout the country. While the sparse mountain regions are largely empty, there are almost three million people in Lisbon and almost one million in the greater Porto region. Cork is one of Portugal's best-known agricultural products: the country has more than eighty-six million cork oaks and they have to be twenty years old before the bark can be peeled for the first time. Today one in three of the world's wine corks still comes from Portugal.

As with most European countries, Portugal, too, has a diverse historical and cultural heritage to look back on. Unique throughout all of Europe, however, is the Manueline architectural style, which enjoyed its heyday during the reign of King Manuel I (1495–1521), arguably Portugal's "golden age". The Manueline is

The dream destination for many holidaymakers is situated in the south of Portugal: the Algarve, with its magnificent beaches and deep blue ocean.

Bragança Citadel enjoys a strategic location on top of a knoll and once served as a place of refuge.

a mixture of Gothic and Renaissance elements, supplemented with frenzied decoration inspired by exploration.

The cultural influence of the Portuguese voyages of discovery saw the development of exotic, maritime ornaments that were utilized in abundance everywhere. The azulejos, the usually blue and white tiles that can be found almost everywhere in Portugal, are a Moorish legacy and, in addition to their aesthetic function, they protect against heat, provide sound insulation, reflect light and liven up surfaces. Those hoping to immerse themselves in the world of the Portuguese will not be able to avoid *saudade*, a word that somehow defies translation because it denotes a sentiment that seems to exist only in Portugal and that is also intricately linked to the language's long development. The word derives from the Latin "solus", meaning loneliness, and therefore also expresses feelings such as solitude, yearning, melancholy, mourning, pain, and a restrained joy of life. *Saudade* is best expressed in *fado*, the traditional Portuguese folk song alleged to originate from Lisbon's Alfama district and from Coimbra. They are tristful songs mostly concerned with unfulfilled longing, lost love or despair. In Lisbon, *fado* is primarily performed by female singers accompanied by two guitarists, while in Coimbra it is typically young men who convey this sense of "fatum" (fate) deriving from social and political circumstances, like Jose Afonso with his fado number "Grandola", which accompanied the 1974 Carnation Revolution leading to the overthrow of the Salazar dictatorship.

It is a telling reflection of Portugal – a beautiful country with a hint of sadness.

On the outskirts of Lisbon, in Benfica: the Palacio Fronteira boasts magnificent gardens.

Sintra and the Palácio Nacional da Pena

This former Moorish town and later summer residence of the Portuguese kings and aristocracy lies at the base of a rocky outcrop with dense vegetation. It is characterized by winding alleyways, picturesque street corners and charming quintas. In the town center is the Paço Real, the Manueline city palace (15th/16th century) that offers a mixture of diverse architectural styles. Its oversized chimneys are the landmark of the town. The Palácio is visible from a distance and dominates the town of Sintra from atop the highest of its rocky promontories.

Sintra: The remarkable Palácio Nacional da Pena was built in 1840.

This Portuguese fairy-tale creation is a pseudo-medieval fortified castle with a truly bewildering mix of styles, from Gothic doors, Manueline windows, Byzantine ceilings and minaret-like towers to Moorish azulejos and other Romanesque and Renaissance elements. The whole thing is fascinatingly bizarre.

It was built between 1840 and 1850 by the Baron of Eschwege on behalf of Prince Ferdinand of Saxe-Coburg.

This circuit of Portugal begins in Lisbon and takes you west from the capital as far as Cabo da Roca before heading north to the culturally exciting cities of Porto and Braga. After a detour to the ancient town of Bragança, it then turns to the south passing through the Ribatejo and Alentejo regions on the way to Faro in the Algarve before returning to Lisbon along the coast.

1 Lisbon (see page 259)

2 Cascais The long beaches here have transformed this fishing village into a popular destination with plenty of cafés and boutiques. The daily fish auction provides something of a contrast to the main sightseeing attractions, which include the Parque da Gandarinha as well as the ornate azulejos in the old town hall and in the Nossa Senhora de Nazaré chapel.

A scenic coastal road takes you to Europe's western-most point north of Cascais. Cabo da Roca rises up 160 m (525 ft) out of the pounding Atlantic.

3 Sintra (see sidebar left)

4 Mafra North of Sintra is Mafra, home to a colossal palace completed in 1750, with which King João V once aimed to overshadow the Spanish El Escorial. Behind the 220-m-long (241-yd) façade are 880 rooms, a chapel the size of a cathedral and a sizable basilica.

5 Óbidos From Mafra, you continue north along the coast

as far as Peniche, one of Portugal's largest fishing ports. Situated on a prominent headland jutting out into the sea, Peniche has an 18th-century maritime fort that is worth visiting before heading inland toward Óbidos. Óbidos, also known as the Queen's Village, is a must-see in Portugal. The fortified hilltop village boasts charming alleys with tidy white houses decorated with flowers, all contained within a picturesque medieval town wall that is up to 15 m (49 ft) high in places.

1 The view over the old part of Lisbon from Largo das Portas do Sol.

2 The picturesque village of Azenhas do Mar is north of Praia das Maçãs near the Cabo da Roca.

3 You can walk around the town wall in Óbidos in around 45 minutes.

Travel Information

Route profile
Length: approx. 1,250 km (775 mi)
Time required: 14–16 days
Start: Lisbon
End: Setúbal/Lisbon
Route (main locations):
Lisbon, Cascais, Sintra, Peniche, Óbidos, Leiria, Coimbra, Porto, Braga, Guimãres, Vila Real, Guarda, Marvão, Estremoz, Évora, Moura, Mértola, Faro, Portimão, Lagos, Sagres, Setúbal, Lisbon

Traffic information:
The speed limit on the motorways is 120 km/h (75 mph), on national roads 90 km/h (55 mph), in towns 60 km/h (35 mph). The legal blood alcohol limit is .05 and it is strictly enforced. Seatbelts are compulsory.

The motorways are also subject to tolls.

When to go:
The best times to visit Portugal are spring and autumn. Summer can be gruellingly hot.

Accommodation:
State-run hotels, or *pousadas*, in historic buildings and/or scenic locations, are a popular form of accommodation in Portugal. Check this site for more information:
www.pousadas.pt

Further information:
Here are some websites to help you plan your trip.
www.justportugal.org
www.travel-in-portugal.com
www.portugal.com

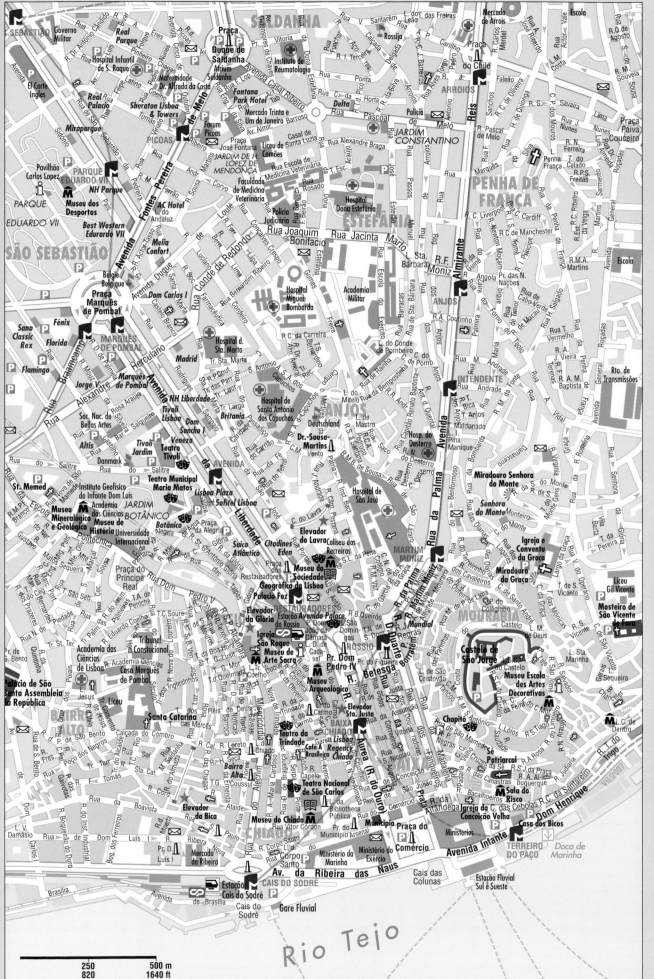

Lisbon

The sea of buildings in the "white city" extends from the wide mouth of the Tagus River up the steep hills of the Barrio Alto. Lisbon's wonderful location attracts visitors from all over the world who, like the locals, navigate the hilly city in eléctricos, creeky old trams.

Sights particularly worth seeing in Lisbon include: Alfama, the oldest and most picturesque district with labyrinthine streets on a fortified hill, dominated by the ruins of the Castelo de São Jorge; the two (of many) lovely miradouros, or viewing terraces, that make Lisbon so enjoyable, are tucked between the ruined fortress and the medieval Sé Cathedral; the Avenida da Liberdade, a 90-m-wide (98-yd) boulevard from the 19th century; the Barrio Alto (upper town), an entertainment district with countless bars, restaurants and fado taverns; Baixa, the lower town rebuilt in a regimented fashion following the devastating earthquake of 1755, today a banking and shopping district; Chiado, the former intellectuals' district in Belle Époque style; the Elevador de Santa Justa (1901) between the upper and lower town; the Museu do Azulejo in the Madre de Deus monastery; the Museu Calouste Gulbenkian, an oil magnate's founda-

Top: Rossio, the center of the Baixa.
Middle: Old Town buildings decorated with azulejos.
Bottom: The Torre de Belém, built in the 16th century.

tion with top-ranking European art; the Museu de Arte Antiga, the largest museum of Portuguese art; the Oceanário, a magnificent aquarium; and the Palácio dos Marqueses da Fronteira, a castle complex with a magnificent baroque garden.

Fátima and Tomar

Fátima is in fact an unassuming place on the Cova da Iria plateau north of the Tagus, but it has also been one of the most important Catholic pilgrimage destinations since 1917. The Virgin Mary allegedly appeared before three shepherd's children on a total of six occasions. At the last appearance, 70,000 people witnessed the "Milagre do Sol", when the sky is said to have darkened and the sun, blood red, circled around itself.

Following an eight-year period of research, the Vatican ultimately recognized the apparition of the Virgin and had the Rosary Basilica built at the site in 1928, which attracts hundreds of thousands of pilgrims every year. The square in

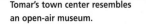
Tomar's town center resembles an open-air museum.

front of the basilica is twice the size of St Peter's Square in Rome.

Not far from Fátima is the small town of Tomar, which is dominated by the fortress-like former convent belonging to the Order of Christ, an order of medieval knights founded in 1314, following the suppression of the Knights Templar (founded in 1119) and which was subject to the will of the king and not that of the Pope. The order's red cross was long resplendent on the sails of Portuguese caravels.

The former Templar fort was later converted to a monastic castle in the Manueline style and is now a UNESCO World Heritage Site. At the center of the complex is the rotunda, built by the Templars in 1160. Be sure to see the high choir, the chapter house and the inner cloister.

6 **Alcobaça** It is hard to believe that one of Christianity's largest sacral buildings – the former Cistercian Mosteiro de Santa Maria de Alcobaça – was built in this town of just under 6,000 inhabitants north of Caldas da Reinha. Founded in the late 12th century and completed in about 1250, it was the first Gothic edifice in Portugal.

The three-storey baroque façade (18th century) is 220 m (241 yds) wide and 42 m (138 ft) high. The three naves of the Gothic interior are also impressive due to their unusual dimensions: 106 m (16 yds) long, 20 m (66 ft) high, but just 17 m (19 yds) wide.

Many of the visitors here are pilgrims visiting the tombs of King Pedro I and his murdered mistress Ines de Castro, who is buried directly opposite him so that, "at the resurrection, each of them should see the other first of all". The complex is a UNESCO World Heritage Site.

7 **Batalha** This simple country town is on the way to Leiria and is also a UNESCO World Heritage Site for the world-famous Santa Maria da Vitoria monastery. Construction began in 1388, following João I's historical victory at Aljabarrota (1385), but it was not completed until 1533. The complex has become a kind of national shrine for the Portuguese as a symbol of the country's independence from Spain.

A 15-m-high (49-ft), elaborately decorated Manueline portal invites you to enter the cathedral, which is nearly as long as a football field and 32 m (105 ft) high. It is adjoined by the "royal" cloister and contains the tomb of King João I.

8 **Leiria** Portugal's coat of arms contains the images of seven castles. One of these is in Leiria and it is one of Portugal's most beautiful. The history of its construction begins with the Romans, is influenced by the Moors, and continues through to the crusaders. The complex is now a mix of Gothic and Renaissance styles and affords a magnificent view of Portugal's largest pine forest.

From Leiria it is worth taking a detour to the south-east, first to Fátima, a pilgrimage site about 30 km (19 mi) away, and then to the Templar castle in Tomar.

9 **Coimbra** This town on the steep banks of the Rio Mondego is one of Europe's oldest university towns (12th century) and in fact was the only one in Portugal until 1910. The center boasts a fortress-like cathedral (Sé Velha, the largest Romanesque church in Portugal), also dating from the 12th century. Behind the cathedral you then continue up to the old university, which is the former royal palace. The highlight here is the library (1716–1728), Portugal's loveliest

baroque construction featuring gilded wood and fresco ceilings by Portuguese artists. Not far from the library, in the former bishop's palace, is the Museu Machado de Castro, with the Sé Nova (new cathedral), a former Jesuit church (1600) high on the slope above it.

A short walk takes you through a maze of alleys to the Mosteiro de Santa Cruz, a former Augustinian monastery. Take a break in the Parque de Santa Cruz, part of the monastery grounds. The Quinta das Lágrimas estate was the setting for the love story between Spanish Crown Prince Pedro and his mistress Ines that ended in such tragedy. The Fonte las Lágrimas (Fountain of Tears) supposedly originated with Ines' tears after her death. Life in Coimbra is heavily influenced by the 20,000 students who still wear the traditional *capa* gown, and not just for special occasions like the Queima das Fitas festival.

⑩ Porto It was no coincidence that Portugal's second-largest town on the Costa Verde was the European Capital of Culture in 2001. The port at the mouth of the Rio Douro has a great deal to offer visitors. Five bridges now link Porto with Vila Nova de Gaia, where a majority of the port wineries are based.

The streets and rows of houses in Porto's Old Town seem to cling precariously to the steep granite cliffs. At the lower end of the Avenida dos Aliados is the Praça Liberdade with the Torre dos Clerigos, the highest church tower in Portugal at 75 m (246 ft). At the other end is the town hall with its 70-m-high (230-ft) bell tower. The huge azulejo scenes on the wall of the São Bento railway station are especially worth seeing as well.

En route to the Ponte de Dom Luis I you come to the cathedral with its sacrament altar made from 800 kg (1,764 lbs) of silver. From here you can go down into the Bairro da Sé district, the oldest part of Porto, or to the Largo do Colegio. The Praça da Ribeira and the Praça Infante Dom Henriques make up the heart of the Ribeira district, where wealth and poverty collide – the stock exchange is juxtaposed with narrow, dingy alleyways.

⑪ Braga This old episcopal city is inland and to the north-east of Porto and is home to twenty churches closely packed together. The originally Romanesque cathedral was frequently remodeled over the centuries and has two massive towers.
Other sites include the 18th-century Palácio dos Biscainhos, surrounded by a magnificent

1 The "royal cloister" in the Santa Maria da Vitória Monastery, Batalha.

2 The Ponte de Dom Luís I in Porto was designed in Gustave Eiffel's office. To the left of the picture is the former bishop's palace; behind it to the right is the Torre dos Clérigos and the cathedral.

3 The University of Coimbra is located on the Alcácova and is the oldest in Portugal.

4 The monumental baroque stairway up the Bom Jesus do Monte pilgrimage church in Braga.

Detour

Bragança

This town in the somewhat spare, north-eastern reaches of Portugal was once the ancestral seat of the last Portuguese royal family. The

The citadel of Bragança

castle, which dominates the town, was built in 1187, has eighteen towers and a mighty keep, the 15th-century Torre de Menagem. In front is a 6.4 m (21 ft) pillory (pelourinho) on a granite wild boar. In the town itself is the Domus Municipalis, a type of Romanesque style town hall. The cathedral was originally Romanesque, but later converted to the Renaissance style in the 16th century.

The Mateus Wine Estate in Vila Real

The splendid Casa de Mateus is featured on the label when you buy a bottle of the famous Mateus Rosé. Situated about 4 km (2.5 mi) east of Vila Real, this country estate from the mid-18th century belongs to the old aristocratic wine-making family Mourão. The grounds have a palace-like character and the building is considered a gem of Portuguese baroque architecture.

The façade itself is indeed impressive enough, with whitewashed walls and granite balustrades, minaret-like towers reflected in the water of the grand pond built in front of it in the 1930s. The gable wall is flanked by classical statues and is crowned by the family's

The magnificent Casa de Mateus country estate in Vila Real.

coat of arms, which you again encounter under the chestnut-wood paneled ceiling of the foyet. The different rooms, including the Four Seasons Room, the Blue Room, the Dining Room and the Four Cornered Room, house magnificent furnishings and valuable porcelain, with impressive paintings adorning the walls. The family chapel and the family museum are also worth a visit.

Afterwards, take a stroll through the surrounding gardens with their boxwood hedges, and down the cedar-lined lane.

garden; the Oratorio São Frutuoso (7th century) is located 4 km (2.5 mi) outside town; the baroque pilgrimage church of Bom Jesus do Monte, 7 km (4 mi) away, is also famous for its elaborate staircase designed to match the Stations of the Cross (18th century). It is Portugal's second-most important pilgrimage destination after Fátima.

⑫ Guimarães This town 22 km (14 mi) south-west of Braga proudly claims to be the "Cradle of Portugal". It was here that the founder of the Kingdom of Portugal, Afonso Henriques, was born in 1111.
His Romanesque castle with its mighty 27-m (89-ft) tower stands high on the "holy hill" above town, and the palace of the dukes of Bragança (15th century) is in the charming Old Town. Nossa Senhora da Oliveira Church is also worth seeing.
From Guimarães, the scenic N206 heads to Bragança in the north-east of Portugal. It is a worthy detour despite the distance (230 km/143 mi).
If you are wanting to head south, the road branches off to the south at Vila Pouca de Aguiar and brings you to Vila Real and the Palácio de Mateus.

⑬ Vila Real This "royal town" on the Rio Corgo has a number of palaces and is famous for its black pottery. The baroque wine estate belonging to the Mateus family is located 4 km (2.5 mi) to the east. Not far from Vila Real is also the magnificent Solar de Mateus country estate.

⑭ Viseu This town's history goes back to the Romans and the Visigoths, whose last king, Roderich, was defeated here by the Moors. A stroll through the picturesque Old Town will bring you to the cubic proportions of the cathedral with its two-storey 13th-century cloister. The Manueline vaults are remarkable. The Museu Grão Vasco documents the history of the famous "Viseu" school of painting.
The scenic N10 now brings you to Guarda 100 km (60 mi) away.

⑮ Guarda Portugal's highest town is situated on a cliff 1,056 m (3,465 ft) up in the Serra de Estrela range and was one of Portugal's most important border fortresses for a long time. The older forts and the cathedral in particular are testimony to this history. It is well worth taking a stroll through the picturesque Old Town.

⑯ Castelo Branco The next stop is the capital of the Beira Baixa, a town which was a political bone of contention for centuries due to its proximity to Spain. Only the ruins of the 13th-century fortress remain. The somewhat bizarre Jardim Episcopal, which belongs to the bishop's palace, is considered to be one of the loveliest baroque gardens in Portugal.
Taking the N18 now to the south, you then turn off at Alpalhão and head for the mountains in the east.

⑰ Marvão This mountain village dating back to the Moors perches like an eagle's nest on the 870-m-high (2,854-ft) cliff. Its mighty fortress once played an important role in the border wars with Spain. You get a magnificent view of the small town ringed by the old town walls, the Serra de São Mamede, the Serra de Estrela and you can even see Spain. With its palaces, townhouses, monasteries, castle, cathedral and medieval town walls, the small town 16 km (10 mi) to the south, Estremoz, is like a open-air museum.

⑱ Estremoz In the Middle Ages this town was home to

one of the most important fortresses in Alentejo, of which only the massive keep (13th century) survives today. It is known for its pottery, which is sold on the large marble-paved marketplace on Saturdays and Sundays. From Estremoz, we highly recommend an excursion to Elvas, situated around 30 km (19 mi) east of Estremoz close to the Spanish border.

⑲ Évora The largest and most scenic town in Alentejo has been declared a UNESCO World Heritage Site because of its historical Old Town, its plazas, 16th- and 17th-century townhouses, palaces, churches and its medieval town wall.
From the Praça do Giraldo, with its lovely Renaissance fountains and Santo Antão Church (1557), you will come to the cathedral, a Gothic church building completed in the 14th century. This fortress-like edifice combines both Romanesque and Gothic elements along with having a Renaissance portal and a baroque altar. Today it adjoins the Museu de Arte Sacra and the Museu Regional.
North of the cathedral is the Templo Romano (2nd century) with fourteen Corinthian pillars.

Their reliefs are in surprisingly good condition despite centuries of misappropriation.
The Casa dos Ossos in São Francisco Church is a somewhat macabre attraction: the walls are "adorned" with five thousand skulls.

20 Monsaraz and Mourão The medieval village of Monsaraz about 50 km (31 mi) east of Evora features an intact town wall, a Castelo (14th century), a Gothic parish church and a *pelourinho*, or pillory, from the 17th century. On the opposite side of the Rio Guardiana, the

road takes you to Mourão, situated on Europe's largest reservoir lakes, the Barragem do Alqueva. It serves as a catchment for the Rio Guadiana. Small country roads lead to the next stop, Moura.

21 Moura The name of this thermal hot springs resort alone (with its well-maintained spa gardens and music pavilion) is indicative of its Moorish origins. A castle (13th century) is also testimony to that fact. The old Moorish district with its simple white houses and curious chimneys is worth a stroll.

22 Beja Passing through Vidigueira you then reach Beja, the second-largest town in Alentejo and one of the hottest towns in Portugal. Originally a Roman settlement, it was then declared a diocesan town under the Visigoths before being ruled by the Moors for 400 years.
It is worth visiting the Old Town for its maze of alleyways, the Convento Nossa Senhora da Conceição with a cloister decorated with lovely old azulejos, and Santo Amaro Church, which dates back to the Visigoth era. The Castelo (1300) is dominated by the highest keep in Portugal.

23 Mértola The terraces of this scenic little town on the right bank of the Rio Guadiana nestle up against the slope beneath the Castelo dos Mouros. The snow-white Igreja Matriz was a mosque up until 1238.

24 Faro Today the "Gateway to the Algarve" is a rather unappealing fishing and industrial town situated on a large lagoon, but it has an attractive Old Town around the cathedral at Largo da Sé and is enclosed by a medieval town wall.
The Carmo Church (18th century) with the Capela dos Ossos (skulls)

1 A wonderful view from the Castello de Vide in Marvão of the Serra de São Mamede.

2 The World Heritage Site of Evora: the Roman Diana Temple dating from the second century.

3 Monsaraz is a commanding mountainous location on the border with Spain. It is dominated by a 13th-century castle.

4 Olive trees and fields of sunflowers near Moura.

5 Mértola's attractions include the castle ruins and a Moorish church.

Detour

Elvas

This town close to the Spanish border is situated among olive groves and plum orchards. The former border town has maintained a Moorish medieval character with its ramparts, fortified towers, terraces and the old aqueduct from the 17th century. Part of this ensemble is the fortress-like Gothic Nossa Senhora da Assunção church with its pyramid-shaped, tapered bell tower, built between 1515 and 1520 on the black and white paved Praça de República. The famous Pelourinho de Elvas, an octagonal marble column with a pyramid-shaped top, is located on the Largo de Santa Clara.

The Aqueduto da Amoreira is the landmark of Elvas.

The town is enclosed by old fortified walls that also include the Fortaleza Nossa Senhora da Graça (1763–1792). To the south of the town lies the Fortaleza de Santa Lucia (1640–1687), today a *pousada*, or state-run guest house accommodation. The 7.5-km-long (4.7-mi) Aqueduto da Amoreira, which is still in use, ends at the Fonte da Vila (1498–1622) and its 843 superimposed arches measure up to 31 m (102 ft) in height.

The Alentejo Coast

Alentejo means "beyond the Tejo" (Tagus) and today the term refers to the entire area south of the Tagus up to the Upper Algarve. It comprises nearly one-third of Portugal's total surface area and extends from the western Atlantic coast across the country to the Spanish border. It can be extremely hot in the interior in summer as none of the cool sea breezes make it this far. Nevertheless, Alentejo has its own character and its own beauty that have been shaped by its climate and rugged location.

Atlantic surf near Carrapateira.

The expansive ochre-colored plains are dotted with olive trees and cork oak plantations as well as scattered wheat and rice fields of remarkable size, vegetable plantations and wine estates. Alentejo is known as Portugal's "breadbasket" and was therefore also a region traditionally controlled by the landed gentry both before and after the Carnation Revolution of 1974. Whitewashed villages and small towns pop up in the wide open landscape. The road network is relatively good, and occasionally lead you past herds of cattle and sheep on your left and right.

The mostly low, one-storey houses often have blue trim, which represents the color that consistent blesses the country's skies. The large chimneys are an indication that it can also be very cold here in the winter. The larger towns in Alentejo are Portalegre, Evora, Beja and Setúbal, while the most attractive coastal towns include Vila Nova de Milfontes, Sines, Carrapateira and Costa de Santo André.

is also worth seeing. You have the option of taking an excursion from Faro to the fishing port of Olhão with its market halls. The Ria Formosa nature reserve extends between Olhão and Faro, with the Cabo de Santa Maria, the southernmost point in Portugal, at its southern tip.

25 Albufeira This former fishing village west of Faro does not have many sightseeing attractions to offer but its favorable Algarve location makes it a tourist stronghold nonetheless. To some extent it is the Saint-Tropez of the Algarve, boasting countless beaches and bizarre cliffs combined with bars and nightlife to suit all tastes.
The buildings in the attractive Old Town sprawl up the steep, scenic coastal slopes.

26 Portimão The second-largest tourist stronghold on the Algarve is primarily known for its 1.5-km-long (1-mi) Praia da Rocha beach, which features beautiful and bizarre cliffs. If you have time, it is possible to take an excursion from here to Silves, a town in the interior that has a striking castle complex and a lovely Gothic cathedral (13th century). In addition to a cork museum, it also boasts the only museum dedicated to Portugal's Moorish era. At that time Xelb, the present-day Silves, served as the capital city.

27 Lagos This was the port from which the droves of Portuguese seafarers used to put to set sail in their caravels. In fact, Lagos has been a shipbuilding center since the time of Henry the Navigator (1394–1460). The slave trade forms part of the darker side of the town's history: Lagos was a market and transshipment center for the trade in African slaves, the first of whom were auctioned on the Praça da Republica in 1443.
The town is dominated by the Ponta da Bandeira fortress, which dates back to the 17th century. The sandy and rocky beaches around Lagos are a very popular destination for water sports enthusiasts. The fortified walls and the baroque Santo Antonio Church (17th century) are worth seeing, as are the magnificent cliffs on the Ponta Piedade around 2 km (1.2 mi) to the south.

28 Sagres This port played a significant role in the 15th and 16th centuries as it is alleged to have been the location of Henry the Navigator's legendary navigation school, a fact that is documented by the giant stone compass on the rocky ledge of the Ponta de Sagres, close to the Fortaleza de Sagres. The rose-shaped compass has a diameter of 43 m (47 yds). The Cabo de São Vicente is close by and has 24-m-high (79-ft) light-

house that protrudes out of the sea, marking the southwesternmost point in Europe. Before Columbus, the 60-m-high (197-ft) cliffs were considered to be "World's End".

29 The west coast of the Algarve From Sagres, the road back to Lisbon largely follows the Atlantic coast. The first stop is the village of Vila do Bispo, where the Ermida de Nossa Senhora de Guadelupe chapel is worth a visit.
From there, the journey continues to Aljezur where the ruins of the Castelo afford a magnificent view. Nearby Carrapateira is to be recommended for anyone wanting to make a short detour to the beach. From Aljezur, the road leads to Odemira, a small country town on the Rio Mira, which is controlled by the 44-km (27-mi) lake above the Barragem de Santa Clara dam 30 km (19 mi) to the south-east.
The next stop is Vila Nova de Milfontes, with sandy beaches and water sport options. The road initially heads inland after Sines, before turning back toward the coast after the fortress-liked town of Alcácer do Sol with its Moorish castle, towards Setúbal.

30 Setúbal Portugal's third-largest port was already an important fishing port during Roman times and the bay formed by the mouth of the Rio Sádo is dominated by the port facilities, sardine factories and dockyards. The lively fishing port is an attractive setting as is the still picturesque Old Town with its winding alleys.
Setúbal is often referred to as a "Manueline jewel", and the Igreja de Jesús (1491) with its elaborate columns is undoubtedly a jewel of this architectural style. The cathedral (16th century) boasts magnificent 18th-century azulejos.
You can get a wonderful view over the town from the Castelo São Filipe to the west. Anyone then wanting to head for the beach should take the ferry over to the Tróia Peninsula. Otherwise, the journey now takes you directly back to Lisbon.

1 Albufeira, with its charming whitewashed buildings, is one of the most popular tourist resorts on the Algarve. Still, by some miracle, it has been able to retain its old fishing village flair.

2 The cliffs on the Ponta da Piedade headland shelter the south side of Lagos Bay.

3 A shrine even in Roman times – the 60-m-high (197-ft) spur Cabo de São Vicente is the weather-beaten south-western tip of Europe.

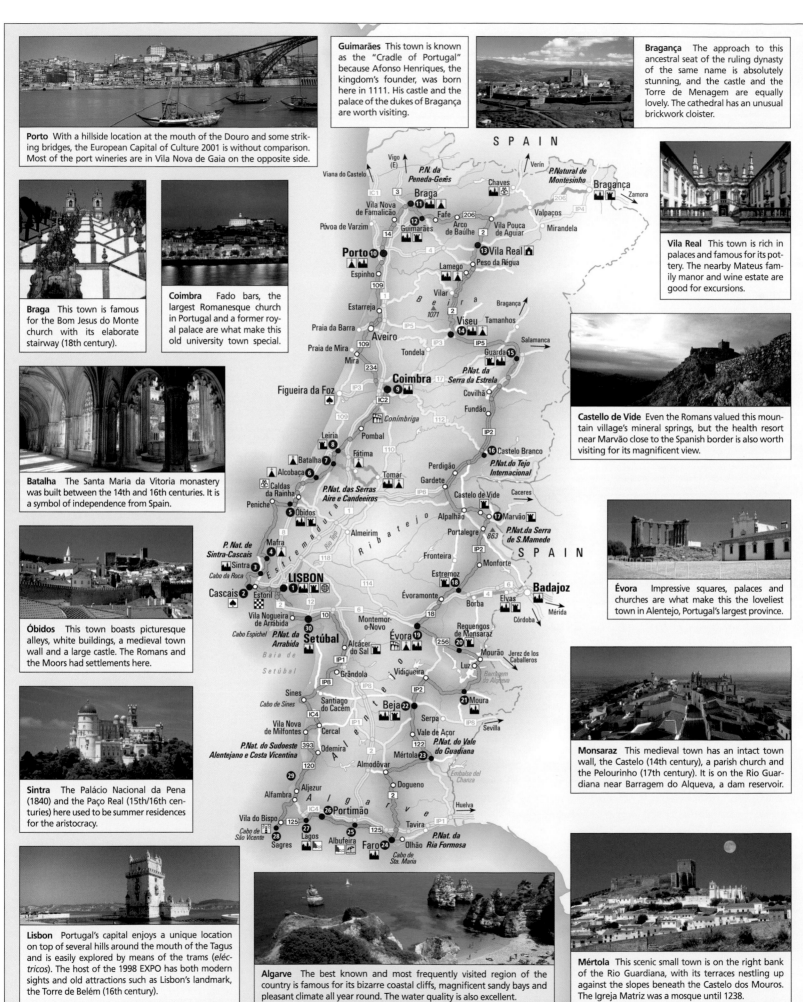

Porto With a hillside location at the mouth of the Douro and some striking bridges, the European Capital of Culture 2001 is without comparison. Most of the port wineries are in Vila Nova de Gaia on the opposite side.

Guimarães This town is known as the "Cradle of Portugal" because Afonso Henriques, the kingdom's founder, was born here in 1111. His castle and the palace of the dukes of Bragança are worth visiting.

Bragança The approach to this ancestral seat of the ruling dynasty of the same name is absolutely stunning, and the castle and the Torre de Menagem are equally lovely. The cathedral has an unusual brickwork cloister.

Braga This town is famous for the Bom Jesus do Monte church with its elaborate stairway (18th century).

Coimbra Fado bars, the largest Romanesque church in Portugal and a former royal palace are what make this old university town special.

Vila Real This town is rich in palaces and famous for its pottery. The nearby Mateus family manor and wine estate are good for excursions.

Batalha The Santa Maria da Vitoria monastery was built between the 14th and 16th centuries. It is a symbol of independence from Spain.

Castello de Vide Even the Romans valued this mountain village's mineral springs, but the health resort near Marvão close to the Spanish border is also worth visiting for its magnificent view.

Óbidos This town boasts picturesque alleys, white buildings, a medieval town wall and a large castle. The Romans and the Moors had settlements here.

Évora Impressive squares, palaces and churches are what make this the loveliest town in Alentejo, Portugal's largest province.

Sintra The Palácio Nacional da Pena (1840) and the Paço Real (15th/16th centuries) here used to be summer residences for the aristocracy.

Monsaraz This medieval town has an intact town wall, the Castelo (14th century), a parish church and the Pelourinho (17th century). It is on the Rio Guardiana near Barragem do Alqueva, a dam reservoir.

Lisbon Portugal's capital enjoys a unique location on top of several hills around the mouth of the Tagus and is easily explored by means of the trams (eléctricos). The host of the 1998 EXPO has both modern sights and old attractions such as Lisbon's landmark, the Torre de Belém (16th century).

Algarve The best known and most frequently visited region of the country is famous for its bizarre coastal cliffs, magnificent sandy bays and pleasant climate all year round. The water quality is also excellent.

Mértola This scenic small town is on the right bank of the Rio Guardiana, with its terraces nestling up against the slopes beneath the Castelo dos Mouros. The Igreja Matriz was a mosque until 1238.

The area north of Siena is the traditional wine growing region for Chianti Classico.

Italy

From Riviera di Levante fishing villages to famous Renaissance cities

From golden rolling hills, aromatic pine forests and stylish cypress boule-vards to extraordinary art treasures and mouth-watering cuisine – Tuscany is a perfect holiday destination for nature lovers, art connoisseurs and gourmets. With rustic villages, a rich history and unique landscapes, this attractive region presents itself as one of Europe's 'complete artworks'.

Travelling in Tuscany is simply an intoxicating experience for the senses. Your eyes feast on the magnificently cultivated landscape, the delicate hints of rosemary and lavender please the nose, and your palate is spoilt for choice with world-famous Chianti wines and a cuisine that, with great help from the Medici family, had already begun conquering the world during the Renaissance. If that were not enough, nearly all Tuscany's charming ancient towns offer abundant art treasures as well.

Historically, central Italy is a region that has been inhabited for thousands of years, and proof of that fact is not hard to find. The ubiquitous remains of Etruscan necropolises, ruins from Roman settlements or the medieval town of San Gimignano make the point clear enough. Tuscany reached its zenith primarily during the medieval and Renaissance periods, and rightly regards itself as the 'Cradle of European culture'. Modern art, including painting, sculpture and architecture, can be traced back to this region.

Michelangelo's *David* in Florence.

The most important role in the region's rise to glory was played by the Medici, a Florentine family of vast wealth and influence that decisively dictated politics and the arts in that city for almost three hundred years, between 1434 and 1743. The pronounced cultural interest of the Medici drew the renowned artists of the time into their fold and, as patron of the arts, the family commissioned some of the most important works of the Renaissance period.

The cultural bounty of Tuscany attracts a great number of tourists every year. But a visit to Tuscany should include not only the well-known towns but also the countryside, as Tuscany is as famous for its ancient rural aesthetic as it is for its urban culture. This extraordinary countryside was planned in incredible detail and cultivated for centuries, with the landed

Cypresses, wine, an isolated farmhouse in the rolling hills – Tuscany presents a unique cultural landscape.

View from Pienza across the Tuscan plain with the cathedral tower in the background.

gentry as well as the farmers playing a part in the development. The farms, with a geometrical layout unchanged over the years, were placed on hilltops and all boasted a cypress-lined drive to their entrances. These splendid, centuries-old cypress lanes indicate their penchant for precise planning here.

Geographically, Tuscany stretches from the Apennine Mountains in the north to the Monte Amiata in the south, offering a varied landscape with rugged mountains, gentle rolling hills, the fertile coastal area of the Maremma and the green valleys of the Arno river. Southern Tuscany differs considerably from other Tuscan regions, being much hotter and having a less lush vegetation, dominated by maquis – dense, evergreen shrubs.

Industry and tourism are the economic backbones of Tuscany. Agriculture's main product is olive oil, but agriculture nowadays only supports a small part of the population. As a holiday destination, Tuscany is almost perfect all year round – between May and June an abundance of plants blossom in an extraordinary range of colours, while summer is dominated by the radiant red of the poppies and the glowing yellow of sunflower fields. Autumn is the time of the grape harvest, when the chestnut trees and the beeches change colour in late October and transform the landscape into a sea of mellow golden and red.

Your tour also enters the Emilia, a region between the river Po and the Apennine Mountains where Bologna is the city of note. On the west coast you reach Liguria with the Riviera di Levante and the tourist mecca, La Spezia. And from the hills of eastern Tuscany you finally reach Umbria.

Built on cliffs, the coastal village of Rio Maggiore in Cinque Terre.

The Medici

Almost no other Italian family managed to attain as much power and influence in politics and the arts as the Medici. A Florentine family of wealthy bankers, the Medici began their rise under Cosimo 'the Elder' (1389–1464) and reached their peak under the tutelage of Lorenzo 'the Magnificent' (1449–92).

Cosimo was basically able to rule his home town without ever holding any political office. He and his grandson Lorenzo were generous patrons of the arts and sciences and, under their auspices, geniuses such as Brunelleschi and Donatello eventually made Florence their home.

Equestrian statue of Cosimo I at Piazza della Signoria, Florence.

In the 16th century the family rose to princely status, but its decline began soon thereafter, continuing until the Medici line died out in 1737. The Grand Duchy of Tuscany then fell to the Habsburgs.

Tuscany – your tour through this magnificent region is also a journey through the Middle Ages and the Renaissance, starting in the lovely city of Florence. A highly recommended day trip leads to three towns on to the Ligurian coast, and the romantic country roads offer you a unique chance to get to know the varied Tuscan landscape in all its glory.

① Florence (see p. 269). Your circular tour through Tuscany begins in beautiful Florence. Only 8 km (5 miles) north of there is the village of Fiésole.

② Fiésole Founded in the 6th century BC by the Etruscans, this hilltop village is a far cry from the hustle and bustle of the big city and offers a fantastic panoramic view of Florence. In centuries past it was an ideal summer retreat for Florence's aristocracy, who were looking for respite from the city's heat and dust.

The wide Piazza Mino da Fiesole with the San Romolo Cathedral (begun in 1028) is the center of the village. North-east of the cathedral, remains of some partially well-preserved Roman settlements were discovered, including the ruins of a theater that seated up to three thousand people. Continuing via Florence you come to lively Prato, Tuscany's third-largest town.

③ Prato With its daring mixture of medieval buildings and modern architecture, Prato is a city of stark contrasts. As it was the metropolis of textile manufacture, wool-weavers began

settling here in the Middle Ages. Medieval ramparts enclose the historic town center, which has a cathedral modelled on the cathedrals of Pisa and Lucca. The imposing Castello dell' Imperatore, built by Emperor Frederick II between 1237 and 1248, is a remarkable sight.

④ Pistóia Following the SS64, an often very winding road that negotiates considerable differences in altitude, you reach Pistóia, a lively town steeped in tradition that is surrounded by nurseries and colourful flora. The picturesque markets and the beautiful 9th-century church of Sant'Andrea is worth a visit with its legendary pulpit by Pisano (1298).

⑤ Bologna Tuscany is not alone in the area as a custodian of Italy's art treasures. The SS64 leads you to the neighbouring province of Emilia-Romagna and three cities that are as richly steeped in history as any Tuscan locations.

Like so many of the cities in this area, Bologna, the capital of

Travel Information

Route profile
Length: approx. 1,200 km (745 miles), excluding detours
Time required: at least 2 weeks
Start and end: Florence
Route (main locations): Florence, Bologna, Parma, La Spézia, Livorno, Piombino, Siena, Arezzo, Florence

Traffic information:
Drive on the right in Italy. There is a toll-charge for Italian motorways, but these are rarely used on this trip. Tuscany's roads are well-planned and free of charge.

Accommodation:
Tuscan farmhouses and wine estates (generally known as agritourismo) offer modest to

luxury accommodation and are a great alternative to hotels. Try:
www.agrotourismo.net

Weather:
Italy is dry and hot in the summer, mild in the winter. The rain falls in the autumn, October and November mainly, and July and August can be oppressively hot.
The recommended travel season for Tuscany is therefore spring (20–22°C/68–72°F).

Information:
There is an abundance of information on travelling in Italy. Here are a couple of helpful resources:
www.enit.it
www.toskana.net
www.anitalyattraction.com

1 The Ponte Vecchio was built in 1345 and is the oldest bridge in Florence. Since 1593, goldsmiths and jewellers have been working in the bridge's workshops.

2 The Romanesque church of San Sepolcro houses the tomb of Saint Petronius and is one of Bologna's many artistically and historically significant ecclesiastical buildings.

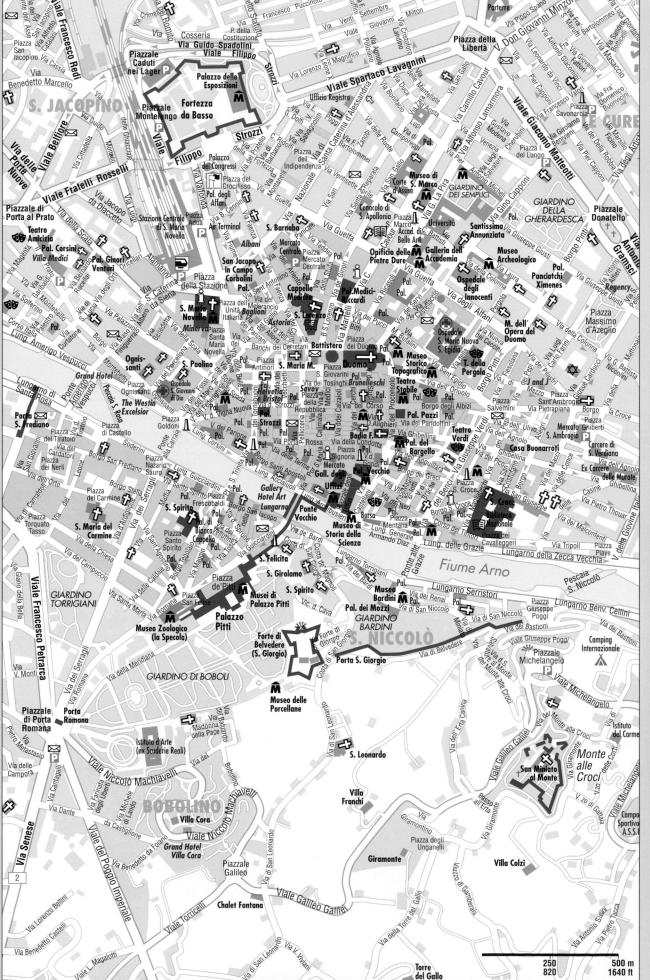

Florence

Florence's influence on the history of Western civilization is unequalled – it is considered the birthplace of the Renaissance. The city boasts a long list of famous sights, and attracts a phenomenal number of tourists each year. If you want to see the city from above, go to the Piazzale Michelangelo, situated 104 m (341 ft) above the historic town center – the view of Florence stretching picturesquely over both sides of the Arno river is breathtaking.

Almost all the sights in the old part of town are within walking distance of one another. Florence's architectural jewel, the 'Duomo' (Santa Maria del Fiore, built 1296–1436), dominates the Old Town with its magnificent octagonal dome by Brunelleschi. Opposite that is the Baptistry of San Giovanni (11th–13th centuries) with its three sets of bronze doors by Pisano and Ghiberti, and the famous 'Gates of Paradise' doors.

The Uffizi Gallery houses one of the oldest and most important art collections in the world, including masterpieces by Giotto and Botticelli. Nearby, the Ponte Vecchio, Florence's oldest bridge, is famous for the goldsmiths' and jewellers' shops built on it in the 16th century.

Top: Duomo Santa Maria del Fiore.
Bottom: The Fountain of Neptune.

Back on the Piazza del Duomo, be sure to take a stroll along the Via Calzaiuoli to the Piazza della Signoria, Florence's most beautiful square and home to the 14th-century Palazzo Vecchio, the city's massive town hall with a slim, crenellated tower. A visit to the Giardino di Boboli is then a lovely finish to your leisurely stroll through town.

View from the south over the red rooftops of Florence. The Arno River is spanned by a number of bridges, the most famous of which is the Ponte Vecchio on the far left. The apartments on the bridge are still used for commercial purposes and shops. The campanile (bell tower) of the Palazzo Vecchio on the

Piazza della Signoria (middle of picture) rises above the sea of buildings along with the 85-m-high campanile and the red dome of the Santa Maria del Fiore cathedral by Brunelleschi.

Portofino

An excursion to the picturesque village of Portofino is highly recommended – but leave your car behind! This swanky seaside resort is among the most beautiful on the Italian Riviera coast, and as such

Luxury yachts anchored in Portofino's port.

the traffic on the one small road to get there is generally horrendous. It's better to take the ferry over from Santa Margherita Ligure. The charming fishing village of Portofino and its cute little port is surrounded by olive groves, vineyards and cypresses. In the 19th century, rich industrialists started to come to the village with its tidy red- and ochre-coloured houses and left their imprint by constructing luxurious villas.

After strolling through the narrow alleys and hilly streets, you come to the medieval church of San Giorgio on the esplanade. The location offers a spectacular panoramic view. The Castello di San Giorgio (16th century) is your next stop. Towards the end of the 19th century, Baron von Mumm converted this former military hospital into a luxury villa.

If you follow the picturesque path up to its southern peak, you reach the lighthouse of Punto Capo, which affords magnificent views across the Tigullian Gulf.

Emilia-Romagna, was founded by the Etruscans. It lies in a fertile plain in the foothills of the Apennines and is home to one of Europe's oldest universities, dating back to 1119.

Important churches, arcaded lanes, towers and palaces bear witness to Bologna's period of prominence back in the Middle Ages. Among other sights, the Church of San Petronio is worth visiting. Its interior ranks up there with the most exemplary of Gothic architectural works. The two 'leaning towers', built

in brick for defense purposes, are the hallmark of the city.

The SS9 now leads you on to Módena, about 40 km (25 miles) to the north west.

6 Módena Located in the Po river valley, Módena is worth a visit for its magnificent cathedral and celebrated art treasures. The center of town boasts extensive squares and leafy arcades. The Cathedral San Geminiano (1184), with its impressive 88-m (288-ft) bell tower, and the Piazza Grande have been given

joint status as a UNESCO World Heritage Site.

7 Réggio nell'Emília Like Módena, Reggio nell'Emília was founded by the Romans and mainly belonged to the House of Este. The town is situated on the edge of Italy's northern plain, a fertile area with great agricultural yields.

The cathedral, whose construction began in the 9th century, the 16th-century San Próspero Church and the Church of the Madonna della Ghiaira, a baro-

que edifice featuring stucco and frescoes (1597–1619), are all well worth visiting.

8 Parma The city of Parma, near the Apennine Mountains, was founded by the Etruscans, but now has a modern layout due to reconstruction after devastating bombings in World War II. The Piazza Garibaldi, with the Palazzo del Governatore, marks the center of town.

On the Piazza del Duomo stands the 12th-century Romanesque cathedral with its famous fres-

coes, while further west you'll find the Palazzo della Pilotta. Inside this unfinished brick edifice is a beautiful inner courtyard and some museums, such as the Galeria Nazionale.

The journey continues now across the 1,055-m (3,460-ft) Cento Croci Pass (SS62 and SS523), a very curvy road with breathtaking scenery that runs from Varese Ligure via Rapallo along the Riviera di Levante.

9 Cinque Terre These five legendary coastal villages built on the cliffs of the Riviera di Levante have become one of the most popular tourist areas in all of Italy. Ever since the steeply terraced landscape in the area was made accessible to automobiles, the villages – Monterosso, Vernazza, Corniglia, Manarola and Riomaggiore – are practically household names.

However, visitors are strongly recommended to leave their cars in Levanto and take the train instead. The roads leading to the villages are very steep and winding – and often full of traffic.

10 La Spézia One of Italy's most beautiful bays is located at the southernmost point on the Gulf of Genoa, with the spectacular Apennine Mountains as a backdrop. La Spézia, Liguria's second-largest town, is one of Italy's most important military and commercial ports, a fact that has rendered the town less attractive over the years.

However, its charming shopping streets date back to the 19th century and the museum of archaeology and the shipping museum make a visit worthwhile. A short trip south leads to Lerici.

To be able to enjoy the natural beauty of this place to the full, you need to take the five-hour walk on the footpath that links the five villages. Italy's most beautiful walking trail offers absolutely awe-inspiring views of the Mediterranean and the magnificent cliffs.

After a short excursion to Portofino, another elegant former fishing village, the journey continues south to La Spézia.

11 Carrara Here in the northwest of Tuscany, Carrara marks

1 Baptistry on the Piazza del Duomo in Parma.

2 Módena's Romanesque cathedral also has a leaning tower – the Torre Ghirlandina.

3 Vernazza on the Italian Riviera, one of the five villages of beautiful Cinque Terre.

4 A medieval castle rises above Lerici's marina.

Detour

Lucca

Lucca, situated in a fertile plain near the Appuan Mountains, is rightly regarded as the archetypal Tuscan city. It boasts a number of palaces and towers and fully intact Old Town walls. This erstwhile Roman settlement retained its independence for a very long time and only fell under the rule of nearby Pisa for a brief period.

The traditional trading city today has an important silk, paper and

Medieval edifices surround the Piazza del Mercato.

textile industry. You enter the historic center through one of the seven old gates and are immediately enthralled by the ambience of its tiny streets and alleyways.

The Duomo San Martino (c. 11th century), with its magnificent arcaded facade, is Lucca's most prominent religious structure. Its nave and transepts were rebuilt in the Gothic style in the 13th and 15th centuries. The Church of San Michele in Foro has a spectacular Romanesque arcaded facade and is named after the Roman forum that once stood here. For centuries the Piazza San Michele was regarded as the center of town, with its exquisite medieval houses built by the wealthy merchant classes of old. Nearby is the villa of the Guinigi family, with an unusual tower that has trees sprouting from it. After a climb to the top, you are rewarded with a wonderful view across the red roofs of the Old Town. Afterwards you should consider taking a walk on the 4-km (2.5-mile) wall around the Old Town, which offers magnificent views of the surrounding countryside.

On the way out of town to the resort of Bagni di Lucca you come to the famous Ponte del Diavolo – the 'Devil's Bridge' – from the 11th century, which dramatically spans the River Serchio.

Elba

Even the ancient Etruscans and Romans recognized the unique beauty of this mountainous island. Its iron resources were already wellknown in Roman times when mines were established. Due to its mild climate, Italy's third-largest island offers a diverse natural landscape that includes not only chestnut trees, vineyards and olive groves, but also Mediterranean scrub brush. Hills, mountains and low plains are all wonderfully mixed together.

Taking the ferry from Piombino, you reach the island's capital of Porto-ferraio on the north coast in one

Porto Ferraio on the island of Elba.

hour. Napoleon's former summer residence, with the somewhat uninspired name of Villa Napoleonica, is in San Martino just 6 km (3.7 miles) from the dock.

On a round trip of the island, you first arrive in Procchio, with a beautiful bay that is ideal for swimming. Continuing along the picturesque winding road, you come to the island's favourite seaside resort, Marciana Marina, where the Pisan Tower offered shelter from the Saracens. Shady pine forests stretch from here to the sea.

Marina di Campo on the south coast has a broad sandy beach and is the island's main tourist resort. Porto Azurro is popular because it is sheltered from the constant wind. Above the town rises the star-shaped Fort Longone, which has served as a prison for the last 150 years.

the beginning of the Versilia Coast, a beautiful stretch scattered with white sandy beaches and the Apuan Alps providing the film-set backdrop.

The road takes you through a unique marble region where exhausted marble quarries have left rather bizarre formations that now seem to dominate the landscape. Even in Roman times, Carrara was famous for its fine-grained white and grey marble. Today, Carrara is home to an academy for sculptors, where artists have the luxury of learning to work with the rock directly at its source.

In the workshops of the Old Town of Pietrasanta, you can see stonemasons at work, happy to let tourists watch while they create. It is also well worth taking a stroll through the historic town center to admire the 13th-century Cathedral San Martino with its charming brick campanile.

12 Viaréggio Even in the coastal resort town of Viaréggio, people's livelihood depends to an extent on the marble industry. Other options, however, include shipbuilding and, of-course, tourism. Europe's high

society discovered this picturesque fishing village in the 19th century, as the art deco villas and audacious rococo-style cafés will illustrate.

From Viaréggio it is only 25 km (15 miles) to Lucca, which is not to be missed on your trip. The road now leaves the coast and runs parallel to the regional nature reserve, Parco Naturale Migliarino-Massaciúccoli, which stretches all the way down to Livorno.

13 Pisa About 21 km (13 miles) south of Viaréggio is Pisa, well-known for its unique buildings around the Campo dei Miracoli, the 'Field of Miracles'. Among the masterpieces here are the Duomo (the cathedral) and the Baptistry – and most important of all, the Leaning Tower of Pisa, which began leaning to the south-east almost immediately after construction began in 1775. Although these structures were built at different times,

they were all erected with white Carrara marble and therefore have the effect of being one harmonious entity.

Pisa's role as an important commercial and naval port earned the city the epithet of 'Queen of the Sea', and its influence was considerable. Its decline came when Pisa was defeated by powerful rivals from Genoa and Venice, and the port silted up. The only leading institution remaining in Pisa is its university,

proof of a deep-rooted educational tradition. If you wish to relax, visit the romantic botanic gardens, established in 1543.

14 Livorno One can hardly believe that Livorno is part of Tuscany, its ambience is so different. But this is probably due to the late construction of the town. It was not until 1571 that this small fishing village was expanded into a port by Cosimo I (see the Medici sidebar p. 268)

because Pisa's port was in danger of silting up. The dyke protecting the port here was built between 1607 and 1621.
Today, Livorno is Tuscany's most important port. At the seaside visitors can admire the 'Old Fortress' (1521–23) and the 'New Fortress' (1590) and enjoy a visit to the aquarium.
South of Livorno the route continues along the cliffs to San Pietro in Palazzi, past some sandy bays. From here you take the exit onto the SS68 heading east and continue for another 33 km (20 miles) inland until you get to Volterra, high above the road on a hillside.

15 Volterra Medieval ramparts surround Volterra's historic town center with its narrow and dark little alleyways and tall rows of houses. The town's livelihood comes mainly from the alabaster industry. The Etruscan Museum, containing thousands of funerary urns and sarcophagi, is a must for anyone interested in this ancient culture.
The view from the top of the city hall's tower is breathtaking – on clear days you can even see the sea. The old town has been left

intact for a rather dramatic reason – Volterra is in danger of subsiding because the steep hill it is built on frequently suffers landslides, making the town unattractive to developers.
A turn-off from the SS68 leads onto a small road of outstanding natural beauty – this is the heart of Tuscany, with its typical landscape of vineyards and olive groves.

16 San Gimignano For a time, the merchant families of San Gimignano built tall towers to display their wealth – the taller the tower, the richer the family. Seventy-two of them guarded the dreamy Piazza della Cisterna in the historic center of town. Only fifteen are standing now, but these perfectly preserved 14th-century towers, the iconic skyline of San Gimignano, make you feel as if transported back to the Middle Ages.
Returning along the same route, you reach the coast again about 72 km (45 miles) further along. Follow the old Via Aurelia south to San Vincenzo, and continue on a small coastal road until you get to a series of beaches that look inviting for a dip.

17 Piombino The ferries for Elba leave from Piombino, a port town with an interesting port promenade and charming views of the old anchorage and the island of Elba. Populonia, an ancient Etruscan port town with the impressive necropolis of San Cerbone, is nearby and worth a visit.
Getting back on the S1 at San Vincenzo, continue to Follónica, where the SS439 turns inland.

18 Massa Marittima Roughly 26 km (16 miles) from the sea, the small town of Massa Marittima lies on the edge of the Maremma, a former marshland that was drained in the 19th century. From the upper part of town – in particular the Torre del Candeliere – you can get a magnificent view of the Old Town's red roofs and the surrounding

1 View across the plains of the Maremma, from Massa Marittima on the hills of the Colline Metallifere. The Romanesque-Gothic cathedral is the town's icon.

2 Pisa's famous symbols – the Baptistry, Duomo and 'Leaning Tower' in the Field of Miracles.

Dynastic towers

In the medieval towns of yore, noble families who had made it rich in the wool, wine or spice trade competed with one another by erecting fortified towers that also served as dwellings. These rivalries between families were focused mainly on the height of the towers – the height being an indication of power. But apart from being symbols of power, the towers actually

The medieval 'skyline' of San Gimignano.a

served the very real purpose of providing shelter from enemies. They were also the sites of family feuds.
The 'skyline' of San Gimignano is unique – fifteen towers of varying height are still intact and have earned the city the rather fanciful name of the 'Manhattan of the Middle Ages'.

The cathedral of Santa Maria Assunta, built between 1136 and 1382, rises high above the medieval rooftops of Siena. It is one of the most beautiful Gothic structures in Italy. The facades of the cathedral and its campanile (bell tower) are striped with black and white marble from the region. The richly-adorned

south-west façade is particularly impressive. To the right is the façade of the unfinished nave. The campanile of the Palazzo Pubblico (left of the dome) is the second-highest medieval tower in Italy at 102 m (320 ft).

Assisi

A short trip to Assisi in nearby Umbria is highly recommended. The famous basilica in Assisi is entirely dedicated to St Francis (1182–1226), who was born here. Everywhere you will find churches and memorials

Frescoes in the Basilica di San Francesco.

erected in honour of this worldly saint, also known as the 'Patron Saint of Animals and Ecology'.

Since the time of Francis, the impressive layout of the small village on the flank of Mount Subasio has hardly changed. One event, however, was far-reaching – the construction of the basilica, three years after the saint's death. The upper church houses works by many of Italy's renowned late-Romansque and early-Gothic artists. Nowhere else in Italy can you find a collection of this calibre. The lower church, where the saint is buried, is the pilgrimage site. Damage from the earthquake in 1997 has been almost completely repaired.

Tuscan countryside. A diocesan town in the 12th and 13th centuries, Massa Marittima boasts magnificent medieval buildings such as the Duomo San Cerbone (1228–1304).

Stay on the SS441 and SS73 for 75 km (46 miles) to Siena.

⑲ Siena Siena's red-brick palaces and extraordinary flair often give this town a more authentic ambience than its great rival Florence. The 'Gothic City' stretches over three hillsides in the heart of the rolling Tuscan countryside. Its historic center has long been designated a UNESCO World Heritage Site. Siena is also home to what is arguably Italy's most beautiful square, the shell-shaped Piazza del Campo, surrounded by Gothic palaces. Twice a year it hosts the legendary Palio horse race, which attracts up to fifty thousand spectators and causes total chaos throughout the city.

The Duomo (12th century) is Siena's cathedral and one of the jewels of the Gothic period. It should not be missed. Other architectural treasures include the Palazzo Pubblico (1288–1309) and the slim 102-m (334-ft) Torre del Mangia, one of the most daring medieval towers.

The center of the Chianti area is north of Siena. From here, small roads lead to the domain of Chianti Classico, carrying the emblem 'Gallo Nero' (black cockerel) as proof of its outstanding quality. The vineyards advertise 'Vendita diretta' for wine tasting and direct sales.

Follow the S222, S249 and S408 in a clockwise direction to visit a number of quaint villages – Castellina in Chianti, Radda in Chianti, Badia a Coltibuono, Moleto and Brolio with its castle Castello di Brolio.

⑳ Montepulciano About 70 km (43 miles) south-east of Siena is Montepulciano, a Renaissance town of outstanding beauty on top of a limestone hill. The small town, with its lovely brick buildings, is a Mecca for wine and art connoisseurs. Just outside Montepulciano you'll find San Biagio, an architectural treasure dating back to the 16th century. The pilgrimage church is laid out in the form of a Greek cross and is surrounded by cypresses – in perfect harmony with the landscape.

From Montepulciano the S146 leads to Chiusi and south-east to the junction of the S71, which runs along the west side of the Lago Trasimeno before bringing you to Cortona 40 km (25 miles) away. From the lake we recommend a detour of about 75 km (46 miles) to visit Assisi on the S75 – birthplace of the legendary St Francis of Assisi.

㉑ Cortona Cortona, one of the oldest Etruscan settlements, is another Tuscan hill town situated above the plains of Chiana. We recommend a stroll through the maze of the Old Town, full of alleyways and steps. The Piazza Garibaldi offers a spectacular view of the Lago Trasimeno.

㉒ Arezzo Arezzo, 80 km (50 miles) south-east of Florence, is the last port of call on your journey. The palaces of rich merchants and influential families dominate the scene, along with the ubiquitous religious buildings. The town is wealthy, partly due to its worldwide gold jewellery export industry.

The Gothic Basilica of San Francesco has become a Mecca for art lovers. The main attraction is the *History of the True Cross*, a series of frescoes by Piero della Francesca. *La Leggenda della Vera Croce* (The Legend of the True Cross) is also one of Italy's most beautiful frescoes. Its theme is the wood from the tree of knowledge in the Garden of Eden that became the cross on which Christ was crucified. The colour and the perspective are extraordinary.

1 The pilgrimage church of Tempio di San Biagio (1518–34) is a masterpiece by architect Antonio da Sangallo just outside Montepulciano.

2 The Duomo and the 102-m (334-ft) bell tower of the Palazzo Pubblico dominate the modest skyline of Siena.

3 Because they grow so straight and tall, cypresses are the local favourite for delineating recreation areas or a landmark.

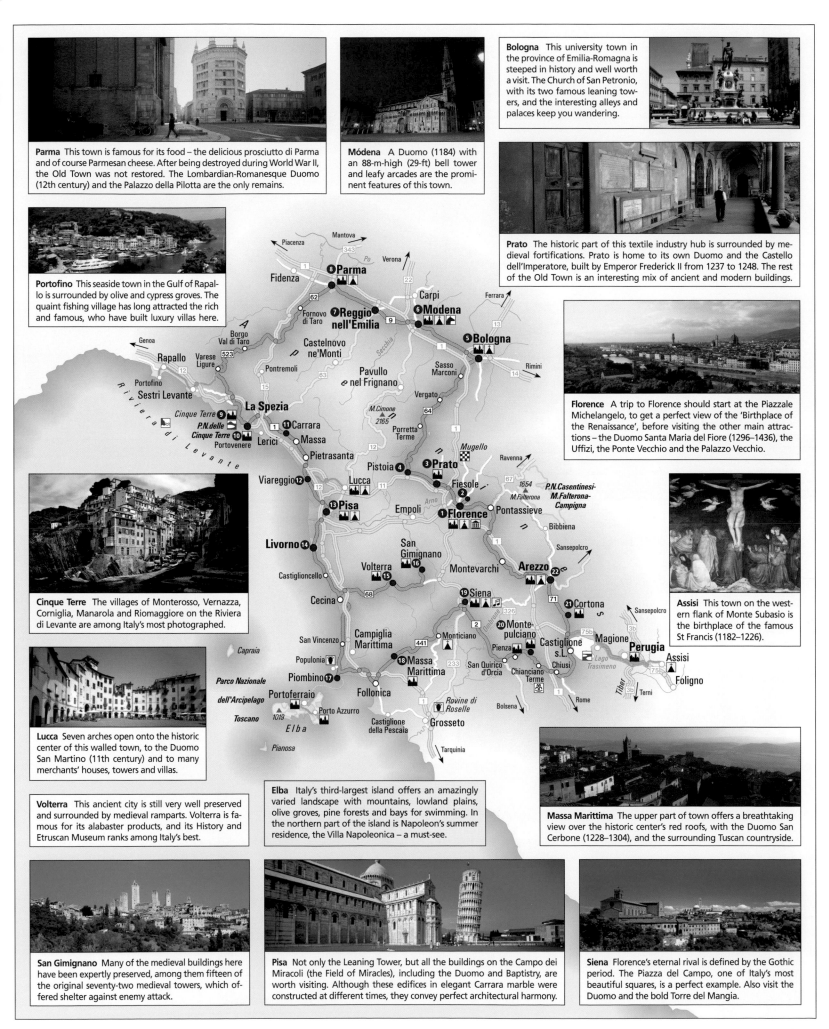

Bologna This university town in the province of Emilia-Romagna is steeped in history and well worth a visit. The Church of San Petronio, with its two famous leaning towers, and the interesting alleys and palaces keep you wandering.

Parma This town is famous for its food – the delicious prosciutto di Parma and of course Parmesan cheese. After being destroyed during World War II, the Old Town was not restored. The Lombardian-Romanesque Duomo (12th century) and the Palazzo della Pilotta are the only remains.

Módena A Duomo (1184) with an 88-m-high (29-ft) bell tower and leafy arcades are the prominent features of this town.

Prato The historic part of this textile industry hub is surrounded by medieval fortifications. Prato is home to its own Duomo and the Castello dell'Imperatore, built by Emperor Frederick II from 1237 to 1248. The rest of the Old Town is an interesting mix of ancient and modern buildings.

Portofino This seaside town in the Gulf of Rapallo is surrounded by olive and cypress groves. The quaint fishing village has long attracted the rich and famous, who have built luxury villas here.

Florence A trip to Florence should start at the Piazzale Michelangelo, to get a perfect view of the 'Birthplace of the Renaissance', before visiting the other main attractions – the Duomo Santa Maria del Fiore (1296–1436), the Uffizi, the Ponte Vecchio and the Palazzo Vecchio.

Cinque Terre The villages of Monterosso, Vernazza, Corniglia, Manarola and Riomaggiore on the Riviera di Levante are among Italy's most photographed.

Assisi This town on the western flank of Monte Subasio is the birthplace of the famous St Francis (1182–1226).

Lucca Seven arches open onto the historic center of this walled town, to the Duomo San Martino (11th century) and to many merchants' houses, towers and villas.

Volterra This ancient city is still very well preserved and surrounded by medieval ramparts. Volterra is famous for its alabaster products, and its History and Etruscan Museum ranks among Italy's best.

Elba Italy's third-largest island offers an amazingly varied landscape with mountains, lowland plains, olive groves, pine forests and bays for swimming. In the northern part of the island is Napoleon's summer residence, the Villa Napoleonica – a must-see.

Massa Marittima The upper part of town offers a breathtaking view over the historic center's red roofs, with the Duomo San Cerbone (1228–1304), and the surrounding Tuscan countryside.

San Gimignano Many of the medieval buildings here have been expertly preserved, among them fifteen of the original seventy-two medieval towers, which offered shelter against enemy attack.

Pisa Not only the Leaning Tower, but all the buildings on the Campo dei Miracoli (the Field of Miracles), including the Duomo and Baptistry, are worth visiting. Although these edifices in elegant Carrara marble were constructed at different times, they convey perfect architectural harmony.

Siena Florence's eternal rival is defined by the Gothic period. The Piazza del Campo, one of Italy's most beautiful squares, is a perfect example. Also visit the Duomo and the bold Torre del Mangia.

The Temple of Hera in Paestum, also known as the 'Basilica', was built around 530 BC.

Italy

On the Via Appia from Rome to Brindisi

In the time of the Imperium Romanum, the motto of the day was 'All roads lead to Rome', when Romans saw their capital as the cradle of not only their own empire but of the civilized world. Large parts of Europe and the entire Mediterranean were ruled from here, and military roads ensured the necessary logistical infrastructure. Probably the best known of these ancient roads is the Via Appia Antica, the basis for your journey.

Relatively little remains of the brilliant splendour of ancient Rome, but what is left is indeed impressive enough – the Colosseum, the Baths of Caracalla, the Pantheon, Domus Aurea, the Arch of Titus, Forum Romanum, the emperors' forums and the Capitol. Contemporary Rome, on the other hand, is defined more dramatically by the unremitting desire of the popes to build magnificent churches, palaces, squares and fountains using the best architects of their times. The popes

were particularly active during the Renaissance and baroque periods. To this day, St Peter's Square and St Peter's Cathedral remain the heart of the city and of the Catholic Christian world.
The ancient Via Appia began at what is today Porta Sebastiano, and originally only went as far as Capua. It was then extended past Benevento and Taranto to Brindisi in 190 BC. Around AD 113, Emperor Trajan added yet another ancillary road that led through Bari.

Statue of Emperor Marcus Aurelius in Rome.

The 540-km-long (336-mile) basalt route, lined as it is by countless ancient tombs, temples, villas, ruins and even early Christian catacombs, can still be driven today and is considered 'the longest museum in the world'.
The road initially takes you out of Rome and into the hills of the Colli Albani where, in the Middle Ages, popes and Roman nobles had numerous villas and castles built – collectively known as the Castelli Romani. From Velletri, the Via Appia continues in almost a dead straight line to what is today Terracina on the Tyrrhenian Sea, then through Gaeta and inland towards Cápua.
From here, there is still an access road to the former Greek city of Neapolis, known today as Naples. This is home to the infamous Mount Vesuvius, a still-active volcano that once destroyed Pompeii and

The Ponte Sant'Angelo bridge in Rome leads over the Tiber to the Castel Sant'Angelo, built in AD 139 as a citadel, prison and papal residence.

The 13th-century Cathedral of Matera (Apulia) is maintained in the late Romanesque style.

Herculaneum, and whose next eruption remains a concern for some geologists. For the time being, the view from the crater's rim provides a wonderful view of the bustling city of Naples and the Island of Ischia in the Gulf of Naples.

From Naples, the journey continues along the sea around the Gulf to Sorrento. Since the time of the Roman emperors this picturesque area has been a meeting place for aristocracy. The southern side of the Sorrento Peninsula is where the steep cliffs of the Amalfi Coast begin, with its quaint, pastel-coloured villages nestled between the azure sea and the brilliant yellow lemon trees. At the end of the famous Amalfitana coastal road lies Salerno, where the actual Mezzogiorno begins. The stunning coastal road then continues on to Paestum, with ancient golden-yellow Greek temples that are some of the most beautiful examples of their kind in Europe. Indeed, the Greeks settled in southern Italy long before the Romans and left some magnificent relics of a blossoming civilization.

After Sapri the route leaves the coast and heads east through the inland province of Basilicata towards the Gulf of Taranto. At Metaponto on the gulf, the route again swings inland towards Matera, whose 'sassi' – former ancient cave dwellings – are a UNESCO World Heritage Site. Taranto marks the starting point for the journey through the 'Land of the Trulli', whose capital is Alberobello.

After passing through Ostuni you finally arrive in Brindisi, where one of the two ancient port columns is a reminder of how important this city at the end of the Via Appia once was for the mighty Imperium Romanum.

Remains of a colossal statue of Constantine the Great in the Palazzo dei Conservatori in Rome.

The Imperium Romanum

History teachers of every generation will tell their students that 'Rome was born in 753'. However, the creation of Rome more likely took place around the turn of the 6th century BC. It began with the merging of several towns into a municipality (still) under Etruscan rule.

In 510 BC the citizens chased away Tarquinius Superbus, their Etruscan king, and created an aristocracy from which the Roman republic eventually emerged. This officially lasted until 31 BC when Emperor Augustus came to power.

The expansion of Rome initially proceeded very slowly and was hardly noticed by the Greek colonists in southern Italy or the Carthaginians in North Africa (present-day Tunisia). However, after the three Punic Wars (264–241

Stairway to the Palazzo Senatorio.

BC, 218–201 BC, 149–146 BC), almost all of Italy, including the surrounding islands, was under Roman rule. Victories over the Etruscans, Greeks and Carthaginians further guaranteed Roman dominance in the western Mediterranean and the Imperium Romanum was born.

The advances of Roman legionnaires were highly visible throughout almost all of Europe, sections of North Africa and in the Near East. At its largest, under Emperor Trajan (AD 98–117), the Imperium Romanum stretched all the way from the British Isles to the Persian Gulf. It had reached its zenith, which in turn marked the beginning of the end. By AD 395 the no-longer governable western Imperium and the East Roman Empire were divided, with Byzantium as the capital of the eastern part. Germanic tribes then invaded the West Roman Empire and in AD 476 the Germanic ruler Odoaker dethroned the last West Roman emperor, Romulus Augustulus.

On the trail of the ancient Via Appia: this route begins in Rome and follows the famous highway of classic antiquity to Cápua, where it was later extended to Benevento, Taranto and then Brundisium (Brindisi). The stations recall the country's important historic periods.

❶ Rome For a detailed description of the myriad attractions here, see pp. 284–285.

Porta Sebastiano used to be known as Porta Appia because this ancient city gate marked the start of the Via Appia. The area around the porta includes the burial site of the Scipios, the famous Temple of Mars and the tomb of Cecilia Metella on the cypress-lined road to Frascati.

❷ Frascati This is the most famous town of the Castelli Romani. Its glorious location, numerous patrician villas (e.g. the 17th-century Villa Aldobrandini), its exceptional white wine

and 'porchetta', crispy grilled suckling pig, all contribute to this renown. And the popes enjoyed it all, which is why Frascati was their long-time summer residence before they moved to Castel Gandolfo. Roughly 5 km (3 miles) east of the city are the ruins of the ancient Tusculum, the favourite abode of Cicero, one of Rome's greatest orators and philosophers.

A few smaller places around Frascati are also worth a visit. The main attraction of the Grottaferrata, 3 km (2 miles) south of Frascati, is the castle-like monastery of San Nilo, founded in 1004, with frescoes from Domenichio (17th century).

see pp. 284–285.

Travel information

Route profile
Length: approx. 650 km (404 miles), excluding detours
Time required: 10–12 days
Start: Rome
End: Bríndisi
Route (main locations): Rome, Frascati, Velletri, Latina, Terracina, Gaeta, Cápua, Naples, Sorrento, Salerno, Paestum, Rotondella, Metaponto, Matera, Taranto, Martina Franca, Bríndisi

Traffic information:
Drive on the right in Italy. Speed limit in built-up areas is 50 km/h (31 mph), on highways 130 km/h (81 mph). International licences are required unless you have a new photocard licence from a European nation. Spare

bulbs and warning triangle required.

When to go:
The best times to travel are spring and autumn, as temperatures are pleasant. In summer, temperatures can rise to over 40°C (105°F), though by the sea it is often cooler with the breezes.
For current weather conditions at many holiday destinations visit:
www.italy-weather-and-maps.com

Information:
www.italiantourism.com
www.justitaly.org
For accommodation and events:
www.slowtrav.com/italy

St Peter's Basilica

Until a larger replica was built on the Ivory Coast in the 1990s, San Pietro in Vaticano was the world's largest Christian church. San Pietro was built under the auspices of master architect Giovanni Bernini between 1656 and 1667, and towers above St Peter's Square (Piazza San Pietro). This absolutely massive plaza is in turn lined with four semicircular colonnades containing a total of 284 columns and 88 pillars. In the middle of the square is the 25.5-m-high (84-ft) Egyptian obelisk, to which two fountains were added, one in 1613 and the next in 1675.

St Peter's Basilica was originally built in 1506, on the site where Constantine the Great had previously placed a basilica over the tomb of Petrus in 320. The most reputable Renaissance builders and artists helped construct the church, including Bramante, Raffael, Michelangelo and Bernini.

The enormous double partition cupola, started by Bramante and finished

The light-filled altar area with Bernini's altar canopy.

It's worth taking a small detour into the Alban Hills (Colli Albani – 740 m/2,427 ft) to see the township of Rocca di Papa, some 8 km (5 miles) south-east of Frascati. Monte Cavo at 949 m (3,114 ft) provides a wonderful view out over the province of Lazio.

The town of Marino is also located roughly 8 km (5 miles) away to the south of Frascati. During the wine festival on the first weekend of October, wine flows from the Fontana dei Mori instead of water!

❸ Castel Gandolfo This small town, idyllically located on Lake Albano (Lago Albano), has been the summer residence of the popes since 1604. The Papal Palace (1629–69) and other impressive homesteads like Villa Barberini and Villa Cyco, are the defining buildings in the area. The Piazza, with the Church of

San Tommaso and a stunning fountain by Bernini, is also worth seeing.

❹ Albano Laziale High above Lake Albano, the legendary Latin Alba Longa is said to have once been located here before the rise of Rome even began. The remains of a villa belonging to the famous general Pompeius is still open to the public. In Arrica, the neighbouring town designed by Bernini, it's worth visiting the Palazzo Chigi and the church of Santa Maria dell' Assunzione (1665) at the Piazza della Republica.

❺ Genzano This small town between the Via Appia Antica and Lago di Nemi is famous for its annual 'Infiorata' – on the Sunday after Corpus Christi a carpet of flowers adorns the Via Italo Belardi all the way up to the church of Maria della Cima.

The flowers come from the neighbouring town of Nemi, which is also a local strawberry-growing center.

❻ Velletri The southernmost of the Castelli Romani communes is Velletri, located at the edge of the Via Appia Antica. Like Frascati, it is known for its excellent wines, but apart from this there are architectural attractions including the Piazza Cairoli with its 50-m-high (164-ft) Torre del Trivio from 1353, the Palazzo Communale from 1590, and the cathedral, which was completed in 1662.

The Via Appia then continues from Velletri to Latina.

❼ Latina This township is a good starting point for a day trip to the lovely forests and lakes of the Circeo Nature Park, which stretches over the mountainous promontory of Monte Circeo. At

the tip of the peninsula is the alleged grotto of the sorceress, Circe, from Homer's *Odyssey*.

From Latina, the route leads into the coastal town of Terracina.

❽ Terracina This town, which is today a famous spa resort,

1 The impressive complex of St Peter's Square, Rome, a masterpiece created by Bernini between 1656 and 1667. The obelisk in the middle of the square was erected in 1586 with the help of horses and winches.

2 The Arch of Constantine in Rome, constructed in AD 315, is next to the Colosseum, the largest amphitheater of ancient times and the scene of countless gladiator battles.

3 An icon of Rome and a popular meeting place – the Spanish Steps. They get their name from the Piazza di Spagna.

by Michelangelo, is 132 m (433 ft) high. Michelangelo also created the famous Pietá statue in the aisle.

St Peter's itself is 186 m (610 ft) long and 136 m (446 ft) wide, with a height in the main aisle of 45 m (148 ft). It has capacity for up to 60,000 people. The papal altar stands over the tomb of Petrus and beneath the Confessio, which is vaulted by Bernini's 29-m-high (95-ft) bronze canopy.

Over the centuries, the faithful have kissed the right foot of the bronze statue of Petrus at the Longinus pillar so often that it is now shiny. Bernini's Cathedra Petri lies in the Apsis while left of the main altar is the papal treasury and the Vatican grotto, a crypt with the tombs of many popes.

Rome

The 'Eternal City', with its unparalleled artistic treasures and architectural monuments from basically every period of Western culture, is the center of the Catholic world and at the same time the lively and vibrant capital of Italy - you just have to see Rome at least once in your life!

Rome, built on seven hills around the Tiber River, obviously has a long and eventful history that has left endless marks on the city. Its neighbourhoods, squares, monuments, buildings and architectural treasures have been built in every style imaginable.

Today, not all seven of the ancient hills are recognizable in the sea of houses, but from the Piazza del Quirinale on the Quirinal, the highest of these hills, you can get a fantastic view over the entire city. It is said that Rome was founded in 753, but the first traces of

the city eventually regained political importance in the 19th century when Italy was reunited and Rome was made the capital of the Kingdom of Italy.

Ancient Rome includes the Forum Romanum, the main square of the Old City; the Colosseum with its four-storey arena; and the Pantheon, the domed masterpiece of ancient architecture. In the Vatican City is St Peter's Basilica, the domed, Renaissance-style monument; the Vatican museums and galleries, probably the largest collection of art in the world; the Sistine Chapel;

Top: Nicola Salvis' masterpiece, the Trevi Fountain, was completed in 1762.
Bottom: The view of Ponte Sant'Angelo and the Castel Sant'Angelo.

settlement are clearly older. In fact for centuries before that there was significant activity here. The year 509 BC, for example, was a dramatic one in which the Roman Republic was established – and one oriented towards expansion. Rome soon became the mistress of the Mediterranean and ultimately, during the time of the emperors, the ruler of the known world. The Age of the Popes began after the fall of the Roman Empire. Rome then became primarily a religious center. However,

and the Santa Maria Maggiore with original mosaics from the 5th century (exclave of the Vatican). Be sure to visit the Villa Giulia, once a papal summer residence with the national Etruscan museum.

The baroque square of Piazza Navona, the baroque fountain Fontana di Trevi, and the Spanish Steps are great meeting places.

For day trips, take the Via Appia to the catacombs of San Callisto and San Sebastiano, or go to Tivoli.

Rome, "the Eternal City", was the center of the Roman Empire and later the Christian world. Impressive ruins testify to the former might of the empire, and the countless religious buildings are evidence of the former power of the popes. Seen here: the portico of the Pantheon, with its many granite columns, built in

25 BC in honor of the "many gods". The building was given its present form under Emperor Hadrian, and its interior is unique for the single light portal (ocultus) in the middle of the dome that provides daylight for the 43-m-high (140 ft) circular structure. The dome's diameter is also 43 m (140 ft).

The frescoes of Pompeii

On 24 August in AD 79, the enormous plug that had sealed the cap of Mount Vesuvius for centuries exploded out of the mountain into the sky above the volcano. A huge cloud of cinders, stone and ash obscured the sun and glowing red magma spilled over the edge of the crater into the valley, burying the Roman cities of Pompeii and Herculaneum.

It all happened so quickly that some people could not get away. Like their cities, they were buried under 6 m (20 ft) of ash, lava and cinders – virtually mummified. Due to the sudden nature of the event and the quickness with which it engulfed these towns, it actually preserved homes and people in precisely the positions they were in when the eruption happened. As a result, much of what we know today

The portrait of Terentius Nero and his wife (1st century BC).

about ancient Roman life was discovered in the ruins of the towns.

Following the disaster, Pompeii was subsequently forgotten until the 16th century. Excavations only began in 1748 and gradually uncovered an almost completely preserved ancient city – not only temples, theaters and forums, but also houses and many other aspects of everyday Roman life – shops, kitchens, hostels, latrines, tools, public baths and, of course, the famous Pompeii Red Frescoes.

The most beautiful and best-preserved of these are in the Casa del Menandro, the Casa dei Vettii and the Villa dei Misteri, including a 17-m-wide (56-ft) series of images depicting the mysteries of the cult of Dionysus.

It is no wonder that Pompeii has long been designated a UNESCO World Heritage Site. However, the hordes of visitors and vandalism mean the excavation site is unfortunately in disastrous condition.

was once an important Roman trading town. Evidence of this can still be seen here.

The devastating bomb attacks during World War II actually had one fortuitous result – they uncovered a number of ancient sites, including a section of the Via Appia and the original foundation of the Roman Forum.

The cathedral is from the Middle Ages and is located on a former temple site. It contains some artistic treasures such as a mosaic floor dating back to the 13th century. The spectacular coastal road leads from here to your next coastal town.

⑨ Gaeta The Old Town, whose silhouette is dominated by the Aragonian fort and the Church of San Francesco, has a picturesque location on a small peninsula. However, the town is particularly worth visiting for the unique bell tower in the 12th-century cathedral – its bricks are fired in bright colours.

The small Church of San Giovanni a Mare, dating from the 10th century, also contains a small oddity – the builders wisely designed the floor on a slope so that the sea water could run off again at high tide. For a long time Gaeta was a fortress for the kingdom of Naples.

After a few kilometers, the road leaves the coast and heads inland towards Cápua.

The ancient Via Appia

The most famous of ancient Rome's legendary roads was named after its builder, Appius Claudius Caecus, and was designed using large hexagonal blocks laid on an extremely solid foundation. First constructed as a military transport route, it was later used more heavily for trade. It originally led from the Porta Sebastiano in Rome to Cápua, but was extended through Benevento and Taranto to Brindisi in 190 BC. As Roman road archtiects mainly preferred straight lines, the road actually runs 'perfectly straight', despite steep rises in the Alban Hills and the Pontine Marshes. The Via Appia is 4.1 m (13 ft) wide, enough for two large transport wagons to pass each other at the time. You can still drive its complete length of 540 km (336 miles).

⑩ Cápua When it was initially built, the first 'section' of the Via Appia ended here in Cápua. This former Etruscan center, with its enormous amphitheater from the 1st century AD, was destroyed after the collapse of the West Roman Empire and rebuilt by the Lombards in the 9th century. The cathedral's bell tower dates back to this time. The Museo Campagna on the nearby Palazzo Antignano houses numerous discoveries from the city's ancient burial sites.

The tour now leaves the Lazio landscape and continues on towards Campania.

⑪ Caserta Just a stone's throw away from Cápua is the town of Caserta, sometimes boastfully called the 'Versailles of the South' – Bourbon King Karl III built the monumental French-style Palazzo Reale here. The palace is grouped around four large interior courtyards and is

Vesuvius

Mount Vesuvius is the youngest and only remaining active volcano in mainland Europe – it's 12,000 years old and last erupted in 1944. It is unknown how long its current dormant phase will last, but one thing is for certain – the pressure is rising inside. At present, a 3-km-deep (2-mile) plug is blocking the crater hole, and the magma continues to bubble up from a depth of 5–7 km (3–4 miles).

In the event of another eruption, more than 600,000 people living around Mount Vesuvius are potentially in harm's way. Since the last eruption, the volcano now has two peaks – Vesuvius itself at 1,281 m (4,203 ft) and Monte Somma at 1,132 m (3,714 ft). The main crater has a depth of up to 300 m (984 ft) and a diameter of about 600 m (1,969 ft).

The crater of Mount Vesuvius.

For those adventurous enough to climb the mountain, the view over the Gulf of Naples from the edge of the crater is gorgeous. These cinder cones and their most recent lava layers have virtually no vegetation, but halfway up are some sturdy oaks and chestnut trees making a go of it. Below 500 m (1,640 ft) there are even oleander, gorse, silver lichen, olive and fruit trees as well as the vines of the 'Lacrimae Christi' wine region. Despite its deadly outbursts over the millennia, the fertile soil on the slopes of Vesuvius continues to draw people back after every eruption.

There are a number of options for getting right up close to Vesuvius. The simplest is taking a ride on the Circumvesuviana, a train ride around the volcano that takes about two hours. Alternatively, there is a bus ride from Ercolano that takes you to the former chairlift station. From there, it takes about half an hour to climb to the top.

church of Gesù Nuovo, dating from the 16th century. The Old Town of Naples, with its 300 churches, castles and town houses, was declared a UNESCO World Heritage Site in 1995.

In addition, there are three castles in the center of the city: Castel dell'Ovo from 1154, the residence of the Normans and Hohenstaufen of Swabia; Castel Nuovo (1279–82) in the port area; and the star-shaped Castel Sant'Elmo (14th–16th century) on Vomero Hill, just opposite the former Carthusian monastery of Certosa di San Martino. The Palazzo Reale and the Teatro San Carlo (1737) are also worth visiting.

Next to the Gothic Duomo San Gennaro (13th century) is the Gothic church of Santa Chiara (14th century), burial place of the Anjou kings with an interest-

1 The view over the Bay of Naples with the yacht port and Vesuvius in the background.

2 One of the important country villas of the ancient city of Pompeii – the Villa dei Misteri. Its wonderfully colourful paintings (80–30 BC) depict occult celebrations.

3 The church of San Francesco di Paola in Naples was modelled after the Roman Pantheon. Its cupola is 53 m (174 ft) high.

an impressive five storeys high. The whole complex – declared a UNESCO World Heritage Site – is 247 m (810 ft) long, 184 m (604 ft) wide and has 1,200 rooms with 1,800 windows.

No less extraordinary are the 120-ha (297-acre) baroque gardens with statuaries and water features including the Great Waterfall, which are a mighty 78 m (256 ft) high!

Somewhat in contrast to this extravagance here is the modest medieval mountain town of Caserta Vecchia 10 km (6 miles) to the north-east. There is a Norman cathedral here that was consecrated in 1153.

From Caserta, it's roughly 40 km (25 miles) to Naples, originally founded as Neapolis by the Greeks in the 7th century BC.

⑫ Naples Italy's third-largest city is often considered the 'most Italian' in the country. It is probably the noisiest and most hectic, but also the most likeable of Italy's big cities, where washing lines still hang over the narrow alleys and the gap between rich and poor provides a somehow fascinating cultural mix.

The Spaccianapoli (literally 'split Naples'), a boulevard that cuts right through the city, widens at the turn-off to the north-south axis, Via Toledo, and leads you into the Piazza del Gesù Nuovo. At the center of the square is a 34-m-high (112-ft) baroque column dedicated to the memory of plague victims from the 17th century. Opposite this is the

The view from the road along the Amalfi Coast, one of Italy's steepest coastlines, alternates between breathtaking views of the blue Mediterranean, magnificent coves, picturesque towns and the island of Capri. This is the land of lemon trees and sunshine, of spectacular cliffs plunging into the sea and lush vegetation.

The highlights of any trip here are Positano and Amalfi. Although tourism has long roots in these former fishing villages, the now world-famous seaside resorts still possess a nostalgic flair that cannot be taken from them.

Capri

Emperor Augustus and his successor, Tiberius, had already discovered the beauty of Capri's legendary sunsets before the birth of Christ – ruins still remain from Tiberius' Villa Iovis on the island.

With a length of just 6.25 km (4 miles) and a width of just 2.5 km (1.5 miles), Capri is relatively small, but the jagged and, in parts, bizarre

Top: The 'Faraglioni' rocks off the south-east coast of Capri.
Bottom: Marina Grande, Capri.

limestone cliffs soar to heights of 589 m (1,932 ft) out of the Gulf of Naples. Along the coast is a series of caves and grottoes formed over the last 2,000 years because the island has sunk some 15 m (49 ft). The entrance of the Blue Grotto, for example, is only 1 m (3 ft) above the waterline. The grotto itself, how-ever, is quite big at 54 m (177 ft) long, 15 m (49 ft) wide and up to 30 m (98 ft) high. The Grotta Azzurra gets its name from the mystical blue light that glows inside it from the early morning sun.

Ferries from the mainland dock at Marina Grande. A trip to the island would be incomplete without seeing the towns of Capri and Anacapri on the slopes of Monte Solaro, the rock cliffs of the Arco Naturale in the east and the three 'Faraglioni', rock formations in the south-east.

ing cloister. Behind the church Della Madre de Buon Consiglio is the entrance to the catacombs from early Christian times with frescoes dating back to the 2nd century. After the caves take a ride on the Funicolari, cable cars that bring you to the higher parts of the city.

The Museo Archeologico Nazionale has some priceless discoveries including the 'Farnese Bull' from the Baths of Caracalla in Rome and the mosaics from Pompeii depicting Alexander the Great's battle. A must on the way to Sorrento is Pompeii, which documents the devastating powers of Mount Vesuvius like no other place on earth.

⑬ Sorrento A beautiful coastal road leads you around the Gulf of Naples to Sorrento, with gorgeous views over the sea on the opposite side of the peninsula from Capri. The Roman emperors had villas and temples built in this small town upon high, steep rock faces as if on their own natural throne.

Sorrento experienced a Renaissance in the 18th century, when it was inundated by artists. Today, the birthplace of the poet Torquato Tasso in 1544 is one of Italy's most popular health resorts and artist colonies. A marble statue in the Piazza Torquato Tasso pays homage to the poet. The iconic 14th-century cathedral is worth seeing for its inlay work alone, and the Villa Communale provides wonderful views out over the Gulf of Naples. Another popular holiday destination in the area is the medieval town of Massa Lubrense, south of Sorrento.

⑭ Positano One of the most beautiful spots on the Amalfi Coast is at the beginning of the Amalfitana. Famous for its picturesque location on two slopes of the Monte Angelo a Tre Pizzi (1,443 m/4,738 ft), Positano has been transformed from a once quaint fishing village into a sophisticated spa resort. Dominating the scene over Spaggia Grande Beach is the glazed cupola of the Church of Santa Maria Assunta.

⑮ Amalfi The cultivated fields dotting the Amalfi Coast, itself a UNESCO World Heritage Site, stretch out along the southern side of the Sorrento peninsula. Amalfi, today a lovely resort with a population of 6,000, was an important maritime republic between the 9th and 11th centuries that competed with the likes of Genoa, Pisa and Venice – it was home to 50,000 people back then. The rowing regatta held every four years between these former rivals is now the only legacy of those times. In the 14th century, Amalfi was extensively destroyed by a heavy storm tide. Little of its history has been preserved.

In the middle of the maze of alleys is the monumental cathedral dating back to the 9th century. It was built in 1203 in an Arab-Norman-Sicilian style. Two former monasteries have been converted to luxury hotels where the likes of Henrik Ibsen and Ingrid Bergmann have stayed.

A worthwhile day trip from Amalfi takes you into the Valley of the Mills where some of Europe's oldest paper mills were constructed. Make sure you see

the wild Castania forests on Monte Lattari, which form the impressive hinterland of the Amalfi Coast.

16 Salerno The capital of the province and gulf of the same name had its heyday under Norman rule in the 11th/12th centuries when it was home to the Scuola Medica, Europe's first medical school. The Duomo San Matteo, with its 56-m-high (184-ft) campanile, was also built during this time. After passing between the Roman lions you enter a large forecourt with arcades of twenty-eight ancient columns brought from Paestum. The crypt is a gem of baroque marble inlay work. The Castello di Arechi towers over the city.

17 Paestum In 1752, road workers on the southern bend of the Gulf of Salerno came across the ruins of the ancient city of Poseidonia, which was founded by the Greeks in 600 BC and later called Paestum by the Romans. After being extensively destroyed by the Saracens in the 9th century, it was forgotten until the road came. The imposing temple complexes (the Temple of Neptune, Temple of Ceres, Temple of Hera) have now been excavated and preserved.
Other attractions include the 4.7-km-long (3-mile) city wall, a forum, the Via Sacra and a Roman amphitheater. Herds of placid buffalo now graze be-

tween the monuments and supply milk for the reputedly best mozzarella in the world.

18 Agrópoli South of Paestum is Agrópoli, a fishing town that clings to a rock cape. It has picturesque alleyways, ancient steps, a Saracen castle and more wonderful views of the gulf. East of Agrópoli, the hilly Parco Nazionale Del Cilento surrounds Monte Cervati (1,898 m/6,227 ft). You can go hiking, enjoy the serenity of the idyllic mountain village of Castellabate, or bathe in the turquoise-blue bays at Capo Palinuro.
Circling the promontory separating the Gulf of Salerno and the Gulf of Policastro, you finally ar-

Amalfitana

The coast road running along the Sorrento Peninsula is considered by many to be the most beautiful in Italy. Hewn mercilessly from the steep cliff walls, the 45-km-long (28-mile) route makes its way along the sea through narrow serpentines and hairpins providing you with non-stop panoramic views over the azure blue sea and the Costiera Amalfitana. Villages dot the coastline like pearls amid lemon groves and vineyards, while the sturdy houses cling to the cliffs and cover the dramatic slopes. The road serves as a connection for the villages between Nerano and Salerno.

rive in Sapri. From here, the route leaves the southbound coastal road and heads east overland to Brindisi, the historic end terminus of the Via Appia. Just under half way to Metaponto, about 30 km (19 miles) out of Sapri, you should take a detour south at Lauría into the Parco Nazionale del Pollina. The rugged landscape of the Basilicata is home to some lovely verdant forests, and peaks like Monte Pollina (2,248 m/7,376 ft). Two of this region's specialities are the rare stone pines and the Apennine wolf.

19 Metaponto Founded by the Greeks, this ancient city on the Gulf of Taranto used to be called

Metapontion before it fell to the Romans. It was also where the philosopher Pythagoras died in 497 BC. Numerous artefacts from excavations in the surrounding area are exhibited in the Museo Nazionale. The ruins of four temple complexes, the agora and amphitheaters are located in the Parco Archeologico. Drive to the Lido di Metaponto for a swim.

20 Matera Matera owes its fame to its 'sassi' – medieval cave dwellings dug into the steep tuff walls of the Gravina (gorge). Inextricably nestled into one another, houses later built in front of them stretch up the western slope. The caves were originally inhabited by Benedictine and Greek monks who built chapels, halls and altars and painted priceless historic frescoes.

1 The Duomo di Sant'Andrea in Amalfi was rebuilt in Romanesque style in the 11th century. An impressive perron leads from the Piazza Duomo up to the church.

2 The Costiera Amalfitana near Positano – pastel-coloured houses cling to the steep slope in terraces.

3 The Temple of Neptune in Paestum was built in 450 BC and is one of the best-preserved Greek temples in all of Europe.

The Greeks in southern Italy

Greek sailors had settled in southern Italy and Sicily back in the middle of the 8th century BC, long before the Romans arrived. On Sicily they found-

The Temple of Hera in Metaponto dates from the 6th century BC.

ed the city of Siracusa which, in its heyday in the 4th century BC, was the most important Greek city outside Greece and a metropolis of the ancient world. There were early Greek colonies on Ischia as well, just as the later Roman city of Cumae was also a Greek colony. These settlements were all grouped under the term 'Magna Graecia'.
Some of Europe's most beautiful Greek ruins can still be found in southern Italy – on the mainland are the Temple of Paestum and the ancient sites in Metaponto, while on Sicily there are the amphitheater and the Temple of Segesta, the Valley of Temples near Agrigent, the Temple of Tyndaris and the Taormina Theater.

The trulli of Alberobello

These traditional stone dwellings (trulli) are only found in the Apulia region, more precisely in the hilly Murge dei Trulli, a high karst plateau where the sparse landscape is defined by olive groves, vineyards and some fruit orchards. The word 'murge' itself comes from the Latin meaning 'sharp stone'.

It is here in the Itria Valley that you will find thousands of these small, round, stone houses with cone-shaped roofs topped with capstones called 'cippos' or 'pinnacolos.' Some of the houses have even been connected.

Until the 1930s, no one was really interested in the cute whitewashed houses of the poor farmers of the Apulia hinterland. Today, they are a national legacy and a UNESCO World Heritage Site.

Farmers used to store their crops in the high cone-shaped roofs. Many of the trulli were extended with another trullo by breaking through a wall each time a new child was born. Unique and bizarre structures were

The classic cone-shaped roofs of trulli in Alberobello.

thus created, the sizes of which were an indication of the owner's wealth. The clever Count Gian Girolamo II originally designed these strange little houses back in 1635 to save taxes. At the time, brick houses were subject to tax so he got his starving farmhands to pile rubble slabs on top of each other, without any mortar, to form round constructions with cone-shaped roofs. Using mud for grouting he developed the trullo – a non-brick building that helped him avoid further taxes.

The trulli were originally located on fields before entire trulli settlements were later formed. Alberobello, with around a thousand trulli, is the capital of the Murge dei Trulli and is located just a few kilometers northeast of Martina Franca.

Farmers later followed their example. Almost 20,000 people lived here in incredibly tiny spaces and in very primitive conditions until the start of the 1950s – sometimes even with their animals.

To eradicate them as a source of 'national shame', the sassi inhabitants were eventually relocated. Since the 1970s the structures were restored and made into a very popular tourist attraction. The town's other sights include the Norman-Roman cathedral (13th century), the Castello Tramontano (1515) and the Chiesa del Purgatorio (1770) with macabre depictions of purgatory. In 1993, UNESCO declared the city with its two sassi areas a World Heritage Site.

The route heads through Castellanetta towards the coast near Chiatona. The next stop on your trip is Taranto.

21 Taranto Also originally a Greek settlement (Taras), Taranto became one of the richest and most powerful cities in Magna Graecia in the 4th century because of its colour production using the spiny dye-murex snail. Most of its inhabitants were still Greek at the time of Emperor Augustus.

Taranto is divided into three sections connected by two bridges. The Old City is perched on a small rock island and is still quite charming despite a long decline. It is dominated by the towers of the Castello Aragonese (15th century). The Museo Archeologico Nazionale is really worth seeing, with its precious gold

and silver treasures. The cathedral in the Città Vecchia (Old City) was built in the 12th century but later remodelled. Its cave-like crypt and ancient marble columns are worth a look.

22 Martina Franca Further down the road you cross the Zona dei Trulli and reach the town of Martina Franca. In contrast to the nearby trulli style, this town is defined by baroque and rococo buildings like the Palazzo Ducale (1668–1742). The Church of San Martino, built from 1747–75, has a beautiful altar and is located at the gorgeous Corso Vittorio Emanuele. A detour to the trulli after Alberobello is a must (see sidebar left).

23 Ostuni The 'white' town lies at the eastern edge of the Zona dei Trulli, just 6 km (4 miles) from the sea. The picturesque village

is full of tiny alleyways and terraced white houses sprawl over its three hills. The late Gothic cathedral (15th century) and the town hall at the Piazza della Liberta (14th century) are also worth visiting.

24 Bríndisi The ancient city, Brundisium, has been the terminus of the Via Appia since 190 BC. Its original icons were two 19-m-high (62-ft) marble columns down on the waterfront. As back then, Bríndisi continues to be a gateway to the eastern Mediterranean – it isn't much further to Greece and 'Asia Minor' from here.

A plaque on the Colonna Romana pays homage to the poet Vergil who died here in 19 BC. Not far from the Colonna Romana is the cathedral square complex, a 12th-century work that was later given a baroque look in 1743.

Other churches include the Temple Church of San Giovanni al Sepolcro (12th century) and, further west, the church of the same name with a Norman cloister. The Church of Santa Maria del Casale has striking frescoes and the castle on the Seno di Ponte was built under Friedrich II from 1227.

1 The cave dwellings in Matera are divided into an upper and lower district, which are in turn made up of Sasso Barisano and Sasso Cavoso. Over thousands of years, new caves and houses were continually dug into the tuff in the two horn-shaped rock gorges. A total of 150 rock churches have been preserved here.

2 Trulli are the round white houses made of stone with a cone-shaped roof that is really a false dome. The architecture is unique to Apulia.

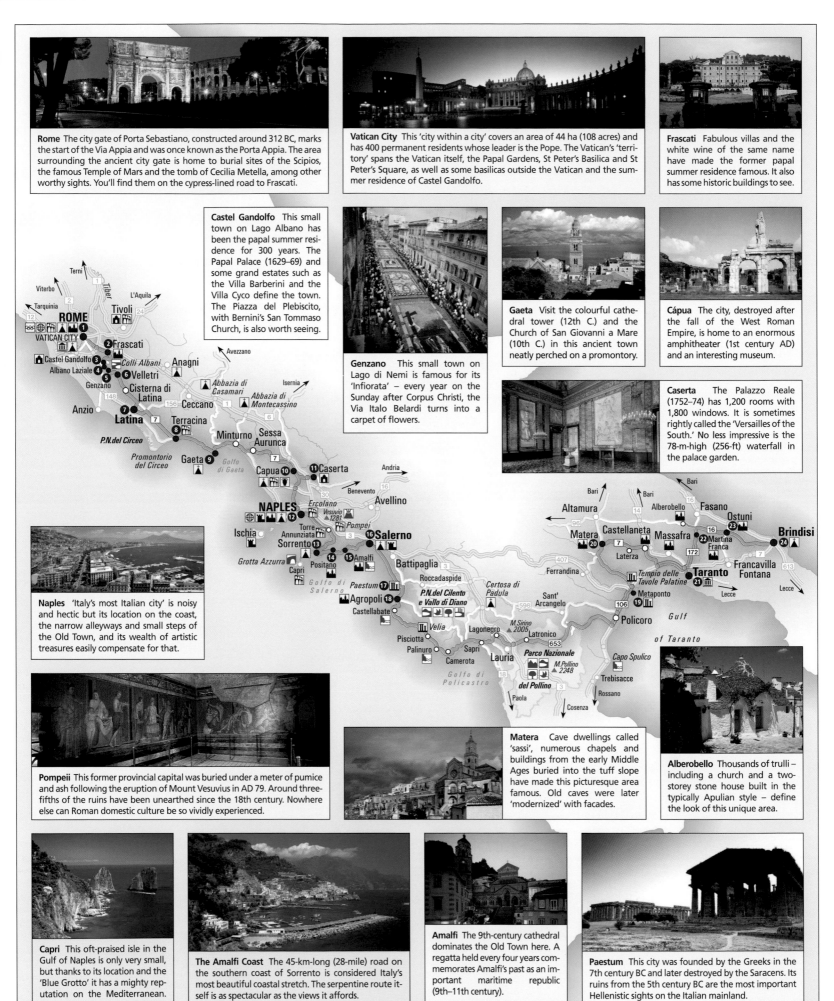

Rome The city gate of Porta Sebastiano, constructed around 312 BC, marks the start of the Via Appia and was once known as the Porta Appia. The area surrounding the ancient city gate is home to burial sites of the Scipios, the famous Temple of Mars and the tomb of Cecilia Metella, among other worthy sights. You'll find them on the cypress-lined road to Frascati.

Vatican City This 'city within a city' covers an area of 44 ha (108 acres) and has 400 permanent residents whose leader is the Pope. The Vatican's 'territory' spans the Vatican itself, the Papal Gardens, St Peter's Basilica and St Peter's Square, as well as some basilicas outside the Vatican and the summer residence of Castel Gandolfo.

Frascati Fabulous villas and the white wine of the same name have made the former papal summer residence famous. It also has some historic buildings to see.

Castel Gandolfo This small town on Lago Albano has been the papal summer residence for 300 years. The Papal Palace (1629–69) and some grand estates such as the Villa Barberini and the Villa Cyco define the town. The Piazza del Plebiscito, with Bernini's San Tommaso Church, is also worth seeing.

Genzano This small town on Lago di Nemi is famous for its 'Infiorata' – every year on the Sunday after Corpus Christi, the Via Italo Belardi turns into a carpet of flowers.

Gaeta Visit the colourful cathedral tower (12th C.) and the Church of San Giovanni a Mare (10th C.) in this ancient town neatly perched on a promontory.

Cápua The city, destroyed after the fall of the West Roman Empire, is home to an enormous amphitheater (1st century AD) and an interesting museum.

Caserta The Palazzo Reale (1752–74) has 1,200 rooms with 1,800 windows. It is sometimes rightly called the 'Versailles of the South.' No less impressive is the 78-m-high (256-ft) waterfall in the palace garden.

Naples 'Italy's most Italian city' is noisy and hectic but its location on the coast, the narrow alleyways and small steps of the Old Town, and its wealth of artistic treasures easily compensate for that.

Pompeii This former provincial capital was buried under a meter of pumice and ash following the eruption of Mount Vesuvius in AD 79. Around three-fifths of the ruins have been unearthed since the 18th century. Nowhere else can Roman domestic culture be so vividly experienced.

Matera Cave dwellings called 'sassi', numerous chapels and buildings from the early Middle Ages buried into the tuff slope have made this picturesque area famous. Old caves were later 'modernized' with facades.

Alberobello Thousands of trulli – including a church and a two-storey stone house built in the typically Apulian style – define the look of this unique area.

Capri This oft-praised isle in the Gulf of Naples is only very small, but thanks to its location and the 'Blue Grotto' it has a mighty reputation on the Mediterranean.

The Amalfi Coast The 45-km-long (28-mile) road on the southern coast of Sorrento is considered Italy's most beautiful coastal stretch. The serpentine route itself is as spectacular as the views it affords.

Amalfi The 9th-century cathedral dominates the Old Town here. A regatta held every four years commemorates Amalfi's past as an important maritime republic (9th–11th century).

Paestum This city was founded by the Greeks in the 7th century BC and later destroyed by the Saracens. Its ruins from the 5th century BC are the most important Hellenistic sights on the Italian mainland.

Piran, Slovenia, is a sailing port that juts into the Adriatic with buildings from the Venetian era.

Around the Adriatic

The Realm of the Winged Lion

Sometimes rather sparse, sometimes lush Mediterranean vegetation – but always a view of the sea. Journeying along the Adriatic through Slovenia, Croatia and Italy you will encounter medieval towns, art and culture in spades, as well as tiny rocky coves and beaches stretching for miles.

The northern reaches of the Mediterranean were originally named after the ancient Etruscan town of Adria on the Po Delta, which today is a good 40 km (25 mi) inland to the south-west of Chioggia and is now only linked to the sea by a man-made canal. The town was taken over by the Greeks after the Etruscans, and since that time the mouth of the Po has moved eastwards at a rate of up to 150 m (164 yds) per year. The Adriatic is actually a shallow arm of the Mediterranean, reaching depths of no more than 1,645 m (5,397 ft) between Bari and the Albanian coast.

Venice, the first stop on your journey around the Adriatic, is a trip in itself. The gondolas, palaces and unique cultural monuments of the lagoon city are the result of its rise to power in the 13th century, when influential patrons attracted the greatest artists of the age. It was the Renaissance in particular that shaped not only the city but also the entire look of coast's culture. For it is not only at the start of the journey through the autonomous region of Friuli-Venezia Giulia that you will encounter Venetian towns. Venetian architectural jewels are also scattered along the adjoining coastline

Fresco in the Capella degli Scrovegni in Padua.

of the Istrian Peninsula as well as along the entire Croatian coast.

Many foreign cultures have laid claim to Istria over the centuries due to its fortuitous geographical position. With 242 km (150 mi) of coastline and idyllic medieval towns, the peninsula has now developed into a popular holiday destination, with tourism providing the coastal residents with a lucrative livelihood.

Between Istria and the mainland is the Kvarner Gulf, which includes the islands of Cres, Lošinj, Krk, Pag and Rab, but the lively port city of Rijeka is the starting point for our journey along the Croatian coast. The coastal road is lined by relatively barren landscape, an intense mix of light, sea and limestone. All the more surprising, then, that the valleys behind the ridge are so fertile, protected from the infamous *bora*, an icy autumn wind.

The port of Vieste in the north-east corner of the Gargano Peninsula in Apulia, southern Italy.

The Church of San Giorgio Maggiore in Venice, built between 1559 and 1580 and designed by architect Andrea Palladio.

Vineyards and lush Mediterranean vegetation are pleasing to the eye and provide a refreshing contrast to the lunar landscape of the limestone cliffs. With its steep coastline, the Adria Magistrale is considered one of the most dangerous stretches of road in Europe. On the other hand, there are many interesting destinations and worthwhile attractions that can only be reached via this route. And, with the Serbo-Croatian War having left very few scars along the coast, tourism has undergone a revival in recent years. As a result, the service sector has also become the most important economic engine for the whole coastal region.

The ferry from Dubrovnik to Bari links the Croatian and Italian coastlines, which are at once similar and different. The section along the Italian side of the Adriatic covers a total of five regions: Apulia, Abruzzi, the Marches, Emilia-Romagna and Veneto, each with an individual culture and landscape.

The settlement of the area goes back a long way. The Etruscans, the Greeks, the Venetians and the Romans all established towns throughout this coastal region. And the coast itself is as diverse as the region: the cliffs of the Gargano Peninsula rise dramatically from the water while south of Ancona the foothills of the Apennines protrude into the ocean. The tourist centers beyond Rímini are very different again. There, sandy beaches stretch for miles and have mutated into centers of mass recreation.

Veneto, on the other hand, paints a very different picture with canals, lagoons and tidy little islands off the coast at about the same latitude as the university town of Padua.

The defiant St. Nicholas Monastery on the island of Korčula off the Dalmatian coast.

Murano and Burano

For centuries, Murano glass was considered the best in the world and the small island has served as the headquarters of the Venetian glass industry since the 13th century. A museum provides interesting insights into the art of glass blowing.

In addition to the quality glass products, the triple-nave Maria e Donato Basilica from the 12th century is also worth visiting. The building with its wonderful apse design is a mixture of Venetian-Byzantine and Early Romanesque elements and boasts a fine mosaic floor dating back to 1140.

Venetian nobility discovered the island in the 16th century and made it their their summer holiday location of choise, the elegant villas and parks bearing witness to this golden era.

The high church tower is the icon of Burano.

Burano paints a different picture. This lively little fishing island has wonderfully vibrant cottages and is the center of the Venetian lace industry. A small museum proudly displays a collection of the finest lacework covering two centuries and includes veils, dresses and fans.

An incomparable landscape combined with cultural diversity are what characterize this tour around the Adriatic, but a number of things remain constant as you pass through Italy, Slovenia and Croatia: the idyllic nature of the coastlines and clear seas, dramatic rock formations and cliffs, the gentle valleys and the tantalizing coves with magnificent beaches.

1 Venice (see page 299) Following one of the undisputed highlights of this tour right at the outset, namely a visit to Venice, you continue along the B14 as far as the intersection with the B352.

2 Aquiléia Aquiléia was one of the largest towns in the ancient empire of Augustus, but today it is home to just 3,400 inhabitants. The remains of the Roman town as well as the Romanesque Basilica of Our Lady, with its magnificent 4th-century mosaic floor, have both been declared a UNESCO World Heritage Site.

3 Údine It was only in the late Middle Ages that this former Roman settlement developed into the region's main city. The influence of Venice can be seen throughout the town, as well as on the Piazza Libertà, whose loggias and the splendid clock tower (1527) truly make it one of the loveliest squares in the world. The Renaissance Castello di Údine towers over the Old Town and the Santa Maria Annunziata Cathedral (14th century) features masterful altar pieces and frescos by Giambattista Tiepolo.

With its high limestone cliffs dropping sharply to the ocean, the Riviera Triestina has very little in common with the rest of the Italian Adriatic. Continuing from Údine via Monfalcone to Trieste along the B14 you get a taste of the craggy, bizarre landscape that awaits in Dalmatia.

4 Trieste This Mediterranean port was part of Austria for

1 The imposing baroque church Santa Maria della Salute on the Grand Canal has a foundation of more than one million piles.

2 A spectacular sunset near Grado over the Gulf of Trieste, the northernmost part of the Adriatic.

Travel information

Route profile
Length: : approx. 2,125 km (1,320 mi)
Time required: at least 3 weeks
Start and end: Venice
Route (main locations):
Venice, Trieste, Pula, Rijeka, Split, Dubrovnik, Bari, Pescara, Ancona, Ravenna, Padua, Venice

Traffic information:
The motorways in Austria, Switzerl and Italy all require a vignette. You also need to carry the Green Insurance Card with you.
Warnings of live landmines have been issued in Croatia; these warnings should obviously be heeded when making excursions into the coastal hinterland between Senj and Split as well as in

the mountains south-east of Dubrovnik!
Information regarding the ferries from Cres and Rab as well as to Bari:
www.croatia-travel.org
www.croatiatraveller.com

Entry requirements:
Slovenia, Croatia, Bosnia-Herzegovina require a valid personal identity card or passport. In Bosnia-Herzegovina you need to register with the police for a stay of over 24 hours.

Information:
Here are some websites to help you plan your trip:
www.traveladriatic.net
www.slovenia.info
www.croatia.hr
www.ciaoitaly.net
www.venetia.it

Venice

A visit to the magnificent lagoon city is simply unforgettable, regardless of the time of year.

If you can somehow avoid the high season when thousands of tourists jam the narrow alleys around Piazza San Marco, you are lucky. But Venice (a UNESCO World Heritage Site) is so extraordinarily beautiful that it is a treat all year round.

As a maritime power, Venice was once the queen of the eastern Mediterranean. The city is unique, and not least because of its medieval architectural design that is an amalgamation of Byzantine, Arab and Gothic elements. This capital of the northern Italian province of Venezia includes over one hundred islands in a sandy lagoon in the Adriatic. The city is linked to the mainland via causeways and bridges, and was built on piles. There are over 150 bridges and 400 canals.

Originally, Venice was a refuge built after the invasion of the Huns, and its inhabitants actually remained independent for centuries in what was then a remote location. They even managed to take over the legacy of Ravenna in

The Doge's Palace in Venice was the residence of the Doge from the ninth century as well as the seat of the Venetian government.

the eighth century, but by the 15th century, the flow of world trade had shifted, leaving the former queen without its foundation. Venice stagnated thereafter, stuck in the early stages of becoming a metropolis.

Sights here include: the Piazza San Marco, city center for the last thousand years; the Basilica di San Marco with its priceless décor (11th century); the Doge's Palace, a masterpiece of the Venetian Gothic; the Grand Canal with the Rialto Bridge; the Church of Santa Maria Gloriosa dei Frari; the Scuola Grande di San Rocco, the Galleria del L'Accademia with collections of Venetian paintings from the 14th to 18th centuries; and the other islands of Murano, Burano and Torcello.

The lion of San Marco guards the Molo San Marco above the Grand Canal. On the other side of the canal is the Santa Maria della Salute, one of the most impressive churches in this lagoon city at the confluence of the Grand Canal and the Canale di San Marco.

Top: Gondolas bobbing on the Canale di San Marco with the monastery island of San Giorgio Maggiore in the background. **Middle:** The Grand Canal is 3.8 km (2.4 mi) long and lined with magnificent palaces. **Bottom:** The Piazza San Marco, the Basilica di San Marco and the sun shining through the Doge's Palace.

Detour

Rab and Cres

Whether you are a fan of culture or the sea, Rab island will not disappoint. Revealing all of its magic behind a protective row of cliffs, Rab is an oasis with forests and a wealth of agriculture.

A former Roman colony, the island has been under Croatian, Venetian, and even Austrian rule. The picturesque Old Town of Rab, with the unmistakable silhouette of its four bell

The Old Town of Rab.

towers, is tiny, its waterfront and the medieval alleyways inviting visitors for an easy stroll. For swimmers, the road continues to Suha Punta with its oak and pine forests and numerous small coves.

The neighboring island of Cres has a more rugged charm of its own. Journeying along the main road you get the impression that you are in the mountains but then every now and again you get a breathtaking view of the ocean. Cres is also linked

Top: Coastal landscape on Cres.
Below: Cres' idyllic port.a

by a small spit of land to the nearby island of Lošinj. The port of Mali Lošinj, with its vibrant late baroque buildings, is a popular stop with magnificent yachts from all over the world anchoring here.

over five hundred years, from 1382 until 1918, when the city was annexed by Italy after World War I. Open squares and cozy cafes are testimony to the former presence and influence of the Austro-Hungarian monarchy, before it lost influence as a center of trade and culture. The atmosphere of the Grand Canal with its small boats is dominated by the imposing Sant' Antonio Church (1849).

⑤ Koper und Piran The Slovenian coast is only 40 km (25 mi) long and yet three towns here offer you virtually all of the aspects of the sea and seafaring you could want: Koper, the country's trading port, Izola the fishing port and Piran, where the beachgoers sun themselves. Formerly an island, Koper is now linked to the mainland by a causeway. The center of the historic Old Town has a Venetian flair and is dominated by the Titov trg and the Praetorian Palace, the cathedral and the bell tower. One palace loggia on the square has been converted into a relaxed coffee house. Izola was also built on an island and before being later linked to the mainland. There are ample signs of a Venetian past here

too, but Izola is primarily a fishing village and port.

Piran, on the other hand, is one of the loveliest towns along the Adriatic, and lives primarily from tourism. The town's focal point is Tartini Square, lined by a semi-circular row of old buildings on the one side and with views of the small fishing port on the opposite side. In Piran, the best thing to do is go for a stroll and let yourself be enchanted by the delightful details of the loggias, fountains and wells.

The onward journey now takes you onto Croatian soil.

⑥ Umag The craggy west coast of Istria, from Savudrija to Rovinj, has lively coastal resorts,

fishing villages and small Venetian towns on the seaside that feature a varied landscape. The road initially travels through reddish, open countryside where you arrive in the "breadbasket" of Istria, the focal point of which is the lovely town of Umag. This former Venetian port on a spit of land has a historic Old Town that is surrounded almost completely by the sea. In the Middle Ages, Umag – then still an island separated from the mainland – belonged o the Bishop of Trieste. The route then continues along small, scenic roads along the coast to Poreč.

⑦ Poreč Headlands covered in pine forests, lagoons with crystal-clear water and craggy

cliffs of marble are the hallmarks of the 70-k-long (43-mi) riviera between Poreč and Vrsar, and it is no surprise that the little town of Poreč, originally settled by the Romans, has developed into Istria's tourism center. The main attractions include the towers of the former town walls, the 15th-century bell tower and the Euphrasian Basilica with its elaborate décor and fine mosaics – the most significant monument to Byzantine sacral architecture from the 3rd to 6th centuries.

In order to reach the medieval coastal town of Rovinj by car you will need to round the Limski zaljev bay on the E751 and, after a very short drive through the interior, turn off to the west of the peninsula.

3

The Plitvice Lakes

An unforgettable natural spectacle awaits visitors to the Plitvička jezera National Park in the north Dalmatian hinterland. The waters of the Korana River plunge down a total of 156 m (512 ft) into a series of stepped lakes and waterfalls over dolomite and limestone terraces. There is a total of sixteen lakes in the park, each one as beautiful as the last, glistening in shades of deep blue and green. The unmistakable hues come from the limestone, which is the dominant type of stone in the region. The ninety waterfalls and cascades are located in what is largely still pristine mixed forest, which has a particular appeal in autumn.

The national park's most impressive waterfalls are the Plitvice Falls where the waters of the Plitvice River plunge 72 m (236 ft) down into the canyon. One of the park entrances is located conveniently close

There are more than ninety waterfalls in this national park.

to the falls while another gate opens at the largest of the Plitvice lakes, the Kozjak jezero. The idyllic landscape is easily accessible on the many miles of boardwalks and the 40 km (25 mi) of hiking trails. Electric boats and a mini tourist railway also help to ensure that the longer distances can be negotiated comfortably. Caution: brown bears, wolves and wildcats roam through the forests and canyons, with otters living in the lakes.

The lake landscape has countless whitewater sections and crashing waterfalls. They have been used in a number of films. The wild landscape around the Plitvička jezera covers an area of 295 sq km (114 sq mi) and was made into a national park back in 1928. It was then declared a UNESCO World Heritage Site in 1979.

Riviera, with the charming 19th-century seaside resorts of Lovran and Opatija. Brestova marks the end of the Istria region, which is now Kvarner Bay.

11 Opatija Belle Époque styles, blossoming gardens and elegant coffee houses are all traces of the Austro-Hungarian monarchy here in Opatija. After being designated as a spa in 1889, this seaside resort developed into an urban work of art.

In addition to the obvious beach pursuits, Opatija offers splendid walks along the 8-km (5-mi) waterfront promenade. European high society used to meet in Angiolina Park (1885) in the town center, and the glamour of those days can still be relived with a walk under the acacia, cedar and lemon trees.

1 Sailing yachts with the historic town of Trogir in the background. The medieval Old Town is enclosed by an impressive town wall.

2 Old Town Rovinj, dominated by the 60-m (199-ft) campanile.

3 The port of Piran has charming townhouses dating from the Venetian era.

8 Rovinj Insiders know that this coastal village, with its Venetian bell tower, numerous brightly painted houses, charming alleyways, and myriad swimming options is one of the country's loveliest. The rocky island has been settled since antiquity and was a prosperous fishing and trading center under the Venetians.

A stroll through the Old Town should begin at the waterfront promenade with its lovely views. The unique flair of Rovinj's center is formed by the Trg Tita Square, which opens out onto the waterfront with welcoming cafés, a town museum and a splendid late-Renaissance clock tower. The imposing St Eufemija baroque church (1736) with its

bell tower is also worth visiting. The route now returns to the E751 in order to reach the next stop. After passing through the very impressive limestone landscape you ultimately reach the southern part of Istria in a wine-growing area interspersed with stone walls.

9 Pula This port and industrial town with its imposing Roman arena is located at the southern end of the peninsula. Pula had developed into a prosperous provincial capital even during the era of Emperor Augustus. With its 62,400 residents, it is today still the peninsula's cultural and economic center.

Visitors are drawn by the museums and the ring-shaped Old

Town laid out around the castle hill, but the most impressive sight remains the amphitheater, a huge structure with arcade arches up to 33 m (108 ft) in height. Pula's undisputed landmark is of course also a UNESCO World Heritage Site.

10 Labin The journey now takes you along the east coast of Istria to the north-east.

The E751 crosses the Raša Valley, which is a steep canyon in places, and then climbs rapidly up to the delightful medieval town of Labin, high above the sea. The stretch along the winding east coast is now dominated by Ucka, Istria's highest mountain at 1,400 m (4,593 ft). This is the beginning of the Opatijska

Korčula

There are only a few places along the Adriatic coast where an island is this close to the mainland, in this case Korčula and the Pelješac Peninsula.

Top: The Venetian fortress in the island's capital.
Bottom: View of the picturesque island of Korčula.

Korčula, a mountainous island with comparatively lush vegetation, covers 276 sq km (107 sq mi) and has a good variety of activities to offer visitors. Legend has it that the famous Moreška sword dances, performed only on specific feast days, derive from the threat posed by the Ottoman Empire. The island's capital has Venetian-style architectural gems combined with a walled medieval Old Town, a triumphal arch, St Mark' Cathedral and the bishop's palace.

⑫ Rijeka The port and industry town of Rijeka often serves only as the starting point for a drive along the coastal road. But that would not do the city justice. One of its attractions is the 33-m-high (108-ft) bell tower of the St Marija Cathedral (13th century, façade from the 19th-century), known as the "Leaning Tower of Rijeka" due to its angle. There are also a number of museums and the pedestrian zone lined with boutiques and shops. Be sure to visit the Trsat fortress (13th century), which towers above the town affording a fantastic panoramic view of the mountains and the sea. The journey continues along the Croatian coast on the E65, also known as Adria-Magistrale, a 600-km (373-mi) stretch between Rijeka and Dubrovnik that follows the coastline almost the whole way, passing through a unique landscape comprising limestone mountains, shimmering, crystal blue water and – typically – bright sunshine.

Anyone with time for a longer detour should turn off at Kraljevica towards Krk and cross over at Valbiska to the island of Cres with its impressive, barren lunar landscape.

⑬ Crikvenica This seaside resort is situated about 30 km (19 mi) away from Rijeka. In the summer it attracts tourists with a wide sandy beach and the 8-km-long (5-mi) waterfront promenade, which extends as far as Selce.

A visit to the aquarium is also worthwhile and provides an insight into the wealth of Mediterranean fish and plant life. About 30 km (19 mi) further on is

the town of Senj. From there it is worth taking the detour to the Plitvice lakes, roughly 90 km (56 mi) away.

Back on the coastal road this stretch is lined with small towns inviting you to stop over. The ferry port of Jablanac is located halfway between Rijeka and Šibenik and from here it is worth taking a detour to the scenic island of Rab – the crossing only takes ten minutes.

⑭ Zadar The Dalmatian capital boasts some historic buildings from the Venetian era such as the circular St Donatus Church and the campanile of St Anastasia's Cathedral dating from the 12th and 13th centuries. The ruins of the medieval town fortress and the Roman forum are also worth visiting.

⑮ Šibenik This charming port is dominated by the glistening white cathedral by Jura Dalmatinác (1441). The talented builder spent most of his life working on

his masterpiece, which is a unique embodiment of the transition from the Gothic to the Renaissance style. The apses contain a row of seventy-four heads, each of which displays an individual vitality and are especially intriguing.

The surrounding landscape is a bit more hospitable here than the northern section of the coastal road. The vegetation also becomes more Mediterranean. Close to Šibenik is the start of the Krka National Park, a singular landscape of natural springs, babbling brooks and tumbling waterfalls – the realm of Croatian fairies and water sprites. The route continues via Primošten. Wine has been produced in this area for centuries, with elaborate walls of white stone built to protect the vines from the cold winds of the *bora*.

⑯ Trogir The charming Old Town of Trogir is situated on a small island. The winding alleys and a cathedral by the famous

master builder Radoan transport visitors back to the Middle Ages. The town, which only has 7,000 residents, was once a Greek and then a Roman colony before becoming Croatia's political and cultural center from the 9th to 11th centuries, as is evidenced not only by the very impressive cathedral (13th–16th century), but also by the many splendid churches and palaces.

The magnificent Old Town has since been declared a UNESCO World Heritage Site.

⑰ Split The stunning port of Split, with 188,700 residents, is the cultural and economic center of Dalmatia and has numerous museums and theaters. It is out on a peninsula dominated by Marjan hill. The Old Town has a curious mixture of Roman, medieval and modern buildings, with the impressive Diocletian Palace (built at the turn of the 4th century) and the 13th-century cathedral – the entire Old Town was declared a UNESCO

Detour

Kotor, Budva and Sveti Stefan

You can make a very interesting detour now from Dubrovnik into Montenegro. Awaiting you in the quaint coastal town of Kotor are narrow, labyrinthine alleyways, charming little squares and a number of well-preserved medieval buildings. The fortress, which was intended to protect against attacks from the sea, has a wall around it measuring 4.5 km (2.7 mi) at a height of 20 m (66 ft). Of the three city gates still standing, the ninth-century south gate is the oldest.

The Cathedral of St. Tiphun, completed in 1166, has magnificent 14th-century frescoes and is an important example of Romanesque architecture. In fact, Kotor is one of the best-preserved medieval towns in the region.

In Budva, situated on a small island linked to the mainland by a cause-

Top: The Old Town of Budva.
Bottom: The tiny but luxurious island of Sveti Stefan.

Large parts of the region surrounding Bari are used for agriculture, in particular olive cultivation.

The onward route takes you along the Autostrada 98 for a few miles before turning off at Ruvo di Púglia onto a smaller road towards Castel del Monte.

㉑ Castel del Monte This hunting castle from 1240, also known as the "Crown of Apulia", towers up from the plain and can be seen from quite a distance. The castle was built according to the laws of numerical mysticism by the German Staufer Emperor Frederick II (1194–1250) who had a passion for science and magic. The symmetrical, octagonal castle has a ring of octagonal towers, so that the only variations are those brought about by the changing daylight, an impressively active design element within the building.

The route continues along an equally small road to Barletta and from there 39 km (24 mi) along the coast to Manfredónia. A few miles further on it continues up to Monte S. Angelo.

1 The Biokovo Mountains form a wonderful backdrop for sailing yachts in one of the coastal resorts on the Makarska Riviera.

2 The Old Town of Split from the marina.

3 Sveti Ivan fortress is one of Dubrovnik's most popular photo motifs. The Old Town and the port create a picturesque backdrop.

4 View over the sea of buildings in the Old Town of Dubrovnik looking toward Lovrijenac fortress.

World Heritage Site. Unfortunately, it suffered significant damage during the Serbo-Croatian War, but that is slowly being repaired.

⑱ Makarska-Riviera This stretch of the Croatian coast becomes narrower and narrower as the journey progresses, until there is only the Biokovo mountain range separating the coast from Bosnia-Herzegovina. This is home to the once popular seaside resort area known as the Makarska Riviera, which was a passenger liner stop back in the 19th century. Sadly, a great many of the historic buildings from that era were destroyed by an earthquake in 1962.

The high mountain ridge results in a mild climate that has inspired wine grape and olive cultivation. The picturesque fishing villages, pleasant pebble beaches and pine forests invite visitors to stop in.

A few miles before Donta Deli there is a turnoff leading to the Pelješac Peninsula. You can catch ferries from here to the island of Korčula. In order to provide Bosnia-Herzegovina with access to the sea, Croatia had to surrender a tiny piece of its coast. The road to Dubrovnik therefore passes through another border crossing.

⑲ Dubrovnik Viewed from the air, this town looks as if it is clinging to the rocks like a mussel. In the Middle Ages, Dubrovnik was known as the seafaring republic of Ragusa. The Old Town, which features a mix of Renaissance and baroque buildings, winding alleys and a wide main street lined with cafés, is surrounded by mighty walls that open up toward the sea in only a few places. Basically impregnable for centuries, the town nevertheless faced near complete destruction on two occasions: from a strong earthquake in 1667, and from shelling by the Yugoslavian army in 1991. Fortunately, the bombed-

out roofs of the public buildings were rebuilt with a great deal of effort, such that the townscape has largely been restored. Other attractions include testimonies to the golden 15th century when Ragusa vied with Venice for power. The Rector's Palace with its arcades, harmoniously round arch windows and baroque staircase dates from this era, as does the completely intact town wall with a total length of 1,940 m (2,122 ft).

Kotor, Montenegro, is roughly 90 km (56 mi) from Dubrovnik, but the small medieval town is worth the detour. Bari, on the east coast of southern Italy, can be reached from Dubrovnik on a 16-hour ferry crossing.

⑳ Bari The capital of Apulia (331,600 residents) was initially founded by the Romans and was long subject to changing rulers. Foreign trade with Venice and the Orient brought wealth to the city, which still has a historic Old Town of Byzantine origin.

way, visitors are also immersed in the Middle Ages. The historic Old Town with its narrow alleys and valuable cultural monuments such as St Ivan's Church (17th century) and St Sava's Church (14th century), is surrounded by a fortress boasting gates and towers.

The medieval fishing village of Sveti Stefan lies in the middle section of the Budvanska Riviera. The 15th-century town, originally built on an island to protect it against pirates, has today become a comfortable seaside resort.

Detour

Urbino

Urbino, the cradle of humanism and the birthplace of Rafael, lies amid a graceful landscape of rolling hills, fields and forests. It was here that Duke Federico di Montefeltro lived, a patron of the arts and sciences in the mid-15th century who turned the town into the center of humanist philosophy. The magnificent brickwork buildings of the Old Town are protected by a medieval wall and are entirely dominated by the gigantic Palazzo Ducale. This imposing building is a UNESCO World Heritage Site.

All of the main streets lead to the Piazza della Repubblica. From there the Via Vittorio Veneto leads up the

Top: Palazzo Ducale (1444–1482).
Bottom: Piero della Francesca painted this portrait of Federico da Montefeltro who built the Palazzo.

hill to the Palazzo Ducale. The ducal palace is considered one of the most important Italian Renaissance buildings and, with its elegant courtyard lined with round arched arcades, it is an absolute highlight in the history of architecture.

The journey now takes you past two lagoons: Verano and Lesina. At Térmoli the route joins the N16. Térmoli itself holds little appeal, but the road now twists through the hilly, coastal landscape, revealing consistently good views. Inviting coves and picturesque villages like Vasto or Ortona perched on the cliffs tempt a stopover.

22 Vieste and the Gargano Peninsula The spur of the Italian boot consists of a wild limestone massif (1,000 m/3,281 ft) that is mostly uninhabited. Monte San Angelo is the highest town on the Gargano Peninsula at 850 m (2,789 ft). You have a wonderful view of the plateau and the Gulf of Manfredónia from the town, which has been an important southern Italian pilgrimage destination ever since the apparition of the Archangel Michael in a nearby grotto at the end of the 5th century. A 12th-century bishop's throne and other valuables adorn the grotto, which is shielded by bronze gates from Constantinople (1076).

Vieste is on the eastern tip of the peninsula. It has splendid beaches and a lovely medieval Old Town where the traditional outdoor *mignali* (staircases) are linked by narrow archways.

23 Pescara The largest town in the Abruzzi region always seems to be bustling. Large sections of the town were sadly destroyed in World War II but they have been rebuilt with generous, open architecture. Only a very small historical Old Town still exists now around the Piazza Unione. The town's attractions include its fine sandy beaches and the annual jazz festival in July, where legendary musicians like Louis Armstrong have performed. Pescara is at the mouth of the river of the same name.

24 S. Benedetto del Tronto Italy's largest fishing port is a lively and vibrant place. The town's icons include the splendid, palm-lined promenades, the

elegant villas and a long sandy beach. The fishing museum and the fish market are also worth a brief visit.

The steep Riviera del Conero, with the Monte Conero promontory, features stunning limestone cliffs, forests and narrow pebble beaches. It is worth taking some detours inland from here, for example to Loreto, perched like a fortress on a hill above Porto Recanati.

25 Ancona The foothills of the imposing Monte Conero drop down to the sea in steps while Ancona, the attractive regional capital of the Marches, sits down at sea level on the natural port. Although the port and industry town with 98,400 residents was originally founded by the Greeks

and boasts a rich history as a seafaring republic, its historical monuments unfortunately tend to be second rate.

In Ancona you should immerse yourself in the port atmosphere, which actually might be a welcome change from all the beach time and medieval towns. The San Ciriaco Cathedral (dating from the 11th–14th centuries) is perched high above the town. The Byzantine-influenced building is one of the most impressive Romanesque churches in Italy. En route to Pésaro there are a number of historical villages inviting you to stop a while, including Senigallia, the first Roman colony on the Adriatic coast. The Old Town there features the imposing Rocca Roveresca fortress.

San Marino

On the eastern edge of the Apennine Mountains, which form the spine of Italy, is Monte Titano with its towering fortresses built on a promontory to protect the world's smallest republic, San Marino, from potential harm. The republic comprises the capital of the same name and eight other villages.

The stonemason Marinus, thought to be from the island of Rab in what is now Croatia, originally sought refuge here in around AD 301 after fleeing persecution as a Christian in Diocletian times. The inhabitants drew up their own

The La Guaita fortress on Monte Titano from the 10th/11th centuries.

From Pésaro it is worth taking an excursion to the Old Town of Urbino 35 km (22 mi) to the south-west.

27 Cattólica to Rímini This is where you will find the tourist strongholds of the Adriatic, coastal resorts which, with their sandy beaches stretching for miles, a diverse range of sporting opportunities and vibrant nightlife are focused on entertaining the masses. Rímini's history goes back a long way, however, so make sure you enjoy that aspect too.

Having first gained major significance as an Etruscan port, Rimini is divided into two districts that could hardly be more different. While the site of the Roman town is still recognizable

1 Castel del Monte is visible from a distance, rising up from the plain. The two-storey castle was built in 1240 by the German Staufer King Frederick II and is one of the most fascinating buildings from the Middle Ages.

2 Typical for the Apulia region, the labyrinthine Old Town of Vieste is dominated by white stone buildings.

3 The Gargano National Park also protects the high, rocky coastline of the peninsula of the same name. There is a series of caves and grottos to be visited.

4 Cervia, around 15 km (9 mi) south of Ravenna, is a small fishing village from the 18th century. The charming houses of workmen from the nearby salt works line the bay.

constitution in the 13th century and declared themselves an independent commune – and so it has remained to this day. San Marino's livelihood is based on stamps and coins as well as on handicrafts, agriculture and tourism.

Parking is available in the lower town of Borgo Maggiore. From here you continue either by foot or via the Funivia, a cable car with wonderful views. The historic Old Town has tiny alleys and surrounded by a wall. There is a fantastic panoramic view from the Piazza della Libertà and the Palazzo del Governo. In addition to the Old Town, it is also worth visiting the San Francesco Church (1361) with a collection of paintings. The three fortresses of Monte Titano are also worth seeing and are reached via the Salita alla Rocca steps.

26 Pésaro At the exit from the Foglia Valley is the industrial town and port of Pésaro. The Old Town, with its Palazzo Ducale (15th–16th centuries) on the Piazza del Popolo is worth visiting. Continuing now toward Rímini the, coastal strip becomes noticeably narrower and the hinterland more mountainous.

Early Christian-Byzantine Churches in Ravenna

The Roman imperial star was already sinking when Ravenna experienced its golden age: Honorius made Ravenna the capital in 395. He and his sister Galla Placidia had Ravenna built up into an imperial city; the Germanic military leader Odoaker took over power after 476 and ruled his empire from Ravenna. Numerous early Christian churches survive from this glittering era. The mosaic cycles here were created by unknown artists and display a remarkable degree of technical perfection. The stylistic similarities seem to

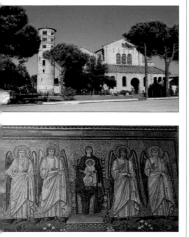

Top: Sant' Appolinare in Classe
Bottom: A Madonna mosaic

indicate that the mosaics were created by Roman craftsmen or by artists from Ravenna who had at least learnt their craft from the Roman masters. The luminosity of the mosaics derives from their material: the individual pieces (tesserae) were made from glass and carefully positioned so as to reflect the light to tremendous effect.

San Vitale Church (526) is well worth seeing: it is based on the Hagia Sophia in Istanbul and its greatest treasures are the elaborate Byzantine mosaics. Behind this is Galla Placidia's mausoleum, an unassuming brick building from the outside but the interior is also decorated with exceptionally grand mosaics. The mosaics cover the cupola and the barrel vaults and are even older than those of San Vitale.

in the Old Town, the coastal section is one of the liveliest seaside resorts on the Adriatic.
After San Marino there is a tiny scenic road for about 20 km (12 mi) that leads past Rimini. You can also take the SS72.

28 Ravenna Art metropolis as well as an industrial city, Ravenna is a multifaceted place surrounded by the nature reserves of the Po Delta region. Indeed, as port in Roman times, imperial Ravenna was once directly on the coast. But the port silted up and the location's importance dwindled. Only when the marshlands were drained in the 19th century did the economic recovery begin. Further impetus came in 1952 with the discovery of natural gas.

Ravenna draws visitors with its early Christian churches and the charming Old Town. The numerous cultural monuments include the San Vitale and Sant' Apollinare Nuovo churches; the mosaics in the Sant' Apollinare Basilica in Classe; the Orthodox baptistery; the Arian baptistery; Galla Placidia's mausoleum; and the tomb of Ostrogothic King Theoderich. Santa Maria in Porto fuori, the Sant' Orso Cathedral and Dante's tomb date from later eras.

From Ravenna the route then takes you to Chióggia, where the unique coastal landscape south of the main Po Delta has been made into a lovely nature reserve. The lagoons and hidden channels as well as the vast fields of the open plain are quite beautiful. Along the river causeways anglers can try their luck with the legendary Po catfish.

29 Chióggia Gracious palaces with their "feet in the water", three canals with boats and a number of charming bridges, those are the things that justify this baroque lagoon town's nickname of "Little Venice". Initially founded by the Romans, Chiógga was once very powerful but was ultimately overshadowed by La Serenissima for many centuries. In addition to enjoying the charming Venetian ambience, it is also worth visiting the baroque St Maria Assunta Cathedral. Lovely beaches are to be found at Sottomarina and Isola Verde.

30 Padua This ancient university town on the edge of the Euganean Hills is the last stop on our tour around the Adriatic. The long arcade corridors and historic buildings characterize

the town's appearance and Padua is one of the loveliest of the Italian towns from antiquity. The main attractions are the Cappella degli Scrovegni, where Giotto painted his most important series of frescos in 1305, in a simple chapel; and the magnificent Basilica di Sant' Antonio from the 15th/16th centuries, which is still one of the country's most important pilgrimage destinations to this day.

Other buildings that are significant for their art history and ought to be visited are the 12th century-Palazzo della Ragione, the former Augustinian Eremitani Church (13th century) with frescoes by Mantegna, the Santa Giustina Church (16th century) and the monument to the military leader Gattamelata, an equestrian statue by Donatello, most of whose works are otherwise to be seen in Florence. It

is worth taking a detour to the Abano Terme and Montegrotto Terme hot springs to the southwest of town. The springs are a blazing 80°C (176 °F).

1 The mosaics in the apse at San Vitale in Ravenna date from the first half of the sixth century.

2 Giotto's famous cycle of frescoes in the Capella degli Scrovegni (1305) in Padua depicts scenes from the life of Christ.

Padua This ancient university town is arguably one of Italy's loveliest. Its particular attractions include the Cappella degli Scrovegni with Giotto's cycle of frescos (1305), and the Basilica di Sant'Antonio (15th/16th centuries), which is visited by millions of pilgrims every year.

Venice The "Queen of the Eastern Mediterranean" is a combination of splendor and disrepair, land and water, Gothic, baroque and Renaissance. The list of attractions includes the Canal Grande, the Piazza San Marco, the Bridge of Sighs, the Accademia and the Palazzo Ducale.

Piran This is one of the Adriatic's most charming towns. On a peninsula on Slovenia's 40 km (25 mi) of coastline, it resembles a small version of Venice. Particularly impressive is Tartini Square, with a monument to composer Giuseppe Tartini, and the view of the Church of St George over the rooftops.

Opatija The blossoming gardens, coffee houses and the waterfront promenade in this spa resort town are all reminiscent of the Austro-Hungarian monarchy.

Murano and Burano Two islands in the Venice lagoon are especially noteworthy: Burano, a fishing island with bright buildings and small lace-making workshops, and Murano, the embodiment of quality glasswork since the 13th century, and home to a remarkable early Romanesque and Byzantine basilica.

Pésaro, Cattólica, and Rímini The Palazzo Ducale in the Old Town of Pésaro is a beautiful sight. Cattólica, on the other hand, attracts visitors with its long beaches. Nearby Rímini – once an Etruscan port – is one of the most popular sea resorts in Italy. The Old Town has Roman ruins and the good food.

Rovinji The best view of this Istrian port is from the water. The Venetian influence is easily recognizable in buildings such as the campanile, the splendid late-Renaissance red clock tower, the waterfront promenade, the Church of St Euphemia and the countless cafés.

The Plitvice Lakes The sixteen turquoise-colored lakes and over ninety waterfalls provide a superb nature experience here.

Split This port is the cultural and economic center of Dalmatia. The center boasts Roman sites such as the Palace of Diocletian (c. AD 300) and several other medieval buildings such as the cathedral.

Ravenna Once the capital of the Ostrogothic King Theoderich the Great's empire, this town is primarily known for its early Christian-Byzantine churches.

Gargano The spur of the Italian boot is made of limestone mountains reaching an altitude of up to 1,000 m (3,281 ft). Monte Sant' Angelo is the highest.

Trogir Winding alleyways and a cathedral (13th–16th centuries) characterize the old heritage-protected town situated on an island. The numerous churches and palaces make the former political and cultural center of Croatia between worth seeing.

Castel del Monte The hunting castle of the Staufer Emperor Frederick II (1194–1250) is visible from a distance and is enchanting with its perfect octagonal symmetry and strict simplicity.

Dubrovnik Only a few years after the severe damage caused by the Balkan war, this former seafaring republic is again intact and an idyllic location in many respects: Renaissance and baroque buildings, cafés and the sea, and especially the splendid fortified walls are what give "Venice's competitor" its unique magic.

Kotor This medieval town in Montenegro has a 4.5-km-long (2.8-mi) wall that is 20 m (66 ft) high. One of the town gates is from the ninth century and the cathedral is from the 14th.

Korčula This mountainous island is famous for its sword dancers and lush vegetation. The sights in the capital of the same name include the cathedral and All Saints Church.

Route 25

Italy

Sicily: in the footsteps of the Greeks, Normans, Arabs and Staufers

Remains of ancient civilizations: the amphitheater in Taormina.

Italy's largest island offers such great cultural diversity that it seems to embody an entire continent. Classic Greek temples, Norman cathedrals and baroque palaces have transformed the island into a larger-than-life open-air museum of art and cultural history. Nature in turn provides a powerful complement to the scene, offering dramatic rocky coasts and superlatives like the home of Europe's largest volcano.

On the edge of Europe, yet at the center of the Mediterranean world – there is no better way to describe Sicily's role in history. For lovers of antiquity, this island between the Ionic and the Tyrrhenian seas is a piece of Greece. For the good citizens of Milan and Turin, it is a stumbling block in front of the Italian boot that is dominated by shadowy powers and slowing down the pace of the country's progress. For Sicilians, despite the fact that many of its people suffered under the feudal conditions and were forced to emigrate due to the pressures of poverty, it will always remain "terra santa" – their sacred homeland – and it is all too often being kicked around by the Italian boot.

Historically, when so-called "world" politics revolved more or less around the Mediterranean, Sicily was the strategic crown jewel at the heart of the battle for dominance of this preeminent domain. In early antiquity, it was the Greeks, virtually dragged along by the Phoenicians, who colonized the island and made Syracuse

Mosaic of Christ in Monreale Monastery.

the center of the ancient world – before the era of the Roman empire. They were then followed by the Romans, Vandals, Byzantines, Arabs, Normans, Staufers, Aragonese and Neapolitans. Many of these conquerors ruthlessly plundered the country and fought bloody wars on its soil. By contrast, the Arabs cultivated growth between the 9th and 11th centuries by planting citrus and mulberry trees, sugarcane and date palms. They made the island into a gateway for Europeans to experience their more highly developed civilization.

Almost all of them, however, left behind stone reminders of their presence. The result is that, in terms of cultural and art history, Sicily now presents itself not as just an island, but as a continent in miniature, a rich fabric of tradition contained in one island. From the classic Greek temples at

The Concordia Temple in the Valle dei Templi near Agrigento dates back to the 5th century BC.

Mount Etna is one of the most active volcanoes in the world today. It has more than 1,000 minor craters as well as eruption points that regularly spew lava. It is closely monitored from a dedicated observatory.

Agrigento, Segesta and Selinunt to the Norman-era cathedrals of Monreale, Palermo and Cefalù, or the baroque Old Towns of Noto, Ragusa and Modica: Sicily has all these styles in their purest forms. Of course it is not only these and other civilizations that fascinate today's tourists on a visit to the "Continente Sicilia". The land and the people leave an equally inspiring impression. Whether you come in the spring, when a paradisical sea of flowers cloaks the entire island with its aromas, or in the summer, when the gruelling heat parches the soil, Sicily rarely fails to enchant. Its ancient beauty, which neither earthquakes, volcanic eruptions nor outbreaks of human violence have been capable of destroying, looks destined to remain.

The juxtaposition of contrasts, passions and an almost fatalistic lethargy; the ei-ther–or, friend or foe, love or hate, life or death attitude is an essential element of the Sicilian mentality. On the piazzas of Palermo or Catania, life pulsates chaotically and yet elegantly. The other side of the coin, however, can be seen in the economy and politics. The spirit of the Mezzogiorno, the Mafia, the bureaucracy and the corruption forms an unholy alliance, exercises a painful lack of consideration for nature.

But one thing is certain: This small piece of land nearly equidistant from the African and European continents, will undoubtedly awaken the senses of any visitor and enchant them with its exotic fragrances, vibrant hues and unique light. It will inspire a desire in you to return before you even complete the journey back across the Straits of Messina at the end of your trip.

Solitude can still be found on the Isola Salina, the second-largest of the Aeolian Islands.

Detour

Aeolian Islands

A lovely excursion takes you from the ferry ports of Milazzo, 40 km (25 mi) north-west of Messina, or Cefalù over to the Aeolian Islands. This group of islands consists of solidified lava and volcanic tuff, and is the mythical realm of Aeolius, Greek god of the winds and the inventor of sailing.

The islands feature steep, dramatic coastlines around nearly their entire circumferences, and they are un-spoiled by human activity, offering inviting little coves that are often only accessible by boat.

The main island of Lípari, with about 4,500 inhabitants, has the most tourism. Vulcano is also well-visited thanks to its two sandy bays and the healing powers of its sulfurous mud. Salina, meanwhile,

Isola Filicudi in the Aeolians.

is primarily agricultural. Capers and sweet Malvasia wine are the main local products.

Far from the crowds you'll find Filicudi, Alicudi and Strómboli. The active volcano on Strómboli is fascinating to visitors for its regular displays of glowing magma .

The greatest cultural attraction in the archipelago is the National Museum, on the acropolis of Lípari, with a wealth of discoveries.

Driving around the largest island in the Mediterranean along 850 km (528 mi) of coastline provides visitors with an excellent overview of Sicily's rich history, the wealth of its historical monuments and the diversity of its landscapes. All of this is then complemented by de-tours into the island's interi-or and to the small neigh-boring islands.

① Messina Located just 3 km (2 mi) from the Italian mainland, this port town has served as a first stop for conquerors since it was founded by the Greeks in the 8th century BC. It is of course still the "gateway to the island", despite having been de-stroyed several times: in 1783 and 1908 by earthquakes, and by bombing in 1943.

Among the remnants of ancient civilizations are the small Nor-man church of Santa Annunziata dei Catalani. From the upper dis-tricts of the town, a beautiful view unfolds of the checker-board layout of roads, the har-bor installations, the infamous straits and the wooded hills of Calabria nearby.

The winding scenic road also af-fords some grandiose views while taking you around to the north coast. After some 80 km (50 mi) you arrive in one of Sicily's most famous pilgrimage destinations.

② Tindari From the top of the steep cliff 260 m (853 ft) above the sea is a modern sanc-tuary with its striking black Madonna. The location affords

some fantastic views down to the sandbanks and across to the Aeolian Islands. The views from the adjacent ruins of ancient Tyndaris are no less magnificent, where the remains of a theater, a Roman basilica, the residential districts and the town fortifi-cations have been preserved.

Along the busy SS113, the jour-ney continues toward the west, passing sandy beaches, rocky cliffs, seaside resorts and indus-trial complexes. After 130 km (81 mi) you finally come to Cefalù, located on a narrow spit of land.

③ Cefalù Cowering under a mighty limestone face, this small fishing town would be worth a stop just to see its Oriental-style Old Town and the sandy beach. After all, it boasts the ruins of an ancient sanctuary, Arabic washhouses and a delightful pri-vate art collection in the Museo Comunal Mandralisca.

All of this, however, pales in comparison to Cefalù's cathedral. The foundation stone for Sicily's oldest religious building, which dates back to Norman times, was laid in 1131, by King Roger II. The façade alone is impressive

Travel information

Route profile
Length: approx. 850 km (530 mi), without detours
Time required: 8–10 days
Start and finish: Messina
Route (main locations): Cefalù, Palermo, Segesta, Trápani, Selinunt, Agrigento, Ragusa, Noto, Syracuse, Catania, Taormina

Traffic information:
The speed limit in town is 50 km/h (31 mph), on country roads outside of town 90 km/h (56 mph) and on mo-torways 110 or 130 km/h (70 or 80 mph). Seatbelts are re-quired only in the front seats of the car. The blood-alcohol limit is .08.

When to go:
Spring and autumn are the best times to go. Starting April to mid-May, the flowers are in bloom all over the is-land (20–25 °C/68–77 °F). Summer temperatures can be extremely hot, but in au-tumn, the water and air tem-peratures typically stay at a comfortable 20 °C (68 °F) until November. Winters are brief, mild and only moderately rainy.

Information:
Here are some websites to help you plan your trip.
www.bestofsicily.com
www.initaly.com
www.sicilian.net

enough to etch itself forever in your mind, with its Romanesque vaulted portal and the defensive posture of the mighty towers. The tall, narrow interior is simply brilliant. Even during the lifetime of its patron, master craftsmen from Constantinople came to create the magnificent golden mosaics in the choirs.

1 The charming port of Cefalù is surrounded by the picturesque fish-ing quarter and lined with small houses used since medieval times.

2 In Tindari, the ruins of an ancient theater, the Teatro Greco, are situated high above the steep rocky coast on the Tyrrhenian Sea in the north-east of Sicily.

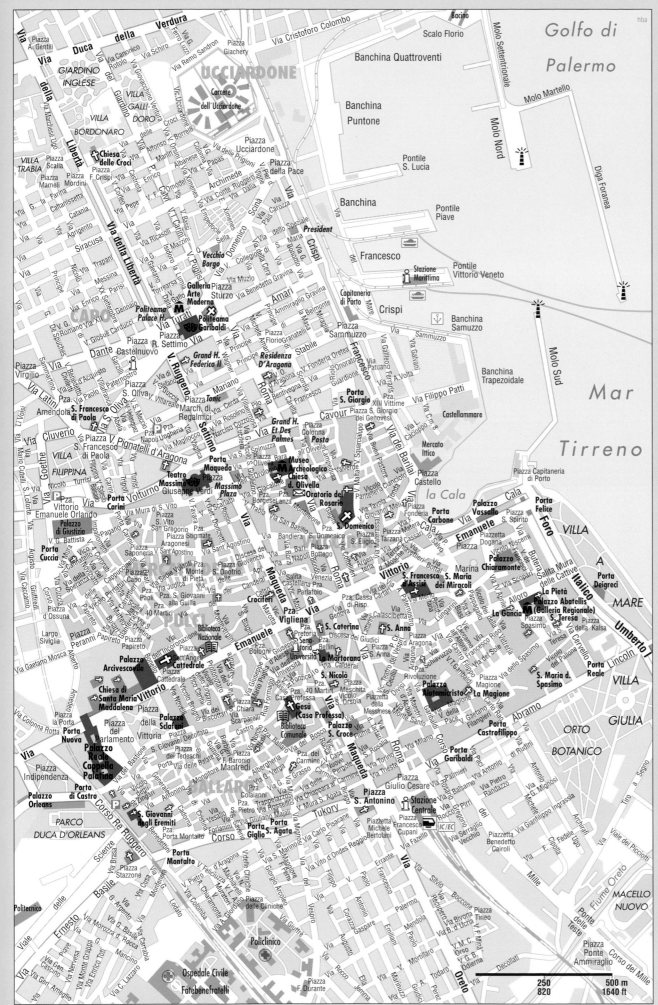

Palermo

During the First Punic War, Palermo was the main base for the Carthaginian fleet. Stationed here, Carthage flourished in unparalleled ways even during periods of Arab, Norman and Staufer rule. Superb architectural treasures have been preserved from all of these eras.

In Palermo's Old Town, Byzantine churches stand next to mosques, baroque and Catalan estates, neo-classical barracks and Arab pleasure palaces. Among the highlights are the vast cathedral and the Norman Palace with its Cappella Palatina, richly adorned with mosaics; the churches of San Cataldo, La Martorana, San Giovanni degli Eremiti; the La Zisa Palace; the Teatro Massimo; the catacombs of the Capuchin Convent; and the National Gallery and the archaeological museum.

One of Europe's most splendid imperial cities only two hundred years ago,

Top: The cathedral, 1184.
Middle: The harbor in Palermo.
Bottom: Lively Vucciria Market on Piazza Caracciolo.

Palermo was seemingly abandoned after World War II. In the 1990s, however, the "beautiful city" shed the stigma of Mafia corruption and, after a long malaise, is being busily renovated. Success can be seen in the vibrant markets, elegant promenades and charming piazzas.

The remote location of the temple of Segesta creates an impressive and mystical atmosphere. It was built opposite Monte Barbaro, where the ruins of the ancient city of Segesta and its theater can be seen. The ancient Greek peripteros, a temple surrounded by a portico with columns, was built in the 5th century BC.

It has thirty-six well-preserved Doric columns, six on its narrow sides and fourteen on its long sides, and covers an area of 61 x 26 m (200 ft x 86 ft). The temple was never completed, and the cella that is typically found at the center of this type of temple is also missing.

Detour

Erice and San Vito lo Capo

You should take two excursions from Trápani: the small medieval mountain town of Erice and the beach town of San Vito lo Capo.

Top: San Vito lo Capo.
Bottom: Erice, Monte San Giuliano.

The Elymians and the Carthaginians came to Erice to worship the goddess of fertility, known as Astarte or Aphrodite. Norman fortifications stand today where once a Roman sanctuary of Venus stood. Ancient temples and town walls are still intact in town and you get lovely views of the coastal plains.

The coast road to San Vito lo Capo is also impressive. After 40 km (25 mi) you arrive at a shallow sandy bay with a lighthouse. The Zingaro nature reserve is just inland.

④ Bagheria In the 17th and 18th centuries, this village was the favorite summer resort for the aristocratic families from the nearby town. Constant sea breezes here promised relief from the heat amidst idyllic lemon and orange groves, inspiring numerous baroque country manors to be built. Some of these palaces can still be visited today, including the Villa Palagonia with its superb Mannerist sculptures.

From Bagheria, it is about 14 km (9 mi) to Palermo.

⑤ Palermo (see page 313)

⑥ Monreale A visit to Palermo is unthinkable without an trip up to the small bishops' town of Monreale just 8 km (5 mi) away. The lofty environs of Monte Caputo make for spectacular views of the Sicilian capital and its neraly perfectly round bay, the Conca d'Oro.

The main sight, however, is the cathedral. In 1172, William II, King of Sicily, commissioned a Benedictine Abbey here, around which a town soon began to develop. In its center, he had a cathedral erected, a basilica with three aisles that was meant to symbolize the triumph of Christianity over Islam. At a length of 102 m (112 yds) and a width of 40 m (44 yds), it is Sicily's largest church, and rests on eighteeen ancient columns. It is home to the sarcophagi of kings William I and II, and has superb bronze portals and marble floors. The cathedrals's most impressive elements, however, are the unique mosaics, which cover an area of 6,300 sq m (67,788 sq ft), telling the stories of the Bible in exemplary splendor.

The cloisters feature a remarkable 216 pairs of columns.

West of Palermo, the Tyrrhenian Sea is occasionally hidden from view as the SS113 leads into the island's interior, to Segesta.

⑦ Segesta In antiquity, the Elymians, supposed descendants of the Trojans, were said to have settled in this now uninhabited mountainous landscape. What remains of this ancient tribe's town are a majestic but unfinished Doric temple and a gracefully situated amphitheater.

⑧ Trápani The provincial capital, spread out across a narrow spit of land, forms the western end of the SS113 and the A29. Drepanon, as Trápani was called in ancient times, was a naval base for the Carthaginian and Roman fleets. It flourished under the rule of the Normans and Staufers, and opened its arms to all Mediterranean peoples as a sanctuary of religious freedom.

At the height of its powers it was also a main trading port for salt, fish and wine. The numerous splendid buildings in the baroque Old Town testify to its former prosperity, and the Museo Regionale Pepoli has a wealth of archaeological treasures. The pilgrimage church of Santuario dell' Annunziata, a colossal structure in Catalan Gothic style, and an excursion to Erice or San Vito lo Capo are worthy destinations here as well.

⑨ Aegadian Islands These three islands off the western tip of Sicily were once infamous as pirates' bolt holes. They make for an interesting day trip from Trápani. Maréttimo is a pristine paradise for hikers. On Lévanzo you can admire the Stone Age rock paintings in the Grotta del

Via del Sale

To make the journey from Trápani to Marsala, we recommend using the 55-km (34-mi) "salt route" along the coast, where sky, water and earth all seem to melt into one another. The main attraction in this protected nature reserve are the salt gardens with their quaint windmills. Also worth visiting are two museums featuring the history of the desalination plants as well as the island of Mozia with its remains of a Phoenician harbor.

Genovese. Favignana is known for the mattanza, a ritual tuna hunt in the spring.

⑩ Marsala This town's name is now synonymous with a dessert wine, but its port, founded by the Phoenicians near the Capo Lilibeo, Sicily's westernmost tip, has more to offer that just a

drink. It features a tidy baroque Old Town with a lively piazza, a Norman cathedral, a museum featuring Flemish tapestries, and a Roman archaeological excavation site. The city owes its Oriental appearance to Mars al-Allah, or "port of God", from its time under Arab rule after 827.

⓫ Mazara del Vallo This former administrative capital of the Val di Mazara, an emirate with a majority Muslim population, has two faces: a rather unsightly side in the form of a vast fishing port, and a more attractive side in the form of a baroque Old Town with an idyllic piazza and an opulently adorned cathedral. Roughly 3.5 km (2 mi) west of the little town of Castelvetrano is another architectural jewel: the tiny domed Santa Trinità church, built by the Normans more than 900 years ago.

⓬ Selinunte This city, which thanks to its wheat trade was one of Sicily's most important Greek towns, was founded in the 7th century BC by the Dorians before being destroyed by the Carthaginians in 250 BC. Despite numerous earthquakes and the plundering of ancient sites for building materials, impressive remains have been preserved on the vast field of ruins. A total of nine temple complexes have been excavated on the acropolis and two other hills. Some have been reconstructed and represent perfect examples of the monumental sanctuaries of the ancient Greek empire.

You follow the coastline southeast now, taking a delightfully scenic road to the next stops: Sciacca, where a thermal hot spring rises from the sulfurous soil that was rated so highly even back in Roman times; and a short detour into the interior, to Caltabellotta, a spectacular "falcons nest" tucked up against the 1,000-m-high (3,281-ft) rock face. From the Norman castle ruins that stand here you get breathtaking panoramic views across large parts of the island. Back at the coast, after about 12 km (8 mi) you arrive at the next ancient sight.

⓭ Eraclea Minoa The few foundations and the beautiful theater in this town, which was founded in the 6th century BC, are situated on a plateau with strikingly white, 80-m (262-ft) limestone cliffs that plunge dramatically down to the sea.

⓮ Agrigento About 30 km (19 mi) farther along you arrive in the provincial capital, which initially makes a rather ambivalent impression. Its slopes have been developed in a fairly unattractive manner with high-rise blocks and industrial complexes. But hidden in the primarily baroque Old Town are quite a few cozy spots and architectural gems, in particular the Norman cathedral in the center. The Old Town itself is also pleasantly void of the uncomely growth of modern buildings.

⓯ Valle dei Templi The "Valley of the Temples", or to be more precise, this protracted mountain ridge, fascinates with its harmonious melding of ancient architecture and Mediterranean landscape. In the 5th century BC, this town rose to prominence as the second most powerful city on Sicily after Syracuse. The monumental Doric temples that adorned ancient Akragas are strung next to one another like pearls on a necklace.

Via the harbor and industrial town of Gela – which is worth a stopover for its ancient Greek fortifications and the archaeological museum – your journey continues to south-east Sicily, a region of barren karst mountains and opulent baroque relics. Vittoria and Comiso are the first two towns along this route into the interior (SS115), and they offer a taste of the sumptuous local architecture to come.

⓰ Ragusa This town was already an important center at the time of the Siculians, the ancient inhabitants of eastern Sicily.

1 Clouds darken the sky above the acropolis of Selinunte.

2 The interior of the cathedral of Monreale, south-west of Palermo.

3 The Doric temple of Selinunte, built in 490–480 BC, was probably dedicated to Hera.

4 Caltabellotta is on a rocky ridge almost 1,000 m (3,281 ft) high.

Detour

Villa Romana del Casale

A day's excursion to the west from Catania takes you into the interior of Sicily and gives you a good impression of the charms of the hilly and mountainous land that used to be Rome's breadbasket. During this 250-km-long (155-mi) circle tour, you will get acquainted with Caltagirone, the picturesque capital of ceramics in Sicily, and with Enna, the heavily fortified "belvedere of Sicily".

The magnificent mosaic floor in the Villa Romana in Casale.

The highlight, of course, will be the late-Classical Villa Romana del Casale. Some seventy years ago, the foundation walls of a country mansion were discovered about 6 km (4 mi) south of the small village of Piazza Armerina. No one could have foreseen what treasures would be unearthed here: forty-two rooms with mosaic floors dating back to the 4th century and regarded as among the best of what remains from antiquity.

Mount Etna

Mongibello (from Italian monte and Arabic gebel, both meaning "mountain") is what the Sicilians call it, fully aware of its perilous mood swings. However precarious

Etna's eruption in 2001.

life might be in the shadow of Europe's largest volcano, an excursion to the 3,323-m (10,903-ft) peak is not dangerous as long as you stay on the signposted paths – and it is an unforgettable experience.
From Nicolosi and Zafferana, the Strada dell' Etna winds its way up to the Sapienza refuge at a height of 1,910 m (6,267 ft). You then continue by cable car to 2,600 m (8,531 ft) before a guide in a four-wheel-drive vehicle takes you to the edge of the crater. If you wish to keep a bit more of a distance, there are walks along the volcano's slopes. The area was declared a national park in 1981.
A comfortable alternative is the Ferrovia Circumetnea, a narrow-gauge railway that takes three hours to circle Etna. It leaves from Catania and passes takes you to Giarre-Riposto, 114 km (mi) away.

Following the devastating earthquake of 1693, Ragusa was completely rebuilt. The nooks and alleyways of its eastern part, Ragusa-Ibla, are jammed onto a narrow spit of rock while the San Giorgio Basilica towers above. The western half of the city is one hundred years younger than the rest, and here you will find the cathedral, splendid palaces and the Museo Archeologico Ibleo. Both districts are superb examples of a baroque styles.

17 Módica The venerable small town of Módica hugs the steep slopes of two karst gorges in an even more picturesque fashion, and is similarly dedicated to an omnipresent baroque architectural style. Its main attraction is San Giorgio Cathedral. All these stops, however, are but a prelude for the delights that await you just 50 km (31 mi) to the east from here.

18 Noto Founded on the low foothills of the Iblei Mountains, this small town is considered the most exemplary work of urban art created in the Sicilian "post-quake baroque" style. The main axis of the grid of roads, which cover the slope in terraced steps, is formed by the Corso Vittorio Emanuele. The stucco-adorned façades of the Franciscan church, Capuchin convent, San Nicolò Cathedral, the town hall and the archbishops' palace, combined with artistic staircases, parks and squares all create a dramatic display that is virtually beyond comparison. It is also delightfully morbid: all of

the splendor and elegantly golden-yellow hues are threatened by imminent decay, and the sandstone and gypsum are crumbling. The preservationists and restorers cannot keep up.

19 Siracusa (Syracuse) At first glance, the faceless new structures of Syracuse make it hard to believe that 2,300 years ago this provincial capital was home to more than one million inhabitants, and that it was once the mightiest of the Greek towns in southern Italy. It was a center of trade but also of philosophy and the sciences.
A walk through the picturesque Old Town, however, is indeed an eye opener. For on the tiny island of Ortigia, which has been the historic heart of Syracuse since it was founded by the Corinthians in around 740 BC (and still is the center), many remains of its early heyday can easily be found: a temple of Apollo, for example, or the Arethusa springs, and a Doric temple that was transformed into the present cathedral in the 7th century AD.

Some parts of the ancient acropolis on the mainland have also been preserved. The archaeological park there features, among other things, a Roman and a Greek theater, a multitude of catacombs, the giant altar of Hiero II, hewn out of the soft chalky rock, and a large grotto known as "the ear of Dionysus". In addition to the relics from antiquity, attractions from the Middle Ages and more recent times, the regional gallery and the Castello Maniace, built under the Staufer King Friedrich II, are also worth a visit.

20 Catánia As the crow flies, Sicily's second-largest town is less than 30 km (19 mi) away from the summit of Etna, and has often had to endure the wrath of its active neighbor. During its 3,000-year history, lava currents and earthquakes have repeatedly destroyed the city. After a devastating quake at the end of the 17th century, Catánia was rebuilt according to original plans in late-baroque style using dark lava stone. The

cathedral stands out among the numerous ostentatious palaces and churches.
The municipal museum inside the Castello Ursino, the Roman theater – Bellini's birthplace –, the Teatro named after him, and the larg baroque church of San Nicolò are all worth a visit too. From Catánia, a detour via Nicolosi to Mount Etna is well worth your time.

21 Taormina The journey now continues toward its grand finale, half way from Catánia going north toward Messina, in the most-visited town on the island, Taormina, where a fabulous location on a rocky cliff high above the sea and an ancient amphitheater have attracted droves of tourists since the 19th century.

1 The Old Town of Ragusa-Ibla, with its baroque buildings and Byzantine fortifications.

2 The ruins of a Greek amphitheater in Taormina, with Mount Etna and the rocky bay in the background.

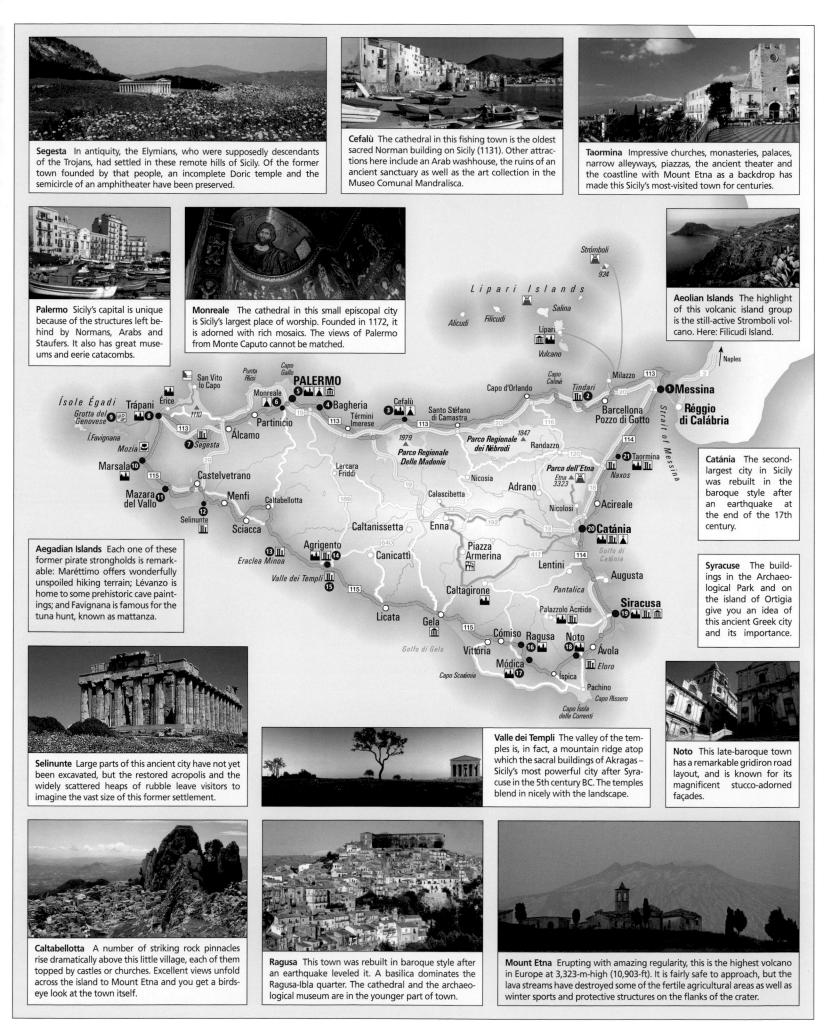

Segesta In antiquity, the Elymians, who were supposedly descendants of the Trojans, had settled in these remote hills of Sicily. Of the former town founded by that people, an incomplete Doric temple and the semicircle of an amphitheater have been preserved.

Cefalù The cathedral in this fishing town is the oldest sacred Norman building on Sicily (1131). Other attractions here include an Arab washhouse, the ruins of an ancient sanctuary as well as the art collection in the Museo Comunal Mandralisca.

Taormina Impressive churches, monasteries, palaces, narrow alleyways, piazzas, the ancient theater and the coastline with Mount Etna as a backdrop has made this Sicily's most-visited town for centuries.

Palermo Sicily's capital is unique because of the structures left behind by Normans, Arabs and Staufers. It also has great museums and eerie catacombs.

Monreale The cathedral in this small episcopal city is Sicily's largest place of worship. Founded in 1172, it is adorned with rich mosaics. The views of Palermo from Monte Caputo cannot be matched.

Aeolian Islands The highlight of this volcanic island group is the still-active Stromboli volcano. Here: Filicudi Island.

Aegadian Islands Each one of these former pirate strongholds is remarkable: Maréttimo offers wonderfully unspoiled hiking terrain; Lévanzo is home to some prehistoric cave paintings; and Favignana is famous for the tuna hunt, known as mattanza.

Catánia The second-largest city in Sicily was rebuilt in the baroque style after an earthquake at the end of the 17th century.

Syracuse The buildings in the Archaeological Park and on the island of Ortigia give you an idea of this ancient Greek city and its importance.

Selinunte Large parts of this ancient city have not yet been excavated, but the restored acropolis and the widely scattered heaps of rubble leave visitors to imagine the vast size of this former settlement.

Valle dei Templi The valley of the temples is, in fact, a mountain ridge atop which the sacral buildings of Akragas – Sicily's most powerful city after Syracuse in the 5th century BC. The temples blend in nicely with the landscape.

Noto This late-baroque town has a remarkable gridiron road layout, and is known for its magnificent stucco-adorned façades.

Caltabellotta A number of striking rock pinnacles rise dramatically above this little village, each of them topped by castles or churches. Excellent views unfold across the island to Mount Etna and you get a birds-eye look at the town itself.

Ragusa This town was rebuilt in baroque style after an earthquake leveled it. A basilica dominates the Ragusa-Ibla quarter. The cathedral and the archaeological museum are in the younger part of town.

Mount Etna Erupting with amazing regularity, this is the highest volcano in Europe at 3,323-m-high (10,903-ft). It is fairly safe to approach, but the lava streams have destroyed some of the fertile agricultural areas as well as winter sports and protective structures on the flanks of the crater.

The Parthenon on the Acropolis was built under Kallikrates and Iktinos in 447 BC.

Greece

Classics of antiquity up close

Greece is the cradle of western civilization, and it is no surprise that the legacy of the ancient Greeks and its classic antiquities have inspired waves of fascination in the country. But a trip to *Hellas* is more than just a journey back through time: Greece is also a place of great natural beauty, with impressive mountainous landscapes, idyllic islands, wild coasts and pristine white-sand beaches.

One-fifth of Greece's total area comprises islands. No place in the entire country is farther than 140 km (87 mi) from the sea, and the 14,000 km (8,700 mi) of coastline offer endless possibilities for spectacular hiking, swimming, sailing or just relaxing on the beach.

On the mainland and the Peloponnese, less than one-third of the land is suitable for farming. Agriculture is therefore concentrated on the plains of the country's north-east. The national tree of Greece, for example, the olive tree, can thrive up to elevations of around 800 m (2,625 ft), and does so on the mainland as well as on the islands.

Greece's mountainous landscape and its proximity to the sea have obviously shaped civilization here for millennia. The most significant evidence of this is that, throughout the country's long history, the combination of mainland and archi-

The Virgin Mary in a Meteora monastery.

pelago prevented the formation of a central power. Instead, small city-states were the natural entities created here since ancient times, despite the fact that these were more easily conquered and ruled by foreign powers than a centralized structure might have been.

When the Roman Empire broke up in AD 395, Greece was part of the Eastern Roman Empire (Byzantium). It became Christian very early on. After the Crusades (11th–13th centuries), and in some cases well into the 16th century, large parts of the country fell under the rule of the Venetians, whose legacy can still be seen in various place names and architecture. In 1453, the Ottomans seized Constantinople and later large parts of Greece. When it came to beliefs, the Turks were tolerant, and their Greek subjects enjoyed religious freedom. The Orthodox Church

The spectacular "Shipwreck Beach" on the north-west coast of Zákinthos. This southernmost island in the Ionic Sea was called the "Flower of the Levant" by the Venetians.

The island fort of Bourtzi protected Nauplia from enemies attacking from the south.

thus became a unifying and protective force for all Greeks during the Ottoman era. Isolated from the important cultural and intellectual developments in the rest of Europe, Greece remained untouched by the Renaissance, Reformation and Enlightenment.

National pride, which emerged in the late 18th century, finally led to revolution in 1821, but it was quashed by the Turks. It was not until 1827 that the Greeks, with help from the British, French and Russians, were able to shake off Turkish rule and proclaim a sovereign state. After independence in 1830, the Greeks made Bavarian Prince Otto von Wittelsbach the king of their nation as Otto I, after which a number of German architects worked in Athens to ensure the nation was transformed into worthy capital of the new Greece after centuries of decline.

At the time, however, some areas of Greece were still under Turkish rule, which again led to wars with the Turks – with varying success – and it was not until the early 20th century that Crete and a number of other Aegean islands were returned to Greece.

As a travel destination, Greece is often presented with deep blue skies above a turquoise sea, with whitewashed houses on a hillside above a quaint port – and not incorrectly. Regardless of whether you are hopping around the more than 2,000 islands or exploring the mainland, Greek hospitality is an exceptional national quality here.

A word of warning, however: their driving can be rather "adventurous" at times. Some think the middle of the road belongs to them, even on curves, so make sure you drive with caution!

Such vibrantly colored fishing boats are typical of many Greek port towns.

Detour

Euboea

A bridge connects the mainland with Greece's second-largest island, which has still somehow remained largely untouched by mass tourism. Long stretches of the two main roads in the north and south head alternately along rugged cliffs and sandy beaches, passing picturesque fishing villages and small seaside resorts. The mountain roads and between remote villages provide spectacular views of the island. Halkida is the capital of Euboea, and its main attractions include the Turkish-Venetian Kastro quarter with an imposing mosque, an aqueduct and a fortress.

Heading north, Route 77 initially skirts the west coast. After Psahná , however, it becomes more mountainous, and the scenery is characterized by olive groves and pine forests before you are taken into the narrow Kleisoura Gorge. The mountain village of Prokópi lies at

A monastery on an island between the ferry ports of Skala and Euboea

the foot of Kandillo, the highest peak in the northern half of the island at 1,246 m (4,088 ft).

Anyone not wanting to miss out on seeing the sandy beaches on Euboea should continue on to Agriovótano on the northern tip. The interior of Euboea is similarly rugged, and from Sténi Dírfios you can climb Dírfis, the highest mountain on the island at 1,745 m (5,725 ft) in about four hours.

Expressway 44 connects you with the south of the island along the west coast to Erétria. The few ruins of the ancient city include the theater, the acropolis and a temple of Apollo. Following the Gulf of Euboea you reach Alivéri, with its interesting Venetian tower. The nearby mountain village of Stíra is known for its "dragon houses". The journey ends in Káristos, which is dominated by the mighty Venetian fort Castello Rosso.

This journey through the Greece of antiquity will take you through majestic mountains and glorious coastal landscapes to the most important remnants of this ancient civilization, as well as to the legacies of Roman, Byzantine and Venetian eras on the southern mainland, Attica and the Peloponnese peninsula.

1 **Athens** (see pages 324–325)

2 **Cape Sounion** From Athens, you initially head about 70 km (43 mi) south along Highway 91 to the outermost point of the peninsula. The lovely beaches at Voúla and Vouliagméni are worthwhile spots to stop along the Attic Coast between Piréas (Piraeus) and Soúnio. At the bottom of the cape is an amazing temple dedicated to Poseidon, god of the sea, from 444 BC. It provides stunning views down to the Saronic Gulf.

From Cape Sounion, the route continues north along the eastern side of the peninsula. Then, east of Athens, you take Highway 54 toward Marathón. The Marathón Plain was where the Greeks defeated an army of Persians in 490 BC. On the day of the battle, a messenger in a full suit of armour brought news of the victory to Athens and the 42-km (26-mi) stretch became the reference distance for the modern marathon.

Following the coastal road to the north, you can make a detour to Évia (Euboea) Island near Halkída.

3 **Thebes** From Halkída, Highway 44 heads to Thíva, the new name of ancient Thebes, which is today an insignificant provincial town. The few historic remnants from what was once the mightiest city in Greece, in the 4th century BC, are on display in the Archaeological Museum. Continuing north-west you will pass the tower of a 13th-century fort built by Franconian crusaders. Heading towards Delphi, you initially take Highway 3 and then turn onto Route 48. The city of Livádia lies in the middle of vast cotton fields. After Livádia you will get some spectacular views over Mount Parnassus to the north-west.

4 **Ósios Loukás** After about 13 km (8 mi), a road turns off southward toward Distomo, and a 13-km-long (8-mi) street leads to the Ósios Loukás Monastery, considered one of the most beautiful Greek Orthodox monasteries from the Byzantine era

Travel information

Route profile

Length: approx. 1500 km (932 mi)
Time required: 3 weeks
Start and finish: Athens
Route (main locations): Athens, Cape Sounion, Thebes, Delphí, Corinth, Nauplia, Sparta, Máni, Methóni, Olympia, Patras, Corinth, Athens

Traffic information:

Greece has a good network of well-maintained roads. You should have a green insurance card with you. Speed limits are as follows: highways 110 or 120 km/h (70 or 75 mph), rural roads 90 km/h (55 mph), in town 50 km/h (30 mph).

When to go:

The best seasons in Greece are spring between March and May, or autumn from October to November. Summers are extremely hot and dry.

Accommodation:

Greece offers a wide variety of accommodation, from domátias (guestrooms for rent) to expensive luxury hotels. For more information check out: *www.gnto.gr*

Information:

Here are some websites to help you plan your trip.
www.gogreece.com
www.in2greece.com
www.greeka.com

Oracle of Delphí

The Oracle of Delphí began having a significant effect on the fates of many Greek city-states in the 8th century BC. Rulers would address their questions to Apollo, for whom priestess Pythia then communicated his replies. She sat perched over a crevice, out of which hot steam rose, presumably sending her into a trance.

The ruins of the Temple of Apollo in ancient Delphí

(10th century). It houses some magnificent mosaics from the 11th century.

Another 24 km (15 mi) down the often steep and winding Highway 48 and you arrive in Delphí.

5 Delphí Evidence of Delphí's magic can be seen in both its mythology and in its beautiful natural setting. Located amid a picturesque mountain landscape on the steep slopes of Mount Parnassus, the town was considered by the ancient Greeks to be the center of the world. The Oracle of Delphí in the Sanctuary of Apollo was a regular center of consultation between the 8th century BC and AD 393.

The most famous sites of ancient Delphí include the amphitheater from the 2nd century BC, with a stunning view of the Temple of Apollo from 200 years earlier; the Holy Road; and the Sanctuary of Athena Pronaia with the Tholos, a famous circular temple. The Archaeological Museum's many sculptures and a recon-

struction of the sanctuary is also worth a visit. The highlight is the life-size bronze charioteer, which had been dedicated to Apollo as a reward for a victorious chariot race in 478 BC.

From Delphí, it is worth making a 220-km-long (137-mi) detour to the Metéora monasteries (see pp 326–327) in the mountainous heart of northern Greece.

Anyone wanting to omit the detour north will initially follow the same route back to Thíva, then continue along Highway 3

1 The icon of Athens: a view from the south over the Acropolis, with the imposing Parthenon in the center of the complex and Mount Lykabettos on the right in the background.

2 The ceiling of the Caryatid Porch at the Erechtheion on the Acropolis is supported by columns in the shape of young women, so-called caryatids.

3 Three of the twenty columns were rebuilt at the Tholos, a round building at the Sanctuary of Athena Pronaia in Delphí.

The wisdom of the oracles was often ambiguous and therefore required interpretation by a priest of some ranking. Roman emperors tried to resurrect the cult in the 2nd century, but the oracle fell silent in AD 393 and the sanctuary was eventually shut down.

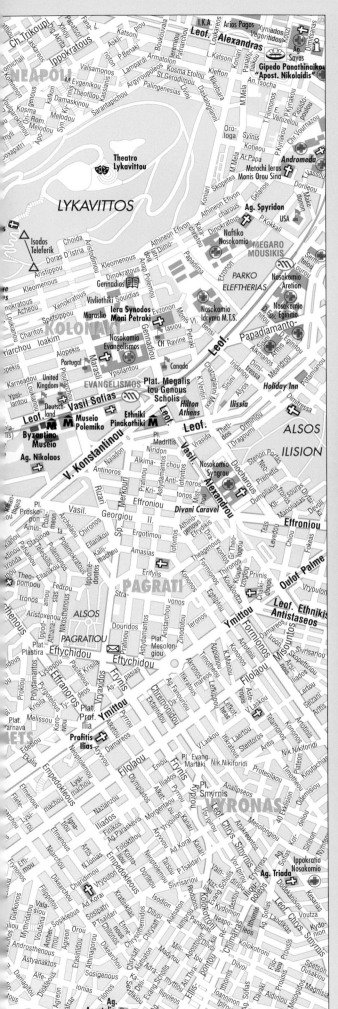

Athens

The Greek capital is a pulsating, modern metropolis with three million inhabitants, approximately one third of whom live in the greater Athens area. The city's most recognizable icon is visible from afar and is the epitome of ancient Greece: the Acropolis.

Athens is a city of contrasts: chaos on the roads, traffic jams, complicated environmental problems and oppressive smog polluting the entire valley, while the greatest ruins from antiquity, especially the Acropolis, still stand tall on the south side of city center. Athens' most famous site is the mighty Acropolis – a UNESCO World Heritage Site –, the castle hill of the ancient city that was converted into a holy district around 800 BC and mainly used to worship the goddess Athena, the city's patron saint. The Acropolis sits atop a steep, rugged, 156-m-high (512 ft) pale limestone plateau and was an important place of refuge for the population in times of need. The early beginnings of a castle wall already existed in the 13th century BC. After the old temple was destroyed by the Persians in 480 BC, the complex of monumental

where the dramas of Aeschylus, Euripides and Sophocles premiered in front of an audience of 17,000; and the Roman Odeion (AD 160), a construction commissioned by the wealthy Athenian, Herodes Atticus.

The Acropolis project ultimately required a huge sacrifice from the Athenian taxpayers: the total costs were more than 2,000 ancient gold talents, an enormous sum of money for a city-state the size of Athens.

Clustered around the Agora, the ancient market place from 600 BC and the center of public life for centuries, you will find the Doric Temple of Hephaistos, or Theseion (449–440 BC); the Attalos Stoa portico, once an artisans' center with discoveries from the ancient Agora, now reconstructed as a museum; the octagonal Tower of the Winds (1st century BC), formerly a clep-

the Roman Library of Hadrian at Monastiraki Square.

Around the bustling Syntagma Square in modern Athens, you should see the Parliament building (Vouli), built by the architect Friedrich von Gärtner in 1842; the national garden created in 1836 with exotic plants; the Numismatic Museum in the home of Heinrich Schliemann; the ruins of Hadrian's Gate and the Temple of Zeus (Olympieion) dating back to Roman times; the ancient Kallimármaro Stadium, reconstructed for the first modern Olympic Games in 1896; the National Archaeological Museum with a unique collection of ancient Greek art; the Museum of Cycladic Art; the Byzantine Museum; and the Benáki Museum (Byzantine works, Coptic textiles).

The surrounding area features: the Kaisariani Byzantine monasteries with

In the 5th century BC, Pericles was able to gain support from the citizens Athens for the city's most ambitious building programme: the construction of the Acropolis, initially with three temples.

marble buildings with the Propylae gate construction, the small Temple of Nike, the imposing Doric Parthenon (447–432 BC), and the Ionic Erechtheum with its Caryatid Porch were all created in the first half of the 5th century BC, the time of Pericles.

The most extensive damage to the Parthenon dates back to the 17th century when a Venetian grenade hit the Turkish powder warehouse in the Parthenon and sent the roof flying into the air. Important sculptures and reliefs are also on display in the Acropolis Museum.

The main attractions below the Acropolis are the Theater of Dionysus,

sydra and sundial with a weather vane; the Roman Agora, from around the birth of Christ; and the adjacent Fethiye Mosque (15th century).

In the Plaka, the picturesque Old Town quarter with narrow alleyways, small shops, cafés and taverns, are several Byzantine churches, such as the beautiful Little Mitropolis (12th century) and Athens' oldest Christian church, the 11th-century cross-in-square Kapnikarea church on the fashionable Ermou shopping street. Also worth seeing is the Panagía Geogoepíkoös cross-in-square church (12th century) at the Plateía Mitropóleos, as well as a small bazaar mosque and the ruins of

the St Mary's Church, built around 1000, and 11th-century Dafni, which has some ornate gold leaf mosaics in the main church, UNESCO World Heritage Site.

It is worth taking a day trip out to Piraeus, Athens' port since ancient times, with the Mikrolimano fishing port, Hellenic Marine Museum and the Archaeological Museum. Also visit the Poseidon Temple on Cape Sounion, 67 km (42 mi) away, and the islands in the Saronic Gulf, home to Aegina with the Temple of Apollo and the Temple of Aphaia, the island of Poros with its charming scenery, and the artists' island of Hydra.

Detour

Metéora Monasteries

The name Metéora means "floating rocks" – and the literal sense of the term becomes apparent to any visitor as soon as they arrive at this vast monastery complex. The Metéora monasteries are some of the most beautiful and impressive attractions in all of Greece.

From Delphí, the road initially heads west as far as Ámfissa, where you turn onto Highway 48 towards Brálos. From there, Highway 3 passes through Lamía to Néo Monastíri, and continues along Highway 30 through Tríkala to Kalambáka.

The first sandstone towers can be seen on the horizon from quite a distance. The monastery buildings sit atop high cliffs, which soar up vertically out of the Thessalia Plain to heights of 300 m (984 ft). The roughly 1,000 sandstone formations are deposits from a large lake whose waters eroded out the pillars before the sea level dropped.

After the 9th century, when foreign invaders began their conquest of the region, some hermits sought refuge in this remote world of rock towers. One of them was a recluse named Barnabas, who settled here at the end of the 10th century. Many others soon followed suit on the nearby towers. The monasteries themselves were not built until the 14th and 15th centuries, when the Serbs threatened with invasion. In 1336, the monk Athanásios from Athos established the first monastery, which was followed by twenty-three others. The buildings on the cliffs were used by the recluses as both places of refuge in the face of foreign invaders, as well as places of worship. The foundations were financed by wealthy private individuals looking to secure themselves a place in heaven; some monasteries still even bear the names of their founders. The monks lived according to strict monastic rules that prohibited women from entering the monasteries. Even in times of need, they were not allowed to accept food from women.

The monasteries were built in places out of the military's reach and could only be accessed in a very circuitous

route using rope-ladders or other climbing aids. If a situation appeared unsafe, the monks could retract their ladders; or they could receive welcome guests, drop down a basket or net and pull the visitors up. Everyone visiting Metéora for the first time will automatically ask themselves, when looking at the steep cliffs, how the first hermits climbed these tall, sharp rocks, which can today only be mastered by sport climbers.

One supposes they beat pegs into narrow crevices and worked their way up. The paths quarried into the rock were only created in more recent times. The architectural construction of the individual monasteries is largely a function of their varying positions on a crag or over an abyss. The internal structure of the monasteries is relatively uniform, and they have all the essential facilities required by occidental monasticism: a prayer chapel, a kitchen, a refectory (dining hall), a cistern, monk cells, a library and a treasure chamber.

The Metéora monastery frescos

Even in ancient times, painting the walls was a common form of artistic and spiritual expression. Indeed, these colorful murals fulfilled an important role in the Byzantine Empire (Eastern Roman Empire) and the form even experienced a sort of heyday in the 9th century.

Frescos (from the Italian "fresco", meaning fresh) were created by applying fresh watercolors to wet lime surfaces. The mineral dyestuffs penetrated the fresh rock and bonded chemically with the lime and sand to form a hard surface.

Top: Agíos Stephanos Convent
Bottom: Fresco with Jesus and saints

Built by Eastern Orthodox monks hoping to escape the imminent conquest of the Turks, some of the Metéora monasteries are still home to rich murals from the 14th to 16th centuries. Due to their natural inaccessibility perched on top of dramatic limestone towers, many of the frescos have in fact been very well preserved, for example the ones in the small Stéfanos Chapel, which date back to the early 16th century.

The Ágios Nikólaos Monastery, built in the late 14th century and expanded in 1628, also houses a vast collection of frescos. A monk named Theophanes painted some of the most beautiful frescos here around 1527. The nuns of the Ágios Stéfanos Convent continue to operate an icons workshop even today.

Rousánou Monastery, perched atop a crag and founded by two brothers from Epirus in 1545. For a long time the location was only accessible using rope-ladders and was often used by the people from the surrounding area as a place of refuge. The oldest preserved monastery in Metéora bears the name Moní Hypapante.

Three monasteries are particularly worth seeing: Várlaam was founded in 1518 and its church (Katholikón) is home to beautiful frescos. Perched 623 m (2,044 ft) up, Megálo Metéoro is the highest and largest monastery, and the hermit caves of its founder can still be visited today. Ágios Stéfanos is a convent and was founded by Byzantine Emperor Andronikos III in 1332.

From 1490, all monasteries were subordinate to the abbot of the Metamórfosis Monastery, built between 1356 and 1372, and one of the oldest monasteries in Metéora. The monks stayed in their monasteries even after the Turkish conquest of northern Greece and new monasteries were still being founded in Metéora in the late 15th century. Some of the monasteries were large properties and were thus subject to tribute to the Turkish rulers.

The 16th century was the heyday of monastic life in Metéora, but also a time of fierce conflicts between the various monasteries. Towards the end of the 18th century, the first monastery complexes had already fallen into ruin because of difficulty in maintaining their basic structures. Today, there are still thirteen monasteries that are in parts completely impoverished and have largely fallen into disrepair, but some of them still have valuable libraries. In total, six monasteries can still be visited. The most spectacular of these is undoubtedly the little Moní

1 The view from the Metéora monasteries stretches far into the Thessalia Plain.

2 The Metéora monasteries were inaccessible to unwelcome guests.

3 An impressive fresco in the Várlaam Monastery, founded in 1518.

Built in 444 BC, the fifteen gleaming white columns of the temple on Cape Sounion create an ideal location for a sanctuary to worship Poseidon, god of the sea. Looking out over the Saronic Gulf, this temple on a cliff soaring 60 m (197 ft) above the sea was used by seafarers as an orientation point even in ancient times.

Dream Routes
Europe